A HISTORY OF TIVERTON

by Mike Sampson

Published by the Tiverton War Memorial Trust

Published by the Tiverton War Memorial Trust

© Mike Sampson 2004

ISBN 0-9548788-09

Jacket design by Peter Skeet.
Typeset and printed by Maslands Limited of Tiverton.

Contents

Foreword

The Trustees of the Tiverton War Memorial, under the chairmanship of Sir John Palmer and following an idea suggested by Eric Shapland, commissioned a new History of Tiverton from Mike Sampson in the hope that he would produce a much needed, up-to-date and comprehensive work. They have not been disappointed. The author has filled this book with an immense amount of material, much of it new, drawn from a wide range of original sources encountered during years of patient, skilful and enthusiastic research. In its compilation he has been advised and encouraged by Brian Jenkins and both of them have contributed enormously to a new understanding of Tiverton's past.

I am very grateful to them both and I thoroughly commend their work to all who are interested in local history.

Sir Ian Amory, Bt.

Acknowledgements

The long-term task of producing this book has necessarily involved the help of many individuals and organisations. For their efficient and courteous service, I would like to thank the National Archives (Public Record Office), the Royal Institution of Cornwall, the Record Offices of Cornwall, Dorset, Somerset, and North Devon, the archives of the Dean and Chapter of Exeter Cathedral, and the Devon Sites and Monuments Register. I must extend special thanks to John Draisey and all the staff of the Devon Record Office at Exeter, for providing such a warm, friendly and helpful atmosphere in which to pore over the many thousands of documents which they produced, without complaint, at my persistent and constant requests. There can be few better places to study than the Devon and Exeter Institution; I have appreciated the assistance given by its staff and volunteers. The collections of the Westcountry Studies Library and the University of Exeter Library have been of immense value in my research, and I am indebted to the staff of both for enabling me to find the more obscure material.

Local help and support for this project has been given by Leslie Boyce at the East Devon College Library, and by Alison Rennie and Hazel Skinner at Tiverton Library, and their assistants. I am also indebted to Brian Jenkins for introducing me to the Blundell's School Archive and to David Gibling for permitting me to work on the material kept at the Newte Library in Saint Peter's Church, as well as to the Town Clerk of Tiverton and Mid Devon District Council for giving me access to some of their documents. I am extremely grateful to John Leach and the Tiverton Museum of Mid Devon Life for the support and encouragement given throughout this project, and to the Museum's Trustees for allowing me to use material from their extensive collections. Many people have unselfishly shared their personal research and knowledge with me over the years. They are too many to list fully here, but heartfelt thanks are offered to Landeg White for his comments on John Gabriel Stedman, Peter Maunder for sharing his work on the Chancery Court cases relating to Tiverton, to Rosemary Nicolaou and the Dunsford family for the loan of some of Martin Dunsford's personal papers, and to Eric Shapland, Dot Butler, Tom McManamon, Oliver Nicholson, Bob Lush, Alan Voce, Les Davey, Peter Jones, Jane Evans, Bill Jones, Pat Lovering, Frank Merrick, and Bob Clark for the wealth of material given. Barbara Keene deserves special mention for her kind assistance throughout the project; for helping me to abstract information in the Newte Library, for her work on the Knightshayes Estate papers and the archaeology of the area, and for patiently answering my never-ending questions. The combined knowledge of such local enthusiasts is boundless.

I shall always be grateful to the Tiverton War Memorial Trustees for their vision to produce a new history of the town and for what was in essence an act of faith in commissioning me to undertake the work. They have been totally supportive in all aspects of the project, and, when a suitable publisher could not be found, resolved to take on that role themselves. I would also record my sincere thanks to their successive secretaries, Tony Wyatt and Carol Gaskell, and to the two Chairmen of the Trust, the late Sir John Palmer who, sadly, did not see the culmination of this work, but whose personal interest and encouragement at every stage is fondly remembered, and the present Chairman, Sir Ian Amory. The production of the book itself has been conscientiously undertaken by Maslands Limited of Tiverton, and I am deeply indebted to their professional expertise, especially that of Andy Jackson, and Louise Boniface, and to the design skills of Peter Skeet.

Brian Jenkins has been the supervisor of this project since its inception, and without his extensive knowledge and editorial skills, this book would have been much the poorer. He has helped me place events in Tiverton in a wider context, intercepted my many schoolboy howlers, and revived in me a respect for the English language. I am also grateful to his wife, Catherine, for her kind hospitality and for enduring our frequent, disruptive meetings. Special mention is also due to the proprietors of the Butterleigh Inn for providing much-appreciated sustenance during those daylong and arduous editorial sessions. I owe the greatest debt, however, to my wife, Sue, and children, Paul and Becky, without whose constant love, support, encouragement and sacrifice this work would never have begun, let alone been completed.

Illustrations

I would like to thank Tiverton Town Council for permission to use a representation of the Borough Seal on the jacket, and Mark Britton of Rowridge Farm for providing the photograph of his grandfather on page 1, to Brian Jenkins for the illustration on page 142, and the Tiverton Museum of Mid Devon Life for permission to use the photographs and illustrations on pages 9, 63, 85, 105, 110, 129, 131, 133, 156, 158, 203, 207, 217, 249, 255, 263, 267, 283, 286, 310, 315, 323, 331, 335 and 337. I am extremely grateful to Peter Skeet for the jacket design of this book. All other photographs and drawings have been produced by the author.

Introduction

Before work on this book could begin, certain perameters had to be set. How were we going to define Tiverton? At what date should the history begin and end? We decided it should be concerned with the ancient parish of Tiverton, whose boundaries were later to be those of the borough. The starting-point had to be the very earliest evidence of human activity in the area, although this was long before any permanent settlement. Various dates were suggested at which to bring things to an end; the Second World War, the accession of the present Queen, or the demise of the Borough under the Local Government Act of 1974. As most of today's population has arrived since those events, it seemed best to try to take the story as far as the present will allow.

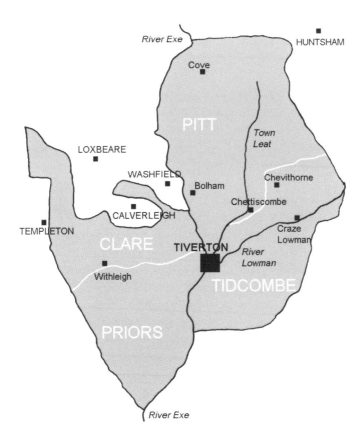

Map of the ancient parish (and borough) of Tiverton.

The first task was to survey all published material on Tiverton, beginning with its histories, which range from the widely accessible Dunsford, Harding and Snell, to the more obscure and rare Blundell and Boyce. Several monographs have been produced on various aspects of the town's past and its personalities, such as Brian Jenkins' book on the 1882 removal of Blundell's School, and Mary de la Mahotière's work on Hannah Cowley. Local contributions often appeared in the *Transactions of the Devonshire Association* and the *Devon and Cornwall Notes and Queries*, from such Tiverton worthies as Emily Skinner, Stanley Mahood and Bill Authers. Much of their work, though well-known, is now too often ignored, and, while it would have been easier simply to review what was accessible the challenge of incorporating new material from unexploited sources was irresistable.

Fortunately, the Trustees set no dead-line for completion, and this gave me time to trawl for information about Tiverton from books and collections which yielded unexpected and surprising detail. Especially rewarding were the abundant volumes published by the Public Record Office, as, for example, the calendars of *Patent Rolls* and the *Acts of the Privy Council*. Evidence was found of gun-running by one of the Borough's M.P.s, the privateering activities of a Tivertonian previously thought to be engaged only in trade, and men of the town involved in conspiracies to overthrow the government and monarchy. Tiverton's colourful, forgotten past was already coming to life.

Most time in research was spent locating and studying original documents. Some, such as title deeds belonging to the Greenway Charity and the miscellaneous collection of the War Memorial Trust are held in the town itself, but others are kept elsewhere. The Somerset Record Office has a large collection of papers of the Wyndham family among whose possessions was the manor of Pool Anthony which included property in the town, and smaller collections concerned with Cove and Chevithorne. By far the greatest number of documents, however, is to be found in Exeter, some in the Dean and Chapter's Archives, but the vast majority at the Devon Record Office. There, nearly four years were spent looking at more than 5,000 documents, many concerned specifically with Tiverton, while others were county-wide papers containing information on the parish. One set of very early records uncovered some exciting details about the town's trade. The *Exeter Customs Accounts* reveal that, from as early as the 14th century Tivertonians were importing goods by ship into Exeter, generally from France or Spain but, later, from as far away as Africa. Other revelations came from the borough and manor court rolls, which begin in the 15th century, and contain the earliest mention of Greneway, Blundell and Slee, as well as fascinating details of life in late medieval Tiverton. The Devon Record Office houses the longest complete run of County Quarter Sessions records, dating back to 1592. Within this collection the Act Books were extensively used as were various miscellaneous documents, but time prevented close study of the bulky rolls. Another omission had to be an in-depth examination of material held in the National Archives (formerly, the Public Record Office). Their publications have been used, but there is much scope in the collections to add to our knowledge, as Peter Maunder's work has shown. From his studies on the Chancery Court material relating to Tiverton he has found, for example, the exact dates for the building of the Great House and Gotham House.

The Record Office also holds photocopies of the *Harrowby MSS*, the unique collection of 18th and 19th century correspondence between Tiverton and its patrons, the Ryder family, parts of which have been published by Chalk and Bourne. Shortly after the enactment of the Local Government Act of 1973, the Record Office received the papers of the defunct Borough Council. This collection contains scores of documents, many of which have probably never been inspected since they were written. Each morning, anticipating the boxes full of unsorted papers, was like Christmas morning - what secrets would they yield? There was the earliest list of byelaws of the Borough, highly detailed property deeds, voting lists for elections of burgesses or the mayor, and much more. Although Council papers increase in volume as the years go on, by the end of the 19th century the number of other sources decrease; many documents are simply not yet available in the public domain. Newspapers, however, go some way to filling the gap. Regionally, they begin with *Trewman's Exeter Flying Post* in the middle of the 18th century; in 1856 the *Tiverton Gazette* was founded, and still is published every week. Early newspapers carried verbatim reports of court cases and other events, but reporting has changed over the years, and now we demand, or at least are served reports that are all-too brief. The local historian of the late 20th century is armed often only with newspapers and memories, both of which tend to be fickle tools and seldom corroborate each other.

The importance of Tiverton in national history is illustrated by the fact that very few sources fail to mention it. Indeed, references turn up in the most unlikely places, such as the Dutch National Archives, which contain volumes of correspondence between Tiverton and Exeter merchants and their Amsterdam counterparts. The excitement of discovery was sustained; indeed, it has never waned, and continued to demand frequent revision of the text even to the end. It is in the hope of sharing such delights as it has brought to me that I offer you *A History of Tiverton*.

1 The First People of the Area

How far back can we trace Tiverton's past? Before the earliest buildings we now see around us were built, before the familiar hedgebanks and lanes in the countryside were made, back to an age where even the landscape would be unrecognisable to us. Evidence of human activity from such a remote time is rarely found; most things used then have simply perished, yet some clues to life in that distant past have been found locally. While working in his fields in the late 1920s, Mark Britton of Rowridge Farm, Halberton, noticed some yellowish-brown stones in the plough soil. He had never seen such stone in any of the local quarries and realised his finds were unusual. He sent some to the British Museum, and was excited when they were identified as tools used as much as 250,000 years earlier[1].

Front and side view of a Palaeolithic hand-axe from Rowridge Farm, Halberton (shown at half the actual size), and Mark Britton, the farmer who found them.

Encouraged by what he had found, he continued his searches and by 1968 had accumulated thousands of items. His collection eventually embraced the immense span of time from the Lower Palaeolithic through the Mesolithic and Neolithic periods to the Bronze Age, which ended about 750 BC. His pioneering work has fired the enthusiasm of archaeologists ever since. The Tiverton Archaeological Group has recently found more very early material near Pool Anthony, Craze Lowman, and Little Gornhay in the Lowman Valley, and Rix in the Exe Valley. Archaeologists are now able

---

[1] some of the finds were published in 1934 and 1935, in the *Antiquaries' Journal, vol 14,* p.177, and *vol 15,* pp.343-5.

to recognise the different types of tools, and give them approximate dates, and the earliest local objects, handaxes, come from the Lower (or earliest) Palaeolithic period. By fieldwalking, that is systematically walking over ploughed soil and plotting finds on a grid, some 20 examples have been found locally[1]. They are all made of chert, a stone similar to flint, and vary in colour from yellow to brown. This particular type of chert has usually been thought to come from the Axe Valley, but fieldwalking in the Lowman Valley and near Chevithorne has led to the discovery of naturally occurring pieces of it, indicating the likelihood that the handaxes were made locally.

Who made the tools and how did they live? The vast expanse of time covered by the Palaeolithic has been termed the Ice Age, when glaciers advanced southward across Britain. The countryside would have looked like modern-day northern Scandinavia or Siberia, and even in the milder spells Southwest England lay on the northern fringe of the area visited by man[2]. Palaeolithic settlements were, almost exclusively, made in caves, such as Kent's Cavern near Torquay. Occupation was seasonal as the winters were too severe, and seems to have coincided with the migration of herds of reindeer, mammoth, bison, horse, and woolly rhinoceros. Archaeological evidence indicates that reindeer were the favourite prey, providing meat, antlers for tools, and clothing. The most common early Palaeolithic tools were handaxes, whereas later times show a greater dependence on flakes, then blades. Rowridge has produced just a single example of each. The development of these later types of tools is usually seen as a result of a growing ability to perform a wider range of tasks. Handaxes would have been used for crudely dismembering and chopping-up animals, whereas activities such as dissecting and skinning would call for the more refined flakes and blades. The Tiverton material possibly accumulated from a succession of seasonal visits by hunters following the migrating herds. The animals used well-defined routes, so the hunters could often lie in wait for their prey. All the local find-spots are on slight slopes, rising above relatively wide, shallow, marshy valleys; Rowridge, Pool Anthony, Craze Lowman, Little Gornhay being by the Ailsa Brook or River Lowman, and Rix beside the River Exe - excellent positions from which to observe the herds and attack them. But any notion of continuous settlement during the Palaeolithic period must be discounted. In view of the small number of finds, the visits to this inhospitable area could have been separated by periods of tens of thousands of years.

The Mesolithic Age may be said to date from about 10,000BC when the climate improved dramatically. The glaciers covering most of Britain retreated northwards, and

---

[1] this is an unusually large number, as most Palaeolithic material comes from cave deposits or gravel beds. In Devon, surface finds of these handaxes seem to centre on the Exe, Culm, Otter, and Axe valleys (Todd, 1987, 41).

[2] Roe 1981, 135.

the melting ice caused sea levels to rise. The harsh steppe and tundra landscape gave way to dense forests, first of birch and pine, but later oak and hazel predominate. A range of grasses and plants more suited to the warmer climate colonised the region as did the animals that fed on them. The Tiverton area would be a more appealing place to live. Instead of having to rely on a limited range of species in a barren landscape, an ever-widening variety of animals and plants were now available as food. The changes prompted new types of stone tools and weapons. Small blades and tips, called microliths, were produced in a variety of forms. They were particularly suitable for tipping arrows and spears used for killing smaller prey, such as deer, birds, and fish. Hundreds of these have been found locally. The earliest were still mainly of chert, particularly a type called Greensand chert, which occurs naturally in the Blackdown Hills and the Vale of Taunton[1]. The greatest concentration of Mesolithic material was recently found near Craze Lowman in advance of the building the North Devon Link Road, when fieldwalking produced 165 flint pieces and 566 of chert from an area just 46 metres by 80. Research elsewhere in Mid Devon[2] has shown that the greater the percentage of chert the earlier the date, consequently, the 77% chert found in this particular concentration has been dated to before 7,000BC. The Craze Lowman area has also yielded bladelets, borers, and scrapers, used for scraping hides, making wooden objects, and sewing garments. Such smaller tools were chipped from a large piece of chert or flint, which, when all had been removed, is known as a core. Several of these have been in the same area, indicating that tools were being made on the spot. This was clearly a place where Mesolithic groups came, stayed, and, as well as hunting, undertook a variety of domestic tasks.

This period is often seen as a time of gradual transition from a nomadic life-style to a sedentary one. People attempted to control animals like wild cattle and deer. One way of doing this was to clear small areas of woodland, so encouraging the growth of grasses which, in turn, attracted grazing animals. Possible evidence of this practice was found during the excavation of a later feature at Long Burrow, on the Uplowman Road, where fragments of oak charcoal were found alongside early Mesolithic tools. The charcoal was radiocarbon-dated to about 6400BC, and interpreted as being from a phase of primary woodland clearance[3]. As the period progressed, better materials, including a grey chert originating from Portland, Dorset, supplemented the local variety. By plotting similar finds of this in the Southwest, it has been shown that[4] once it was brought to the mouth of the Exe it either continued along the coast to Cornwall, or turned north-west up the River Exe and its tributaries. Flint, which is more easily

---

[1] Norman 1975, 28.

[2] Silvester et al. 1987, 18.

[3] Smith, 1990, 19.

[4] Palmer 1970, 92.

worked than chert, was also being brought to the Tiverton area, especially the finer-grained black type occurring at Beer in South Devon. Even at this early date, trade and communications were becoming important.

Palaeolithic and Mesolithic worked flint and chert has been discovered all along the lower Lowman Valley, as well as on the eastern slopes of the Exe near Bolham and on the higher ground near Chevithorne. However, it is almost certain that these find-spots do not represent the full geographical range of early human activity, but they are the only the places that have so far been investigated. The major part of the Tiverton area, including all the land west of the River Exe and the large expanses of higher ground to the north and south of the town, has not been looked at. Who knows what lies there, waiting to be discovered?

Permanent settlements can be recognised from about 4,000BC, and characterise the beginning of the period archaeologists call the New Stone Age or Neolithic. First, clearings needed to be made in the woodland. The polished stone axes used to cut down the trees and work the felled timber have come to epitomise this period and are considered by many to be the most aesthetically pleasing objects made by prehistoric man. Usually made of flint, they were worked to a perfectly smooth finish before being secured to a handle. Experiments have shown, perhaps surprisingly, that a smooth finish is more resilient than a flaked one. Local examples have come from Withleigh, Tidcombe, the River Exe, as well as the highly productive area around Craze Lowman. Typical settlements of this period appear to consist of a number of enclosures near to a dwelling, which is often a roughly rectangular hut, surrounded by a ditch broken only to provide an entrance. Settlements like this have been recognised by using aerial photography[1]; two sites near Chettiscombe and Chevithorne show possible signs of enclosures and huts covering quite a large area. Permanent settlements required an easily available source of food, and so probably accelerated the domestication of animals, which also provided skins for clothing and shelter. Scrapers, small circular tools held between the thumb and index finger, were used to clean and treat hides, and are common finds from this period, especially in the Craze Lowman area. Cleared land would have been used for growing cereals as well as for animal enclosures, and some sites in the Southwest have produced remains of primitive strains of wheat and barley dating from about 3,000BC. Tiverton, however, has produced only indirect evidence in the form of the large stone pounders and rubbers found at Rowridge, used to break down grain.

As settlements increased in number, greater importance was placed on defining boundaries. One method was to set up markers, often in conspicuous places such as the

---

[1] ditches, although filled in, retain more moisture and produce a stronger growth of grass or crops, which is visible from the air, similarly, remains of stone features will not retain moisture, so sparse growth will be noticeable.

summit of a hill. Wooden posts, of course, have not survived, but on Exmoor and Dartmoor many stone markers remain. Another could have stood on the high ground north of Tiverton near the farm of Firebeacon, where a group of fields once bore the name 'Long Stone'. Large burial mounds were also characteristic of the Neolithic period, and were probably yet another way of marking out territory. In Devon and Cornwall, the most common form was the chambered tomb, a circular mound with an entrance formed of large stones leading to a series of chambers where either individual or multiple burials were placed. Although none survive locally, the place name 'quoit' may be a clue to where they once stood[1] – in Stoodleigh we find Quoit-at-Cross.

Further afield, the chalk lands of Wessex are dotted with another type of mound known as the earthen long barrow, like that at West Kennett in Wiltshire. The westernmost examples were thought to be confined to south Dorset, until a proposed building development in 1985 on a site at Long Burrow, beside the Uplowman Road, began to interest archaeologists. The site contained part of an unclassified and undated feature marked on the Ordnance Survey map as 'mound'. An incomplete, yet detailed excavation, revealed that the mound was originally a metre high and more than 50 metres long, and was, at least partly, surrounded by a ditch, three metres deep[2]. The mound had been formed from soil removed for the ditch, probably with a slight core of turf and sandstone slabs. Although there was no secure dating evidence to place this monument firmly in the Neolithic period its form suggests that it is a Wessex-type long barrow – the farthest west so far recognised[3]. Who built it? Were they simply descendants of the local Mesolithic population who had, through trade and exchange of ideas and fashions, adopted a Wessex-type burial practice, or were they immigrants from that area? We can only speculate.

Metalworking was introduced to Britain from the Continent before 2,000BC. The first objects, made of copper or gold, were employed mainly for ceremonial, ritual or decorative purposes: both metals are relatively soft, so are not suited to repeated physical use. Copper was put to greater practical use, however, when it was combined with tin to produce bronze, giving rise to the name of the period, the Bronze Age. The earliest metalwork found locally comprises a copper flat axe from Rowridge Farm, and two bronze items, a blade discovered on the slopes of Exeter Hill, and a palstave[4], found some years ago 'near Tiverton'[5]. The most

---

[1] Todd 1987, 86.   [2] Smith 1990, 15
[3] ib., 24.
[4] a metal axe-head which was lashed to a cleft wooden handle.
[5] cited in Pearce 1972, 238.

important items have been found near Washfield. A reputedly large group of objects was found near Beauchamp Farm in the 19th century, but all were quickly sold and dispersed, except for one decorated palstave. The second site, near a ford across the River Exe at Worth, produced a hoard consisting of a leaf-shaped sword blade, two spearheads, and a circular sheet of bronze, dating to about 1,100BC. The sheet would possibly have been worked, with others, into a cauldron or similar vessel[1]. Hoards are common during this period and, when they contain unfinished items, are often seen as the stock-in-trade of an itinerant smith, hidden in times of danger.

The custom of placing the dead in an earthwork continued into the Bronze Age, but then cremation was preferred to burial and circular barrows to long ones. Bronze Age barrows are more likely to contain the remains of a single body which, judging from the range of valuable goods placed with the remains, would be that of a person of substance. Groups of these tombs are still visible on nearby Gibbet and Witheridge Moors. Though only one well-preserved example exists within the bounds of Tiverton parish, lying just to the south of Craze Lowman, aerial photographs suggest that there is a group of five in the lower Lowman Valley, three of which are immediately to the south of Chettiscombe. As yet no settlements related to these barrows have been identified, but, considering the amount of flint found from this period, there is no doubt they existed. The likeliest site is near the Craze Lowman barrow, but shards of Bronze Age pottery have also been found at Bolham, indicating domestic activity there as well[2].

Throughout the late Neolithic and the Bronze Age, southern England came to be dominated by a culture originating in Wessex. Society was controlled by an élite warrior-class who regulated the trade and ownership of luxury goods so characteristic of this culture. Many of these exotic items were placed in graves with their owners, such as the Egyptian glass beads found with a burial at Bampfylde Hill, North Molton. Weapons, which make up a large proportion of Bronze Age finds, were more important as visual symbols of authority than as tools of warfare. In fact, bronze was seldom used for practical purposes, and rarely fell into the hands of anyone outside the controlling élite. The introduction of iron, however, had a profound effect on this society. Its abundance meant that it could not command such a high prestige value, and it became available to a wider section of society. The warrior-class monopoly of metal was broken. Because of these changes, the power-base slowly shifted away from the chalk lands of southern England to the iron-rich Southeast. Consequently, Devon's situation, already peripheral during the Bronze Age, was now far removed from the main developments in society; culturally, the region stagnated to some extent. Nevertheless, and yet again, Rowridge possibly has provided important material from this time. Two currency bars,

---

[1] Evans 1881, 402.   [2] Brown 1991, 58-9.

iron ingots used in trade, were supposedly discovered there although their description was vague and they have not survived.

Overlooking the modern town of Tiverton, Cranmore Castle sits conspicuous near the top of Exeter Hill. This well-known landmark has often been described as a hill fort, although the element 'fort' may be misleading. Cranmore consists of a large elliptical area of 28 acres enclosed by a bank which, in many places, has been incorporated in later hedges. This rampart is particularly impressive on the north, where stock damage has revealed a stone core. Perhaps this is the 'wall of uncemented stone' noticed in the 1860s[1].

The best-preserved sections of the ramparts of Cranmore Castle, as seen from the north (top), and from the south, overlooking the town of Tiverton (bottom).

[1] Skinner 1906, 380.

To interpret the site as defensive does not bear scrutiny. It is on a spur rather than a hilltop, the approach from the south being downhill. The interior is not flat, so an enemy could enter at one point without ever being noticed from other areas. An interpretation as a stock corral, a meeting-place, or even a market is much more attractive.

One piece of evidence, admittedly tenuous, in support of Cranmore's being a focal point was the coin discovered on its northern slopes. Found in the 1990s with the aid of a metal-detector, the silver coin was minted in the first century BC. The Dumnonii, the tribe that occupied Devon and Cornwall at that time, did not mint coins and it is supposed that they relied largely on barter. Coins were known to them, however, as many sites in the two counties have yielded examples from the tribes to the east, the Durotriges and Dobunni[1]. In fact, the coin found at Cranmore Castle was Durotrigian.

By this time many tribes to the east of the Dumnonii enjoyed close contact with Roman Gaul – so close, in fact, that some of their rulers were little more than puppets of the Empire. In 42AD, one of them sought protection from the Emperor Claudius, who had always intended to conquer Britain, if only to achieve what the great Julius Caesar had failed to do almost a century earlier. Four legions with a host of auxiliaries, some 40,000 trained soldiers, landed in Kent in the spring of 43AD, and by the end of the year they had subdued almost all of southeastern Britain. When the legions were assigned their tasks for the following year, *Legio II Augusta*, commanded by the future Emperor, Vespasian, was given the task of clearing up resistance in the west. Although its exact movements are largely unknown, the historian Suetonius says that this legion subdued two of the region's strongest tribes[2], usually taken to be the Durotriges and Belgae who lived in the eastern half of the Southwest peninsula. The nature of the legion's earliest contacts with the Dumnonii is unknown, but it must be emphasised that the Romans put their enemies to the sword only if they resisted. They preferred to enter into treaties and set up client-kingdoms with more peaceful tribes.

The *Legio II Augusta* established a fortress at Exeter in about 50AD[3]. Its size, about 38 acres, implies that either the whole legion was living under extremely cramped conditions or that only a part of it was stationed there and the rest deployed elsewhere. Aerial photography has led to the discovery of many Roman military sites in the mid-Devon area. During the past 20 years forts have been discovered at Bury Barton in the parish of Lapford, on the outskirts of Cullompton, straddling the Clayhanger-Bampton parish boundary near Cudmore Farm, and at Bolham, just outside of Tiverton.

---

[1] Clarke 1971, 153. [2] *Vespasian*, 4, 1.

[3] the date of its foundation is still a matter of contention, but arguments (Todd 1987, 195-6) for a date near to 50AD seem to be well-founded. The main thoroughfares of the fortress are still apparent in the lines of North Street and South Street, and High Street and Fore Street.

Samian bowl, dated 75-85AD, found in the fill of the west ditch, near the gateway of the Roman fort at Bolham. It bears the stamp RVFINI, indicating it was either made by, or for, Rufinus.

The Bolham site was recognised in 1978, during a survey in advance of the building of the North Devon Link Road. A trial trench soon yielded pieces of *terra nigra* ware, a fine pottery used by the Romans. The fort, a typical Roman rectangular shape with rounded corners, was built on a slight spur with extensive views up and down the valley of the Exe and its confluence with the Lowman. From the air, the lines of the rampart, the ditch, and all the gates, except that at the east, can be recognised. The fort covered just over three and a half acres. Judging by other examples of a similar size, where the barrack-blocks have been excavated, it could have held between 500 and 800 soldiers. What a striking impression such a large body of well-equipped troops would have made on the local Dumnonii – sounds of soldiers practising their drill in a foreign language, the sight of cavalry detachments in the surrounding countryside, and the noise and smells of iron smelting and forging[1] emanating from the fort. It would have been unlike anything they had previously experienced. Thorough excavation of the western entrance to the fort was carried out in 1982-6[2], and showed that the rampart of the fort was about five metres wide and outside it there was a ditch three metres across. The entrance area itself was made up of pebbles and gravel rammed into clay covered by a layer of river stones, with gutters to channel rainwater. The gate structure was substantial, being almost 40 feet wide, and, surprisingly, of distinct phases, datable by the pottery found in the ditches. When first built, in about 65AD, there were two gates flanked by guard-towers, but this was replaced less than ten years later by a different structure without towers. This second, and final phase, lasted until about 90AD, when the fort was abandoned.

---

[1] evidenced by slag and smelting debris.　　　[2] Maxfield 1991, 25-98.

Presumably, the troops left Bolham because they were no longer needed. The threat, real or perceived, that had prompted the building of a fort had passed. Similarly, about 75AD, *Legio II Augusta* had departed from Exeter, although it is likely that auxiliary forces remained. The conditions in Devon on the withdrawal of the legionaries are uncertain; Exeter became the administrative capital of the Dumnonii, and was possibly run by native men, aided by Romans in essential positions. As with other regional centres during the period Exeter displayed the full range of characteristically Roman buildings, such as a forum, basilica, and baths. Away from Exeter, villas have been found at a handful of locations, including Topsham and Crediton[1]. Although no civilian settlement has yet been discovered in the Tiverton area, there is distinct evidence of a continued Romanised presence. In the first half of the 19th century, several hundred small silver coins, *denarii*, were found in a pot buried near Little Gornhay Farm, and dated to the late 2nd and early 3rd centuries[2]. Fifty years ago, in 1954, a local schoolboy, Nigel Cross, noticed something shining in a section of roadwork in Castle Street which turned out to be three Roman coins dating from the later 1st century. In 1973, during archaeological excavations at 18-22, Saint Andrew Street, a single piece of 3rd or 4th century pottery was found. These finds are important in that they are the earliest evidence of activity within the area of the present town and hint at the possibility of a settlement here during the Roman period. A piece of stone, said to have been decorated with horses and numerals, found in the 1950s near Rix Farm may also date from this time. Unfortunately, it was not properly recorded and was left where it was found, a spot since forgotten.

From the late 4th century, large numbers of Roman troops were withdrawn from Britain, not only to support imperial contenders but also to fight against barbarians who threatened Rome itself. By 410, Britain had become isolated from Roman administration and had to find its own means of defence. Centrally organised activities like coinage and the mass production of pottery ceased almost immediately. Even before the Romans departed raiders from Scotland and Ireland were attacking parts of northern and eastern Britain, and as soon as they saw there was no organised defence the attacks increased. Some of the Britons invited Saxon mercenaries from Germany to help repulse the northern raiders about 430. These Saxons, however, soon turned against their hosts and called on their Germanic neighbours, Angles, Jutes, and Frisians, to join them. By the end of the 5th century they had gained control of the whole of the south and east of England. Their attempts to extend their territory met with little resistance from the native Britons until about 516 when they suffered a heavy defeat at *Mons Badonicus*[3]. This, it seems, checked their westward advance for almost 150 years.

---

[1] Jarvis & Maxfield 1975, 227; Griffith 1988, 137.

[2] Shortt 1846, 140.

[3] although the location of the battle has never been established, a site near Bath seems likely (Burkitt & Burkitt 1990, 93).

Outside the area of Saxon domination, in the north and west of Britain people developed their native cultures from the 5th century, which both looked back to earlier times and made exciting new advances. In Wales and the Southwest several Iron Age hilltop sites were re-occupied and refortified, hinting at possible political continuity from pre-Roman times. The area covering Devon and Cornwall became known as the kingdom of Dumnonia, recalling the pre-Roman tribal name of Dumnonii. Significant amounts of pottery, originating from the eastern Mediterranean and North Africa, have been found at places all around the coasts of the Southwest, Wales, Ireland, and Scotland. Much of it comes from amphorae, large jars used to hold oil or wine. What was being taken back from the Celtic lands to the Mediterranean region in return? Precious metals, perhaps, such as gold and silver from Ireland and Wales, and tin from Cornwall and Dartmoor. It is likely that this same trade brought the type of Christianity that was adopted by the Celtic peoples of western Britain and Ireland. Celtic Christianity was monastic in nature, with a strong emphasis on an austere, contemplative life. The date of Easter was fixed by using the same method as the earliest Christians, not the system laid down by the bishops of the Western Roman Empire in 314. Celtic monks, their heads shaved in a line from ear to ear, unlike the Roman practice of removing the hair from the crown of the head, travelled throughout the lands bordering the Irish Sea and the western Atlantic, spreading the word. Many of them, later elevated to the status of saints, are commemorated in Irish, Welsh and Cornish place-names and church dedications. There are but a few examples in Devon, although Saint Petroc does have more dedications in this county than in Cornwall. Of these, three are at Petton, near Bampton, West Anstey, and West Worlington[1], so it is possible that he came to the Tiverton area. Many churches originally dedicated to him, such as those at Berrynarbor and Combe Martin, were later 're-dedicated' to Saint Peter; perhaps this also occurred at Tiverton. To the east, the Saxons received Christian missionaries from the Roman Church, beginning with Augustine in 597. Kent was the first kingdom to be converted, and Canterbury became the first archbishopric in Britain. From this solid base Christianity, as promoted by the Church at Rome, spread northwards and westwards.

The cultural and political independence of Celtic Dumnonia was, inevitably, short-lived. In the mid-7th century, the Saxons renewed their push westward to conquer and settle the Southwestern peninsula. The *Anglo-Saxon Chronicle* relates that in 658 the King of Wessex forced the Britons back to the River Parret, which enters the Bristol Channel near Bridgwater. Fifty years later, Bishop Aldhelm of Sherborne wrote to the Dumnonian king, Gereint, ordering him to correct the Celtic usage in the dating of

---

[1] Grant 2000,13.

Easter[1]. Apparently he refused, for two years later a combined army from Wessex and Sussex attacked, Gereint is said to have been killed in battle, bringing to an end the independent Dumnonia (in Devon, at least). Apart from a few who moved into the unconquered Cornwall or even crossed the seas to the remaining Celtic lands of Brittany, Wales, or Ireland, most Dumnonians carried on farming their land.

Place-names are a useful guide to settlement in this period. As time went on, and the number of Saxon settlers increased, the majority of Celtic names were replaced. Devon is full of parishes and farms ending in -cott, -worthy, -hayne, or -ton, all of which were Saxon introductions. Nevertheless, a few Celtic names have survived, including Duvale, near Bampton, and Morchard, composed of *mor* and *cet*, meaning 'great wood'. The names given to rivers seem to have been unusually resilient; in the Tiverton area, the River Exe takes its name from *uisc*, Celtic for water, and the Lowman, from a word meaning 'elm tree'. The Celts held land in common; it belonged to the tribe and not to the individual; so, many of their place-names consisted of simple topographical descriptions - 'high ridge', 'wet marsh' - which would have been immediately translated into Saxon forms. On the other hand, Saxon land was divided into distinct units, or manors, owned by a particular individual whose name has often survived. Although many have been changed over the centuries, they are often still recognisable from earlier versions. So Chevithorne derives from 'the thorn tree of Ceofa', possibly the 8th century coloniser, Lurley was Leofhere's clearing, Patcott was the cott of Peatta, who is possibly the same man who is remembered in Peadhill, and Tidcombe was Tida's valley[2].

What is probably more surprising than the survival of place-names is that the administrative system of the Saxons proved so efficient that much of it is either still in use or died out only in the 19th century. Saxon kingdoms, such as Northumbria and Mercia, covered vast areas, so there was a need to create subdivisions in order to control and rule more efficiently. Shires were brought into being, with Dorset, Devon, and Somerset in existence by the late 8th century[3]. Over each shire was placed an *ealdorman*, the main royal official, who performed both military and administrative duties. Justice was meted out through the shire-court, presided over by the *ealdorman* and the bishop of the diocese. Every shire was sub-divided into hundreds[4], each of which had a court that met once a month, usually in the open air, attended by all the free tenants in the hundred. We do not know whether the hundred of Tiverton was one of the earliest to be established or a later creation, but it has been suggested[5] that it may have been linked at an early date to the hundred of Halberton. In that case one would expect to find a

---

[1] although the Synod of Whitby (664) had ordered the Celtic Church to fall in line with that of Rome, it took another 200 years before it grudgingly abandoned its practices.

[2] Mawer & Stenton 1932, 540-6.   [3] John 1982, 172.

[4] probably originally meaning the area covered by, or assessed for, 100 hides, one hide being the land necessary to support a family, varying in size according to the terrain.

[5] Thorn & Thorn 1985, Appendix.

meeting-place for the court somewhere on the border between the two hundreds. Shamel's End is the name of the crossroads just to the east of Copplestone Farm, and lies on the Halberton-Tiverton parish (and hundred) boundaries. There were hundreds in Cambridgeshire, Kent and Essex containing the element *sceamol*, a Saxon word meaning 'bench', evidently referring to the place where the members of the hundred court sat. It is quite possible that Shamel's End was the site of the early hundred court for the Tiverton-Halberton area.

By 830, Viking raids on the West Country had become commonplace. Sailing from their colonies in Ireland and northwestern France, they mainly targeted coastal areas, especially north Devon and Exeter, although sometimes they ventured further inland. There are no specific references to Viking activity in the area around Tiverton, but on many occasions the *Anglo-Saxon Chronicle* states that 'the raiding-army rode over Wessex'. Within a generation, those parts of England east of a line from London to Chester were under Viking control, and they had installed a puppet-king in Mercia (the west Midlands). Wessex, under Alfred, remained undefeated and, indeed, achieved a great victory in 878 at Edington in Wiltshire over those Vikings based in England. Nevertheless, raiders sailing from the Continent still posed a potent threat. To counteract their raids an organised system of defended towns was devised in the mid-9th century, but not completed until well into the 10th. They certainly seem to have proved effective during Alfred's reign; whereas in the 850s and 860s the Viking raiders could range throughout the whole of Wessex, by the 890s they were hard-pressed to penetrate the inland areas. In Devon, these defended towns, or *burhs*, were sited at Pilton (Barnstaple), Exeter, Halwill (Totnes) and Lydford. Men from its surrounding region garrisoned each one, so Tiverton men probably helped to defend Exeter. Alfred also divided the army into two halves; for every man on active duty there would be one at home working on the land. So successful were these measures that Wessex alone of the English kingdoms did not to succumb to the Scandinavians.

Alfred died toward the end of 899, but had written his will as much as 20 years earlier. Many of his estates passed to his elder son, Edward, while to the younger, Æthelweard, he left 17 holdings, of which nine lay in Devon. Included in the list are Cullompton, a place called *Mylenburnam* (possibly Silverton), and *Twyfiride*. Early commentators believed this last place was Twyford in Hampshire, but now it is generally agreed that Twyfiride, 'two fords', is indeed Tiverton. What can we say about Alfred's Twyfiride? Tiverton's most important historian, Martin Dunsford, states[1] that the settlement was a village on a little hill, composed of 12 tithings and governed by a

---

[1] 1790, 169

portreeve. There is no evidence for his statement, however. We do not know how long Tiverton had been in royal hands, but its strategic position as a crossing-point of both the Lowman and Exe had probably been of importance for a long time. The Saxon settlement would have been located on the high ground between the two rivers, in the same place as the present town centre. Tiverton's royal status gave it administrative, ceremonial and economic importance[1], all of which would have provided an impetus for growth. By the 10th century, Tiverton could also have had a minster, that is a church staffed by monks or clergymen sharing a communal life. Research in Hampshire has shown that minster churches had been established there by the 8th century based on royal estates that were hundred-centres[2]. As regards Devon, two more indicators of the existence of a minster have been suggested[3] – having a large parish, and a church in the charge of several priests. Tiverton fits all these criteria, so there could well have been a minster church here, perhaps having its origins much earlier in the Celtic period. There are no surviving remains of Alfred's Tiverton. Almost all buildings would have been made of timber and roofed with thatch, and the ravages of time and successive fires would have seen to their destruction many times over. We cannot even say whether Twyfiride was a hamlet, village, or a town at this early date, but, at least we do know it existed in Saxon times.

---

[1] Haslam 1984, 276.   [2] Hase 1988, 45-8.

[3] Orme 1991, 9.

2 The Town Established

It is likely that 10th century Tiverton, as a royal estate, shared in the prosperity of Alfred the Great's successors, who extended their rule to cover all England. Trade was strongly encouraged, especially by Alfred's son, Edward the Elder, who decreed that buying and selling had to take place in a *port* – the name given to a trading-centre, inland or maritime – and were to be witnessed by a royal official, known as a *reeve*. Tiverton's royal status probably meant that it had a resident *reeve*, and was possibly considered a *port*. Indeed, we still have Newport Street, close to the church, perhaps the site of an early market. Edward's son, Athelstan, the first king of all England, made trading at markets and elsewhere much easier by the introduction of a national coinage with just one denomination, the silver penny. The mixture of races could well have been apparent at the markets. Native Britons, it seems, were still recognisably distinct and, in some cases, lived apart from the Saxons. Following a rebellion in Cornwall Athelstan's plans to subdue the Britons included the expulsion of members of their community at Exeter, where they occupied a special quarter of the city. As well as Britons and Saxons, could there also have been Danes near Tiverton? After all, they occupied most of eastern England throughout the century, and some could possibly have settled as far west as Devon. The place name Veraby, in the parish of Bishops Nympton, has a Scandinavian origin, and is almost identical to Fairby just north of Bolham. Overlooking Tiverton itself, Cranmore is sometimes named in documents as Skrinkhill, which sounds particularly Scandinavian.

Viking attacks were renewed in the 980s, and were often ferocious. Devon was subjected to a fearsome raid in 1001 when Exeter was attacked but managed to repel the assailants. Nevertheless, 'they turned through the countryside, and did just as they were accustomed; killed and burned'[1], until they were defeated at Pinhoe. Most of England was similarly ravaged, and King Æthelred's efforts to buy peace failed. Matters worsened when he issued an order that all Danish men in England were to be killed on Saint Brice's Day, November 13th, 1002. Tiverton's historian, Dunsford, assures us, almost 800 years later, that 'the Danes that were in the town were massacred by the women, with much secrecy, in the night'[2]. In response, the Danish ruler, Sweyn, launched a determined series of attacks on England, with the intention of absorbing the country into his empire. Exeter was attacked in 1003; great riches were taken, the minster was burnt down, and all its charters destroyed. England suffered a further ten years of warfare and heavy tributes in coin were paid to buy off the raiders. By 1013,

---

[1] *Anglo-Saxon Chronicle.*
[2] 1790, 169.

however, the Saxons were so weakened that Sweyn was accepted as king.

When he died in 1014 Æthelred returned from exile to be king again, only to lose the whole of England within four years. The victor was Sweyn's son, the great Cnut, who divided the country into four earldoms. The most important, Wessex, which extended all along the south coast and contained the bulk of the royal estates, including Tiverton, was placed in the hands of Godwin, the son of a South Saxon prince,.Marriages to the royal dynasty helped him and his family achieve great prominence and possessions. While he himself held Wessex, his eldest son Swein was made earl of an area that included the counties of Berkshire and Somerset, and his second son, Harold, controlled East Anglia. When Cnut's son died in 1042 without an heir, the throne of England passed to Æthelred's son, Edward, known as 'the Confessor' or 'the Saint'. Recognising the danger of the over-powerful Godwin dynasty Edward had its leader discredited, and stripped the family of their titles. They left the country in 1051, but returned in the following year, and were allowed to remain. Godwin and Swein died soon after this, leaving the earldom of Wessex to Harold. Tiverton became part of the dower of Godwin's widow, Gytha[1].

Saxon society was by this time divided into distinct classes, each with specified duties and ties of service to the others. Though it was never systematic, or simple, a social pyramid had taken shape. At the top was the King; below him the earls, then came the nobles or *thegns* who had to provide armed service, repair fortresses and work on bridges. Under the nobles were the *geneats*, who seem to have performed personal services for the nobles and, in many cases, were bailiffs or reeves on their estates. Locally, the earliest spelling of Knightshayes is Knyghtenhaie, which could be derived from the *gehæg*, or enclosure, of the *geneat* of the royal estate of Tiverton. Next in rank came the *cottars* who held at least five acres of land, and were required to do, on average, one day's work a week for the lord of the manor, more during harvest. The duties of the *geburs* were even more onerous. Their services varied according to the customs of the individual manor, but a typical list of duties could include work for two days a week on the manor, an annual rent of about ten pence, a tribute of barley and two hens in the autumn, and at Easter a lamb or two pence. The *gebur*, when he first acquired his land, perhaps received two oxen, one cow, six sheep, and seven acres sown with corn. On his death, however, the lord of the manor could take any surplus. The lowest of all the social orders were the slaves, but even they were accorded rights; their food allowances were prescribed by the customs of the manor.

Edward the Confessor died on January 5th, 1066, a day given great significance when the *Domesday Book* was compiled 20 years later. One of the questions then asked

---

[1] Parry 1871, 401.

was 'Who held the land on the day that King Edward lived and died?' In many cases the answers provide us with the earliest mention of places in the Tiverton area as well as the first named individuals associated with them. Identification of the Saxon landholders is inherently difficult. Problems arise as we are usually given a single name with, sometimes, a nickname or a profession. Alstan Tilley, 'cultivator', was the lord of West Manley and Newcott (now called Way, near Templeton), but was he the same Alstan who held a group of manors to the east of Exeter? Two different manors, both called Chevithorne, were owned by Ælmer, who appears to be holding 57 properties across Devon, was this one individual or as many as 57 different men with the same common name? Such questions pose no easy answers. Those who can be identified vary greatly in importance. Hardwulf, the owner of one of the Bradley manors near Withleigh, is not mentioned in any other document. On the other hand, Alfrun, who held Craze Lowman, was clearly a woman of means as she had five other properties in this part of Devon, including Canonsleigh. Brictric, said to be a thegn of Gloucester, held Bolham as well as the more valuable manors of Bideford, Winkleigh, Halberton and Great Torrington in Devon, in addition to property elsewhere in the West. He would have been an absentee landlord, like Mærleswein, the sheriff of Lincoln, who owned the smaller of the manors called Tiverton and one of the two nearby Washfields. Godwin's widow Gytha was the best known owner of land locally. All of her property, covering more than 36,000 acres, lay south of the Thames, mainly in Wiltshire, Somerset, and Devon, and earned her an annual income of about £600. In Devon, she owned the important hundred-centres of Hartland, Witheridge, and, of course, Tiverton.

The death of Edward the Confessor led to the Norman Conquest, the story of which is well known. William the Conqueror, crowned King of England on Christmas Day, 1066, had to deal almost immediately with a rebellious Gytha, who, with a small army, had made a base at Exeter. The Saxons resisted for 18 days, but before it fell she and her children made their escape. The King confiscated her lands, including the estate of Tiverton, which he possibly reduced in size at this time, giving Huntsham, Calverleigh, and Loxbeare to those who had shown him support. Feudalism, the system by which all land was held in exchange for services, including military, monetary and labour dues, was once regarded as a Norman introduction. Nowadays, it is generally agreed that it had been emerging in many parts of England, especially Wessex. The change brought about by the Normans was to impose it in a systematic and thorough manner. William took great care in distributing land to his followers; no single person was to be allowed to create his own power-base. Even the king's favourites, who held many manors, usually had them scattered over several counties.

In 1085 after 'deep speech' with his closest advisers, William ordered a survey of his country. This was accomplished in two years, and has become familiar to us as the *Domesday Book*. The speed of its completion and the scope of its detail make it probably the greatest achievement of early medieval administration anywhere. Its purpose is still debated, but it seems to have been made to establish the resources of each manor available for taxation, and to provide a definitive listing of who owned what. The information about Devon is found in two separate sources: the Exchequer version, the complete survey as sent to the King, and the Exeter volume, now on display at the Cathedral Library. The Exeter Domesday was probably compiled locally from those who actually made the survey and contains some material which was left out of the final version.

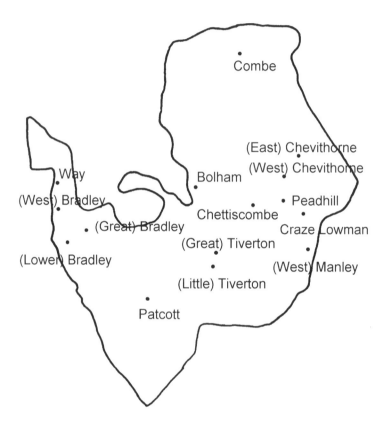

The location of those manors in the parish of Tiverton according to the Domesday Book [1].

---

[1] the smaller Tiverton manor, later called Little Tiverton, should almost certainly be placed in the Little Silver-Collipriest area; the identification of *Petecote* with Patcott has not yet been established; a large area around Cove seems unaccounted for, but was possibly included with Stoodleigh, or may have been one of the manors called Combe, which are usually placed in Uplowman parish.

The Tiverton entries shed light on William's methods of allocating land. He held the manor of Tiverton in his own hands, along with over 70 others in the county, almost all of which had belonged to the Saxon royal family. William's shire reeve, or sheriff, in Devon was Baldwin de Brionne, who was based at his castle of Okehampton. He was tenant-in-chief of almost 180 manors in the county, but most of them were held by under-tenants, including East Chevithorne, Chettiscombe, and Patcott. The Saxon sheriff of Lincoln, Mærleswein, had been stripped of his lands for opposing William, and by the time of the survey, his properties, including Little Tiverton and Washfield were in the hands of Ralph Pagnell, sheriff of Yorkshire. On the other hand, William generously rewarded those who had served in his army; one of his ordnance-masters, Haimeric de Arques, received Great Bradley. An under-tenant of Geoffrey de Mowbray, the Bishop of Coutances, held the other two manors called Bradley, together with Peadhill. West Chevithorne belonged to Ralph of Pomeroy, whose family is still remembered in the Devon names Berry Pomeroy and Stockleigh Pomeroy. Similarly, Walter of Clavile's name survived in the manor and hamlet of Lowman Clavile, until it changed much later to Craze Lowman. Not one of the Norman tenants-in-chief lived on his Tiverton estate, and the same can probably be said of the under tenants named.

The location of the Tiverton manors can be established in almost every case, although it is virtually impossible to define their exact Domesday boundaries. Manors were always fluid entities; they came and went, parts were added and subtracted. They were simply convenient units for administration, and did not always respect parish or hundred boundaries. Judging from later records, other manors infringed on the parish of Tiverton; land around Palmershayes belonged to the manor of Worth in Washfield, and Huntsham probably included the far north-eastern part of Tiverton parish. Some idea of the relative sizes of the manors in the area can be gained from the figures given in the *Domesday Book* as 'land for x ploughs', usually referred to as ploughlands. Historians have attempted many times to evaluate this measure, which probably refers to the amount of potential not actual arable land on the manor. It is generally agreed that each ploughland covered between 100 and 200 acres, therefore Tiverton's 36 corresponded to about 5,500 acres of arable land. At the other extreme, the two smaller Bradley manors covered only 150 acres each. Most of the corn grown on the Tiverton manors would have been ground into flour at local mills, of which four are mentioned. The royal manor had two, which paid 5s 6d a year, a third was probably located in Westexe and the other somewhere on the lower Lowman. Chettiscombe's mill was taxed at 2s, but the most valuable was that at Bolham which rendered 7s. Land other than arable is categorised as meadow, pasture, or what must have been a significant feature of the local landscape, woodland. Baldwin's manor of Chevithorne had 100 acres of it, and Chettiscombe 60 acres. Tiverton manor contained the two largest woods in the area; one of 160 acres and another covering 780 acres which probably stretched from Ashley toward Bickleigh. The three swineherds recorded on the manor would undoubtedly have kept their pigs there.

Heads of families are counted but not named in the *Domesday Book*. They appear under three categories – villagers, smallholders, and slaves. Although the size of the population will never be known with any certainty, by using the formula suggested by Nash[1] the royal manor of Tiverton could have contained 380 persons, Bolham 100, and the remaining manors together would have 370 people. This total of about 850 men, women and children in the parish does seem credible at a time when the population of England probably stood at about two million.

On the death of William the Conqueror in 1087, his sons, Robert, William, and Henry fought over Normandy and England. Eventually, the guile of Henry prevailed and his inheritance was united. From the 1090s one of his chief supporters had been Richard de Redvers, whose family took their name from Reviers in Normandy. Henry, like his father, rewarded his followers with lands in England, and Richard de Redvers received properties in Hampshire, the Isle of Wight, and Devon, including Plympton, where he lived, and the royal estate of Tiverton. Before his death in 1107, Richard founded a priory at Sainte Marie, Néhou, in Normandy, and gave it 60 shillings from his manor at Tiverton to maintain the canons. His son, Baldwin, made a similar foundation for four canons at Exeter in 1126, on land beside the Exe given to him by the King. The house was dedicated to Saint James the Apostle, and placed under the governance of Saint Martin-des-Champs, just outside Paris.

Baldwin de Redvers was based in the castle at Plympton, which was probably built by him or his father. His Devon lands formed the Honour of Plympton, the term 'honour' being given to the group of manors of a tenant-in-chief, generally centred on a town with a castle where justice was meted out at an Honour Court. Peadhill and two of the three Bradleys had become part of the Honour of Barnstaple, under the ownership of Judhael of Totnes. The Pomeroys' manor of Chevithorne was still owned by the family as part of their Honour of Berry, and the other Chevithorne, together with Chettiscombe, formed part of the de Brionne's Honour of Okehampton, where a castle had stood since soon after the Conquest. The descendants of Odo FitzGamelin counted Great Bradley in their Honour of Torrington, and the de Mohun's Honour of Dunster included Bolham. The only other Honour represented in Tiverton concerned the manor of Craze Lowman, whose former tenant-in-chief Walter de Clavile had been made subordinate to the wife of Robert, Earl of Gloucester, King Henry's chief counsellor (and bastard son).

---

[1] Nash 1988.

For years, Robert's half-sister, Matilda, was expected to succeed their father, Henry. However, when the King died, in December 1135, he was actually at war with Matilda's husband, Geoffrey of Anjou, so many of the English nobles refused to accept her as Queen. Henry's nephew Stephen of Blois crossed the Channel and took the crown for himself, but support for Matilda grew, especially in the Southwest. Within a year, Stephen was forced to intervene in a dispute concerning rights over the church of Uffculme. Although one of the parties, Robert of Bampton, had lost the case in court against Stephen's brother, Henry of Blois, Abbot of Glastonbury, rather than repent he 'afflicted all his neighbours with fire and pillage'[1]. He was summoned to appear before the King, but escaped to his castle at Bampton, the slender remains of which can still be seen to the side of the road to Morebath. Stephen himself rode to Bampton and forced the surrender of the castle. This was not to be the end of his troubles in Devon, for news soon came that Baldwin de Redvers had taken the castle at Exeter. Stephen's forces rushed down the Exe valley and, while many of his men laid siege to the castle, another group carried on to Baldwin's base at Plympton, where the garrison soon submitted and the castle was slighted. The siege at Exeter was raised only when those inside ran out of water. Baldwin escaped, and eventually sought refuge at the court of Geoffrey of Anjou and Matilda. He remained there for two years until Robert of Gloucester launched his great assault on Stephen's forces.

Matilda returned from France and established her base in the Southwest, where she acted like a queen and was received as one. Her supporters were given prestigious titles in 1141: Baldwin de Redvers, the only noble never to recognise Stephen as King, was made Earl of Devon, and William de Mohun became Earl of Somerset. It was probably at this date, not 1106, that Baldwin built his castle at Tiverton next to the church. The main objection to the earlier date is that if the castle had existed in 1136 it would surely have deserved some attention from Stephen when on his way from Bampton to Exeter[2]. Tiverton Castle should probably be seen as a response to the ongoing civil war between Stephen and Matilda. The site chosen was on the edge of what can be described as a cliff overlooking the Exe, with wide-ranging views to the north and south along the valley and west to the hills. It almost certainly started as a conical earthen mound, or 'motte', topped with a keep, linked to a large flat open area, known as a bailey, which was possibly ditched or even moated. If its coloured banners were flying, the castle would have made a strong visual impression on those approaching Tiverton as well as those who lived in the town. It proclaimed the presence of Baldwin de Redvers who,

---

[1] *Gesta Stephani*, 29-31.

[2] and would have been recorded, like the slighting of Baldwin's castle at Plympton, in the *Gesta Stephani*. Dunsford's date of 1106 was when Baldwin received the manor of Tiverton.

with the castle at Plympton slighted, made Tiverton his main residence, and, to entertain himself and his visitors, established a deer park at Ashley. At Exeter, Baldwin's foundation of Saint James Priory was in financial difficulty, as the income from its lands at Cowick was not enough to maintain the monks. His solution was simple; in 1143, he gave them the revenues from the church of Tiverton.

Meanwhile, Matilda had failed to extend her influence further than the Southwest. Her weak position, together with the deaths of her two most able supporters, the Earls of Hereford and Gloucester, persuaded her to leave England for good. But what she never gained, her son Henry eventually did. Despite an unsuccessful invasion in 1153, he forced Stephen into naming him as his successor. The wait was not long; Stephen died in the following year and the 21-year old restless, but decisive king began his reign. One of his first tasks was to enquire into certain titles and rights to land that had become confused during the previous years. These included a dispute over the Redvers endowment to Saint James' Priory. The original grant of 1143 clearly states that the gift consisted of the income from all the church of Tiverton. However, the Pope's judgement, made in 1159 was that only one half of it was to belong to the Priory, and the other half was to be kept by two Tiverton clergymen presented by Richard de Redvers, Baldwin's successor[1].

As well as this documentary evidence of Saint Peter's Church and its priests, one feature of the 12th century building has survived, namely the arched doorway in the north wall, facing the Castle ruins. It is not known whether the arch is in its original position, but it was there when the church was virtually rebuilt in the 19th century[2]. The doorway is probably all that remains of the first stone church on the site, which no doubt replaced others of cob or wood. Tradition has it that Leofric, Bishop of Exeter, consecrated Saint Peter's in 1073, but there is no firm evidence to support this claim. The four portions, so clearly in existence during the 12th century, may have dated from Saxon times, or even earlier. The portioners probably served the original three or four (depending on whether Prior's was newly created) divisions of the extensive parish, although the names, Pitt, Tidcombe, and Clare, were not applied until later. Parishes had been defined as early as the seventh century, but their boundaries in Devon did not become firmly established until about the 12th century. At the same time the ecclesiastical administrative hierarchy of diocese-archdeaconry-rural deanery was

---

[1] one passage (*Redvers*, 93-5) seems to read 'the half which the monks possess has four portions', but this probably refers to the time when the Priory did claim the whole of the church. However confusing the situation may now appear, we can take some comfort in the fact that, even the papacy was unclear on this matter: although two bishops of Exeter had already recognised the later agreement, the Pope himself in 1199 confirmed the gift of the whole church to the Priory (see DRO DD6,690).
[2] Hughes 1862, 235.

finalised. Tiverton became the head of a rural deanery controlling a dozen parishes, but subordinate to the archdeaconry of Exeter. The importance in royal affairs and everyday life of the Church, with the Pope at its head, the higher clergy exercising a separate jurisdiction in their courts, and countless priests with a care of souls and a monopoly of education cannot be overstated. As late as the 19th century ecclesiastical courts adjudicated on morals and wills, and the clergy were maintained by the laity's payment of tithes.

The 12th century doorway on the north side of Saint Peter's Church. The chevron ornament is typically Norman and can also be seen at the churches of Sampford Peverell and East Worlington.

Henry II made many changes to the administration of the shires, making sheriffs accountable for the royal finances they handled. The annual payments received in each county were entered on the Great Rolls of the Exchequer, better known as *Pipe Rolls*.

In these, we can find local references from as early as 1164, recording details of the manors of Little Washfield and Little Tiverton, which had been taken into the King's hands. Crown lands, even if they were often only held temporarily, were farmed as efficiently as possible; the aim was to maximise income. This can be seen in 1166 when the keeper of the two manors was made to pay £3 12s as they were understocked by as much as 22 oxen and two horses. Within a couple of years, both holdings were leased to the sheriff of Devon for a payment of £3 a year. In 1179 this post was held by William Briwer, a man who was to play a prominent part in national affairs under Henry's successor, Richard the Lionheart. When the King set sail to fight in the Crusades, just three months after his coronation in 1189, he left the care of England in the hands of four men, one of them the sheriff of Devon. Briwer's interests in the Tiverton area grew considerably during the 1190s when he bought the northern half of the Honour of Berry, which included the Pomeroy manor of Chevithorne, and he also acquired Newcott and the manor of West Manley. How he came by the last two is not clear, but it has been suggested[1] that 'by using his position, he had regularised uncertain, ambiguous tenures, and probably falsified documents accordingly'. Yet he was not always beyond the law; in 1196, he was fined 20d for bringing a false claim in the Redvers' hundred court of Tiverton.

King Richard's overseas exploits, as we well know, ended with imprisonment; England was forced to raise a ransom equivalent to five times his annual income. This drained the nation's coffers and angered the barons. When he died in France in 1199, he had spent only six months of his 10-year reign in England, and was succeeded by his brother. John's subsequent actions aroused such hostility among the barons that they forced him to issue the *Magna Carta* (June 15th 1215), which curtailed his personal power. Nevertheless, neither John nor the strongest-minded of the barons were willing to adhere to the terms of the charter. The outcome was civil war, with the barons offering the crown to the French Prince Louis. Fortunately, probably for all concerned, John died in October 1216. The civil war ended, the anger of the barons subsided, and support dwindled for Louis, who was defeated by a Norman adventurer called Falkes de Bréauté, a man later to figure in Tiverton's history. Although there seems to have been little fighting in the Southwest, the troubled times probably account for the hoard of 17 silver coins of John's reign found near Highgate Cottage at Loxbeare in 1980. Clearly, someone considered it wise to hide this modest amount of money, but never came back to recover it.

Throughout these turbulent times, Tiverton had been in the hands of William de Redvers. He granted borough status to Honiton and Plympton, and it appears that he also did the same for Tiverton. The foundation of boroughs in this period must be seen

---

[1] Halsbury 1960, 31.

as a speculative undertaking by tenants-in-chief, an attempt to attract settlement and increase income, through burgage rents and market and fair tolls. No charter survives, but in the 1220s Tiverton was taxed as a borough, and burgage rents were paid on properties in the town. Payment of these rents would have excused town dwellers from labour duties, unlike those who lived in the countryside. In many ways, however, the borough and its surrounding area had to co-operate. As an example, when the town needed timber to repair houses, it was supplied by the manor, most likely from the aptly named Custom Wood near Ashley. Having the status of a borough did not guarantee success. Unlike Tiverton, places such as Rackenford or Sampford Peverell, also boroughs, never outgrew their appearance as villages.

William de Redvers did not live long enough to see Tiverton develop as a town. He died in 1216, as did his son and heir. His widow, Margaret, was given in unwilling marriage to Falkes de Bréauté, the adventurer whom we have already met. He gained custody of her son, Baldwin as well as the receipts from Tiverton and other lands[1]. On his coming-of-age in 1225, Baldwin claimed his inheritance and married Amicia, the daughter of Gilbert de Clare, the Earl of Gloucester. Baldwin died twenty years later, and, whereas the lands of the Earldom passed to his ten-year old son, yet another Baldwin, the manor of Tiverton was assigned to Amicia in dower[2]. The estate she inherited had been somewhat reduced by her husband, who had carved three new manors out of Tiverton. Cove with West Mere, East Mere, and Lurley had been created by sub-infeudation, that is granting lands to an under-tenant who carried out the military service which went with the property. Other manorial changes took place at this time. A new manor, Southwood, appears, but Patcott disappears. Perhaps a large part of Patcott was included in Ashley Park, so the focus of the manor had shifted toward Southwood. William Briwer's death in 1233, without a male heir, meant that his lands were divided among his daughters. In the Tiverton area, Alice de Mohun received Newcott, while West Manley passed to another daughter, Margaret de la Ferté, and became known as Pool Anthony after its under-tenant, Anthony de Pole.

By this time the Honour of Okehampton, which included the manors of East Chevithorne and Chettiscombe, had passed into the hands of the Courtenay family. Although they had already come to prominence in local affairs, they had as yet given no indication of the part they would play in the future history of Tiverton. In the 1240s, the town received the rarest of commodities: a clean, constant supply of fresh water, the Town Leat. The water stems from a spring on Norwood Common, near Van Post in the far north of the parish, then runs south, fed by many streams on the way.

---

[1] he had been the conqueror of Prince Louis in 1216. De Bréauté's unpopularity as a non-Englishman and implication in the imprisonment of a royal justice in 1224 forced the King to banish him from the country.
[2] *Close Rolls 1242-7,* 301.

The donor was Alice, or Alson de Ros[1], the Courtenay tenant of Chettiscombe. She stipulated that the water was to be parted at Chettiscombe: Tiverton was to have half the water in summer and a third in winter, the rest being for her tenants' use. The water destined for Tiverton was turned into a manmade channel, whereas its natural course was directly south into the River Lowman. Apart from unreliable and unhealthy wells, rainwater, and the filthy Exe and Lowman, the Leat was to be Tiverton's sole source of water until the 19th century and, as such, was always cherished and safeguarded against abuse.

The Town Leat at Chettiscombe.

By the middle of the 13th century it was likely that much of the wool produced locally was sold to a fulling-mill at Tiverton. Whereas wool had been woven into cloth from prehistoric times, it had always been a small-scale operation; family members performed all the tasks, and used the finished products themselves. Fulling-mills, harnessing the power of rivers and streams, would bring about an industrial revolution. As with corn mills, they were driven by a waterwheel, which raised and let

---

[1] the earliest authority on Tiverton's history, John Blundell, in 1712, states that Alson de Ros was the donor of the Leat, but Dunsford (1790, 71) thought that Alson was the name of Isabella de Fortibus's first husband, and so asserted that it was Isabella who gave the stream. This misconception has been perpetuated.

fall one or more hammers, called stocks, that pounded the woven cloth which had been soaked. The result was a heavy, shrunken fabric, compacted into a kind of felt. What is most surprising about the local mill is that it is mentioned in 1225, just 40 years after the first recorded example in the whole of England. Interestingly, at Tiverton, where the corn mills were invariably under direct control of the lord of the manor, the fulling-mill was always leased. It is no coincidence that its potential income was soon recognised, hence the significant rise during the century in the numbers of sheep kept. The woollen cloth industry had clearly begun in Tiverton and would bring the town riches and fame in the centuries to come.

The survival of many 13th century manorial accounts of Tiverton has left us welcome details[1]. The four permanent ploughmen working on the manor were expected to plough half an acre a day, and from May to September, dairymaids were employed. They had to produce a cheese every day and, during the five summer months, about 60 to 70 pounds of butter. Changes took place during the latter half of the 13th century concerning methods of employment on the manor. Nationally, lords were paying out too much for direct labour on their demesne land – that which was not tenanted – and they soon realised greater profits could be made by leasing it for increasingly high rents. On the manor of Tiverton, this had the effect of reducing the demesne from 595 acres to 380 between 1245 and 1293. Another trend was to demand money payments instead of customary labour (days when tenants were obliged to work for the lord of the manor). The lord could then employ men only when he wanted them. Indeed, by 1286 the harvest at Tiverton was performed by twice as many hired hands as those doing labour services. While the lord of the manor's burden became lighter, that of his tenant became heavier. As well as labour services and high rents, he had to pay the lord an *entry fine*, the sum exacted when he took his tenancy; when one of his children married he had to pay a *merchet*, and on his death a *heriot* was due, either in cash or his best beast.

The methods to improve the land were very basic. On the de Redvers' farms, 'beat-burning' was practised. This involved removing the turf by plough or mattock, letting it dry off, then burning it, and afterwards spreading the ashes on the ground just before ploughing and sowing. There was quite a variety of cereal crops grown at this time, with oats being the most common, and wheat and rye next in order. The value of land depended on the terrain. In a rental of Tiverton manor made in 1293, riverside meadow was valued at 4d an acre, compared with hill land at 2d. Most of the farms in the Tiverton area were in existence by the 13th century, and probably had been for a long time before. Some 44 different land-holdings can been identified from

---

[1] best discussed in Ugawa 1962.

documentary sources relating to legal and administrative matters:

Barton	Ford	Landbote	Peadhill
Bingwell	Frogwell	Lurley	Pinnex Moor
Bradford	Gogwell	Manley	Pool Anthony
Bradley	Gornhay	Marley	Prescott
Chettiscombe	Gotham	Mere	Sellake
Chevithorne	Hayne	More	Southwood
Collipriest	Hensleigh	Newcott	Tidcombe
Combe	Holwell	Newland	Warnicombe
Craze Lowman	Honeyland	Palmershayes	Way
Crosse's	Horsdon	Passmorehayes	Withleigh
Fairby	Huntland	Patcott	Yearlstone

The produce of the surrounding countryside found a ready market in the town. It was rapidly emerging from its purely rural origins and was beginning to have more in common with Crediton, Barnstaple, and even Exeter, than villages in the neighbourhood. The Castle provided work for many people, whether as servants or supplying household goods. Masons, carpenters and thatchers were kept busy building and repairing, and the town's bakers and butchers were needed to feed the growing population. Trade was encouraged, locally and nationally. In 1233, Henry III gave travelling merchants a greater sense of security in towns by ordering night watches to be kept by armed men throughout the summer, the fair season. It was already realised that the easiest way to increase trade was by establishing fairs and markets, and the de Redvers held more of each than did any other lord in the Southwest. Tiverton had been granted a weekly market on Mondays and four annual fairs[1], each lasting for three days around the feast-days of the Translation of Saint Thomas (6th-8th July), Saint James (24th-26th July), Saint Giles (31st August-2nd September), and Saint Andrew (29th November-1st December). A lot of thought went into the timing of such events to give them the greatest chance of success, often to the intentional detriment of other lords' interests. Competition with Tiverton's Monday market came only from Exeter, because the markets at Bampton, Cullompton, Crediton, Rackenford, Sampford Peverell, Silverton, and Witheridge, all capable of diverting trade away from Tiverton, were held on other days of the week.

Late 13th century pedlars, hawkers, and merchants would have entered a town that already had its Newport Street, Saint Andrew Street, and a road leading to Westexe[2]. But how did people travel to and from Westexe? A ford, one of those that gave the town its name, existed up river from the present Exe Bridge. It is difficult nowadays to imagine walking across the bed of the Exe, though this was being done within living

---

[1] Kowaleski 1995, table A2.1.

[2] these are all named in deeds. Other streets could have been in use, but not mentioned in documents.

memory. In the early 13th century, there could even have been a ferry service, as litigation survives concerning the oarsman of a boat from which four people drowned[1]. A bridge had been built by 1295, when a grant was made of a shop 'in the south part of the road leading from the Exe Bridge to the mills of Tiverton'[2]. Six years before, a deed mentions the 'chaplain of Saint Mary of Tiverton'. A chapel dedicated to Saint Mary later existed on the bridge itself, so we can assume that a bridge, in almost the same position as the modern one, existed by 1289. Apart from Saint Peter's Church, and perhaps parts of the Castle very few buildings would have been of stone. Houses were likely to have had stone footings, with cob walls and thatched roofs; glazed windows were rare. Behind each house would have stood an assortment of flimsy structures such as a stable, pigsty, woodshed, chicken-house, or storehouse. Most families would have had a small garden, which was put to good use growing vegetables to supplement a meagre diet. Somewhere in the town, we do not know where, in 1238, there was a 'house of the lepers'[3]. Leprosy was not rare at this time, but, apart from this single reference, no further record of it has been found.

Henry III visited Tiverton in 1250. Proclamations were issued from the town on August 10th and 11th. His presence would have caused great excitement, and no doubt many people revelled in a glimpse of the monarch and his entourage. He almost certainly stayed overnight at the Castle, whose resident, Amicia de Redvers, would have been known to him. Indeed, her young son Baldwin was being tutored by one of the King's closest advisers, Peter of Savoy, and later married one of Peter's daughters in 1260. Baldwin died just two years later, leaving a son who failed to survive infancy. With the child's death, the male line of the de Redvers came to an end. Baldwin's sister, Isabella, inherited his possessions, including the earldom of Devon. She already owned many estates which had been the property of her late husband, William de Fortibus, the Earl of Albemarle, a powerful baron with great influence in the North. She did not acquire Tiverton, however, which remained in Amicia's hands until her death. The two women chose not to remarry, becoming powerful dowagers. In many ways their status was enviable: noble women were subject to fathers until they were married, and then to their husbands, but in widowhood they could wield a large measure of control over their own affairs.

Amicia must have taken pleasure from the rising career of her great-nephew, Bogo de Clare. As a younger son, he was destined for a life in the church and, as son of the Earl of Gloucester, had no difficulty obtaining lucrative benefices. He was made a Canon of Exeter Cathedral, then Rector of one of the portions of Tiverton, which, from this time became known as Clare[4]. Isabella's only surviving child, Avelina, married

---

[1] *Devon Eyre*, 31. [2] DRO 3490Z/Z1.

[3] *Devon Eyre*, 127.

[4] Clare House later became the rectory for the portion, and, although now in use as a doctors' surgery, still preserves the name.

the King's son, the Earl of Lancaster, in 1269. Links with the royal family remained close after Henry III's death in 1272, when a bond developed between his widow, Queen Eleanor, and Amicia. In 1282 the Countess and all her household lodged 'in the Queen's great chamber and the adjoining houses at Winchester Castle'[1]. Amicia died in 1284, and her holdings, including the manor, borough and hundred of Tiverton, as well as the proceeds from the fairs and the right to present to the portions of Clare, Pitt and Tidcombe, all passed to her daughter.

In the same year, Isabella instructed the building of a weir across the River Exe at Topsham, Countess Wear. This perhaps hindered the passage of salmon upstream and, more importantly, and definitely, stopped ships sailing up to Exeter. The people of the city were incensed. Isabella was not one to shirk from fighting for her rights, even when they were not justified, and counted men of the cloth as well as laymen among her victims. No doubt, many sighed with relief at her death in 1293. Her many possessions passed to her only surviving child, Avelina, who herself died childless in the following year. Who was now to inherit? Genealogy decided. Royal officials traced the de Redvers line back 50 years to the marriage of Mary de Redvers to Robert de Courtenay, and from that point down to the 16-year old Hugh de Courtenay. This young man had just a year earlier inherited the Honour of Okehampton, which included the manors of Chettiscombe and East Chevithorne, as well as lands in the counties of Berkshire, Buckingham, Dorset, and Somerset. To this sizeable fortune was now added all those lands of the earldom of Devon and of the de Redvers family. Hugh, however, was still a minor, so all his property was temporarily taken into the hands of the king, Edward I.

---

[1] *Close Rolls 1279-88,* 150.

3 Early Courtenay Tiverton

Hugh de Courtenay came of age in June 1297 and received a rich inheritance, of which Tiverton was only a part. As well as the Borough and Hundred, he owned the manors of Great and Little Tiverton, East Chevithorne, Chettiscombe, Newcott, Pool Anthony, Cove, East and West Mere, Lurley and Southwood. Fortunately for historians, a large number of the family's papers have survived, of which the most important are the Courtenay Cartulary[1], containing many detailed early land transactions, and the Trelawne Book[2], a 17th century copy of an earlier list of charters and deeds. In addition to these, the Royal Institution of Cornwall holds a large number of original Courtenay deeds, several of which are concerned with Tiverton[3]. It appears that shortly after Hugh attained his majority, he began to rationalise the Tiverton holdings. Little Tiverton, located in the Little Silver-Holwell area, seems to have been joined to the main manor of Tiverton, probably for ease of administration. The holding of La More or Elmore also features prominently. Dunsford states[4] that the common of Elmore, covering about 150 acres, was given about 1250 by Isabella de Fortibus 'for the benefit of the poor inhabitants of Tiverton, to keep their cattle'. But it was still changing hands among tenants up to 1305 when John Caffyn granted it 'to his lord, Sir Hugh de Courtenay'[5], who, although it is not recorded, probably then gave it to the townspeople. Hugh also established another park. In addition to Ashley, he claimed Godsbear, on the northern edge of the town stretching from the present People's Park eastwards to the Cowleymoor area. It is first mentioned in a reeve's account of 1308[6], when a lot of work was being done to its banks and ditches.

Hugh was the holder not only of large amounts of land, but also the right to present clergymen to several Devon parishes, including all the portions of Tiverton except Prior's. On many occasions men moved between the churches under the family's patronage. William de Belauny in 1308 was rector of one of the Tiverton portions, as well as a portioner at another Courtenay manor, Chulmleigh. Walter de Clopton of Pitt portion went on to become rector of Kenn, then Parkham, and a prebendary of Cutton in Exeter Castle, all in the gift of the Courtenays. Thomas de Teffonte, Rector

---

[1] DRO 1508M/Devon TD51.
[2] DRO 3490 Z/Z1 is a photocopy of this schedule of Trelawny family deeds.
[3] Cowleymoor and Deepaller make their first appearance in these documents, as does Robert Godman, in relation to a property in Withleigh - almost certainly that now called Withleigh Goodman.
[4] Dunsford 1790, 106.   [5] *Courtenay Cartulary* pp235-6.
[6] DRO CR490.

of Clare, was at the same time the incumbent of benefices in Staffordshire and Lincolnshire. Between 1310 and 1330 he often acted as a representative of Bishops Walter Stapledon of Exeter and John de Drokenesford of Bath and Wells. De Teffonte was likely to have been the host when Bishop Stapeldon[1] visited Tiverton in May 1309 and stayed in the town for a night.

Hugh de Courtenay was often called upon for royal service. In 1308 he accompanied Edward II to Boulogne for his marriage to the French princess, Isabella. Like many of his predecessors, Edward was made to acknowledge the power of the barons. A new clause had been inserted in his coronation oath forcing him to adhere to such laws 'as the community of the realm shall have chosen', and the barons soon made it clear that they considered themselves the representatives of the 'community'. In 1311, the King was presented with a list of conditions known as the Ordinances, intended to restrict his spending and appointments; they also called for the exile of his lover, Piers Gaveston. Edward had little choice but to submit to the demands made by the nobles, one of whom was Hugh de Courtenay. The King gave Hugh permission in 1315 to place some of his lands in trust for his mother in her widowhood. These included the manor and hundred of Tiverton, but Hugh retained complete control over the borough.

It was in the interest of any lord of the manor to make the most of his boroughs. With their markets and fairs they were the means of attracting trade, merchants, and, most importantly, income. Although our knowledge of the layout of Tiverton at this time is necessarily sparse, there are a couple of important clues. In 1314 William de Bycklegh gave 'for the common use and profit of all the burgesses of Tiverton' a strip of land just under 250 feet long by eight feet wide 'for a common way at their pleasure'[2]. Documentary references only to Newport Street, Saint Andrew Street, and the road leading to Westexe have so far been found, so where was this new thoroughfare? Could it have been the alley now linking Saint Peter Street with the present Market area? This suggestion is strengthened by the fact that the same William, 20 years later, was selling his interest in some houses in Saint Peter Street. As for the northern limit of the town, a deed of 1350, mentions property at 'the Barr in Tiverton'[3]. A later document[4] also mentions 'la Barre' and states the bounds of the property as the road to Bampton on the east, and the street and the Town Leat on the

---

[1] Walter Stapeldon's brother, Richard, who was to benefit greatly from the Bishop's position, in 1310 was engaged in a case involving land at Fulford, Lurley and Moorhayes in Tiverton, and in Bampton and Washfield. The brothers founded Stapledon Hall (later to become Exeter College) at the University of Oxford, with the intention of educating 13 poor scholars of the diocese of Exeter.
[2] contained in DRO 3490Z/Z1.   [3] ib.
[4] DRO Z12/42/1/1.

south. As the Leat runs in an east-west direction only through Water Lane and Silver Street, the single site where these bounds would fit is at the junction of the present Bampton and Silver Streets. The word 'barre' can refer to a gate or gatehouse of a castle or town, so could Tiverton's Barre have been some sort of physical barrier or boundary of the medieval borough? Significantly, this part of Bampton Street later becomes known as Town's End.

Hugh de Courtenay's desire to promote the borough seems to have led him to further the career of at least one of its inhabitants, Hugh Sampson. This Hugh was the first person from Tiverton, other than nobility, to appear in national, as well as regional and local records. He was admitted as a Freeman of Exeter in 1316, and his entry fee was reduced from two marks to one and a half at the request of de Courtenay[1]. The Freedom of the City exempted him from paying not only market dues and tolls, but, more importantly for Sampson, import duties. Less than a year later, he is recorded as co-owner, with a certain Ives Byrch, of part of the cargo of the *Welyfer*, a ship that arrived at Exeter from Dover[2]. The two men had paid for just under four tons of lead, 50 pipes[3] of potash, ten bales of alum, and half a ton of copper. In addition, Sampson himself owned three tubs of wax. These commodities hint at important industrial activity: potash was used to make soap and fertiliser, alum for dyeing and tanning. What we do not know is whether the items were for use in Tiverton, Exeter, or elsewhere.

In 1323, after the barons' bitter struggle against the King's favourite, Despenser, Hugh de Courtenay gave the profits and tolls of Tiverton market to trustees for the use of the town's poor. Perhaps the gift was a thanksgiving for deliverance from what had been a time of great bloodshed, as well as a sustained period of bad harvests and cattle and sheep epidemics. After a brief peaceful period, Tiverton's lord of the manor was pressed into military action again in 1326. He was to lead the forces raised in Cornwall and Devon against an invasion by Edward II's Queen, Isabella, her lover Roger Mortimer, with the heir to the throne, Prince Edward, as their figurehead. The King was captured, and secretly murdered at Berkeley Castle in 1327. The 15-year old Edward III became king, but then turned on his mother and Mortimer who was executed three years later. The turmoil caused changes to the manors around Tiverton - taking sides always results in winners and losers. The new King confiscated the manor of Craze Lowman as it had been part of Hugh le Despenser's property, but it was

---

[1] *Exeter Freemen*, 14.

[2] the City of Exeter was allowed to levy a duty on every cargo brought into the port (whether it was landed at Topsham, Exmouth or Exeter itself). Records were kept detailing the name of the ship entering the port, its master, and the amount of cargo and its owners. Many of these records, the *Exeter Customs Accounts*, survive for the long period between 1266 and 1611.

[3] a pipe was equal to about half a ton.

restored to his widow in 1328. Early in 1330, the manors of West Chevithorne and Chettiscombe were forfeited after the Earl of Kent's execution at the hands of Mortimer, but were returned to the Countess on Mortimer's death.

Murder and treachery were not restricted to the baronial class, as shown by a case investigated at the Devon Assizes in 1332. It was alleged[1] that William le Tornour had murdered Nicholas de Legh, whose father was tenant of Lurley. Alexander atte Worth, his brother Reginald, and John de Calwodelegh were charged with being William's 'confederates and accessories'. To compound the case Alexander and a certain William Teych harboured the murderer. Le Tornour was found guilty and sentenced to hang and, as was the law, his goods, valued at £14, were forfeit. It seems that the case had been heard previously, probably in the Tiverton Hundred Court, as all except the murderer claimed Hugh de Courtenay had already judged them.

Despite political troubles, further important measures were taken in the 1320s to promote trade, especially in wool and woollen cloth. Nine towns, including Exeter, were named as staples, where all wool for export had to be taken for inspection. The duty collected there amounted to 6s 8d on each sack exported by Englishmen, 10s by foreigners. It was also forbidden to export teasels, fuller's earth, madder, woad, and burs, all used in making woollen cloth, whilst imports were discouraged by banning all people with less than £40 worth of land from wearing foreign cloth. The main intention was to encourage the production of finished cloth in England. In Devon and Cornwall, very little local wool had ever been exported because of its poor quality, so export duty had never been a great burden. On the other hand, the coarse broadcloth made in the region found international markets, and profits had increased. Not surprisingly, many merchants prospered, among them Hugh Sampson. He had moved from Tiverton to Southampton, where, in 1322, he was appointed Collector of Customs. His commercial enterprises were so important that he petitioned Parliament in 1327 after Frenchmen had attacked two of his ships, the *Portepayse* and the *Grace Dieu*, killed the crews, and stolen their cargoes of wine, wool, sheepskins, and coin. He claimed £300 damages, and the Chancery was ordered to reimburse him. Although based outside Devon he was recorded as Hugh de Tiverton, importing into Exeter on four occasions during 1333, and he further maintained his local links by purchasing the tithes of Prior's Portion in the same year. But his name does not appear in the very important Devonshire Lay Subsidy of 1332.

This list is of great significance for local historians as it is the earliest published tax list giving personal names[2]. The tax was assessed in two ways: in the countryside, it was charged on a fifteenth of the value of animals and crops; in the towns, on a tenth of the value of merchandise and domestic goods. A different threshold was also set. Those

---

[1] PRO JI/1/190.

[2] *Subsidy 1332.*

with goods valued at less than 10s in the rural areas and 6s in towns were not assessed. Most people fell well short of these amounts, so the 79 individuals taxed in the rural parts of Tiverton parish and the 29 in the borough represent a very small proportion of the total population. The Hundred of Tiverton produced a little over £6 from this levy, a mere 1% of the assessment for the county. The town raised £1 15s 10d, placing it 16th out of Devon's 19 boroughs, headed by Exeter[1]. Of the individuals, Hugh de Courtenay's 8s was the highest assessment in Tiverton; he also paid smaller amounts at fifteen other places in Devon, including Plympton, Colyton, Okehampton, and Honiton. The tenant of Bolham, Peter de Ralegh, who lived at Fardell near Ivybridge, appears at five other locations in the county. These two apart, the others listed under Tiverton reveal only local interest. Alexander atte Werthe was also taxed for Worth in Washfield, whereas Elias Fitzpayne appears at Stoodleigh as well as Tiverton. Most of the surnames in the list consist of 'de' (of) followed by a place-name, such as Richard de Westbradelegh. These names provide a further 11 previously-unrecorded Tiverton properties:

Berry	Fulford	Norwood	Shortridge
Broadmoor	Hone	Plainsfield	Wormsland
Deepaller	Longhayne	Quirkhill	

The list also contains names that indicate some of the trades carried on at this time. In Tiverton, there was John the blacksmith (*le ferour*), a roofer (*heliere*), two millwards, a tailor, a maker of coats of mail (*hauberger*), a painter (*lytheger*), parker, tanner, as well as two skinners and a merchant.

In 1335, Edward III bestowed the title of Earl of Devon on Hugh de Courtenay, and made him a member of his Council. It is likely that Hugh's elevated position prompted the considerable amount of building work at his castles of Tiverton and Okehampton. At the former various features in the east range, as well as the windows and corbelled fireplace in the southwest turret, date from this time[2]. The stone used was mainly the local red material[3], with a type of volcanic trap, possibly from Thorverton, employed in the more detailed work. Timbers from the gatehouse ceiling have been dated to 1330-1340, coinciding with Hugh's appointment as Earl. What is not certain is whether the work at Tiverton was new building or alterations to an existing structure.

The conflict with France that has become known as the Hundred Years' War began in 1337. The causes of this dispute were many. English rule in Gascony was resented; the new French King was showing support for the Scots; Edward's alliance with the cities of Flanders had angered the region's French overlord, and he had renewed his

---

[1] followed by Sutton (Plymouth), Barnstaple, Totnes and Tavistock.
[2] (Blaylock 1988, 2). The upper floor of this turret has long been considered as the location of the Castle chapel (Hughes 1862, 245).
[3] exposed in quarries such as Ashley and Hensley.

claim to the French crown. Hugh de Courtenay and Bishop John de Grandisson of Exeter were commanded to keep a close watch on the coasts of Devon, and they were expected to summon the men of the county if the French attempted to invade. The King also ordered that in all churches less than seven leagues (21 miles) from the sea one single bell was to be rung on normal occasions, but if an attack came then all the bells should be rung to warn the inhabitants. Tiverton, being less than 20 miles from both the Bristol and English Channels, should have been included in the order. In the event, the French did not launch the expected invasion, and in June 1340 their ships were nearly all destroyed at the Battle of Sluys. Nevertheless, Edward's resources had been exhausted and he was forced to call a truce, albeit temporary.

Upper-storey window in the south-west turret of Tiverton Castle, the building thought to be the solar. It dates to the time of Hugh de Courtenay's appointment as Earl of Devon in 1335, or even earlier.

Hugh de Courtenay died in 1340, and the earldom passed to his son, another Hugh. Like his father, the new Earl was soon summoned into battle, the enemy this time were the Scots. He took with him a contingent of men from his lands, including a banneret, 12 knights, 36 esquires and 60 mounted archers[1], some of whom were likely to have been from Tiverton. Their wages, when they came to be paid in July 1342, were in a curious currency. They received 87 sacks of wool. Hugh obtained permission to ship it to the staple in Flanders and sell it there, to pay the troops in hard cash. Illness, however, prevented him from taking part in the celebrated victory at Crécy in 1346, and the surrender of Calais a year later.

The population of England had been rising steadily since Domesday in spite of occasional disease, bad harvests, and warfare. Even the most conservative estimates suggest it had doubled in that time to about five million, and even a threefold increase has been proposed[2]. Food and housing were needed in increasing amounts, and the cultivation of marginal land was reaching its natural limits. This placed pressure on town and countryside alike. Tiverton was no exception. It was expanding into the surrounding countryside, as seen by a grant in 1344 to Hugh Coleprust of land to be used as burgage plots[3]. The rise in population meant there was a surplus of labour in the rural areas, a situation that lords of the manor exploited to the full. They raised entry fines and imposed further labour services whenever they could, and grew richer in consequence. The status quo was soon to change drastically.

A disease carried by flea-ridden black rats moved out of China in the 1330s and, following the well-used trade routes of the period, rapidly spread through Europe. The Black Death reached England early in the summer of 1348 through the harbours of the south coast. It was unstoppable. People fled into the countryside, but it followed them. The pestilence carried off about one third of the population of Europe. No greater loss of life has ever resulted from any epidemic or war. The Sheriff of Devon was too ill to appear at the Exchequer in June 1348, but there was no chance of a replacement as all his staff had died of the plague. Locally, there is no way of counting the number who died. Only one of Tiverton's four portioners, Thomas de Whistone of Tidcombe, was replaced, and he may have resigned rather than died. What effect did the deaths have? Whereas earlier historians supposed that the Black Death was a large-scale economic disaster, modern research indicates that it may not have greatly altered a settlement's economic effectiveness[4]. Yes, it was an indiscriminate destroyer of life, but it served to

---

[1] a banneret was a knight entitled to lead his men into battle under his own banner, so this was probably Hugh himself; an esquire generally meant a knight's attendant.
[2] Miller 1991, 33.   [3] Trelawne 222.
[4] at Walsham-le-Willows, Suffolk, in March and April 1349, the plague killed 64% of the children, over half of the over-40s and 90% of the elderly. On the other hand, of the parish's working male population aged between 20 and 40 no more than 20% died (cited in Platt 1996,10).

pare down an excessive population that was out-consuming production. If the plague had not occurred, the consequences may have been mass starvation. Perhaps the greatest effect was upon people's way of thinking: life seemed even more precarious, and the will of God yet more mysterious.

Despite the Black Death the woollen cloth industry in Devon and Cornwall made progress during the 1350s[1]. Its manufacture benefited from royal encouragement. Edward III in 1344 had given protection to cloth-workers coming to England, and in the larger towns standards for the industry were being set. The ordinances of Bristol, made in 1346[2], detail the punishable faults or practices, such as having deficient threads in a cloth or working at night. The penalties imposed included fines to the Mayor and Aldermen, having the cloth and loom burnt, and, if caught three times, a weaver could be expelled from his trade for a year and a day. Interestingly, alongside Tiverton merchants in the Exeter Customs Accounts from the 1350s there are a small number of importers from Chulmleigh, another Courtenay manor. It is tempting to see this noble family as promoters of the cloth industry in both towns. To curb excesses as well as further encourage English textile production, a law was passed in 1363, which stipulated the types of clothing different classes of society could wear. The lowest category, those with less than 40s worth of goods or chattels, which would have included the great majority of Tivertonians, were permitted to wear only russet or blanket cloth of wool with linen girdles. The Courtenays, other nobles, and the occasional rich merchant, that is, those who held lands valued at £200 or goods worth £1,000, could dress in fine cloth, silk, furs such as ermine and squirrel, and wear sumptuous jewellery. The rich enjoyed a level of affluence not only indicated by dress but also by diet. In 1366 the breakfast served to Hugh de Courtenay and the rest of the King's Council included ale, beef, calves, sheep, capons, goslings, doves, rabbits, lamb and ten bitterns, and the fish dishes comprised cod, pickerel, plaice, turbot, conger, dory, salmon, shrimp and eel[3].

That meeting of the King's Council no doubt discussed relations with France, which had once more become strained following the accession of Charles V in 1364. Edward had signed the Treaty of Calais in 1360, renouncing his claim to the French crown in return for Aquitaine, but Charles dismissed the Treaty and war was resumed. Attempts were made to keep the men of England alert and, to some extent, trained for military action. In 1363, sheriffs were ordered to prohibit 'useless sports'[4] and to encourage archery, which became compulsory practice. Many of the sites where it took

---

[1] see Gray 1924, 13-35. [2] *Bristol*, 2.

[3] PRO E101/26/8.

[4] the banned games included the throwing of stones, wood or iron at targets, playing handball, football, stick-ball, hockey and cockfighting.

place still retain the place-name *butt*, the word given to archery targets, and in Tiverton there was a field known as Tree at Butt[1] in Elmore. This long period of warfare against the French had stimulated English national pride. One manifestation of this was the replacement of French, the language long preferred by the nobility, by English, which in 1362 became the official language of the law courts.

Saint Peter's Church hosted a series of ordination services during 1370 and 1371, which brought many distinguished people to Tiverton. William de Courtenay, who had been consecrated Bishop of Hereford in 1369, was commissioned to perform the ordinations. He was Earl Hugh's fifth son, and his family connections had enabled him to obtain his first benefice when he was just 13 years old, and the bishopric when only 27, both at an age below the canonical limit. The services at Tiverton would have provided a great spectacle with most of the participants dressed in fine robes, and also generated a great deal of income for the town. At each of the first two services, in May and June 1370, the candidates numbered more than 350. Accommodating such numbers must have stretched the small town to its capacity. A small proportion would have been local and could have travelled to the services on the same day, but the vast majority would have originated from elsewhere in the diocese, which, as well as Devon, included the whole of Cornwall.

In 1374, services began in a private chapel at Farleigh, just outside Tiverton, which was licensed by the Bishop of Exeter. The chapel is the earliest of its kind recorded in the parish of Tiverton, and some of its fabric can still be seen in the present house at Lower Farleigh. The owner of the property was John Asshe, who occurs quite regularly during this period as an importer at Exeter, and had been appointed gauger of wine[2] for Devon in 1371. Two years later he was also required to sit on a commission of enquiry in the county. Asshe is a good example of the growing number of men at this time who were becoming increasingly important in county affairs. Perhaps best described as gentry entrepreneurs, they were not of the nobility, nor were they mere tenant farmers, but rather men with some land who were also involved in trading.

Hugh de Courtenay died in 1377. In the original form of his will he had expressed the wish to be buried in Saint Peter's Church, Tiverton, but by a later codicil he changed this to Exeter Cathedral. He made a bequest of ten marks to the high altar of Tiverton church, and the contents of the Castle chapel – the cross, incense burner, candlestick, vessel for Holy Water, vestments, linen, and the ornaments that hung there – were to pass to his wife Margaret. His three daughters received £20 each, and his son Peter 100 marks[3]. The immediate administration of his lands was of great importance.

---

[1] alternative names for this field were Field at Butt or Gilbert's Close.
[2] requiring him to check, measure and exact any duty payable.
[3] a mark was equal to 13s 4d (67p).

By feudal custom, the lands of a deceased person reverted to the Crown before the new holder swore his allegiance and officially received possession. This enabled the King to swell his coffers, albeit temporarily, while it depleted those of the deceased's family. Many landowners, including Hugh, were avoiding this trap by contracting deeds of enfeoffment. In such documents, an owner granted his property in trust to one or more persons (feoffees), with the condition that the owner should have use of the property until his death, after which the feoffees would grant it to the person named as the inheritor. Some of Hugh's manors, including Cadeleigh, had been granted in this way three years before to trustees who were ordered to pass them on eventually to Hugh's fifth son, Philip. The majority of the Earl's lands passed to his grandson, Edward, who took full possession when he came of age in 1378, but Hugh's widow Margaret received many estates as dower, including East Chevithorne and Newcott.

The income from Edward's Devon lands in 1381 amounted to almost £540: Plympton, accounting for just under £104, was the most lucrative. Tiverton was in second place[1], with £83 19s 5d, of which £53 2s 4d came from the manor, £28 4s 5d from the borough, and £2 12s 8d from the hundred. At the Castle, Edward's personal staff was as many as 61 individuals[2], and the family's presence in the town generated a lot of business. In the markets of Exeter, Tiverton tanners, livestock and meat traders were certainly very active[3], and on the city's quay men such as Alex Legh and John Brasyeter regularly brought in cargoes of wine and herring. Another Tiverton merchant, John Northmore, was trading at this time, although all references to him come after his death. In the *Patent Rolls*, his widow Joan is pardoned in 1382[4] for not paying an £80 debt of his. This picture of a modest Tiverton trader is enhanced by the discovery that he was storing various goods at Southampton[5]. These, however, were no ordinary items; they included luxuries such as beaver, otter, squirrel and Russian furs, Russian linen, cloth, spruce boards and flax. Unless Northmore used an alias, he does not occur in the *Exeter Customs Accounts*, so he probably intended the goods to be transported by land from Southampton to Tiverton[6]. Long-distance transport by packhorse or waggon, although not mentioned in this instance, is well attested later.

Tiverton almost certainly had a school in the 1390s, but the evidence for it consists of a single reference. A list of expenses[7] of the Courtenay household records two pence paid *'as escoliers de Seynt Nich a Tyverton'* – to the scholars

---

[1] DRO CR543.
[2] *BLib AddCh* 64,320.
[3] Kowaleski 1995, 302 and 296.
[4] *Patent Rolls 1381-5*, 170.
[5] cited in Kowaleski 1995, 274.
[6] as Kowaleski states.
[7] DRO CR1466.

of Saint Nicholas at Tiverton. The dedication to the patron saint of children perhaps encouraged a local celebration of the election of a boy-bishop as was common elsewhere[1]. Unfortunately, we do not know where the school was situated, when it was founded, how long it lasted, or whether it was attached to a craft guild, to a chantry or the church. Nevertheless, one thing we can be sure of is that the teacher would almost certainly have been a clergyman. The most likely candidate is the John Scolemaystre who witnessed a Tiverton property deed in 1399[2]. If not him, many others in the town would have been qualified for the task. Walter Netarell and Thomas Tidderson served in the chapel at the Castle at this time[3]. Together with the three portioners, and the curate of Prior's, no less than eight other clergymen had property interests in Tiverton at this period. They included the Rector of Cruwys Morchard, Walter Robert, who owned premises in Saint Andrew Street, and John Snape, a prebendary at Crediton, who had a house and garden on the west side of Saint Peter Street. There was certainly plenty of work for local clergy, for in the single year of 1400 Bishop Stafford licensed no fewer than six chapels within the parish. They were Saint Mary's at Chettiscombe, Saint Bartholomew's at Bolham, one dedicated to Saint Thomas where the Town Hall now stands, one at Craze Lowman called Saint James', Saint Katherine's at East Bradley which stood near the site of the present Withleigh parish church, and finally one at Tidcombe. A few years later the chapels of Saint Luke and Saint Stephen, both said to be in the parish of Tiverton, obtained licences, but their whereabouts remain unknown[4].

The contest between king and barons came to a head in the reign of Richard II. The King was overthrown and subsequently murdered by Henry Bolingboke, Duke of Lancaster, who ascended the throne in 1399 as Henry IV. During his troubled reign, Edward de Courtenay took part against the rebellion of Owain Glyndwr. He was ordered to take supplies of Devon wheat, oats, wine, ale and hake to the troops in Wales, and in 1403 he was to gather men from the county and sail to Cardiff. Devon's long-established trade links with Wales led to one unusual problem during the conflict. Many local men had property of the 'Welsh rebels'; one such person was Thomas Baker of Tiverton, who had three 'rebel' oxen worth 20s[5]. Although Glyndwr's main strongholds were captured by 1409, he continued to harass the English until as late as 1412.

Bishop Stafford of Exeter wrote to the Rector of Pitt in 1413 about the poor

---

[1] Orme 1976, 106.   [2] Saint Peter's ED9.

[3] DRO CR500.

[4] they could possibly have been the private chapels at Farleigh or Tidcombe whose dedications are never stated.

[5] and was probably the Tivertonian of the same name who, at this time, was importing wine into Exeter.

condition of Saint Peter's Church. He commanded the Rector, Walter Robert, to call a meeting of the parishioners and to remind them of their responsibility to repair all of the building except the chancel, which the clergy had to keep in good order. The Bishop insisted that, if necessary, the whole church should be rebuilt. This was not done, but the imposing 99-foot tower of Saint Peter's can probably be attributed to this time, as can the piers of the chancel arcade. Further clues to the appearance of the building in the early fifteenth century were revealed during the 19th century restoration. The tower was apparently built against an earlier wall that had been covered with wall paintings 'of foliage and geometrical patterns in red and blue'[1]. Unfortunately, no Victorian had the presence of mind to record the designs. As the majority of the medieval congregation was illiterate, such paintings served as visual aids to the church services; murals probably adorned most churches at this time, although too few have survived[2]. Who paid for the repairs? The Courtenays would have been expected to contribute, as would other families such as the Redes of Pool Anthony and the Asshes of Farleigh, who resided or had interests in the parish. Merchants would also have made donations. Thomas Baker and John Brasyeter were still actively importing goods into Exeter, while on the Bristol Channel coast a Tivertonian, Peter Plente, was trading from Bridgwater. As for the chancel repairs, it would seem that the only rector able to make a significant contribution was Walter Robert. In addition to Pitt Portion, he held the benefice of Northill as well as a prebend at Ottery Saint Mary, whereas the other portioners, Alan Benet and James Frankcheyne, do not appear to have had any other income. Robert's contribution to the repairs was supplemented by an additional 20s, which he gave to the church on his death in 1414. He left eight marks to a chaplain to celebrate mass in Saint Peter's (and not elsewhere!) for his soul and that of others. He made many bequests to his family, including 3d a week to his mother, his best robe with hood and fur to his sister, and his nephew was to receive six marks to maintain him at school. Among various sums that he was owed, however, was £20 from Edward de Courtenay. Robert was willing to waive the debt as long as the Earl was a good lord to his executors, 'otherwise I hold him accountable to the most high God'[3].

Besides clothing that included a luxurious surplice edged with *gris*[4], Robert left various pieces of kitchen equipment to Walter Colle, his successor at Pitt. Among these items were his 'vessels used for brewing'. Water, of course, was usually too polluted to drink, and wine too expensive, so ale, often produced by clergymen, was consumed in large quantities. A combination of drink and the church in the summer of 1419,

---

[1] Hughes 1857, 43.
[2] but see Black 1987, 35-6, and Glascoe 1987, 182-90, for Devon examples.
[3] *RegStafford*, 406.   [4] a very expensive grey fur.

however, brought Saint Peter's once more to the attention of Bishop Stafford. A fight had taken place in the churchyard between a Tivertonian, Matthew Rowe, and a Bristol merchant, John Barstaple, during which blood was spilt. The Bishop ordered a commission to enquire into this incident, which resulted in church authorities having to perform a service of 'reconciliation of the pollution'.

A long chapter in the manorial history of Chettiscombe and West Chevithorne ended in 1411 with the death of Elizabeth, Countess of Kent. She had received the two manors as dower 59 years earlier, and they now passed to her great-niece, Elizabeth Neville, whose husband, John, was heir to the earldom of Westmorland. Perhaps the longevity of the dower had clouded the issue of tenancy, as Neville petitioned the King that Edward de Courtenay was demanding homage as if the manors were held of him – which, according to earlier records, they were. The King upheld Neville's claim, declaring him the tenant-in-chief[1]. Nicholas Hele held the other Chevithorne manor until his death in 1413, when it passed to his daughter Alice the wife of William Fraunceys. For many centuries it was to stay in this family, as was the manor of Craze Lowman.

Following his father's death in 1413, the ambitious Henry V became King. He was intent not only on reclaiming those territories in France that had formerly belonged to England, but he also wanted new accessions. The first campaign in 1415 included the great victory at Agincourt, and he later gained Normandy. His battles in France were fought by various contingents of English troops, such as the 316 men-at-arms and 632 archers who had sailed from Dartmouth in 1417 under the supervision of Edward de Courtenay, the son of the Earl of Devon. Edward was at the beginning of a promising military career, but died in the following summer, leaving his younger brother Hugh as heir. Within two years, he, too, was pressed into action in France. Death closely shadowed the family at this time, for Earl Edward died at the end of 1419; and his successor, Hugh, lived just three years more. Within the space of five years, Devon and the Courtenays had lost two earls and an heir apparent, and now the future rested precariously on an eight year old boy, Thomas de Courtenay.

---

[1] *Close Rolls 1409-13*, 264.

4 The Courtenay Influence

Thomas Courtenay was too young to inherit, so John Copplestone and Walter Colles, the Rector of Pitt, were chosen to administer his lands. His mother, Anne, received the manor of West Chevithorne as well as the manor, borough and hundred of Tiverton as part of her dower. But did she continue living at the Castle? Possibly not. A chapel in the rectory of Tidcombe was licensed for divine service in her presence. Tidcombe was certainly a residence fit for the Countess of Devon. A document written almost two centuries later[1] could still describe the property as 'a house and garden walled and moted aboute, watered with water issuing from ye hill grounds out of ye come called Mazar Coombe'. In front of this grand building was a field containing five ponds, more than likely stocked with fish for the residents. If she was indeed living at Tidcombe, then was she leasing the Castle? She was more than capable of exploiting her son's minority; she was already paying 700 marks a year for the custody of all his lands, and, with her brother, Lord Talbot, she paid no less than 2,000 marks for the right to contract a marriage for young Thomas. Anne made better provision for her own future in 1432 by marrying John Botreaux. Even for this right, she had to pay £200. This was a time when love and sentiment came a poor second to financial considerations. Thomas Courtenay eventually inherited in 1433. By then, his wife, Margaret Beaufort, had given birth to their first son, also called Thomas. Father and son were both granted 100 marks a year by Henry VI in recognition of Thomas' service in France to the Duke of Bedford, regent for the 12-year old king. While Bedford looked after affairs in France his brother, Humphrey, Duke of Gloucester, did the same in England. Before long, however, Gloucester found himself at odds with the formidable Cardinal Henry Beaufort, who, like Bedford and Gloucester, was descended from John of Gaunt's House of Lancaster, and was also the uncle of Thomas Courtenay's wife.

Tiverton was a valuable asset. From an account roll of 1428 the Devon manors contributed over £924 to the family coffers, of which £107 5s 3d came from Tiverton[2], more than from any other single holding. The manor returned £78 11s 10½d, and the borough £28 13s 4½d. These figures simply represent profit, but sometimes accounts survive showing the details of income and expenses. One example from this period[3] includes payments for three men working on the ditch at Little Tiverton, and for mowing 30 acres of grass there, as well as 21 acres at Fosmead and six acres at Bingwell, and stacking it all. Mills, whether for grinding corn or fulling cloth, always required a

---

[1] DRO PR Glebe Terriers/Tiverton.
[2] DRO CR536.
[3] DRO CR498.

lot of work: the same account notes the purchase of a new pail, the digging of a new leat, making six small ditches and cleaning out silt from the leats. Major works included carrying 41 wagonloads of turf to rebuild the weir at Elmore, and repairs to the lodge in Ashley Park.

From 1434, our knowledge of day-to-day life in Tiverton is greatly enhanced by the survival of the court rolls for both the manor and hundred. Although often written in a minute Latin script these parchment rolls chronicle crimes, debts and debtors, and are full of place-names and family names which soon become familiar. From the very first roll, it can be seen that keeping the local roads clear and well maintained was important. The highway at Tidcombe was in disrepair, the way at Worth and Bolham was blocked, and John Hopere of Cove was fined 4d for allowing the road at Therlehayne to become muddy and full of pits. The same Hopere was involved in another case, accusing Thomas Crydya of letting his cows and pigs stray on to his land. Other actions included William Holwill who, without permission, cut down an alder at Fernham Island, near Ashley, and William Spurway was involved with Roger atte Wode for not paying 3s rent for Gotham.

Thomas Courtenay obtained Tiverton and West Chevithorne on the death of his mother in 1440. In the following year, he replaced William Bonvile as steward of the Duchy of Cornwall. Bonvile, a rising star, took this as a personal affront, and a bitter feud began. The Tiverton Courtenays were jealous of any other group that aspired to challenge their status in the region. They did not even place much importance on family ties; they strongly disliked their own relative Philip Courtenay of Powderham Castle, and Bonvile himself was married to Thomas' great-aunt. On this occasion, the matter was resolved with Bonvile's appointment as Seneschal of Aquitaine, and both men were bound over in the sum of £2,000 to keep the peace.

In 1442, Thomas Courtenay was host to one of the King's secretaries, Thomas Bekynton, who stayed at Tiverton Castle for one night. He was actually on his way from London to Plymouth, from where he intended to sail to Bordeaux. Perhaps his visit to Tiverton was to secure funding for King's College, Cambridge, which had been founded by Henry VI in the previous year. The College was endowed with Saint James' Priory at Exeter, which, in turn, held the advowson of Prior's Portion in Tiverton. As the Earl held the right to appoint the other three portioners, he would have been interested in who was likely to become curate of Prior's, as well as how King's College intended to collect their tithes. Another possibility for the visit could have been to discuss the arrangements for Henry VI's intended marriage to Margaret of Anjou[1]. As Steward of England, Thomas Courtenay played an important role in the ceremony, which took place in 1445.

---

[1] this union was included as a condition of the Treaty of Tours signed by England and France in 1444.

Court rolls of the manors of Cove and Mere survive from the late 1440s[1]. The first document[2] mentions 'the capital messuage', the chief property, of Cove, which is almost certainly the holding which is now known as Court Place. The roll for 1450 records one John Brookland taking the lease of Horscombe in the manor of Mere. In the mid-19th century this property was still a distinct farm covering 77 acres, all of which is now covered by Mere Down Woods. It is almost certain that in October 1450 some of the inhabitants of Cove would have noticed Walter Renell driving six cows and a bullock along the road to Bampton. What they would not have known, however, is that he had stolen them from Peter Wyot and was on his way to sell them[3]. This incident came to court at Tiverton, where such crimes were commonplace, as was another form of theft, poaching. Far more serious, though, was the taking of deer from the Courtenay parks. One case of this was brought before the jury in 1448 by Adam Cokkes, the keeper of Ashley Park, who accused John Webber of Wayland and Thomas Chatehey of killing six fallow deer[4]. The two men had used mastiffs to bring down the deer, and the court roll even gives the name of Webber's dog - Abrache or Abraxas - a word with supposedly magical powers!

As for the borough of Tiverton its court rolls exist from 1451[5] and provide us with fascinating details of misdemeanours typical of a late medieval town. The cases are many and varied. John Pappe and John Cornish allowed their pigs to roam free at night in the town and, later, Cornish let his ducks run loose. Thomas Potyngdon was charged with keeping a 'suspicious hostelry' at the end of the town, where 'suspect men are accustomed to stay awake at night and sleep during the day'. One crime peculiar to Tiverton was the occasional diversion of the Town Leat, the culprit in 1451 was a John Crudge. The reasons are rarely given, but altering the course of the Leat north of the town was usually for watering the fields, whereas, in the built-up area it was generally to wash away various unsanitary and smelly hazards. Violence, as well as petty crime, was commonplace. The incidents detailed in the court rolls were often not simply fistfights, but affrays causing a disturbance of the peace and armed assault. A variety of objects was used, ranging from whatever was to hand in the heat of the moment, like candlesticks and bowls, to sticks, knives, daggers, swords, bows, and even crossbows. A careful distinction is made in the court cases between attacks that resulted in loss of blood and those that did not. Close scrutiny of these rolls occasionally reveals the habitual criminal. John Hopere, already mentioned for allowing his stock loose on the

---

[1] the two manors, along with East Stoodleigh, had passed to John Austell, a man whose sphere of influence was centred in Somerset; he had represented Wells in the Parliament of 1432, and had often sat on commissions in the county.

[2] part of SRO DD/TB/Box 2/6.

[3] DRO CR287.

[4] DRO CR285.

[5] DRO CR227.

roads, first appears as a poacher of fish in 1429. He seems to have turned to violence, however, and in 1451 was charged with three serious matters: he threatened William Tirlake with a dagger: assaulted Nicholas Clarke and his wife Joan with a stick, and John Hukeley with a sword. Evidently, Hopere realised that drastic action was called for and in the following year, while under arrest, he escaped. He rode off on a horse, and disappeared from the Tiverton records.

L ondon witnessed bloody scenes in 1450 when rebels from Kent, led by Jack Cade, succeeded in entering the city and executing the Lord Treasurer before they were dispersed. They had wanted an end to 'bad governance', high taxes, and the recovery of Crown Lands so that the King could live off his own means. They also demanded the return of Richard, Duke of York, who had been virtually banished to Ireland by the mentally unstable Henry VI on the insistence of the manipulative Beauforts. The Duke did, indeed, return, and one of his first duties was to calm the situation that had arisen at Taunton Castle, where William Bonvile was under siege from Thomas Courtenay, Earl of Devon. During this incident, if not before, the Earl seems to have struck up an alliance with the Duke of York, for in January 1452 together they advanced on London in an unsuccessful attempt to overthrow the King. In the same month Bishop Lacy of Exeter warned one of his tenants, John Copplestone, not to take part in any 'gatherings against the King'[1], and urged those already assembled at Tiverton to return home. No reason is given for the presence of this crowd of people, but probably they were there under orders from the Earl. The peace of England could not survive long when Henry VI suffered bouts of insanity. In 1453, Parliament approved the protectorate of Richard, Duke of York, but he was dismissed when a son and heir was born to Queen Margaret, and the Beauforts were restored. Then began the sporadic fighting of the Wars of the Roses, a bloodletting of the leading families.

The feud between Thomas Courtenay and William Bonvile simmered throughout 1454[2], and came to a head in the following year. Courtenay supremacy in Devon was challenged in July 1455 when Parliament was summoned, for among the members were two of the Earl's enemies, Philip Courtenay of Powderham, representing the county, and John Radford, the member for Barnstaple. John's father, Nicholas Radford,

---

[1] *RegLacy III*, 137.
[2] in July 1454 they were bound over to appear in the Court of Chancery, Courtenay having to provide surety for 4,000 marks and Bonvile for half as much. The tension grew in the following year, when the Earl and his son, Thomas, found themselves with Bonvile on a commission enquiring into the dilapidation and sale of crown lands in Cornwall - a subject guaranteed to arouse deep-seated emotions in both families.

was a rich lawyer who, at this time, was selling much of his land and giving a large part of the money to the Dean and Chapter of Exeter Cathedral for safekeeping. A combination of Radford's wealth and his position as one of the foremost lawyers in the county, in addition to his being a close acquaintance of William Bonvile, induced a mounted group numbering over 90 men to leave Tiverton on the night of October 23rd 1455. Led by Thomas Courtenay the younger, they reached their destination, Nicholas Radford's house at Upcott Barton in the parish of Cheriton Fitzpaine. The events that followed are related in a contemporary petition[1] and reveal that Radford was robbed of £300 in cash and valuables worth 1,000 marks before being viciously murdered by Nicholas and Thomas Philip and John Amore. A few days later, a smaller group returned to Upcott where Radford's body was lying in the private chapel. A sham inquest was held with one of those present, Richard Berthelot, playing the part of the coroner, and naming fictitious persons as the murderers. The corpse was then taken to the churchyard at Cheriton Fitzpaine and unceremoniously dumped into a grave. One week after the murder, a force said to number over a thousand men assembled at Tiverton with the Earl of Devon and his son at its head. They set out for Exeter, where the guards of the city's gates were forced to hand over their keys. Once entry had been gained, the ramshackle army divided. The larger part pressed on to Powderham where they besieged Philip Courtenay, who summoned assistance from William Bonvile. At Exeter Cathedral, the remaining group demanded the goods that Radford had deposited. They took away gold and silver plate worth £600 as well as £700 in money. The Earl asked the Mayor of Exeter if he would help hold the city against the approaching Bonvile, but he refused. Courtenay left the city and met his enemy on December 15th on Clyst Heath. A pitched battle was fought and Bonvile was put to flight.

The Tiverton Courtenays seem to have been satisfied that their potential challengers in the region had been humiliated. But what of the offenders? Eight months after the murder a commission was appointed to arrest and imprison a number of men, including 17 from Tiverton, among whom were Nicholas and Thomas Philip and Richard Berthelot. They were all said[2] to 'wander within the counties of Somerset, Devon, Dorset and Cornwall spoiling the King's lieges of their goods and chattels and intending to slay some and stirring up others to fulfil their wicked presumption'. This implies that after Radford's murder the perpetrators continued their lawless spree. Their fate is not recorded. It is worth noting that the names of the 17 Tiverton men involved, with two exceptions, are not found elsewhere in connection with the town, not even in the court rolls. Had they been hired from elsewhere for the express purpose of committing the crime? The Earl of Devon was pardoned in April 1457 for all crimes

---

[1] see Radford 1903.

[2] *Patent Rolls 1452-61*, 310-1.

concerning the Radford incident, as were his sons, Thomas and Henry, and a John Brymmore[1] later in the year. A pardon, however, did not necessarily imply innocence, rather that Henry VI dared not alienate any potential supporters.

Thomas Courtenay died at the end of 1457, and was succeeded by his eldest son, Thomas. As well as the earldom, Thomas also inherited his father's debts, and was obliged to sign a bond for 5,000 marks promising to repay them within five years. Fortunately, his finances were improved at the end of 1459 by the profits of the Somerset manor of Donyatt as well as 100 marks a year from other lands in the county. These grants were made by the King in recognition of his services against the Duke of York. The income would have been most welcome, as the Tiverton borough rents[2] had not risen significantly during the previous generation. One of the reasons for this was the large number of customary rents, which, by definition, were constant, such as the trifling amount of 3d paid by Thomas Cornewale for a piece of land by one of the leats. On the other hand, some rents could be considerable; the heir of Hugh Bridham paid 44s 10d for land which included Wilcombe Parke. The tolls of three fairs brought in just 8s 4d, probably indicating that they were being leased. On the debit side 5s was needed to repair the shambles, the market stalls and booths, and a similar sum was paid for a millstone. Thomas was trying to exploit any opportunity; the reeve's account of 1459[3] records Richard Pigge paying 3d rent for a plot of land 'in which the lord is building', and a very large rent of 33s 4d was paid for stables which had recently been built in the *forum*. This word usually refers to an open area in the middle of a town, so it is possible that the stables were built where the Pannier Market now stands, an area which curiously never appears to have supported houses.

Henry VI's forces defeated Richard, Duke of York, in 1459, causing him to flee to Calais. He returned in the following summer, however, and captured Henry. Although the King was forced to declare Richard his successor, the Queen took up arms on behalf of her son, the Prince of Wales. In the last week of 1460, her troops won a great victory at Wakefield in which Richard was killed, leaving his son Edward to further the Yorkist cause. Henry was deposed in March and soon after the Yorkists won a ferocious and unyielding battle at Towton. The 19-year old Duke of York was proclaimed King Edward IV in June. Thomas Courtenay's fortune had turned full circle. His fate was to be a traitor's death. He was executed and his head placed on the city walls at York. His lands were also forfeit to the crown. Thomas' brother, Henry Courtenay, won back the King's favour and the Courtenay possessions, but not for long. He was implicated in a plot against Edward, attainted of treason, and beheaded.

---

[1] Brymmore is the contemporary spelling given to the Courtenay manor of Breamore in Southampton, perhaps lending weight to the notion that the Courtenays had hired these men.
[2] DRO CR494.   [3] DRO CR493.

49

The manor, borough, and hundred of Tiverton were then granted to Sir Humphrey Stafford, a man from a minor Dorset family, who, like many others, had received a knighthood following the Battle of Towton. He was also given some of Courtenay's personal property. From the Castle at Tiverton his haul included two suits of clothing, two beds of silk, five books from the chapel, and three bombards[1]. Stafford, too, soon found himself on the wrong side of a dispute between the Earl of Warwick and the King. His execution meant that Tiverton reverted to royal hands once more. Edward IV appointed John Dynham temporary keeper of the manor, and Richard Milton was made parker of Ashley and Godsbear for life[2].

Did all this have any effect on Tiverton? For those living in the borough, the imposed changes of lordship must have caused concern, but no sources exist to fill in the details. On the other hand, an account of 1469-70[3] does survive, and seems to show one major difference on the manor. Before the attainder of Thomas Courtenay, labour services are not mentioned in his accounts, but one dating 1469-70 records either payment in place of service or performance of the service itself. The sale of due-days brought in 77s 5d, of which 40 days should have been spent cleaning the Leat. Those labour services actually performed included 25 days ploughing, two days mowing, 171 days harvesting as well as 78 'works' for harvesting[4]. This was one of those rare times in history when the labourer's lot was probably a happier one than that of many a noble, whose plight was best summed up in the will of John Blount, Lord Mountjoy, where he advises his sons

> 'to live rightwisely and never to take the state of baron upon them if they may lay it from them, nor desire to be great about princes, for it is dangerous'[5].

Early in 1470 Tiverton was granted to John Neville, the Earl of Northumberland, and brother of the Earl of Warwick. Later in the year, Warwick, along with the King's younger brother, the Duke of Clarence, succeeded in restoring Henry VI to the throne. However, this too was not to last. Edward defeated Henry's army at Barnet in April 1471, and the Queen's forces three weeks later at Tewkesbury. She was captured, the

---

[1] the meaning of bombards is not clear in this instance, the word can mean cannon, jugs or bassoon-like musical instruments.

[2] (*Close Rolls 1468-76*, 55). One feature of Milton's position was that his wages of 6d a day were to be paid by the farmers and occupiers of the manor and borough.

[3] DRO CR292.

[4] these 'works' were calculated by the area rather than the day.

[5] PRO PCC 27 Logge.

Prince of Wales was killed, as was Henry Courtenay's son, John, who had temporarily been re-instated as Earl of Devon. The King himself was murdered shortly afterwards, leaving Edward in an almost unchallenged position. At last strong, if ruthless rule was restored, at least during Edward's reign. He had granted Tiverton to his brother, the Duke of Clarence, but plotting led to his murder in 1478. Yet again, Tiverton became forfeit to the crown. The manor and castle were placed in the custody of John Hayes, who was to take £5 a year from the manor as wages[1]. He was already an important figure in Devon, having served as a Commissioner in many enquiries, and in 1480, Edward IV appointed him receiver of the crown lands in the county. Hayes was also appointed parker of Ashley and Godsbear with Richard Milton[2].

When Edward IV died in April 1483, conflict again seemed imminent. Richard III was crowned King and Edward's two sons died in the Tower. Any rivals were promptly executed. The only hope for the Lancastrian cause came from an obscure Welsh claimant, Henry Tudor, safely exiled in France. When in 1485, Henry landed in Wales with a small force of French mercenaries and Lancastrian supporters he managed to reach Bosworth, Leicestershire, and surprisingly defeat the Yorkist forces. The King was killed and the crown handed to Henry. His marriage to Edward's daughter, Elizabeth of York, seemingly united both causes, and bode well for peace. Henry VII rewarded those who had helped him obtain the crown, among them Edward Courtenay of Boconnoc, who was made Earl of Devon. The last earl of the Tiverton branch, John, had died childless; now the Cornish line claimed the earldom because of direct descent from the second Earl[3]. Tiverton, once more, became the seat of the Earl and the administrative centre of the earldom.

Meanwhile, developments decisive to its future prosperity were occurring in Tiverton's trade. The absence of the Courtenays had coincided with the reappearance of Tiverton merchants importing goods into Exeter. Before 1473, apart from a single cargo of honey brought in by John Collys in 1432, the last mention of a Tivertonian in the *Exeter Customs Accounts* had been in 1419. During 1473 three men from the town, Henry Roper, James Curham, and Thomas Taylor, brought in wine and crestcloth[4]. What could have been the reason for this 50-year absence? There is sufficient evidence to show that local trade did not decline, but continued in Tiverton during this period: John Curham took the tenancy of no less

---

[1] *Patent Rolls* 1476-85, 128.
[2] it is doubtful whether Milton agreed with this appointment; after all, he had been granted the post for life in 1469, and probably never envisaged sharing the position.
[3] Hugh Courtenay, who died in 1377.   [4] a type of linen, made in northern France.

than eight fulling mills in 1445[1], and Richard Spurway owed John Taylor money for making cloth in 1451[2]. There are many more examples. The surnames of the three 1473 importers are often encountered earlier in the century at Tiverton linked to the cloth trade, so they are not likely to have been newcomers but townspeople continuing their family craft. Possibly, the Courtenay family itself was to blame for the lack of Tiverton importers. The gap does coincide with the height of Courtenay power. By not encouraging Tiverton men to conduct trade on a large scale, or by ensuring goods were brought in under their strict control, it is possible that they had brought about the situation.

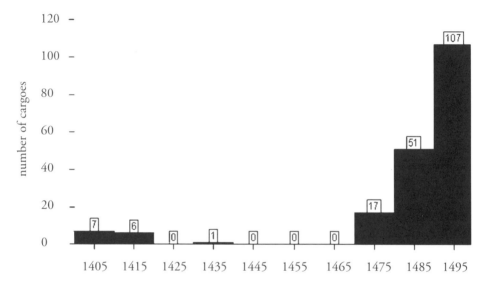

Graph showing the number of cargoes imported into Exeter by Tiverton merchants during the 15th *century (compiled from data extracted from the Exeter Customs Accounts).*

Taylor and Roper maintained their initial impetus, and in 1476 a trader called John Greneway joined them. He first appears in July as owner of three bundles of crestcloth carried on the *Anne* of Ottermouth[3]. In the following year, he imported four further consignments of cloth, as well as one cargo comprising eight tuns of iron, ten bags of cork and six bags of woad[4]. Not since the early fourteenth century had Tiverton been

---

[1] DRO CR287.   [2] DRO CR285.
[3] DRO ECA16EdIV.
[4] the city's quays were also the place where such exotic cargoes as sugar from Madeira, banyan wood, frankincense, and, on several occasions, barrels of puffins, were unloaded.

home to a merchant of the calibre of Greneway[1]. During the next ten years, his list of imports grew to include wine, herring, figs, raisins, tar, alum, woad, canvas, sugar, madder, hops, soap, haberdashery, teasels, vegetables, as well as crestcloth. The three men, Greneway, Roper, and Taylor were not alone in their endeavours: John Glovier, Thomas Skinner, and William Gray, all of Tiverton, were operating through Exeter by the mid-1480s. John Hayes, the parker of Tiverton, also imported wine, woad, iron, salt and, on one occasion, forty millstones.

The assessment of Tiverton manor and borough made for the parliamentary tax of 1488 contains the names of 82 people[2]. Of this total, 61 were taxed in the town and 21 in the manor. The townspeople were assessed at just over £80 and those of the manor £105, compared with the 1332 subsidy when the amounts were £17 and £53 respectively. From these figures, it would appear that whereas the wealth of the rural area had doubled that of the town had risen nearly fivefold. The countryside was still the domain of the well-established families with strong manorial interests; about 85% of the assessment was levied on the Earl of Devon and the families of Denys, Worth and Calwodelegh[3]. Although this group was also represented in the borough by the Earl and Calwodelegh, as well as by Edward Wadham, and John Bere of Huntsham[4], its share there was much less. For the borough of Tiverton, those individuals importing goods into Exeter had become significant; eight of them can be recognised in the assessment and they account for a sixth of the money collected. The social balance of Tiverton was changing slowly and silently in favour of the merchants who were becoming prominent. The Courtenays had returned to a town of growing prosperity, where their relationship with the inhabitants would have to be one of mutual respect not of domination.

---

[1] there is no doubt that Greneway was resident in Tiverton: in 1477 he appeared at the Tiverton borough court for allowing the Town Leat to become diverted from near his property (DRO CR233), and three years later he again appeared, and was fined 2d for brewing (DRO CR235). Conversely, earlier in the year he had served as one of the twelve jurors at the borough court (DRO CR234)

[2] (DRO CR557). The list includes surnames like Crudge, Sellake, Pleymarke, Deyman, Curham, London, Skinner, Veysey and Coterell - long established by 1388 and, in many cases, still recognised today.

[3] the family of Denys had inherited Farleigh, but lived at Orleigh, near Bideford; the Worths of Worth in Washfield; Calwodelegh of Calverleigh.

[4] Edward Wadham had inherited the manor of Pool Anthony which included properties within the town; similarly, John Bere held three burgages there.

5 The End of Courtenay Tiverton

John Morton, Archbishop of Canterbury, came to Tiverton in June 1492, as part of his visitation of the Deanery of Exeter[1]. He was one of the most powerful and influential men in the kingdom. Not only was he Primate of England but also Lord Chancellor, and he was to become a cardinal in the following year. He spent the night of the 15th in the town, probably at the Castle, and on the next day, he presided over the visitation in Saint Peter's Church before the assembled clergy. A few months later Edward Courtenay asked the Archbishop to become a trustee of his properties in Tiverton as he was about to leave for France as part of Henry VII's army. Edward served the King for a year with six men-at-arms (himself included), two cavalrymen carrying light lances, 25 archers on horseback and 66 on foot. He was accompanied by his son, William, who took six lancers, eight mounted archers, 32 archers on foot and four billmen. War was avoided when Henry wisely relinquished his claim to any French territory, apart from Calais, in return for a payment of £159,000.

The Earl's help was needed much nearer to his home five years later. Early in the summer of 1497, an army of Cornishmen, headed by a blacksmith, Michael Joseph, marched on London, complaining of the high level of taxation. Although their numbers had grown considerably by the time they faced the King's troops at Blackheath in June, they were heavily defeated. Another force of rebels marched out of Cornwall three months later. They were led by Perkin Warbeck, who claimed to be Richard, brother of Edward IV and rightful king of England. Exeter was besieged, and during its relief, the Earl of Devon was wounded in the arm by an arrow. Warbeck and his supporters moved on to Taunton, but he was soon captured[2]. For his loyalty on this last occasion, the Earl of Devon was given the power to enquire into the rebellions (and exact some retribution).

Meanwhile, the Courtenay family's elevated status enabled the Earl's son, William, to take a royal wife. In 1495, he married Princess Katherine, the daughter of Edward IV. Tiverton Castle was not to be their home at first; the couple spent the early years of their marriage at the royal court, where young Courtenay received a 50 mark annuity 'for his daily and diligent attendance on the king's person'[3]. He took a prominent role in the marriage of Henry VII's son Arthur to Catherine of Aragon in 1501, especially in the lavish celebrations following the ceremony, which included a jousting tournament. Prior to each bout the main participants entered the arena in spectacular

---

[1] *RegMorton*, 62.
[2] and was eventually executed in 1499.
[3] *Patent Rolls 1494-1509*, 223.

fashion, and before one of his contests William Courtenay arrived 'enclosed in a chapel all curtained with rich cloth of gold'[1].

Although they were prominent national figures few Tiverton localities of the time recall the Courtenay name. Not so the merchant John Greneway, whose Chapel and Almshouses are still standing and in use today, reminding us of his generosity to the town. While William Courtenay was flaunting his popularity at court, Tiverton's John Greneway was making his mark both locally and among London merchants. This was not the man first noticed in 1476 importing goods into Exeter[2], however, but his son. During 1494, the *Exeter Customs Accounts* record both of them, and soon they were using their own ships. One vessel named the *George Greneway* of Dartmouth occurs in 1498, and later the *Trinity Greneway* appears[3].

Carving of a ship from the exterior of the Greenway Chapel at Saint Peter's Church.

---

[1] *London*, 251-2.
[2] see p.52. John Greneway sr had been the most prolific Tiverton importer from the late 1470s to the 1490s; a time that had seen the number of the town's importers increase from four to 16, and the average number of their cargoes rise from less than six to over 15 each year.
[3] Nicholls 1960, 62.

The junior John Greneway was admitted to the London Worshipful Company of Drapers in 1497. This powerful city guild held a virtual monopoly of buying and selling cloth in the capital, and the young man from Tiverton was soon to become a member of its governing body[1]. He continued to use Exeter, importing mainly linen cloth from northern France, but also such diverse commodities as the 150 reams of paper carried on the *Juliane* of Poole in March 1502, and a quantity of figs and raisins later in that year.

By the beginning of the 16th century, the cloth trade had become Tiverton's main industry, giving work to a large number of people, including women and children. Many of the clothworkers, especially the weavers, worked on the land during the day but spent their evenings at the loom. All aspects of the trade were carried on in and around Tiverton: from sorting the raw wool then combing, carding, spinning, weaving, dyeing, fulling, to packing and transporting the finished cloth. Although farming involved more people, it was largely geared towards subsistence, whereas the cloth industry could generate large profits. Much of the money was reinvested in the industry, for example by building more fulling mills. This was happening at Tiverton, but they were not restricted to the town itself. One at Whitwell in East Chevithorne manor was begun in 1507, and the farmer, John Bluet, was told to construct a weir on the river there[2]. Once the mills were built, of course they needed constant maintenance; Exe Mills had fallen into disrepair and the manor court in 1505 ordered the replacement of the decayed timbering[3].

The importance of the developing cloth trade to Tiverton cannot be overestimated, for it permeated most aspects of daily life. Even reports of local crime contain abundant references to cloth and cloth making. In 1501 John Philip, armed with a staff and dagger, broke into William Wyot's house at Craze Lowman and took 31s 8d in cash[4]. Philip's goods were forfeited and delivered to the Tiverton manor court, where they were sold. They consisted of two dozen woollen cloths of kersey plonket[5] and 16 pound of white wool which were sold to Richard Horne, 15 pound of white wool to John Style, 2s 10d in cash, a dozen teasels[6], and half a piece of woollen cloth called canvas to the victim Wyot. The rest of his possessions comprised 5s in gold, a honey-coloured russet gown, a worsted doublet, and a pair of white hose.

Not for the first time, a Courtenay fell under royal suspicion in 1502. William, the heir to the Earldom of Devon, had been keeping company with members of the Yorkist Pole family. This was enough for the ever-vigilant Henry VII, who arrested all those

---

[1] Welsford 1984, 4. [2] SRO DD/CN/2/2.
[3] DRO CR303a. [4] DRO CR355.
[5] a type of heavy woollen cloth, for which Tiverton would become world-famous.
[6] thistle-like plant, used to raise the nap on woollen cloth.

nobles he thought were plotting against him. William Courtenay was attainted along with Humphrey Calwodelegh, who held the manors of Cove and East Mere as well as lands in Chettiscombe. Their lands were forfeited to the King despite their previous record of loyalty. William Courtenay stayed in the Tower until Henry VIII succeeded to the throne in 1509 and restored him to favour. But he was soon to mourn the death of his father, Edward. The Earl, in his will, had made arrangements for the provision of a chantry in the church, as well as stating his wish to be buried 'near his lady' in their chapel at Tiverton. Apart from that in the Castle, this is the first mention of a Courtenay chapel at Tiverton[1]. The building no longer exists, but was attached to the outside of Saint Peter's Church, probably with access both from without and within the church. Although its exact location is unknown, it was almost certainly on the northern side of Saint Peter's, close to where the modern vestry now stands. It is likely that it had been constructed to house the remains of Edward's wife, Elizabeth, who had died in 1493.

In spite of his release, William Courtenay's attainder initially remained in force. This meant that he was deprived of most of his inheritance, although he did receive the Boconnoc estates. The other lands, including Tiverton, were in Henry VIII's hands, and he appointed a host of officers to administer them. William Legh, a yeoman of the Royal Chamber, was placed in charge of the Tiverton parks, temporarily at first, but subsequently for life[2]. One apparent result of the royal administration of the manor was the unusually high number of new tenants. The court roll for 1510[3] also shows that higher entry fines were being demanded; East Barton was taken by Richard Vautard for £6, John Hoygge alias Saddler took Collipriest at £7 (previously £4), and Edward Hoper was admitted to a holding in Cove for an £8 fine. Whether this was due to a growing population or increased prosperity from cloth making, the King was not one to pass over the opportunity to reap the rewards.

The Courtenays were soon back in favour, spending much of their time at the royal court. Henry VIII made William Earl of Devon in the spring of 1511, and in the same year, he played a principal part in the tournament to celebrate the birth of the King's short-lived son. But fate dealt the family a heavy blow. Before his investiture as Earl of Devon could take place, William died of pleurisy. Henry VIII mourned his loss and ordered that he should be buried in the manner befitting an Earl. A grand funeral ceremony took place at Blackfriars Church in London. His widow, Princess Katherine, still only 32, now took a vow of chastity, wisely withdrawing herself from the marriage market. Her nephew, the King, granted her lands that included Tiverton, where she decided to live at the Castle. For the first and only time in the town's history, it became the seat of a member of the Royal Family.

---

[1] Risdon's assertion that Edward Courtenay, the Blind Earl, was buried there in 1419 with his wife Kate is incorrect. Edward's will stipulated that he should be buried at Forde Abbey, and Edward's wives were named Eleanor and Matilda, not Kate.

[2] *LPFD 1509-13*, 405.   [3] DRO CR306.

A remarkable transformation was begun at Saint Peter's Church in 1517. John Greneway the younger had undertaken to enlarge the south aisle and add a chantry chapel to the building. Dunsford states[1] that he had also offered to replace the tower with 'one more curious and magnificent', but was dissuaded by the people of Tiverton who feared his ability to complete the work. The chapel was probably built to house the remains of John Greneway senior, who disappears from any records at this time. Although the blinding creamy-white Beer stone must have caused a logistical nightmare to transport, it provided a gleaming advertisement of pious endeavour and commercial success. The noble Courtenays had their new chapel on the north side, the Castle side, of Saint Peter's, and now the leading merchants were to have theirs on the south side, the town side. The Greneway Chapel was the first conspicuous sign of merchant wealth in the town. Emblazoned across the front of the church, the first part of the structure seen by all that enter the building, are the merchant ships, which carried Greneway's cloth and brought in his goods. As well as his merchant's mark, there are the arms of the family, along with those of the Drapers' Company, the Merchant Adventurers, and, taking pride of place in the porch, those of Princess Katherine Courtenay[2].

The arms of Katherine Courtenay above the porch of Saint Peter's Church

The earthly adornments are matched by those of a more spiritual nature showing a series of scenes from the life of Christ. The Chapel was dedicated to Saints Christopher,

---

[1] 1790, 325.

[2] Prideaux 1918, and Blaylock 1986.

Blaise and Anne: the patron saints of travellers, cloth workers, and Brittany respectively, reflecting Greneway's interests. The finished interior made such an impact locally that less than a decade later many aspects of it were the inspiration for the magnificent fan-vaulted aisle at Saint Andrew's, Cullompton, constructed by its own wealthy merchant, John Lane[1].

Saint Peter's Church and the Chapel of Saint Mary on Exe Bridge were endowed in 1518 by David ap Thomas alias Phelip[2]. He granted land near Howden for the benefit of the church and chapel, and to maintain the bridge. The donor was said to be the heir, probably the grandson, of John Phelip alias Weyber. The Welsh 'ap' (meaning 'son of') probably indicates that David ap Thomas' father was called Thomas ap John or Thomas Phelip. One of the murderers of Nicholas Radford in 1455 was called Thomas Philip (see page 48). So, perhaps David's gift was an act of atonement for his father's misdeeds. We can only speculate.

Dynastic politics in Western Europe were soon to be dominated by the rivalry between the Bourbon Francis I and the Hapsburg Charles, Archduke of the Netherlands, King of Spain, and, in 1519, Holy Roman Emperor. Marriage had contrived a unique situation by which England became involved; Henry VIII's queen was Charles' aunt, and the nation's trading interests needed the alliance with the Netherlands. Henry sided with Charles, and sent a number of fruitless military expeditions to fight against France. His interventions were so costly that novel and heavy taxation expedients were necessary. They do, at least, help local historians.

The tax assessment of 1524 lists 289 households in Tiverton parish. Taking into account those too poor to contribute, the population of the parish was therefore well in excess of 1,000, and probably nearer 2,000. The number of Tiverton's taxpayers places the town fourth in the county, behind Exeter, Crediton, and Plymouth, and 52nd in the whole country[3]. There were three categories of assessment: land, wages, and goods. As with many of the neighbouring parishes the number of Tivertonians taxed on land is very low, only eight individuals. Nevertheless, this small group included Katherine Courtenay, assessed at £64, as well as John Spurway who was lord of the manor of Peadhill, and John Way who held Newcott near Templeton. These three individuals were the only resident manorial holders in the parish. Wage earners made up a quarter of those paying tax in Tiverton. Within the group can be recognised

---

[1] the craftsman responsible for the work on the ceiling of the Greneway porch could well have been the same man who worked on the vault of Bishop Oldham's chantry in Exeter Cathedral a few years earlier, and also executed some of the work in the Dorset aisle of Ottery Saint Mary church (Blaylock 1986, 104).
[2] cited in Harding 1845, iii, 67.   [3] Dyer 2000, 762.

Thomas ap Howell who was a member of the Courtenay household, as probably were many others of this category. At least four men paying tax in Tiverton may be termed foreigners; probably all involved in Tiverton's cloth trade. They were John a Gaunt, possibly of Ghent in Belgium; John Cleve, perhaps from the town of Cleves or Kleve, on the Dutch-German border; John Frenshman; and Bartholomew Nove, who is specifically termed 'Dutchman'. By far the biggest group was assessed on goods, among whom were men bearing such recognisable names as Tanner, Bere, Crosse, Land, Deyman, Prouse, Sharland, and Chamberlain. Besides Katherine Courtenay, Tiverton was home to four other individuals assessed at £40 or more. Richard Parkhowse, at £40, was a considerable importer into Exeter, although in the Customs Accounts his origin is never stated. John Skinner, taxed on just under £67, held extensive lands at Elmore, which probably included the mills. The two conspicuously rich individuals were the ubiquitous John Greneway assessed at £150 and William Selake at £100.

Selake died in 1524, leaving a will[1] that bears witness to his commercial interests and spiritual beliefs. To each of his sons, Andrew and Robert, he left two packs of kersies, and to each of his godchildren ten yards of crestcloth. His brother John received 40s and a mulberry-coloured gown lined with satin from Cyprus, as well as William's best gown and two doublets. His widow Joan was given £40, two silver goblets, and other bequests, whereas his three daughters were promised 40s when they married. Selake left money to the rectors of Tidcombe and Pitt for 'forgotten tithes', and he gave the sum of £36 to Saint Peter's Church to build a roodloft. He expressed the wish to be buried in the church, and made provision for the ceremony; 10s was given for a trental (30 masses) as well as five masses of *Scala Celi*. Joan, his wife, was instructed to use the remainder of his estate to establish a chantry 'for the wealth of his soul'. In the foundation document[2] it states that a daily mass was to be said at the 'Pytte awter' in Saint Peter's by a chaplain, and a mass of Our Lady was to be sung with 'the orgones' for his soul and those of his family.

An account of Katherine Courtenay's household[3] made in the same year as Selake's death, 1524, shows in detail the luxuries enjoyed at the Castle. Items bought included sugar, a great rarity costing 5¼d a pound, honey at 8s 8d a gallon, ginger at 2s 4d a pound, three pounds of marmalade for 15d, half a pound of cinnamon at 3s, as well as cherries, sweet and sour oranges, pomegranates and raisins. The most expensive commodity, however, was saffron, which was bought for 17s a pound – in stark contrast to the 7d paid 'to a woman weeding in the garden six days'. The fish and meat consumed were similarly varied: 383 hake, 800 bokhorn[4], conger, porpoise, wild boar

---

[1] *Moger Wills.*
[2] NDRO B1/4930.
[3] *LPFD 1524-30*, 338-42.
[4] buckhorn, dried whiting or other fish (so called because of its hardness).

and deer, in addition to the more common beef, pork and mutton. The kitchen also prepared swan, heron, peafowl, woodcock, snipe, mallard, teal, cormorants and puffins. Entertainments after the feasting were also of the highest quality. Payments were made to a harpist and tumbler, as well as to minstrels. The number of people employed in the Castle to provide this quality of service can be judged by the fact that during this one year the Princess gave livery cloth to 91 servants. Out of all these people, one was clearly especially close to Katherine. Her laundress, Philippa, was married in 1524 and a lot of money was lavished on the event. Three yards of velvet were bought for her wedding dress, and various amounts were paid for making it, as well as £6 13s 4d for her 'marriage money'. A later account[1] mentions that in the living quarters at the Castle there were as many as 40 standing bedsteads, and in the stable 'my lady's litter, covered with black velvet', probably the ideal transport to convey the Princess between Tiverton and her other residences. In spite of her relative isolation in Devon, Katherine kept in close contact with London, especially by letter. Payments were made for the delivery of messages to the King, and to Cardinal Wolsey.

At eight o'clock in the evening of November 15th, 1527, Princess Katherine peacefully passed away at Tiverton Castle. The daughter of Edward IV, sister of Edward V, and, by marriage, aunt of Henry VIII, she had proudly styled herself simply Katherine Devonshire. Despite her royal birth she did not choose to be buried in an abbey or cathedral, but rather expressed a wish to remain at Tiverton, her home. Soon after her death, her body was embalmed, placed in a lead coffin, and taken to the Castle chapel. A black velvet cloth with a white satin cross upon it was laid over the coffin. In turn that was covered with a pall of cloth of gold on which was a cross made of silver tissue, embroidered with her coat-of-arms. Her remains rested there for 17 days, bathed in the light from countless candles. Dirges and masses were sung daily, and attendants kept a constant vigil. Two officials of the College of Arms were despatched from London especially to conduct the funeral ceremonies. These began on December 2nd; Katherine's body was taken the short distance from the Castle to Saint Peter's Church in a formal procession. As a spectacle, it has probably never been equalled in Tiverton's history. At the head of the solemn cortege was carried the Holy Cross, followed by many important clergymen, among them the principal officials, the abbots of Montacute, Torre and Forde. Next walked 100 men. Then six yeomen of equal height carried the coffin, above which was held a black velvet canopy supported by six local notables including John Chichester, John Fulford and two members of the Fortescue family. At each corner of the canopy was a saint's banner, carried by George Carew, Nicholas Ayshford of Burlescombe, Richard Chudleigh and Alexander Wode. This leading group was flanked by eight gentlemen, four on each side, each carrying a small

---

[1] *LPFD 1524-30, 1677-8.*

banner. Lady Carew, the chief mourner, came next, assisted by Piers Edgcombe and a multitude of the region's dignitaries. Katherine's body was received into a church bedecked with black cloth and illuminated by 800 candles. The coffin, after it had been sprinkled with holy water by the abbots, was left in the Courtenay Chapel with attendants. The procession went back to the Castle for the night, and returned at seven o'clock the next morning. The funeral service itself now took place with the three abbots singing the masses of Our Lady, the Trinity and Requiem, aided by choristers drawn from near and far. The chief mourner, the attendant knights and nobles, the Mayor and Aldermen of Exeter, local yeomen, attendants, and others all made offerings. Peter Carslegh, the Rector of Pitt and one of Henry VIII's chaplains, delivered a sermon on the words 'the hand of God touches me', and, finally, the body was lowered into the vault below the Courtenay Chapel[1]. At this instant, Katherine's officers broke their wooden staves. The congregation then returned to the Castle, where a banquet was held for 500 people, and a gift of 100 marks was made to 8,000 poor to pray for the Princess' soul[2].

Two years later, Tiverton lost its most affluent merchant. John Greneway died in London. It is hard to imagine that his death was not marked locally with great ceremony, but there is no record of the event. His body was placed in the vault[3] below the Chapel in Saint Peter's Church, and he left money for an obit and 5s to keep a light burning in his memory at the high altar. Notwithstanding the magnificence of the Greenway Chapel, his enduring legacy is the Almshouses in Gold Street. The money to support the bequest came from some of his properties in Tiverton and the farms of Frogwell and Delbridge, in the parish of Diptford in south Devon[4]. The building fronting Gold Street, nowadays often ignored and unrecognised, is not the original structure; that was built with galleries. Parts of the adjoining chapel, on the other hand, are original. The almshouses were established to provide shelter for five poor aged men unable to find themselves meat, drink, or cloth.

---

[1] in Katherine's will (Oliver & Jones 1853, 53-8) there are references to two separate chapels at Saint Peter's. One of these, the 'Courtenay Chapel', was where she was actually laid to rest, and was situated near the north door of the church. However, Katherine herself desired to be 'buridd in the new Chapell lately edefyed and bylded in the southe syde of the churche', clearly a reference to the Greenway Chapel. Are we to read from this that Katherine personally wished to be buried there rather than in the family chapel, but her family had other thoughts on the matter?

[2] Tiverton's population would not have exceeded 2,000 persons at this time, so the gift to 8,000 poor must have been distributed over a very wide area.

[3] according to Dunsford (1790, 318-9) the vault measured eight feet square and lined with glazed brown tiles.

[4] it is likely that Diptford was the ancestral home of the Greneways - in the early 14th century a man of that name from nearby Dartmouth was a ship's master.

Each was to have a separate chamber and to receive 8d a week. Over the years, the numbers of those benefiting from the foundation have increased, as has their accommodation. Now administered as part of the Tiverton Almshouse Trust, additional buildings have recently been erected behind the street frontage, stretching down to the Lowman.

Greenway's Almshouses in Gold Street, built in 1529.

Catherine of Aragon's apparent inability to provide Henry VIII with a male heir caused him to consider divorcing her in favour of the young Ann Boleyn. Although he had received special Papal dispensation to marry Catherine, who was his brother's widow, Henry now pointed out that such a union was forbidden by the Bible, and therefore unlawful. He realised that an approach to the Pope would be difficult; Catherine was the aunt of the Emperor Charles V, who had complete domination over Italy and the Papacy. To prepare the best possible case Henry enlisted many scholars, including Peter Carslegh, the Rector of Pitt. The King wanted divorce proceedings to be heard in England, but the Pope ordered the case to Rome in 1529. Henry knew he would not receive a favourable hearing under the gaze of Catherine's uncle, so, somewhat reluctantly, he decided to dispense with appeals to Rome and strike out alone. In 1532, the English clergy were made to submit to him, and in 1533, using the authority given by Act of Parliament, Archbishop Thomas Cranmer pronounced his previous marriage invalid. Henry married the pregnant Ann, who, in September, gave birth to a daughter, Elizabeth. At the christening, Henry Courtenay carried a taper of golden wax and his wife acted as godmother.

Henry had obtained his divorce through the support of Parliament, and the manipulation of anit-clerical sentiments fostered by Lollards and reformers, who had grown in number and confidence after the protest and trial of Martin Luther the German monk. He had preached that God's mercy alone was necessary to save sinners and through the printing press gained political support. The Rector of Pitt was fully aware that Henry, when it suited him, fostered such feelings of anti-clericalism. In a sermon given before the King, he said that if the Pope could deliver souls from purgatory but would do so only for money rather than charity, then he deserved to be in purgatory himself[1]. Perhaps a series of assaults on clerics in the Tiverton area can be attributed to these sentiments. The manor court rolls record the beating of William Brytan, a chaplain, in 1532, but much more seriously in the following year, the Rector of Calverleigh, William Olyver, suffered five separate attacks[2].

Parliament passed the Act of Supremacy in 1534, effecting the final break with Rome, and declaring Henry the Supreme Head of the Church of England. Thomas Cromwell was appointed Vicar General, in church matters subordinate only to Henry[3]. An administrative genius determined to enrich his king, he embarked almost immediately on compiling the *Valor Ecclesiasticus*, a valuation of all church possessions. It contains information about the income of parishes and monastic lands, detailing revenue from tithes, glebe land, and other sources. The various amounts due from the Tiverton portions are set out below.

	PITT	CLARE	TIDCOMBE
Rent from glebe	£4 10s	-	£3 16s
Tithes of Corn	£16	-	£12
Tithes of Wool	£3 15s 9d	-	£2
Tithes of Lambs	£1 13s 4d	-	£1 3s 4d
Easter Dues	£10 4s 9½d	-	£8 4s 5½d
Total	£36 3s 9½d	£27 3s 9d	£27 3s 9½d
Clear	£36	£27	£27

There is no breakdown of the Clare total as the tithes were leased to Robert Brodemede for an annual payment, and Prior's Portion belonged to King's College, Cambridge.

---

[1] cited in Whiting 1977, 45.   [2] DRO CR367-9.
[3] one of the first matters dealt with by the Vicar General concerned Tiverton's Peter Carslegh. The Rector of Pitt had been reported by the Bishop of Wells (*LPFD 1535*, 98) for making a notorious (and potentially dangerous) blunder. During a service at Wells, Carslegh asked for prayers to be said for Catherine of Aragon instead of Queen Anne, but his slip of the tongue was dismissed as coming from a man 'not much under 80'.

The deficit between the total due and the clear amount was taken up by payments made to both the Bishop and the Archdeacon of Exeter.

Henry VIII soon tired of Anne and had her executed in 1536 for adultery. He next married Jane Seymour, and at last a male heir, Edward, was born on October 12th 1537, although his mother died twelve days later. At the christening, Gertrude, Henry Courtenay's wife, carried the young prince, but she, too, soon became a victim of Henry's dangerous suspicion. Gertrude had continued to communicate regularly with Catherine of Aragon, and had refused to denounce Catholicism. Furthermore, Henry Courtenay had maintained a close friendship with the Pole family. Just like his father, Henry VIII constantly suspected any dynastic challenges to his throne, and he knew that both Courtenay and the Poles had a valid claim to it. His solution was drastic: both Henry Courtenay and Henry Pole were executed in December 1538. The price of fame once more was death. In what had become almost a regular occurrence, the Courtenay lands became forfeit to the Crown. Surveys were taken to determine their value, and the results shows that the borough, manor and hundred of Tiverton made an annual proft of just over £87, a meagre £9 more than in 1484. The servants numbered in excess of 100, and included John Frye, bailiff of both Tiverton and Cornwood, a man 'who can play well at all weapons'[1]. The most intriguing individual named was Robert Taylor who, as well as being the Rector of Clare, taught Henry Courtenay's son, Edward[2]. Although just 12 years of age, this young boy was incarcerated in the Tower, but his mother was released.

By 1540 Henry VIII's regular annual income was boosted by about one third[3] from the confiscation of monastic lands. The process, masterminded by Cromwell, had begun in 1536 and was virtually complete four years later. Most of the property did not remain in royal hands for long; the prospect of sales for cash and the desire to reward and promote loyal service won the day. Local men took their chance. Roger Bluett of Holcombe Rogus benefited from the first surge of selling. He paid over £500 for lands in his home parish and in Sampford Peverell, Silverton, Clayhanger, and elsewhere. Bluett's purchases had formerly belonged to Montacute Priory, Torre Abbey, and Canonsleigh, and included 10s rent payable out of Passmorehayes in the parish of Tiverton. Another man to take advantage of the situation was Anthony Harvey, who had been appointed surveyor of the Courtenay lands, and already owned a fulling mill and fields called Withymead in Tiverton. He bought estates that had belonged to

---

[1] *LPFD 1538*, 293.
[2] a letter written from Antwerp to Henry Courtenay before his arrest, states (*LPFD 1538, 83*) that Taylor had been discovered in the Flemish city of Louvain, where he had fled because he had been threatened for 'ministering correction' to his young pupil.
[3] Elton 1977, 236.

Hartland Abbey and Plympton Priory[1], and his future was doubly assured when he received more forfeited Courtenay lands, including Columbjohn, which became his chief residence. George Losemore of Tiverton, along with John Strangman of Dorset, received a grant of lands in 1545 that had formed part of the Knights Hospitallers' possessions in Devon, as well as other ex-monastic land[2].

According to a tax assessment of 1546, Losemore was the richest inhabitant of Tiverton[3]. He was followed by such individuals as Robert Colycke, Thomas Deyman, John Prouse of Bolham and Ralph Waldron, merchants to a man. The cloth trade was enjoying such success that even disputes with France were not allowed to disrupt commerce. Licences were issued to English merchants enabling them to take woollen cloth, tin and lead to Guernsey, where they were permitted to be traded for canvas, crestcloth, and cloth such as lockram, dowlas, and poldavys, all brought there from France[4]. Individuals such as Peter Carver 'frenssheman', however, who appeared before the town's borough court in 1540, may not necessarily have been welcome during the hostilities.

Henry VIII died in January 1547 in the middle of a futile costly war against France and Scotland. He was succeeded by his nine-year old son, Edward VI. The boy's guardian was Edward Seymour, Duke of Somerset, who, six months later, was granted the manor, borough and hundred of Tiverton. Edward's short reign would be remembered for the dramatic acceleration of Protestantism. Bibles written in English had been placed in every church; pictures and images were, in most cases, removed. Monasteries and priories were crumbling into ruins or being scavenged for building materials. No doubt spurred on partly by avaricious courtiers the reformers now turned on the chantries. Many parishes contained lands used to support chantry priests and the upkeep of their chapels. Tiverton had two: one begun by the Marquis of Exeter in 1511, the other by William Selake. Henry Bedell was the priest for the Marquis' foundation, and his income of £6 13s came from lands at Hone. Selake's Chantry benefited from the £10 4s a year received from the farms of Gotham, Wood and Honeyland, as well as lesser rents from properties in Saint Peter Street, Fore Street, and Westexe. Both foundations were dissolved, and Bedell received an annual pension of £5.

Initially, the transition from Catholic tradition to Protestant practice produced few problems, but as time passed various sects emerged and religious discord grew. In an

---

[1] *LPFD 1540-1*, 327, and *1542*, 166.   [2] *LPFD 1545*, 663-4.
[3] *Subsidy 1543-5*, 59.   [4] *LPFD 1544*, 376.

attempt at unity, Thomas Cranmer penned the first Book of Common Prayer[1]. Its introduction was enforced by an Act of Uniformity, making any other usage illegal. This had the effect of antagonising Protestant and Catholic alike and spawned the Western Prayer Book Rebellion. Cornwall and Devon rose in favour of 'the old religion', as well as against proposed taxes on wool and cloth. In June 1549, the rebels took Exeter. A force of 2,000 men, under Sir William Herbert aided by John, Baron Russell, relieved the city. Although the main body of insurgents was defeated at Clyst Saint Mary, one group fled up the Exe Valley. Herbert pursued them as far as Cranmore Castle, where they made a stand on August 19th. Not all of them managed to escape; some were taken prisoner, hanged and quartered on the spot, and their remains put on display to discourage others[2]. For their part in the suppression of the rebellion, Herbert received the earldom of Pembroke, and Russell that of Bedford.

Protector Somerset died in 1552, and the manor, borough, and hundred of Tiverton passed back into the King's hands. Edward VI then granted them to one of his servants, Henry Gate, who was already Controller of the Petty Customs of the Port of London and Receiver of the Duchy of Cornwall. The Earl of Bedford surrendered his lifetime grant as keeper of the Tiverton parks in March 1553, and the post was given to Gawen Carew together with the custody of the Castle[3]. The death of Edward VI in July changed everything. His Catholic stepsister, Mary, came to the throne, and soon gave orders for Edward Courtenay to be released from the Tower, where he had spent 15 out of his 27 years. Tiverton was returned to him, as were the other lands of the earldom.

Edward Courtenay was favoured by many as a possible husband for the Queen, but Mary herself was determined to marry Philip, the son of the Holy Roman Emperor. She also made it clear that she intended to restore Papal authority in England. A Protestant insurrection quickly followed in Kent, but gained little support; the rebels were dispersed and the leaders executed. A similar rising in Devon led by Sir Peter Carew was nipped in the bud. In fact, the figurehead of this movement was none other than Edward Courtenay, who informed the Lord Chancellor of the plot. One of the ringleaders, Gawen Carew, keeper of Tiverton Castle, was captured at Bickleigh and taken to the Tower of London. Sir Peter Carew and Edward Courtenay escaped to the Continent, as did many Westcountrymen[4]. Mary and Philip were married in July 1554, and the aged Cardinal Pole returned to England as papal legate in November. By this time, George Carew, for his Protestant leanings (and family connections), had been

---

[1] which was to replace the missal and breviary.
[2] cited in Cornwall 1977, 200.   [3] *CSPDom 1547-53*, 293.
[4] John Chichester of Youlston, Christopher Chudleigh, Francis Russell the second Earl of Bedford, four brothers of the Tremayne family, John Bodlegh of Dunscombe in Crediton etc. (see Garrett 1938).

deprived of his benefice of Tidcombe as well as that of Torbryan and the Deanery of Bristol. On the other hand, Tiverton's two remaining portioners must have showed enthusiasm for the 'old religion' as they benefited under Mary's regime. Thomas Marshall, Rector of Clare, obtained the Archdeaconry of Lincoln, a canonry in Southwell, and the benefice of Saint Bride's in Fleet Street, London. The portioner of Pitt, Thomas Raynold, was chosen as a chaplain to Mary and Philip in 1555, and in the same year was appointed Dean of Exeter.

Meanwhile, Edward Courtenay was in Italy mixing with influential people such as the Doge of Venice. He was warned in June 1556 that if he returned to England from exile 'it would cost him his life'[1]. But he did not have to travel to meet his death, however. He died in Padua on October 5th 1556 as a result, many believed, of being poisoned. With no direct descendants, Edward's possessions were divided between the heirs of the four sisters of his great-grandfather Edward, the eighth Earl of Devon. All four of them had married into the Cornish gentry families of Tretherf, Arundel, Mohun and Trelawney. Tiverton's direct association with the Courtenay family had come to an end after more than 250 years. During that time it had grown from little more than a village protected by its feudal lord to a thriving centre of cloth manufacture, producing men like John Greneway who could take their place in national and international commerce. Tiverton had survived its upbringing, nurtured, protected (and sometimes stifled) by the Courtenays, and had taken on some aspects of maturity.

How different would local and national history have been if Mary had married Courtenay. The Queen, through Parliament, restored Papal supremacy to England, and led the way to a Catholic revival. This was not to be an easy return to 'old religion'. Mary's reign was tainted by the persecution of Protestants, which produced almost 300 martyrs, and her marriage to Philip led many Englishmen to associate Catholicism with Spanish arrogance. An unsuccessful and unpopular war against France saw England lose Calais, its last toehold on the European mainland. Bloody Mary died childless in November 1558 together with her vision of a Catholic England. She knew her successor would be Anne Boleyn's daughter, the Protestant Elizabeth. No one could have predicted the long reign of the Virgin Queen.

---

[1] *CSPFor 1553-8*, 229.

6 Elizabethan Tiverton

From the outset, Elizabeth needed to settle the question of religion. The compromise she arrived at was approved by Parliament in the Acts of Supremacy and Uniformity in 1559. She demanded recognition as Supreme Governor of the Church of England, but Catholics were to be treated with considerable tolerance at first. On payment of a fine they could opt out of the obligatory monthly church attendance, and their private celebration of mass was allowed, unless treason was suspected. Nevertheless, Catholic bishops and priests were replaced. The religious reversal inevitably caused changes in the Tiverton clergy. On Mary's accession George Carew had been deprived of Tidcombe, Stoke Fleming, and Ilfracombe, but was now restored to favour. He did not regain Tidcombe, however, as that remained in the hands of George Harvey. Instead, he was admitted to Clare on the death of Thomas Marshall, and also took Pitt Portion when Thomas Raynold was ejected. A staunch Catholic, and Queen Mary's chaplain, Raynold was Bishop-Elect of Hereford at the time of her death. He was not consecrated, but thrown into the Marshalsea Prison, where he died in the following year. Many of the Protestants who had fled to the Continent during Mary's purges now came back.

As her father had done with monastic and chantry possessions, so Elizabeth did with chapels. As head of the Church she owned most of the sites, and in March 1567, granted ten of them in Tiverton to two Londoners[1]. They were Nicase Yetsweirt, a royal servant for the previous 20 years, and Bartholomew Brokesby, who had already spent nearly £3,000 on land that included former chantry properties. The chapels named in the grant were;

Saint Thomas	on the site of the present Town Hall
Saint Andrew	near the Bridewell in Saint Andrew Street
Saint Mary	on Exe Bridge
Saint Bartholomew	at Bolham
Saint James	at Craze Lowman
Saint Matthew	at Palmershayes
Saint James	almost certainly near Seven Crosses
Saint John	at Church Coombe[2]
Holy Trinity	possibly at Tidcombe
unknown dedication	at Fairby

---

[1] *Patent Rolls 1566-9*, 48.
[2] Dunsford states (1790, 177) that Church Coombe lay in Pitt portion, and the name could refer either to Coombe Farm near Cove or to Lower and Higher Coombeland, which lie about a mile further south.

These, however, were not all the chapels within the parish. A further seven had been listed in a document of 1544[1]

Saint Mary	at Chettiscombe
Saint Peter	near Chilcott's School, Saint Peter Street
Saint John the Baptist	at Cove
Saint Lawrence	at East Mere
Saint Katherine	at East Bradley[2]
unknown dedication	at West Manley
unknown dedication	at Farleigh

The transfer of ten of Tiverton's 17 chapels[3] into lay hands must have brought home the fact to most local people that the Roman Catholic faith was now lost to Elizabeth's England, and its alleged superstition and ritual consigned to the past[4]. Now, the only remaining places of worship within the parish were Saint Peter's and the chapel-of-ease at Cove, though the latter's continuity is not known to be certain.

Saint Peter's parish registers begin in 1560[5], enabling us to chart individuals, families, and the whole parish through the years. As well as fulfilling their purpose by recording all christenings, marriages and burials, they often give additional details such as dates of induction of the clergy, professions of the people referred to, and, in the case of burials, sometimes the cause of death. By using the registers, it is also possible to gauge the population of the town. It has been calculated[6] that Tiverton contained just over 2,500 persons in 1565, a time when no town outside London had more than 20,000 inhabitants, when Totnes was more important than Liverpool, and Birmingham was still a manorial village one sixth the size of Coventry[7].

Meanwhile, work, trade and bargaining went on. There was an upsurge of property sales in and around Tiverton during the early years of Elizabeth's reign. Almost all of them concerned premises or people involved in the cloth trade. One example is John Webber, a clothier of Taunton, who in 1563 disposed of much of his property in Tiverton. The purchasers were Christopher Glover, Thomas Land, and Robert Waldron, all clothiers, and two men described as drapers, John Godbeare and Anthony Pearse. Waldron's acquisition[8] included a field called Boysham, the ground now lying to the east of Heathcoat's factory, where Exeleigh House stands. The bounds given in

---

[1] cited in Dunsford 1790, 177.   [2] on the site of Withleigh's present church
[3] assuming that the chapels of Saint Luke and Saint Stephen licensed in the early 15th century are two of the unknown dedications, rather than additional sites
[4] there could well have been some loss of education: small chapels often housed schools, but there is no evidence of this practice in any of the Tiverton chapels.
[5] but John West copied the entries to 1608 from an earlier volume that no longer exists.
[6] Eden 1797, 142.   [7] Rowse 1950, 159.
[8] *Enrolled Deeds*, 612.

the deed are of particular interest. On the south was Exe Bridge, on the north New Park belonging to the Lord of the Manor, on the west Boysham stretched as far as the 'water coming from the Dyelake'; and the eastern boundary consisted of the 'Town Gardens'. The 'dyelake' probably refers to a leat in the area of the present Factory Leat, but as for the 'town gardens', clearly they must have lain at the foot of the slope below the Castle and Church, but there are no clues as to their appearance or function[1].

The Waldrons were the most prominent family in Tiverton in the 1560s. Robert and his brother John were the sons of Ralph Waldron, who had died in 1559. Six years before his death, Ralph and John had together bought the advowson, of Bampton (that is the right to present the Vicar there) and, after his father's death, John purchased the tithes and advowson of the parish of Coldridge, along with a manor in the parish of Crediton[2]. Although always described as clothiers, they had wider commercial interests. John Waldron supplied the cloth trade with cargoes of madder and woolcards, but his main imports were iron and wine. It also appears that he took a young Tivertonian, a merchant in the making, under his wing. The 24-year old John West, whose father died two years earlier, began importing into Exeter in 1566. On the first two occasions, he and Waldron appear as joint owners of consignments of iron carried on the *Mayflower* and *Trinity* of Kenton[3]. Later, the two men owned cargoes separately, but often on the same vessel. This was not unusual, as there was a growing trend for Tiverton merchants to own cargoes on the same ship. They were apparently pooling resources, or at least co-operating on such occasions.

Towns like Cullompton and Barnstaple were also enjoying success. Cullompton had four merchants importing goods into Exeter at this time; George and Philip Cockram, Humphrey Parys and John Clement. Like their Tiverton counterparts, they often carried goods on the same ship. Although the more accessible documentary sources deal with the trade of south Devon ports, activities on the northern coast must not be ignored. Here Barnstaple, which would be incorporated as a borough in 1577, was by far the busiest. Most of the burgesses first appointed to govern the town were merchants and, interestingly, one of them was a man originally from Tiverton. James Goddysland had been one of John Greneway's apprentices, and soon after his master's death he moved to Barnstaple as a merchant in his own right. English ports, by this time, were reaping the rewards of an ocean trade. To the east, vessels from the

---

[1] one feature missing from the bounds is the River Exe, which we would expect to have formed the eastern limit of Boysham. Its absence can be explained by looking at a 1776 map of the lands of Blundell's School (kept at the School), which shows the previous channel once ran to the west of Boysham; the course of the River Exe had changed with time.
[2] *Patent Rolls 1560-3,* 322.   [3] *ECA 8-9Eliz.*

Southwest were being harassed by Swedish ships[1], and to the west and north the Newfoundland cod fisheries had become very important. Whales were hunted, especially for train oil that was used as fuel in lamps and for making soap. John Waldron imported a consignment of two tuns of this oil in 1574. Further afield, English merchants began impinging on the activities of the Spanish and Portuguese in the Americas, where the chief lure was precious metals. One commodity from the New World which particularly interested cloth makers was brazilwood which, when ground, produced a dye that coloured cloth crimson or purple.

Merchants are relatively easy to find in documentary sources. They were generally the ones who bought land, imported goods, and instigated court proceedings. What about other cloth workers? By the mid-16th century, a degree of specialisation had already taken place in the industry in Tiverton. For example, John Crudge was a maker of coverlets (blankets), Thomas Withecombe a 'yearngrosser' (yarn merchant), and Gilbert Newcome made sleys, the movable frames that separate the warp threads on a loom. Dunsford suggests[2] that societies of weavers and fullers had been formed in Tiverton in the late 1550s to regulate their respective trades, and provide mutual support for their members. These craft guilds were, in essence, the forerunners of trade unions. Their foundation in Tiverton was probably a response to legislation passed in 1558 aimed at defining many of the crafts in the woollen cloth industry. Among other things, it was laid down that weavers had to have served an apprenticeship, fullers could not have looms, nor could weavers own fulling-mills, or have more than two apprentices.

Tiverton's population, like its commercial success, was on the increase, but the cost was a corresponding rise in the numbers of beggars and vagrants. There was a large itinerant population by this time, and they were especially attracted to the more prosperous towns. Many of the wanderers are specifically noted in the parish register, for example 'Kathren, a poor walken woman's child' was buried at Saint Peter's in 1567. A child, such as Kathren, born to a woman on tramp was not likely to live long. Vagrants were tolerated if they were willing to work, but the idle, whether itinerant or native, were despised[3]. Where there was need there was sometimes charity. By his will in 1568, Walter Tyrrell left £200 to buy land, the profits from which were to be used for the poor[4]. He also bequeathed the income from his houses, gardens, and two acres of meadow, which stretched northwards from the western end of Exe Bridge. This money was to maintain the bridge, which would later be administered by the Exe

---

[1] *CSPDom 1547-80*, 313. [2] 1790, 177.
[3] in a case brought before the Tiverton borough court at the end of 1571, Richard Lampray was found guilty of allowing sturdy, idle beggars into his house (DRO CR379).
[4] DRO 3171M/F1.

Bridge Trust[1]. Tyrrell left a further £15 10s for the upkeep of the roads around Tiverton, vital for trade. His executor was John Waldron, who used part of his personal legacy to buy the manor of Doccombe, near Paignton. In turn, Waldron founded an almshouse in October 1577, and endowed it with £24 a year from Doccombe. The site chosen was in Westexe, at the extreme western edge of the town, at this time surrounded by fields. Eight 'poore, impotent and indigent' persons of Tiverton were to be given accommodation and a shilling a week. The building, which included a chapel, was well under way by the time the founder died in July 1579. John Waldron's remains were placed beneath the large chest tomb to be seen in the chancel of Saint Peter's Church.

The administration of the manor and borough of Tiverton had become somewhat confusing since the demise of Edward Courtenay. The simple heading on the court rolls - 'the court of the co-heirs of Courtenay' - legally correct as it may have been, disguised the true situation. The four lines of descent had become five on the death of the Tretherf heir without a male child. That family's inheritance was divided between two heiresses who had married into the Vivian and Courtenay[2] families. This gave rise to entries in the court rolls such as that of John Waldron who, shortly before his death, had been admitted to a half of one quarter (one eighth) of the close called Little Shillands and the garden called Perrymanshay[3]. In practice, what happened usually was that the tenant would negotiate terms with the owner of each fraction of the property. One person occupied the property but paid rent to many owners. Despite this fragmentation, the powers of the manorial courts were not weakened, nor were the customs of the manor. Cases were still brought to the courts. John Stile and Elizabeth Coke were charged in 1576 with taking grain out of the manor of Tiverton to their own mills, thus depriving the Tiverton mills and the lords of the manor of their rightful income[4]. As for the Church, the advowsons of Clare, Pitt, and Tidcombe had also descended to the Courtenay heirs, although the way this was put into practice is unclear. What appears to have happened is that, until 1571, the co-heirs jointly presented the rector when a portion fell vacant. After that date, and for a further twenty years or so, the advowsons of all three portions seem to have been held by the Queen 'by reason of the minority of Jonathan Trelawney'. Although there is no evidence, it looks as if the non-Trelawney heirs sold their advowsons to the Queen.

---

[1] the Exe Bridge Trust was consolidated with the Tiverton market tolls in 1702 (Dunsford 1790, 110-1).
[2] of Landrake, in Cornwall.   [3] DRO CR265.
[4] (DRO CR327). Coke's mills were at Gornhay, and John Stile's at Craze Lowman.

A tax assessment of 1581[1] reveals some of the changes taking place in Tiverton. What is notable is the absence of any members of the ancient families so prominent a century earlier. There is no Courtenay, no Henslegh, Calwodelegh, or Prestecote, nor is there a Sellake or Greneway. The man heading the list is John Prouse, from a family with varied interests and assets. A generation earlier, they were in possession of West Chevithorne, premises in Peadhill and Bolham, as well as properties in the town itself, and even land as far away as Lesnewth, in north Cornwall[2]. Some members were involved in trade; a brother, Robert, appears as a merchant of Barnstaple, and John occasionally imported goods into Exeter as well as selling considerable quantities of cloth in London[3]. Marriage united the Prouses with other important Tivertonians. John Prouse himself had married Elizabeth Colycke, whose father, Robert, had topped the list of taxpayers in 1545, and with her had come the manor of West Mere[4]. Elizabeth Prouse married the most prolific Tiverton importer of the early 1580s, Nicholas Skinner. A Prouse was also living in the Castle. Richord, one of John's daughters, was married to a Braunton man, Roger Giffard. In 1579 the couple were occupying a house in Fore Street[5], but a couple of years later they took the lease of Tiverton Castle, described as 'a court, gardens, pound, stable, barns and mansion house, along with lands called the Little Park'[6].

Roger Giffard and his wife had clearly moved to a more desirable home, but Fore Street, or High Street as it was known at this time, attracted the richest people in the town. Everyone aspired to having a property in the main street. John Hukeley was no exception. In addition to Boysham, fields, and a fulling mill at Little Silver, he had a house and garden in Fore Street. In August 1584 he leased the house and garden[7] to Peter Blundell. Although the rent of the premises was trifling, Blundell paid £100 consideration money. He could afford it, for, like Hukeley, he had the second-highest assessment in the 1581 tax list.

Much of Peter Blundell's life remains a mystery. The family name had been known in Devon for centuries. A Simon Blundell, sometimes called Blundon, became a freeman of Exeter in 1419[8] and was an importer during the following decade, as were other Blundells during the 15th century. As there is nothing in the *Customs Accounts* to suggest they originated elsewhere, it is probably safe to assume that they were Exeter men. The first of the name to be associated with Tiverton was John Blondon, a juror of the borough court in 1531[9], and later in that decade an Edith Blondon is granted

[1] *Devon Subsidies 1581-1600*, 83.
[2] *IPM MS.*
[3] PRO C1/1382/62-3.
[4] *IPM MS.*
[5] Saint Peter GFS23.
[6] SRO DD/CN/Box 24/10.
[7] Blundell's MSS Tiverton 1540-89.
[8] *Exeter Freemen*, 43.
[9] DRO CR248.

rents[1]. In 1556 Peter Bloundon (also called Bloundell in the same document) appears in the borough court trying to recover a debt of 16s 4d[2]. Peter Blundell bought the manor of West Prawle, near Salcombe, in 1568 for the considerable sum of £791[3]. Where had such money come from? He appears, invariably as Peter Blunden, in the records of Blackwell Hall, London, the chief cloth market of the country[4]. Obviously, he was selling cloth, but so were many Tiverton men. He does not re-appear in Tiverton records until the tax assessment of 1581, when he returns as one of the richest men in the town, and the owner of a sizeable manor in south Devon.

The number of Tiverton men importing goods into Exeter reached a peak in the mid-1580s, with no fewer than 16 individuals being recorded. Alongside the well-established names of Amey, West, John Prouse and Skinner, are six new men, Humphrey Cogan, John Lewes, John Glanfilde, Nicholas Clevanger, Richard Voysey and Thomas Snowe. In other sources they almost invariably appear as clothiers, so it can be assumed that the outgoing cargo comprised cloth, mostly kersies, whereas the imports were varied. Eager to find new markets, two of them, John West and Edward Amey, contributed £12 10s each[5] to John Davis' and Adrian Gilbert's journey in 1585 in search of a northwest route to China[6].

At this time, Parliament was exacting tax for maritime defence. Ship money, originally levied on coastal towns, was increasingly demanded from inland centres. Tiverton and Cullompton were ordered to pay the tax in 1588. A letter was sent to the Earl of Bath on behalf of the two communities asking for total exemption or, failing that, a reduction[7]. Would the towns have taken this action if they had known the course of events about to unfold? King Philip II of Spain had been angered by Francis Drake's raids on Spanish territory, by the presence of English troops in the Netherlands, and by the execution of Mary Queen of Scots. His response was to launch the ill-fated Armada of 1588, the first of three in the long war which afflicted the last years of Elizabeth's reign.

War with Spain was bound to affect Tiverton's trade. The range of imports into Exeter became severely restricted; Spanish iron, raisins, and wine ceased immediately. Most cargoes now came from Morlaix in Brittany or Saint Malo in Normandy, and consisted of cloth such as lockram, treger, canvas, or dowlas. New markets were tapped.

---

[1] (DRO CR251). This entry seems to imply that she was the daughter of that John Hukeley (or his son) who leased the Fore Street property to Peter Blundell.
[2] DRO CR257.   [3] Blundell's MSS.
[4] in the records (PRO E159/378 *et seq*) he is fined for selling defective kersey.
[5] DRO 58/7/11.4
[6] although they failed in their goal, Davis sailed further north than any Englishman had done, skirting the west coast of Greenland.
[7] *APC 1587-8*, 50.

Richard Hawkins had already shown that trading in Africa could make great gains, and English merchants took the opportunity to wrest this business from the Spanish by forming the Guinea Company in 1588. One of the first merchants to take a chance on this commerce was the Tivertonian George Slee. Just a few years earlier, when the Caribbean waters were safer, he often imported brazilwood from that region, but his interests soon switched to Africa. In June 1590 Slee owned part of the cargo of the *Phoenix,* which entered Exeter from Guinea. His share comprised four hides and 74 pounds of 'elephants' teeth'. A month later he brought in 645 hides, two hundredweight of wax and three hundredweight of teeth aboard the *Speedwell,* which also carried cargo from Guinea for two other Tiverton men, Edward Amey and William Grigge[1].

During the summer of 1591 Tiverton importers almost completely disappear from the *Customs Accounts.* One reason was the unforgiving spectre of the plague which had returned to the town. The burials entered in the parish register tell the story; in a normal year 100 would be expected, but that year saw 550[2]. The population was rapidly reduced, as, apart from those who died, many fled in the hope of escaping the disease. In the following year, the number of burials totalled just 85, lower than usual, perhaps indicating that several had indeed left the town. Recovery was slow, but within a few years Rewe, Skinner, Amey, Slee, Grigge, and John West were all to be seen once more on the quay at Exeter. They were Tiverton's richest merchants, most able to withstand a temporary setback, no matter how severe. Almost certainly, other anonymous traders had been ruined by the return of the plague.

Apart from Tiverton's home-grown importers, the town had other close links with the sea, especially with seafarers. Few people realise that Sir Walter Ralegh's family owned the manor of Bolham, which they sold at this time. In 1595, Bolham Mill was sold to Henry Worth of Worth, but the major sale took place in the following year, when, for £1,470 the lordship and manor was sold to George Prouse of Wellington and Richard Hagley, a Tiverton clothier[3]. The deed names the vendors as Carew Ralegh of Corsley in Wiltshire and his younger brother, Sir Walter, who had just led an expedition to the interior of Guyana. Ralegh and other seafarers of the time are now seen by some not so much as England's naval heroes, rather as adventurers, even pirates, lured by treasure. This ambiguity is also seen in the activities of Nicholas Clevanger of Tiverton. He first appears as an importer of wine in 1586, and continued to bring in cargoes throughout the rest of that decade. In 1591, he was engaged in the Guinea trade, but also occurs as part owner of a privateering ship, the *Adonie*[4].

---

[1] *ECA 31-2Eliz.*
[2] there were 127 in July, 114 in August, and 74 in September.
[3] DRO 213M/T242.   [4] Andrews 1964, 243.

Tiverton's death rate soared again in 1597. There is no contemporary explanation for the 300 deaths in the year, but a likely cause was an influenza-like disease and dysentery associated with famine[1]. One casualty was Nicholas Mercer, Rector of Pitt and Tidcombe, and also the incumbent of Bishops Nympton, near South Molton, as well as a Prebendary of Exeter Cathedral. His combined income from these benefices probably accounts for the unusually high valuation of his goods, which totalled £308 15s 6d[2]. Mercer would be long remembered in the town for his criticism of the inhabitants for profaning the Lord's Day by working and preparing for the Monday market. William Sharpe took Mercer's place at Tidcombe while William's brother, Lionel, became Rector of Pitt[3]. They were the sons of a London merchant, Robert Sharpe, and had both attended King's College, Cambridge. By the time Lionel was instituted to Pitt he already held livings at Malpas, Cheshire, and Stoke-in-Teignhead in Devon, and was chaplain to Robert Devereux, Earl of Essex, a royal favourite on the verge of disaster.

Shortly after midday on Monday April 3rd 1598 a fire broke out in a house near Wellbrook. The culprit was a woman cooking pancakes[4]. Driven along by a westerly wind, the flames raced and jumped toward the town. They crossed the Exe, and within a few hours, the whole of Tiverton, as far east as the Greenway Almshouses, was engulfed in flames. There was panic: people raced back and forth with bucketfuls of water vainly trying to douse the flames. Above the crackling fire could be heard the screams of its victims and the pitiful sounds of frightened horses which, as it was market day, filled all the available stables. Almost as quickly as it began, the terror was over, leaving a town of smouldering ruins. Many horses perished in the conflagration, but, far more seriously, 33 people lost their lives. Among those that died were the children of two of Tiverton's most prosperous merchants; Joan, daughter of John West, and Eleanor, George Slee's child. Christopher, his surname unknown, a servant of another of the town's merchants, William Grigge, also perished, along with one of Tiverton's butchers, Nicholas Hartnoll, and his servant Mary Morrel. More than 400 houses were destroyed with their contents and many families made homeless. The losses were later estimated at the huge figure of £150,000.

Tiverton could not cope alone with a catastrophe of this magnitude. Help was sought from the highest source. The Privy Council was informed of the situation[5], and the Queen was asked to authorise a nationwide appeal to relieve the sufferers[6]. She duly

[1] Oswald 1977, 86.
[2] *Murray Wills*.
[3] DRO 2960A/PR1.
[4] according to Dunsford 1790, 179.
[5] *APC 1597-8*, 391-3.
[6] *ib*, 452.

obliged. The Devon Quarter Sessions ordered collections in every parish[1]. As for the homeless, the County Justices arranged for several of them to be sent 'into the country' to escape the hardship, permitting them to remain there for a year. Not all these exiles were housed in the neighbouring parishes, as we would expect. One young man, Walter Belman, was sent to Kenton, near Exeter[2].

Although there is no way of gauging the social and economic disruption to the town's trade caused by the fire, it must have been considerable. Many of those people who remained in the town would have been without work, placing a great burden on the providers of poor relief. The fire happened at a time when Parliament was at last defining terms regarding the problem of the poor. Legislation had been introduced in 1598 to institute poor law overseers in every parish. Their duties included levying rates and providing work, although many places had already introduced such schemes themselves. The distinction between poverty through no fault of the individual and idleness was strengthened; the idle were to be punished and put to work in 'houses of correction'. Wills of Tivertonians had long since emphasised the difference. There was an increasing trend toward making loans to poor weavers, fullers, and husbandmen, rather than simply to 'the poor'. Humphrey Cogan bequeathed £10 to be lent to 'poor craftsmen' in 1591, £20 was left to 'four honest householders or artificers of the town and parish of Tiverton' by Humphrey Bonvile in 1593, and Joan Prowse gave £12 to 'six poor artificers'[3].

Yet, in spite of everything it was business as usual for the more prosperous merchants of the town, who carried on importing into Exeter. Amey, Skinner, West, Lewes, Slee, Bennett continued without a break. The one exception was William Grigge, who is styled 'of Exeter'[4] in August, four months after the fire. Whether his move was occasioned by the disaster is not known, but in this same year he was made a freeman of Exeter[5]. Again, it may be coincidence, but John West the merchant made his will in September, bequeathing almost all his goods and lands to his son, also called John[6].

Human nature is such that, after disasters, the finger of blame is pointed in various directions. A later author recalled[7] that the conflagration took place shortly after the death of 'a godly preacher', Nicholas Mercer, a fierce critic of those Tiverton people who worked on Sundays to prepare for the following day's market. As the fire had occurred on a Monday, it was predictably interpreted by many as God's judgement.

---

[1] DRO QS1/1.

[2] he was still there eight years later when he applied for poor relief, but was told to return to Tiverton (DRO QS1/2).

[3] all cited in Dunsford 1790, 112-9.   [4] *ECA 39-40Eliz.*

[5] *Exeter Freemen*, 108.

[6] (DRO 2723M/WW5). By this time, West was living at Yellaford in Thorverton, but his commercial base was at Tiverton.

[7] Bayly 1619.

According to the Tiverton court roll of 1598-9[1], however, the cause was much less spiritual and more a result of building practices. The document contains orders that 'no person shall erect a mantle [fireplace] of wood', on pain of a £2 fine; all bad chimneys and mantles were to be taken down within a year and replaced by stone chimneys and cob mantles. If anyone failed to comply with these orders, a fine of 6s 8d would be charged for every fire lit in the unaltered features. The portreeve was given the authority to pull down or deface the old chimneys and mantles, and was duty-bound to provide enough leather water buckets for the town. The court roll cites previous portreeves, namely John Prouse, Edward Amey, John Waldron and John Chilcott, 'who have omitted this order before this time'. They, or their executors, were given a year to make up the shortfall of water buckets, or face a £1 fine. The corresponding roll for 1595[2] substantiates the reference to a previous order. There, three years before the fire, 18 people were reported to 'have mantells and chymnies dangerous to their own houses and their neighbours', and improvements were ordered. If only this byelaw had been heeded!

The main concern was to rebuild the town. In addition to the 400 houses that had been destroyed, there were countless others that had been partially burnt, as well as outhouses and sheds. Donations of wood and timber made the process much easier, especially the large quantity of timber given by the lords of the manor from the Little Park[3]. Transporting the material over the unmade, muddy, pot-holed roads of the time would have been a problem. One mode of conveyance, sometimes ignored by historians, was by water. Timber was taken down the local rivers, as shown by a letter written to the Privy Council by some inhabitants of Tiverton[4]. They complained that Richard Gober[5] and Richard Vaizey 'who have a mill leat on the river', were refusing to allow timber through their weirs and leat on the Exe, and were threatening litigation. People were given incentives, often financial concessions, to rebuild. John Webber obtained the lease of a plot of land against Greenway's Almshouses on condition that he built a house on it. In return, the Feoffees of Church Lands, its owners, waived the usual consideration money[6]. Even property held by copy of the manorial court roll was sometimes leased without an entry fine; in 1601 Richard Poyer and Elizabeth Cockram were granted premises in Fore Street 'which had been burnt in the late dreadful fire'[7]. Despite boons, some people took advantage of the circumstances. James Rampstert built a house which was partly supported on the church wall, so he was ordered to start again, while Richard Woodward's premises

---

[1] DRO CR272.
[2] DRO CR271.
[3] PRO C91/1/4.
[4] *APC 1598-9*, 564-5.
[5] more probably Gover, or even Godbeare.
[6] Saint Peter's CGS1.
[7] DRO 2723M/MT13.

'encroached on Barrington Street'[1]. A general tidy-up in the town seems to have accompanied the rebuilding. It included repairing 'le cuckinstole', described as 'totally ruinous' in October 1599[2]. This object, situated on the Leat, was the ducking stool, of which, unfortunately, there is no further record.

Elizabethan rebuilding probably gave rise to many of the courts so characteristic of Tiverton until very recent times. They generally comprised a rectangle of cottages surrounding an open courtyard, with access from the street often by a passageway through one of the buildings. The entire court was usually owned by a clothier, but occupied by weavers and woolcombers in his employ. In the central open space the threads for the warp, called long chains, could be laid out, and stretched, and dyeing could take place there. Many courts survived until the 20th century, and even now we can visit Chappell's Square and Cocks Court off Barrington Street, which are largely unaltered from their original form.

Peter Blundell died in London on April 18th 1601, aged about 80. At the time of his death he was living in the capital, and was buried there, in the church of Saint Michael Royal, Paternoster Row. By then, he was a citizen of two towns. In leases of 1596 concerned with parts of his manor of West Prawle he appears as 'clothier of Tiverton', but by 1600 he is designated as 'of London'[3]. It is possible that the Tiverton fire of 1598 prompted him to move, although business interests offer a more likely explanation. He does not appear to have bought any more property in Devon after 1589, when he purchased lands in Tiverton from Nicholas Turner, which included the fields of Boysham and the Rag (at the confluence of the Exe and Lowman)[4].

From Blundell's will, it is notable that his business acquaintances, and friends, were drawn from the highest levels of Elizabethan society. Sir John Popham, the man entrusted to carry out his wishes, and called by him his 'righte deare and honourable friende', had been appointed Lord Chief Justice of England in 1592. Of Blundell's five executors, two were Londoners: William Craven, sheriff of the capital in 1601, and a business partner of his, William Parker. The remaining three were George Slee, and John West senior and junior, of Tiverton.

By whatever means, Blundell had amassed a huge fortune comparable to what we would expect only of an earl or duke. He was able to make substantial gifts to several institutions and individuals[5]. To the governors of Christ's Hospital in Newgate he left £500, and £250 to both Bartholomew's Hospital and that of Saint Thomas in Southwark, as well as £150 to each of the twelve great Livery Companies of the capital.

---

[1] DRO CR273.
[2] DRO CR272.
[3] Blundell's MSS West Prawle 1560-1601.
[4] Blundell's MSS Tiverton 1540-89.
[5] printed in full in Incledon 1790.

As for personal bequests to Londoners, he left £1,000 to Anne Whitmore, and £500 each to three of her sons, and lesser amounts to Elizabeth Craven and Anne Babor (both Whitmore daughters) and Henry Polstead. The Whitmores, with whom he lodged, lived in Lombard Street, in the same area of London as Blundell's burial-place, and a district that was rapidly becoming the city's financial heart. Anne Whitmore, herself the daughter of an alderman and sheriff of London, was well-versed in financial dealings. The Devon Record Office contains an agreement between her and Sir Jonathan Trelawney dated 1601[1], in which it is stated that he owed her the considerable sum of £7,000. Nevertheless, she was prepared to cancel the debt on payment of just £3,740. Where had the Whitmores' money come from? One of Anne's sons, George, along with another of Blundell's legatees Henry Polstead, had, in 1599, 'ventured' £200 towards a voyage to the East Indies[2]. Is this a clue? There were fortunes to be made in the Indies. Those with money were often asked to lend some to the monarch; William Whitmore was among a group of men later granted lands to the enormous value of £50,000 by James I instead of repayment of such a loan[3].

Could Blundell have been part of this money-lending coterie? If he were, it would explain some of the mysteries surrounding his later life. It would account for his close relationship with the Whitmores, Polstead and Craven. Perhaps it would also answer why, given the accepted view that he was a clothier or merchant, he does not occur in the *Exeter Customs Accounts* (as many London merchants do). However, he does leave monetary gifts to six of Exeter's most prolific importers who, presumably, were regular business contacts of his. It would also explain his apparent rapid accumulation of a vast fortune. Moneylending was slowly becoming necessary and acceptable, and fortunes could be made by those with the means to lend. Yet many equated it with the sin of usury. If this was Blundell's line of business, he would not have boasted about it, nor indeed would those who benefited from his generosity. Like Peter Blundell, William Craven does not appear in any of the London port books, and was possibly never personally engaged in overseas trade, yet he was one of the largest wholesale cloth dealers in London at the time. Another similarity is that the source of Craven's wealth was, like Blundell's, obscure[4].

However close his ties were to London, Blundell did not forget his native town of Tiverton or his relatives there. He had never married, so his family consisted of siblings and their partners and offspring. In all, they were left well over £10,000. This was a

---

[1] DRO 651.

[2] *CSPEastIndies etc 1513-1616*, 101.

[3] *CSPDom 1603-10*, 637.

[4] (Lang 1971, 245). It is unlikely to be mere coincidence that the house built at the end of the 16th century for William Craven became the East India Company's first London headquarters.

great injection of capital to a group whose menfolk already formed the economic backbone of the town. He assured the well being of many Tiverton families for generations to come. Moreover, an annual sum of £20 was left to place four boys as apprentices in husbandry. Not only Tiverton boys or farmers benefited from this legacy, as youngsters from Alphington, Tavistock and Silverton became apprenticed to yeomen from Dean Prior, Pinhoe, Luppitt and George Nympton, as well as the parishes adjacent to Tiverton[1]. Furthermore, the considerable amount of £900 was to be distributed by the Mayor and Commonality of Exeter in loans to artificers of their choice, as long as £400 of the money went to men from Tiverton. The money was to be lent at 2% interest, an unusual condition to find in a will, but understandable if the testator was a moneylender. A sum of £400 was to be used as dowry for 20 poor Tiverton maidens, £100 for the poorest of the town, and £100 to mend the road from Tiverton to Silverton. Although he left £50 for the fabric of Saint Peter's Church, there was no legacy for any of the rectors, but there was £4 to Annys Style's son, Roger, who was a curate there.

Old Blundell's, which served as the School until its removal to Horsdon in 1882.

Blundell's name is today known worldwide because of the Tiverton school that bears his name. His will gave detailed instructions on how it was to be funded as well as how it was to be built. Peter Blundell directed John Popham to build a free grammar school costing at least £2,400. A master and an under-master, called the usher, were to teach up to 150 boys, of which as many as possible were to be natives of the town.

---

[1] Blundell's MSS Apprentice Bonds.

Blundell's intention was to create 'the increase of good and godly preachers of the Gospel'. To further his wishes six scholars were to be selected to attend colleges of Popham's choosing at the Universities of Oxford and Cambridge, and their places would be funded by a further bequest of £2,000. Twenty-five feoffees were charged with administering the school's affairs. As well as Tiverton merchants, such as Waldron, Colman, Amey, Skinner, Slee, Prouse, West, and Deyman, Blundell included gentry from the surrounding area, like Pollard of King's Nympton, Bluett of Holcombe Rogus, Bere of Huntsham, Ayshford of Burlescombe and Sir Francis Popham, John's son.

The will seems to have been processed swiftly and efficiently. Letters of administration were granted on 28th April, and Exeter received payment of its £900 legacy by 24th May all within six weeks of Blundell's death. One of the executors' first acts was to secure a site for the school, and in 1602 for £30, they purchased a 4½-acre field known as Brownham, beside the River Lowman. Chief Justice Popham decided that, of the six university places, two should be established at Balliol College, Oxford, where he himself had studied, and two each at Emmanuel and Sidney Sussex Colleges, Cambridge. Emmanuel declined the offer, however, and its two places were added to Sidney Sussex's share. Before the school was built, Popham appointed the first scholars and fellows. John Bury and Christopher West, Tivertonians, took their places at Balliol in 1602, while two 'outsiders' William Durant and John Pocklington were admitted to Sidney Sussex[1]. Tradition, and the inscription above the entrance, gives the foundation of Blundell's School as 1604. The first master, however, is not known for certain. Joseph Hall is supposed to have been appointed by Popham, but refused on the same day and suggested the post should go to his lifelong friend Hugh Cholmeley. Similarly, Cholmeley is also alleged to have turned down the offer in favour of the benefice of Clare Portion[2]. He was, indeed, admitted to Clare in February 1605, but he had been in the town for almost a year by this time, as his son John was baptised at Saint Peter's Church on May 24th 1604. Therefore, it is likely he was acting as Master of Blundell's. When Cholmeley became Rector of Clare he was replaced at Blundell's by Samuel Butler, who brought with him some pupils from his previous school at Bradninch. If, from the beginning admissions registers were kept, as is quite probable, they have not survived. So, apart from the few individuals who filled the scholarships and fellowships or the rare mention of one of the more famous pupils, most of the early scholars remain anonymous.

---

[1] Incledon (1790, li) introduces an element of confusion by stating that Thomas Pell, Richard Perrot and Lewis Land were placed at Sidney Sussex; presumably two of them took the places freed up by Emmanuel's refusal, but the third place is inexplicable.
[2] e.g. Banks 1904, 11.

7 The Chartered Borough

The peaceful accession of James, King of Scotland, in 1603 was widely acclaimed, and so was the end of war with Spain a year later. This prompted John West[1] along with thirteen other Tiverton merchants and numerous traders to petition the King for the establishment of a Company of Merchants of England trading into Spain and Portugal. Their wishes were granted in May 1605[2], just six months before the famous Gunpowder Plot soured all relations with these countries for years. Another venture, the London Company, was set up in 1606. Its intention was to colonise Virginia in America, with Blundell's friend, John Popham as one of the promoters. In the Far East, the East India Company, founded in 1601, was exploiting opportunities initially created by the Portuguese and Dutch. The Tiverton merchant, Nicholas Skinner, was as an 'adventurer' of £150 in this trade[3]. Indeed, the cargo carried on one of the first voyages to the East comprised 80 pieces of broadcloth, 80 pieces of Devonshire kersey and 100 pieces of Norwich stuffs[4]. It is more than likely that some, if not most, of the kerseys had been made in Tiverton.

Robert Comyn alias Chilcott, who had been Peter Blundell's servant and nephew, died in 1609. His uncle had left him the sizeable fortune of £2,000, and this sum was augmented in 1607 by one of Blundell's legatees, George Whitmore, who assigned his stock in the East India Company to him. Chilcott's will[5] shows many similarities to Blundell's, but his could hardly be on the same scale. Apart from £1,000 to his wife and £400 to his brother-in-law George Slee, no other bequest exceeded £100. However, the Whitmores again benefited, including Elizabeth, the widow Ann's daughter, who had married Sir William Craven. Chilcott also achieved lasting recognition in Tiverton by founding a school. It was to take 100 boys, all from the town if sufficient numbers could be found, if not 'foreigners' would be allowed. Trustees were given £400 for the building of the school and a dwelling house for the master, whose salary was to come from lands Chilcott held in Yorkshire and Durham. A plot in Saint Peter Street was chosen, on which had stood a house that was burnt down in the 1598 fire, and work was soon under way. The interior of the school building has been altered over the years, but the master's house, hidden from the street, yet visible from the Exe Bridge, still contains many of its original features. For its time, Tiverton was unquely endowed with schools.

---

[1] who bought a quarter of the manor, borough, and hundred of Tiverton for £2,700 from Sir Reginald Mohun in 1605 (DRO 2723M/TT111).
[2] *SpanishComp*, 98.
[3] *CSPEastIndies etc 1513-1616*, 173.
[4] *Annals EIC vol I*, 129.
[5] DRO 2723M/WC16.

WOFVLL NEWES,

From the West-parts of England,

𝔅𝔢𝔦𝔫𝔤 𝔱𝔥𝔢 𝔩𝔞𝔪𝔢𝔫𝔱𝔞𝔟𝔩𝔢 𝔅𝔲𝔯𝔫𝔦𝔫𝔤 𝔬𝔣 𝔱𝔥𝔢 𝔗𝔬𝔴𝔫𝔢 of

TEUERTON, IN DEUONSHIRE,

Vpon the fift of August last, 1612,

Whereunto is annexed, the former burning of the aforesaid Towne,
the third of Aprill, 1598.

𝔏𝔬𝔫𝔡𝔬𝔫:

Printed by T. S. for Thomas Pauier, 1612.

Cover of pamphlet detailing the 'Lamentable Burning of the Towne of Teuerton' in 1612, as well as noting the previous disaster of 1598. The illustration shows the crude and ill-effective means of putting out a fire in those times.

On August 5th 1612, the dreaded calamity of fire returned once more to the town. This time it started in a dyehouse on Angel Hill, and spread eastwards. Within a few hours more than 600 houses had been destroyed, and 3,000 people were without shelter. The nightmare had returned after just fourteen years. The intensity and destruction of the fire were just as great as in 1598, but, fortunately, on this occasion not a single person died. The only buildings to escape the blaze were Saint Peter's Church, the unfinished Great House in Saint Peter Street, and Chilcott's School opposite, Waldron's and Greenway's Almshouses, Blundell's School, and a few isolated cottages around the town.

If anything about this disaster was fortunate it was that it took place during the week of the County Assizes, so the machinery of relief began promptly. The day after the fire, the Justices sent £20 to be 'specially disbursed to the poor', and it was ordered that 300 of the worst affected were to be dispersed throughout the county[1]. Having learnt lessons from 1598, they also stipulated that none should return without a pass[2]. The King ordered a collection to be made in southern England to raise funds for the relief of the inhabitants and for rebuilding the town, and appointed nine local men as collectors. They were John Deyman and Henry Newte, gentlemen, Humphrey Coleman, George Slee, Richard Spurway and John Blundell, clothiers, and Edward Amey, John West and Richard Prowse merchants. The task of rebuilding homes and livelihood now faced many people for the second time. The supply of timber again caused problems. The *Acts of the Privy Council* reveal that Wonham Wood, near Oakfordbridge, was the source for much of the supply. The members of the Council were asked to summon those who refused 'to permit passage to labourers who are guiding, in that river, timber'[3].

When those sent away by the Justices eventually returned, the amount needed for poor relief increased correspondingly. Tiverton was already spending a considerable amount each year on relief, and the Churchwardens' Accounts bear testimony to the hardships faced by many. Ralph Burrow of Tiverton was reimbursed 12s in 1611

> *for that he was at great charge by reason of a poor woman who fortuned to be delivered of a child in the King's highway and, having no friends to relieve her, Burrow received her into his house to comfort her in extremity as one Christian should do to another'.*

National legislation had authorised parishes to build houses of correction to accommodate many of the poor, where they would be cared for and put to work. In July 1610, the Devon Quarter Sessions had sanctioned such a building at Tiverton, apparently at the insistence of the townspeople who were to bear the cost of its construction[4]. A mystery surrounds this prescribed building; there is no record of its whereabouts or when it was built. However, a Quarter Sessions record of 1615 implies that George Slee's son, Roger, initially provided the money for it[5]. He had been Constable of the Hundred of Tiverton until that date, and therefore, perhaps, he felt obliged to have such a house of correction built.

---

[1] DRO QS1/3.

[2] by May 1614 it was considered that they should return by the following Michaelmas, but further delays pushed the date back to Midsummer 1615 (DRO QS1/4).

[3] *APC 1615-6*, 562-4.   [4] DRO QS1/3.

[5] DRO QS1/4.

The Great House in Saint Peter Street, completed in 1614.

George Slee died in 1613. He had made a lot of money through the cloth trade; over £5,000 worth of stock is mentioned in a Chancery case[1]. His will, made three years before his death, testifies to his wealth and to his puritan streak. He was mindful of those whose labours had helped him become rich: £20 was left to William Ham 'his factor in London', and an equal amount to Robert Crudge 'his tucker' or fuller. Nor did he forget the needy of Tiverton. The sum of £10 was to be distributed among the poorest agricultural labourers, and £100 to 40 or 50 poor artisans of the town. He emphasised, however, that

> *'the money is to be given to industrious workmen and not idlers or loiterers nor those who give themselves to drunkenness in alehouses or use gambling at cards or dice'.*

---

[1] PRO E112/170/76.

He left large amounts of money to his kinsmen, who were mostly the same individuals who had benefited from the wills of Blundell and Chilcott, both close relatives. Whereas their lasting legacies were schools, Slee, like Greneway and Waldron in the previous century, left money for almshouses. He gave £500 to purchase enough lands to produce an annual income of £20 for the maintenance of six 'poor widows or maidens of Tiverton', and sufficient money to buy a house for their accommodation. The site chosen was next to Slee's own home, nowadays the Great House in Saint Peter Street, which was being rebuilt at the time he died[1]. It is sometimes called the Great House of Saint George, perhaps for no apparent reason other than its association with George Slee. The date of 1614 on the rainwater head refers to the date of completion of both this and the almshouses next door[2]. Built largely of Hensleigh stone, it is Tudor in style with Jacobean arched doorways much like Blundell's School. Especially noteworthy are the stud-and-panel partitions, one in the screens passage, and another in the rear wing. It is a unique survival of the domestic architecture of the period and its imposing structure still dominates the approach to the town from Westexe.

The second rebuilding of the town is amazing testimony to the determination of its inhabitants. People returning from their enforced exile, and visitors alike, would have been greeted with the smell of fresh-cut timber, paint and newly-cut reed for thatch, and the sound of hammers on nails would have rung out across the town. The resolution to rise again from the ashes increased ambitions for a charter of incorporation[3]. The fire had again thrown Tiverton on the mercy of the County's J.P.s, for many of whom the town had become a nuisance and a liability. Despite its size[4], Tiverton was virtually powerless to take any legal responsibility over its own affairs. Many similar-sized towns, indeed several smaller ones, had already been granted charters of self-government by means of a corporate body of burgesses. This had happened at Totnes in 1505, Torrington in 1554, Barnstaple three years later, and South Molton in 1590. Encouraged by this, a group headed by Richard Hill alias Spurway[5] began the long and expensive task of obtaining one for Tiverton. No doubt

---

[1] rebuilt on the site of Slee's earlier house in which his daughter is said to have been burnt to death in 1598.

[2] in a Chancery case, it is stated that the Great House was completed by Joan Slee, after her husband's death (PRO REQ 2/304/12).

[3] a full appreciation of the reasons leading to the incorporation of Tiverton and of the Charter itself is best seen in Youings 1967.

[4] the King himself, in his appeal for relief, stated that as many as 8,000 people were reliant on the town for their living, and that upwards of £2,000 a week was spent at the wool and cloth market.

[5] Hill had benefitted from the will of George Slee and, in 1612, already had sufficient funds to purchase the manor and advowson of nearby Oakford, where a descendant of the family still resides.

he received legal help from Henry Newte, but he appears to have borne much of the expense himself. The costs, including bribes, would have been considerable.

King James signed the warrant granting Tiverton its Charter of Incorporation as a borough on August 10th 1615. The document itself, four sheets of parchment[1], now safely housed at the Devon Record Office, defines a *modus vivendi*: which remained virtually unchanged until 1835. The boundary of the Borough was to be that of the parish, covering some 17,650 acres, and including the hamlets of Cove, Chettiscombe, Chevithorne, Mere and Withleigh. It was to be governed by a Corporation comprising a mayor and 24 burgesses, equally divided into capital and assistant burgesses. Richard Hill alias Spurway was rewarded for his efforts by being made the first Mayor. The first Town Clerk was Henry Newte and special provision was made for his son Henry, to succeed him. Humphrey Were of Halberton was chosen as Recorder, a man who had to be 'learned in the laws'. He presided over the town's own Court of Quarter Sessions, and would be a judge of the Court of Record, where pleas involving sums under £100 were heard. The words of the charter had been skilfully crafted so as not to impinge on the rights or courts of the Lord of the Manor, Borough, or Hundred. Indeed, the feudal courts continued, but by this time, they were little more than ceremonial. The Corporation was empowered to pass its own byelaws and summon offenders to courts, and Tiverton was to have a prison with the Mayor as keeper. All of these operations were to be performed in a Town Hall, which was rapidly built at the top of Angel Hill[2]. Official documents would carry a Borough Seal, the design of which portrayed all the elements that had brought Tiverton to this stage in its history. The church, castle and town, with the two rivers uniting, and a woolpack, are all there.

What sort of men formed the Corporation? Of the 25, eight were merchants, another eight were clothiers, two were yeomen, two gentlemen and one was a tanner; the background of the remaining four is unknown. From the outset, those who already controlled the cloth trade were to assume control over the Borough. In fact, they were given additional powers regarding trade, as no stranger or foreigner was allowed to sell his goods except during fairs and markets, or carry on his profession without a licence issued by the Corporation. The Mayor was to be elected annually, and burgesses were replaced only at death, or by a majority vote of the others. They were also given the

---

[1] DRO R4/1/CA.

[2] from a deed cited in DRO R4/1/Z79. Although the first Town Hall stood on approximately the same place as its successor, the streets surrounding it have altered. The early deed places High Street on the east, the lane from the High Street to Saint Andrew Street on the south, Saint Andrew Street itself on the west, and the northern boundary was formed by the lands of John Prowse, so the Town Hall formed an island.

important privilege of choosing the Borough's two Members of Parliament[1]. The burgesses were the obvious beneficiaries of the Charter. They were expected to lead, rule, and safeguard the town's citizens from crime, injury, and poverty. They formed an oligarchy with power and responsibilities.

These extended to the very edges of the large parish of Tiverton, and included maintaining and repairing roads and bridges. For a town so heavily dependent on trade overland transport was of paramount importance. Trains of packhorses loaded with raw wool, finished cloth and many other goods journeyed between the town and the ports of west Somerset and north Devon, particularly Barnstaple, as well as south to Topsham and Exmouth. Many basic commodities made their way to Tiverton along these routes. During the 17th century, coal was brought[2] from Bridgwater, after being shipped from Wales. As much as 70% of the pottery used in the town originated from the kilns of Barnstaple and its immediate area[3]. A well-developed national system of carriers operated on a regular basis to London by this time, handling goods and letters. Soon after the Borough Charter was issued, an agreement was made with the Justices of the Peace by which Tiverton's contributions to the repair of the county's bridges were waived, as long as it took responsibility for its own. As well as those within its boundaries, Tiverton was to pay for half the upkeep of Cove Bridge, Langley Bridge, and Worthy Bridge[4]. Almost immediately, these arrangements were challenged, as the Hundred of Witheridge in 1617 refused to pay its half for the maintenance of Cove Bridge[5].

Tiverton would have seen a colourful variety of people coming and going on its roads. Saint Peter's Churchwardens often gave money to beggars and other unfortunates, although it must be wondered if all were quite as deserving as they claimed. In 1615, a shilling was given to two Irish women 'trying to return to their homes'. The large amount of 13s 3d was spent in the same year on a wounded soldier. This included 5s for dressing his wound, and for making a stretcher to carry him William Read, a cooper, received 22d. A further entry details the gift of 6s to a man who had been imprisoned by the Turks, and in 1617 5s was given to another authorised by the Admiralty to collect for himself and others like him who had 'their tongues cut off by Turks'. Most of these sailors had been victims of piracy in the Mediterranean and collections were often made to raise a ransom for their return, hence the 10s given by Tiverton toward 'certen prisoners in Barbarie'.

---

[1] they would have to wait a further five years, however, until they could exercise that right.
[2] Clark 1960, 77-8.   [3] Grant 1983, 81.
[4] (cited in Dunsford 1790, 182). The last two span the Little Dart.
[5] Witheridge Hundred's position is understandable as it included parishes more than 20 miles distant from Cove that were probably reluctant to pay money towards a bridge from which they derived little benefit.

Two of Tiverton's first capital burgesses amassed considerable property at this time. One, Nicholas Skinner, bought the freehold of Knightshayes and premises at Horsdon, all of which his family had previously held only by lease. The other, John West, purchased five corn mills in Westexe. The properties bought by both men had once formed part of the manor of Tiverton, much of which was being broken up and sold. The situation was probably a result of the fact that it had devolved upon at least four families, rather than staying with just one. Although, as stated above, the Charter was careful not to impinge on any of the manorial rights, changes to the manor itself were taking place. Ashley Park, another remnant of feudal Tiverton, had undergone considerable alterations. A deed of 1611[1] states that George and Roger Giffard, had 'lately severed, enclosed and hedged' Middlehill, a part of the park[2].

A mystery surrounds the disappearance of another feature of Tiverton's manorial past, the Courtenay Chapel. The accepted story is that the building was destroyed much later, at the hands of Civil War troops, but the Churchwardens' Accounts for 1621-2 allow a different explanation. They include payments of 2d 'for carrying in at the window of the chapel the stones that fell down into the vestry', and 1s for 'carrying in of the timber of the chapel which fell down'. This seems to indicate a building already in ruins. There is no mention of the Courtenay monuments inside the chapel, and although no contemporary description survives they must surely have been notable. If the Accounts do refer to the Courtenay Chapel it seems strange that clerical authority had permitted it to decline to this extent. After all, it was less than a century since the remains of Princess Katherine were laid to rest there. Was the memory of Tiverton's feudal past so readily forgotten?

Valentine Carey's enthronement as Bishop of Exeter in 1621 sparked off a close investigation of the moral health of the Diocese. His Consistory Court stamped down heavily on any deviations from prescribed practices, and consequently the Court's Act Books show a sudden rise in the number of cases brought before it. Many of them involved Tivertonians. William Palmer, Nicholas Upcott and

---

[1] DRO 79M/T1.

[2] the hedge boundaries created at this time can be readily spotted on a modern map; the area within the former park boundary is characterised by straight field hedges which contrast sharply with the noticeably more sinuous older hedgelines outside the park. However, the manors to the east of the town were by no means being broken up. East Chevithorne had been granted by the Bluett family to John Fraunceis of Combe Florey in Somerset (SRO DD/CN/Box 21/8), who, added the former Tiverton manor farms of Colcombe and Berry to his holding in 1622 (SRO DD/CN/Box 21/4). Just a little further to the south, the manor of Pool Anthony passed into the Wyndham family of Orchard Wyndham in 1609 on the death of Nicholas Wadham.

John Pinkstone were cited for not attending church and profaning the Sabbath by travelling – it seems they were in the habit of carrying yarn from Launceston to Tiverton on Sundays. William Hill of Cove was charged with abusing the covenant table, Alexander Swiffen of Cove for making hay on Sundays, and one case involved a brawl between six men in the churchyard at Cove. Sexual morals were also scrutinised. Robert Hill of Tiverton appeared 'for being the father of a base child of Frances Baker', and Edward Richards 'for having two of his servants unlawfully begotten with child'[1].

Ideally, the church authorities acted in harmony with the Justices of the Peace and the newly established Borough to maintain moral standards. The earliest surviving list of byelaws for the town dates from 1627[2], although they were no doubt addressing concerns felt for many years. No inhabitant was 'to take a bastard child which, in the opinion of the Mayor, may become chargeable on the parish'. No shop was to be opened, nor any animal killed by a butcher on the Lord's Day. Cleanliness was also apparently considered next to godliness, as all burgesses were to wear a 'decent and comly gowne' at all assemblies. Furthermore, every one of the town's householders was to sweep that part of the street in front of his home on Tuesday morning and Saturday afternoon.

However important Carey's attempts to improve moral standards, he had inherited a far greater problem from his predecessor, William Cotton. Groups that refused to conform to the doctrines or practices of the established Church of England had become common throughout the diocese. Bishop Cotton, writing in 1618, had stated that whereas he had few Catholics in his diocese, there was 'an infinity of sectaries and atheists'[3]. An entry in the Saint Peter's Churchwardens' Accounts for 1617-8, notes that 6s was received from 'certen persons for their absence from church of Sabbath days', pointing to the existence of a dissenting group, probably Anabaptists. Some Protestant congregations had begun to break away from the established church in the previous century, but groups unwilling to compromise and seeking separation from the uniformity of the Church of England become identified during the first decade of the 17th century. For some, the conviction of their beliefs and fear of prosecution persuaded them to cross to the Netherlands. Englishmen established churches at Amsterdam and Leiden; members of these congregations returned to London in 1611 and formed a Baptist church there. Later, some would sail to America in 1620 on board the *Mayflower*.

Tiverton's Anabaptists grew in number and soon attracted the attention of the County Quarter Sessions. In 1624 the Justices placed a clothier, Richard Berry, on bail,

---

[1] all cases in DRO Chanter 763. [2] DRO R4/1/C88.
[3] *CSPDom 1611-8*, 517.

insisting that Tiverton's Mayor was to jail him if he 'makes any conventicle at home or elsewhere'[1]. Anabaptists had earned the dislike of most people. Their rejection of infant baptism in favour of an adult ceremony of immersion, their insistence on the corruption of parish churches, and the general belief that they wished to separate themselves completely from the Church of England[2] had distanced them from the rest of the population. In 1626, letters passed between five English Anabaptist congregations and that in Amsterdam, regarding very earnest matters of doctrine[3]. It is no coincidence that the five groups were based in London, Coventry, Lincoln, Salisbury and Tiverton, all important centres of the cloth trade, and, as such, had long enjoyed close commercial links with the Netherlands. Dutchmen in Tiverton have already been noted in 1524 (see p.60). A further connection with the Netherlands can be glimpsed in 1625, when the wedding took place at Saint Sidwell's Church, Exeter, between an Exeter girl, Sarah Moore, and Jacobus van Kaffelghem[4]. Despite his obvious Dutch name, he was designated 'of Tiverton'. Not only were goods being exchanged, but clearly religious beliefs and ideas as well. The links between the various English Anabaptist congregations have not yet been explored. However, one example can be found in the marriage of Israela Cockram of Tiverton in 1628 to James Toppe of Salisbury, a man from a Wiltshire family of rich clothiers and landowners.

Trade between England and the Dutch was sometimes severely tested. One such occasion had been in 1614 when the Cockayne Project banned the export of unfinished cloth in a misguided attempt to foster the process at home. The Dutch, who had for a long time undertaken the finishing process on much of the English cloth, and had grown rich on their skills, predictably began a boycott of English goods. During this sharp setback, English merchants opened trading stations in India and the East Indies, a region where the Dutch were firmly established. Although direct evidence of Tiverton's involvement in this trade is lacking, many enticing clues imply it. In 1614, the children of one John Chilcott were permitted to lend £200 to the East India Company[5], and in the same year, a certain John West had been refused a post as factor for the Company[6]. Both are instantly recognisable Tiverton names. Following the execution in 1623 by Dutch colonists of 10 Englishmen and 11 other foreigners at Amboina in Indonesia, English enterprises concentrated on the Indian subcontinent. The massacre would one day be avenged but meanwhile trade with Holland prospered.

---

[1] DRO QS1/5.
[2] whereas the earlier Anabaptists wanted total separation, the Particular Baptists, formed in 1616, were non-Separatists.
[3] see Burrage 1912, ii, 233 *et seq.*.   [4] DRO Chanter 42.
[5] *CSPEastIndies 1513-1616*, 273.
[6] (*ib.*, 333). John Jordaine was in charge of the factory at Bantam in 1615 and asked the Company to pay £150 to his cousins Ignatius and John, both merchants of Exeter (*ib.*, 453), the latter with property in Tiverton in the 1620s.

More important than their occasional differences was the fact that the English and Dutch had two common adversaries, Spain and the Catholic Church. Protestant fears, however, were raised by James I's proposed marriage of his son, Charles, to a Spanish Catholic princess. Parliament was critical of his action, insisting they had a say on foreign policy. What part did Tiverton's Members of Parliament play at this time? Although the town had gained the right to elect two members in 1615, it did not get an opportunity to do so until 1620. The long wait was due to the enduring peace; it was usual to have few or no Parliaments during such times, and the King's right to rule was never challenged, though quarrels could break out. In the eventual election the two men chosen by the burgesses were John Bampfylde of Poltimore and John Davy of Crediton, who were both rather innocuous, quiet men, and made no mark on the proceedings whatsoever.

When Charles I began his reign in March 1625 the country was at war. He called his first Parliament then and also in the following year. One of Tiverton's members, John Drake, relinquished his place to take up a county seat. Richard Oliver, an experienced politician who had served in three preceding parliaments, replaced him. Oliver had been employed by the Duke of Buckingham for at least five years, and was now to be his man in Tiverton[1]. Buckingham had become the court favourite of King James by 1623 and had been instrumental in the negotiations of Prince Charles' Spanish marriage, which ultimately failed. He was successful, however, in his arrangements of Charles' betrothal to Princess Henrietta Maria of France. This French wedding also threatened a possible Catholic succession. Buckingham further alienated Parliament by an ill-conceived attack on Cadiz, and by the time it convened it was ready to impeach him. It is likely, therefore, that he took the opportunity of imposing Oliver on Tiverton in 1626 to boost his own support, no doubt providing the burgesses with financial incentives for his election. Parliament was not so easily swayed, and King Charles was forced to dissolve the session to save the Duke. England, nevertheless, was soon at war with both France and Spain.

Charles routinely billeted soldiers on his subjects, often in unacceptably large numbers. This sometimes caused unrest, as in November 1627 when martial law had to be imposed on the troops staying in Plymouth[2]. In the same month, Saint Peter's parish register records the burial of two soldiers, one from Bristol, the other from Essex. The cause of death was more likely through illness rather than because of violence. They were part of a contingent of 168 boarded in the town. Although Tiverton had been promised reimbursement for the costs of their stay, six years later no money had

---

[1] Gruenfelder 1981, 146.

[2] *CSPDom 1627-8*, 440.

been received[1]. The financial burden of maintaining these soldiers came shortly after the King had imposed an oppressive forced loan to pay for the war. The rate was to be five times the normal subsidy, and, according to one source[2], the payment 'of such as are able' was to be made within 24 days; others were to pay half within two weeks and the remainder by the end of three months. In response for granting subsidies the Parliament of 1628 presented the Petition of Right. This demanded an end to taxation without parliamentary consent, imprisonment without cause, billeting of soldiers on subjects, and martial law in peacetime. Both King and Parliament had gone too far. The murder of Buckingham enabled Charles to conclude peace and restore personal rule with no recourse to Parliament.

John West who, according to the 1627 subsidy list, was the richest man in Tiverton, died in 1630 and was buried in the north aisle of Saint Peter's 'under the seat where the serjeants of the mace do usually sit'[3]. A surviving inventory[4] details the contents of his property in Fore Street. It gives us a rare glimpse into a Tiverton town house of the time. Listed by chambers one thing becomes clear – allocating different rooms for separate household functions is a relatively modern fashion. In the study, reams of writing paper were kept beside a box of silk lace and 'some gunpowder', but this was not so bizarre as the collection of goods found in the 'higher gallery'. Here a trundle bedstead, a hackney saddle and a pair of gambadoes[5], two muskets, a corselet[6], and 'other arms' shared the space with two chests containing 'bacon and fish therein'. Curiously, the house was cluttered with beds; there was one in the chamber 'over the shopp', two in the two 'higher chambers towards the street', one in the chamber over the kitchen, and three others elsewhere. In addition to West, three other prominent Tivertonians died in that year: the first mayor, Richard Hill alias Spurway; George Slee's widow, Joan, and Edward Amey. Spurway gave £100 for the support of the Corporation, which he had been instrumental in forming in 1615, and he also left them a house in Saint Andrew Street provided that it was used as a Bridewell or prison[7], so fulfilling a condition of the Charter[8]. Edward Amey had been so successful as a merchant that, on his death, he was in a position to leave many sizeable bequests. He gave £400 each to his three sons and two daughters, as well as 1s each to 200 poor persons, and £50 to ten poor weavers and tuckers of Tiverton[9].

---

[1] *CSPDom 1634-5, 424.*
[2] *Yonge, 100.*
[3] DRO 2723M/WW9.
[4] DRO 2723M/WW10.
[5] leggings worn when riding a horse.
[6] a piece of armour covering the torso.
[7] in DRO R4/1/C93.
[8] there appears to be no mention of a borough prison before this gift, unless Roger Slee's house of correction (see p.86) served the purpose.
[9] TivMus 89/1240/9.

S uch gifts to the poor of Tiverton came at an opportune time. The town faced the return of the plague and soaring corn prices, but, most importantly, a serious slump in the cloth trade was forcing down the price of kersies. The reason for this was partly the New Draperies, the lightweight cloths being developed in East Anglia. The situation was so serious that in 1622 a group of Devon clothiers journeyed to London to complain about the state of their trade. We do not know the names of those in the group, but the Devon Quarter Sessions ordered various parishes to pay their expenses. Crediton and Cullompton together were to pay 20s, Tavistock and Okehampton the same, Torrington 20s, Barnstaple £2, but the largest contribution, £3, was to come from Tiverton[1]. It is likely that these payments show not only the origins of the group members, but also the relative importance to these communities of the cloth trade. The situation had worsened after 1618, when all the major European powers were gradually drawn into the Thirty Years War, and markets were constantly changing.

The West Country's response to the disruption in trade was radical, innovative, and effective. A change was made from manufacturing traditional heavy kersies to the production of much lighter serges, especially the type known as perpetuanas. Unlike those made elsewhere, the local serges were fulled, and, as they were woven from combed worsted warp and carded woollen weft, they were thicker[2]. This combination of lightness with thickness meant that West Country serges could compete with the popular East Anglian cloths. Devon was particularly well placed for these changes. For a long time, local supplies of wool had been insufficient to meet the demands of the county's cloth production, so importing wool, often as yarn, became the norm. Experimentation in cloth types therefore presented no great problems. Another valid reason for change, often underestimated, is that almost all aspects of kersey production had become increasingly hampered by government regulations. The manufacture of serges, on the other hand, was relatively free from such restraints. The change was neither universal nor immediate. In the Southwest serge production seems to have become concentrated around Taunton, in the Tiverton area, and at Exeter. Hoskins says[3] that Tiverton waited until about 1690 before it changed to serge. In taking this view he probably followed Dunsford who states[4] that the manufacture of mixed and shaded worsted serges was introduced at about that time. But other types of serge were evidently being made at a much earlier date. The first reference found to Tiverton serges comes as early as 1620, in an account of a local clothier, George Hartnoll[5]. This is hardly surprising. Tiverton needed the industry to survive; it would not have lagged behind in any aspect of production at this period. Shortly before 1634, John Skinner

---

[1] DRO QS1/5.
[2] Stephens 1958, 3-5.
[3] 1954, 66.
[4] 1790, 201-2.
[5] DRO 1131A/PZ1.

had four new fulling mills constructed on part of the Hams, beside the Lowman[1]. Similarly, from a lease we learn that two new fulling mills had been added to those already standing on a plot of land at Bolham. A large sum of £660 was paid for the lease[2] by an Exeter doctor, named Robert Vilvaine, showing that people not traditionally linked to the cloth industry were eager to invest their money in it. Success and markets were jealously guarded. In 1638, several Tiverton and Cullompton merchants signed a petition from Devon that was sent to the King complaining of the City of London's attempt to monopolise the export of cloth to Spain[3]. Nothing came of the Londoners' proposal.

During these years, Blundell's School flourished under Samuel Butler, the Master, and his various Ushers, among them his sons Jonathan and Amory. The school was clearly fulfilling its founder's purpose. Many 'natives' were progressing through to the Universities, several of them sons of Tiverton burgesses. In 1637, the Tivertonian William Spurway succeeded Thomas Hartnoll[4] at Sidney Sussex. Thomas, whose brother James was Rector of Pitt from 1631, took up residence as Rector of Templeton immediately on leaving Cambridge. Peter Blundell's wish to educate boys to become 'good and godly preachers of the Gospel' was now reality. The survival both of Blundell's Accounts and those of the Churchwardens of Saint Peter's give us an opportunity, in their detail, to glimpse day-by-day administration in and around the two institutions. On both sites, building and repairs were almost continuous. Stone for the School was often hauled from a quarry at Bingwell and, in November 1636 there must have been severe weather, for two men were paid 'for lyme to right that which was hurled by the storm'[5]. In the following year, Saint Peter's was undergoing minor alterations with the 'two great casewayes' being laid. Presumably, these are the same two main paths that still lead to the southern porch. A new sundial was also fixed to the church. This was no mean feat; 6s was paid for a stone which had to be cut and then put up in the porch wall, a Mr Franke was paid 7s 6d to make the dial itself and 7d to carry it from his house. Payments were frequently made, often to boys, for killing animals and birds in the churchyard. The records single out 'grays', the name given to badgers, but foxes, hedgehogs and birds were also caught. As well as ridding the churchyard of vermin, boys are also noted as playing one particular jape at Saint Peter's – on many occasions, the door of the church toilet had to be recovered from the

---

[1] DRO 213M/T270.
[2] (DRO 49/9/1/420). From this date the property was known by the name of its lessee, and is still called Velvains.
[3] *CSPDom 1637-8*, 218.
[4] the son of George Hartnoll, the clothier of Tiverton, whose accounts have just been mentioned.
[5] Blundell's MSS Account Rolls.

bottom of the steep slope to the River Exe. Nor did such behaviour, it seems, improve with education, as the Blundell's Accounts frequently record someone having to retrieve 'the stones of the house of office[1], which were taken out of the water'.

On the death of Edward Toogood in 1638, the portion of Tidcombe fell vacant. Two candidates were put forward; Richard Newte, the son of Henry, Tiverton's Town Clerk, and Thomas Jones. It appears from the *State Papers* of 1637-8 that Jones' presentation had already been obtained for him at least one year before[2], but Bishop Hall of Exeter was delaying the procedure. Hall's reluctance is probably explained by the fact that Jones' sponsor was none other than William Laud, Archbishop of Canterbury. Laud was known for his profound dislike of Puritans, those eager Protestants, strong in Parliament, intent on ridding the Church of England of what they believed were remnants of popery. Because Bishop Hall had been brought up under Puritan influences, Laud always suspected him, hence the rivalry between the two. As for Richard Newte, he had been passed over largely because of a judgement issued by Sir John Lambe, a close friend of the Archbishop[3].

Rather than stay in England and face Laud's persecution, many Puritans preferred to go abroad and some to make the perilous journey across the Atlantic. There, along with like-minded groups, they established settlements on the northeastern seaboard of America. Nicholas Frost was one such person, who, together with his young son, Richard, left their home at Lowman Green and became settled at Piscataqua in modern Maine[4]. For those who remained, but refused to renounce their religious beliefs, gaol was often their fate. This happened to James Toppe, one of Tiverton's most vociferous Anabaptists. Even from Newgate Prison he exclaimed defiantly that 'his offence is not for any evil that he has done to any man, but only for desiring to keep a good conscience in all things towards God'[5].

When Laud attempted to impose a new Prayer Book on Scotland in 1637 it was violently rejected by the Kirk. Charles decided the only way to show the Scots his authority was by force, and musters were called throughout England in 1639. Not everyone, however, was eager to take part. Five Tiverton men were reported for being 'deficient in arms at the musters'[6], and only one of them, Lewis Bray, pleading poverty, offered an excuse. Indeed, by this time the town of Tiverton itself owed £130 in Ship Money, an emergency tax that had been introduced in 1634. In spite of increasing opposition to his actions, the King remained adamant. Although English and Scottish forces did not join battle, Charles demanded more money for his military designs in the north than prerogative expedients could supply.

---

[1] a contemporary euphemism for lavatory. The privies are still to be seen at the back of Old Blundell's, overhanging the River Lowman.
[2] p. 288.
[3] *HMC IVth Report*, 36.
[4] now called Kittery (cited in Case 1907, iv).
[5] *CSPDom 1639*, 438.
[6] *CSPDom 1638-9*, pp. 338, 485 and 488.

Parliament was summoned, for the first time in 11 years, and the session began on April 13th, 1640. Representing Tiverton were Peter Sainthill, educated at Blundell's, and Sir Peter Ball, one of the King's legal advisers. In Convocation Laud pressed through a new set of Canons, including the Etcetera Oath that required all clergy and some laymen to swear to maintain the episcopal hierarchy of the Church of England. This infuriated those in Parliament who saw this as nothing less than a move toward the ultimate abomination, Catholicism. As soon as Charles saw he would gain no taxes without strings, wholly unacceptable to him, he dissolved Parliament. The Short Parliament had lasted less than a month.

The conflict with Scotland was renewed with disastrous results. The Scots took Newcastle, abolished bishops, and allied with Parliament's leaders. At least one Tiverton man became a casualty of the fighting in the North. John Sharp was wounded and subsequently secured an annual pension of £5[1]. When the Scots took Northumberland and Durham, another Tivertonian, Richard Spurway, was placed in danger. He had been a Blundell's scholar at Balliol, where he had been granted a vicarage that was now 'in the midst of the Scottish army'[2] and he was without money. The most disturbing event to affect Tiverton, however, did not take place in the north of England, but much nearer to home. A group of 600 troops, raised in North Devon, arrived on 11th July 1640. While the majority of the men remained in the town, 160 left under the command of Lieutenant-Colonel Richard Gibson and his Lieutenant, Compton Evers[3]. They quartered the night at Wellington and, the following day being Sunday, the troops all went to church, except Evers. Under suspicion of being a Papist, the men dragged him from his lodgings and he was barbarously murdered. The mutineers dispersed, but 140 were captured. Their intention, so they said, had been to kill the officers and 'seize the king's money'[4].

Charles was forced to make peace after the Scots took Newcastle, and Parliament was recalled. Sainthill was returned for Tiverton but not accompanied by Peter Ball. According to one author[5], this was despite the King's wishes. The Mayor and Corporation of Tiverton selected a merchant of the town, George Hartnoll, a man who would be more accountable to them and was not closely linked to the Royal Family. Parliament agreed to pay the Scots army, to punish those responsible for advising the King to impose an arbitrary prerogative government, and to make sure no such government was possible in the future. Over the following six months, Charles agreed to substantial changes. Laud was imprisoned, and the Courts of Star Chamber and High Commission were abolished, along with non-Parliamentary taxes. By the

---

[1] DRO QS1/8.
[3] *CSPDom 1640*, 494.
[5] Gruenfelder 1981, 203.

[2] Blundell's MSS - letters re Balliol.
[4] *ib*, 496.

Triennial Act he agreed to summon Parliament every three years, and not to dissolve this one without its own consent. In the country, the significance of all this may not have been fully understood, but these actions were giving rise to a situation in which the ancient constitution would be threatened. In Tiverton, Thomas Jones preached a sermon in defence of Laud and against Parliament. He was consequently thrown into prison and forced to relinquish his portion of Tidcombe[1]. Richard Newte, on this, his second, attempt, filled the vacancy[2]. In July 1641, Parliament required everyone over the age of 18 to swear allegiance to the King and the Established Church. Until they did, no one was permitted to hold office in the church or state. The resulting lists, known as Protestation Returns, were not completed until the following year and show only the names of males. In Tiverton's list of well over 1,750 individuals[3], only one entry provides more than just the name: John Topp alias Fort, an Anabaptist.

Parliament reconvened in November 1641 after a recess during which a long-simmering rebellion had broken out in Ireland. To many M.P.s it confirmed the worst fears of a Popish Plot. They were reluctant to allow the King to raise an army to deal with the Irish, so they asked him to surrender command of the troops. Charles refused to give them his decision, and was soon confronted with a list of grievances, later known as the Grand Remonstrance. This massive document demanded, among other things, that the King's officers should be approved by Parliament before their appointment, and that a synod of divines, drawn from abroad as well as England, should be asked to resolve the issue of whether the Church of England should be governed by the episcopal or presbyterian model. Charles' response was to attempt to arrest five of the promoters of the Remonstrance on 5th January 1642. He stormed into the chamber of the Commons accompanied by armed soldiers, and demanded that the Speaker of the House reveal the whereabouts of the men he sought. The Speaker claimed 'I have neither eyes to see nor tongue to speak... but as this house is pleased to direct me'. This was the defining moment. Parliament and King were not to be re-united. By the Militia Ordinance, never signed by Charles, command of the army was handed to lords-lieutenant who were to be appointed by Parliament. In June 1642 Parliament announced its Nineteen Propositions, virtually terms of a limited monarchy Charles would not comprehend. On August 22nd at Nottingham the King raised the royal standard. Civil war was inevitable.

---

[1] Walker 1717, 280.
[2] Newte was already the domestic chaplain of George Digby, son of Charles I's newly-appointed adviser, and within a month of obtaining Tidcombe, he was admitted to Clare Portion on the death of Hugh Cholmeley.
[3] *Protestation 1641,* 47-57.

8 England Turned Upside Down

*T*he war broke out between the King and the Parliament, which occasioned great distress throughout the kingdom, not only by the common desolations of war, which were many, but by creating such feuds, animosities, and strongly heated party spirits, as have scarcely subsided to this day [1790]: individuals of the same counties, districts, townships, and even private families, joined opposite armies, according to their different opinions of the justice of the cause, or propriety of the conduct of the two great parties, to promote the future benefit of the kingdom and happiness of the people[1].

Dunsford, writing in 1790, had no doubt of the calamity of the Civil War and its enduring consequences. But when it began, where would Tiverton's allegiance lie? Who in the town would favour either or any side? With its largely artisan population and growing number of dissenters, one would expect most to support Parliament, but we simply do not know. Could the town play any effective military role in the conflict? It was not a defensive location. The Castle, of course, had not been built for 17th century warfare, but for defence against medieval weapons. Yet Tiverton's strategic importance should not be underestimated; it was on the main route out of Exeter to the north-east of the county, as well as the main east-west route running through the northern parts of Devon and Somerset.

The forces of the King and Parliament spent the late summer of 1642 recruiting. Sir Ralph Hopton, one of Charles' most talented generals, had been sent to the Southwest even before the King had raised his standard at Nottingham. Although born in Somerset, Hopton could not evince much support there, and set out with a small force for Cornwall where many of the county's gentlemen rallied to the King's colours[2]. Sir George Chudleigh, an M.P. for Tiverton in the 1620s, was Hopton's counterpart for the Parliamentary forces. He recruited sufficient men to form five or six troops of horse which, threatened by the Royalists in Cornwall, were forced to withdraw to the safety of Plymouth. As a populous town, Tiverton was probably targeted for recruiting, but the number of volunteers or men impressed into either side is not known.

The major Civil War battles took place far away. The first encounter at Edgehill in

---

[1] Dunsford 1790, 48.
[2] among them was Sir John Trelawney, a man still holding a considerable landed interest in Tiverton.

Warwickshire on October 23rd proved indecisive. In Devon by this time, the Royalists had ventured out of Cornwall but were repulsed at Exeter, and had fallen back to besiege Plymouth, which remained in Parliamentary hands throughout hostilities. After a winter truce, fighting resumed in April 1643. Chudleigh defeated a Royalist force near Okehampton, but on May 16th Hopton's Cornishmen won at Stratton, killing over 300[1], and marched east. This was the first Royalist success in what was to be their best year.

The Royalists travelled first to Exeter, then northward towards Tiverton. The town was under the control of Colonel John Were of Silverton with a regiment of foot[2]. This small Parliamentary band had been commandeering supplies from local Royalist supporters, such as Thomas Carew, lord of the manor of Cove and owner of Rifton Barton in Stoodleigh. The troops confiscated 225 sheep, 37 lambs and 13 oxen from him[3]. Though threatened, not everyone in the area supported the King; one group of eager anti-Royalists had insisted that the Mayor give them sufficient warning of Hopton's approach so they could come into the town and resist his forces[4]. This unknown Mayor, however, was either unwilling or unprepared, as he failed to notify the Parliamentary supporters. The consequence was that Were, 'wanting arms, ammunition and men' fled the town on 28th May[5]. Hopton and his men apparently passed through unchallenged.

The summer of 1643 was a time of Royalist successes. Nationally, their victories forced Parliament to seek military assistance from the Scots. In Devon, the Lord Lieutenant, the Earl of Bedford, crossed over to the King's forces; Barnstaple, Bideford and Appledore all surrendered, the Exeter garrison agreed terms with the King's nephew, Prince Maurice, and further afield Bristol fell to Prince Rupert. Was there still Parliamentary support in Tiverton? Dunsford implies that there was[6], stating that in August the town opposed a part of the King's horse. The soldiers overcame the resistance and defeated the townsmen during a skirmish in Gold Street. Some of the locals were wounded or slain, and legend has it that a miller, John Lock, was taken by the soldiers and hanged at the White Horse Inn.

Despite their domination in Devon, the Royalists always found it difficult to obtain supplies. In early 1644 the initiative of Peter Atkins, a Tiverton man, helped ease the situation at Exeter by sending supplies of corn seized at Tiverton market. Another local man, William London, was recruiting in and around the town for Charles' forces, and 'threatened and discouraged any from taking up arms for Parliament'[7]. Feeling sufficiently secure in the region, many of the Royalist strongholds reduced their forces

---

[1] Stoyel 1994, 33.
[2] *Clarendon, VII*, 93.
[3] SRO DD/TB/Bundle 11/FL8.
[4] Thomason E105(27).
[5] Thomason E21 (34).
[6] (1790, 183). Although this incident is not related in any other source, the Tiverton Civic Society has seen fit to commemorate it with a blue plaque.
[7] both appear in *CommAdvMoney 1642-56*, 1411-2.

in order to send men to bolster Prince Maurice's siege of Lyme Regis. Their position was soon threatened, however, by the decision of the Lord General of the Parliamentary army, the Earl of Essex, to free the Southwest from Royalist control. He entered Devon at the end of June, and struck out for Tiverton. The Royalist garrison, mainly Northamptonshire men, deserted *en masse* as soon as they heard the news of his approach[1]. By way of Honiton and Cullompton, Essex reached Tiverton on July 3rd and entered without opposition. He spent his time in the town recruiting new troops, but according to one source[2], these men preferred being under the command of the local gentry rather than outsiders. In a letter written from Tiverton on July 18th Essex declared his intention to relieve Plymouth[3], and two days later he marched off in the direction of Crediton. Saint Peter's Churchwardens' Accounts record a payment of 4s 6d for 'cleansing the churchyard' after the departure of the troops. More serious than this mess, however, was the disease, probably typhoid, which the army brought with them. While they were in the town, 35 troops were buried in the churchyard, and after they had gone, the parish register lists 62 burials in August, rising to 109 in the month of October. In all, 445 people died in this year, more than twice the average. Like most communities Tiverton felt with some justification that soldiers of either side brought only economic spoliation and death. Meanwhile, Parliament's westward thrust had ended in humiliation and defeat at Lostwithiel in September, leaving the greater part of Devon, except Plymouth, firmly under Royalist control. Essex's Western Campaign ruined his reputation, and the Parliamentary cause was compromised soon after it had seemed triumphant in the greatest battle of the War, Marston Moor.

During the following months, the Royalist forces operating in the central part of Devon were commanded by Lord Goring, but rarely controlled by him. They soon earned a reputation for being ill-disciplined, and spent much of their time rampaging around the countryside, taking supplies and quarters as they pleased. Such behaviour led to the formation in Devon and elsewhere of the so-called Clubmen; groups of local people tired of having to sustain successive armies. They refused to quarter or provision the troops, or to help them in any way except under dire threat.

Faced with incompetence and delay, the Parliamentary solution was to recruit a new, highly-trained, disciplined and professional force. They were determined to win the War with this New Model Army, commanded by Sir Thomas Fairfax with Oliver Cromwell in charge of its cavalry. It eventually secured a decisive victory at Naseby, Northamptonshire, on June 14th 1645 over Prince Rupert and Charles I. News of this success probably influenced the Devon Clubmen who now decided to side with Parliament. In July, the town of Bridgwater was taken, cutting off the Royalists in

---

[1] Whetham & Whetham 1907, 70.   [2] Andriette 1971, 115.

[3] *CSPDom 1644,* 358-9.

Devon and Cornwall from the rest of their forces. Once Bristol had fallen, in September, the Parliamentary army headed westwards. At this particular time it seems that Tiverton was occupied by pro-Parliamentary forces[1], possibly Clubmen. Goring, however, soon re-imposed Royalist control over the town. However, having been paid, Fairfax's men moved with renewed enthusiasm into Devon on October 14th, and soon reached Cullompton. A council-of-war there decided that Major-General Massey, with his regiment of horse accompanied by a brigade of foot commanded by Colonel Weldon, were to advance to Tiverton.

Massey's objective, Tiverton Castle, together with Saint Peter's Church, had been strengthened by woolpacks brought from the Church House. The size of the Royalist force under Sir Gilbert Talbot[2] was about 300 infantry and a few cavalry, but, on hearing the news that Massey was on his way, almost 100 of the men deserted, and the rest withdrew to the Castle and church[3]. Massey reached Tiverton on October 16th and immediately ordered its surrender, but was refused. Fairfax himself arrived on the following day and, after setting up his artillery, again demanded that Talbot surrender. He received the same reply. The Parliamentary officers began to plan an assault on the Castle from their quarters at Blundell's School. Several houses were pulled down in the upper part of Saint Peter Street and Newport Street, to give them full sight of their target, and to deny the Royalists any cover for an escape.

On the morning of Sunday October 19th the artillery began to play on the Castle and, about two o'clock in the afternoon

> 'the Generall for the sparing of blood, with the advice of the councell of warre, resolved to sende them a second summons, which was written and signed and parties drawne out, who were reddie with their scalinge ladders to storme, if a deniall were returned, but at that instant it pleased God so to derecte one shott that it cut the chaine of theire draw-bridge which instantly fell downe, and the souldiers spirits were such, that they presently without ordre given, entered theire workes. The enemies heartes failed, and wee became suddenly masters of the church, and castle, and theire strong and regular workes in which they confided. Wee tooke the governour, Sir Gilbert Tawbott, and 204 officers and souldiers of which you have heere enclosed a list, 4 greate gunnes, 30 barrells of powder, with other armes which cannot bee particularized, they being dispersed. Wee loste not a man in the storming, nor put any to the sword'[4].

The incidents were reported to the House of Commons which ordered 'that on the next Lord's Day. God's delivery into the hands of Parliament of Tiverton may be remembered'[5].

---

[1] Thomason E300 (11).

[2] made governor of the Castle after Colonel Amyas Pollard abandoned his command.

[3] Thomason E306(1).

[4] (HMC Portland, vol I, 292). The Churchwardens' Accounts in 1648-9 record that on at least two occasions parts of the walls were pulled down, probably resulting in the state of the building as we now see it.

[5] JHC 1644-6, 317-8.

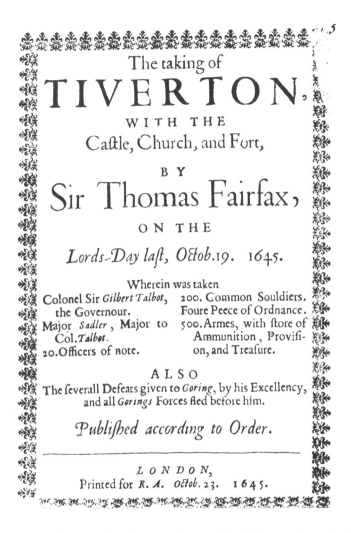

The taking of

TIVERTON,

WITH THE

Caftle, Church, and Fort,

BY

Sir Thomas Fairfax,

ON THE

Lords-Day laft, Octob.19. 1645.

Wherein was taken

Colonel Sir *Gilbert Talbot*, 200. Common Souldiers.
the Governour. Foure Peece of Ordnance.
Major *Sadler*, Major to 500. Armes, with ftore of
Col. *Talbot*. Ammunition, Provifi-
20. Officers of note. on, and Treafure.

ALSO

The feverall Defeats given to *Goring*, by his Excellency,
and all *Gorings* Forces fled before him.

Publifhed according to Order.

LONDON,
Printed for *R. A. Octob.* 23. 1645.

*Title page of the pamphlet issued just four days after the fall of Tiverton Castle. Such publications
as this were used as much for propaganda as news.*

Having accomplished his task late in the year Fairfax departed, leaving Tiverton in
the hands of a Colonel Shapcott. His first duty was to organise the cleaning up of the
Castle area. The Churchwardens' Accounts are once more revealing; they note the
payment of 11s for 'making clean the church', as well as money for four quarts of wine
for the soldiers' communion. Clearly, they were not all anti-sacramentalists in the New

Model Army. The General reached Ottery Saint Mary, but, with his troops suffering from the cold and wet weather, and dying of disease, he decided to return to Tiverton. He was back by the second week of December, and while there he laid plans that would bring about the end of the Great Civil War[1]. In the first week of the New Year, some troops moved off toward Okehampton, where a large force of Royalists had congregated, whereas the main force struck out towards the South Hams. The Royalist threat dissolved before the Parliamentary advance; by January 13th the three-year long siege of Plymouth was lifted. Fairfax now headed north-westwards to engage the enemy at Torrington. On February 16th 1646 the Royalists lost the town when a large store of powder kept in the parish church exploded, killing over 200. This heavy loss sounded the death knell for the King's cause; the Royalists were demoralised, help expected from France failed to materialise, and the army, constantly losing men through desertion, trickled back into Cornwall. The Prince of Wales left for France in March, Exeter finally surrendered on April 14th, the King handed himself over to the Scottish army in May, and the last Royalist garrison in the Southwest, Pendennis Castle, surrendered on August 18th.

Tiverton was in no mood for celebration for disease had returned. The County Quarter Sessions ordered £200 to be raised for the relief of the town's poor 'now visited by the plague'[2]. This was so bad that Parliament ordered a collection to be made in every church and chapel in London, half of which would be sent to Tiverton and Cullompton[3]. One of those ministering to the sick in Tiverton was Richard Newte, who had just returned from Europe to reclaim the portions of Clare and Tidcombe. As he had fled England because of his support for the King and the Church, it was predictable that he would not have the confidence of Parliament. He was forced to hire an assistant, Lewis Stukeley, at a cost of £100 a year. George Pierce, the portioner of Pitt, fared even worse. Accused of being critical of Parliament, he was deprived of his benefice at the end of 1646, and his family harassed and attacked. Pitt was given to John Chishull, a boarding-school keeper from Enfield. Whereas elsewhere an ejected clergyman's family could expect compensation, Mrs Pierce, pleading on behalf of her six children, was told by Chishull that 'he had a pair of geldings and a groom to support, and they were more chargeable than her children'[4]. Chishull and Stukeley were both Independents, or Congregationalists, groups wanting unattached churches, governed only by their individual congregations, unlike Presbyterians who desired a regional organisation.

From the outset of the Civil War special Parliamentary committees had investigated the actions of individuals, and assessed how much they should contribute to the war

---

[1] Gibb 1938, 135-6.
[2] DRO QS1/8.
[3] *JHC 1644-6*, 585.
[4] Walker 1714, 327-8.

against the King[1]. These contributions were in addition to the compulsory monthly payments for maintaining the army; the Parliamentarians took more money than had ever gone to the King. Many people were brought before the Committees to explain why they had favoured the Royalists. This was a time for settling scores. Peter Bartow[2] admitted that he began the War as a soldier in the Parliamentary army, but when the King's forces became dominant he was impressed into their army as a Quarter Master, but later reverted to the Roundheads[3]. Richard Culme of Canonsleigh stated that he 'never took arms or contributed against Parliament but lived quietly at his house'. His accusers, however, insisted that he 'often sat in commission with the malignants in Tiverton' and 'joyfully entertained the Cavaliers'. He was fined £2,906[4], a huge sum.

To avoid possible punishment, Peter Sainthill, one of Tiverton's M.P.s, had left the country. He travelled to Italy to join his brother at Leghorn (Livorno). This left George Hartnoll as Tiverton's only voice in the Commons, but his allegiance was doubted to such an extent that he was 'disabled to sit by judgement of the House'[5]. An election took place on October 5th 1646, when the burgesses chose John Elford and Robert Shapcott[6]. They took their seats in a Parliament that, together with the Army, the Scots, and the King (who had been handed over to Parliament by the Scots) attempted to contrive a political settlement. There could be no peace until the King agreed to it, but Charles I could never contemplate being King under conditions. The Army took him into custody on June 4th 1647 and, amid rumours of a severe reduction in the size of its forces, issued the Solemn Engagement. The men would resist being disbanded until their grievances, including payment of arrears, had been settled. The Army Council defied Parliament, and tried to negotiate their own peace settlement with the King, which included religious toleration[7].

Attempts made during the summer to reconcile Parliament, the King and the Army, ended when Charles escaped. He negotiated a pact with the Scots, promising them the Presbyterian Church they wanted in return for their military assistance. Royalist

---

[1] their proceedings have been summarised in the *Calendar of the Committee for the Advancement of Money 1642-56* and the *Calendar of the Committee for Compounding 1643-60*. The latter also obtained confessions of 'delinquency' and a pledge of adherence to the Parliamentary cause.

[2] from whom Bartow's Causeway derives its name.

[3] *CalCommComp 1643-60*, 1385.   [4] *ib.*, 461 and 1161.

[5] *JHC 1644-6*, 653.

[6] both were probably 'placemen' of Edmund Prideaux, keeper of the Great Seal (Roberts 1985, 8).

[7] the soldiers' political views were varied, but a sizeable proportion followed the ideas of the Levellers, a group which advocated 'the levelling of men's estates', biennial sessions of Parliament, and votes for all men.

supporters, believing that Parliament and the Army were divided, took up arms once more. Risings in Wales, Scotland, and northern England were put down efficiently by the Army. Despite the fighting, talks continued, but a number of officers, including Cromwell and his son-in-law, Ireton, demanded that Charles be tried as a 'Man of Blood'. This group set about organising the removal of potential Parliamentary opposition to their plan. At the end of December 1648 Colonel Thomas Pride with armed troops stood outside Parliament and barred those in favour of continued negotiations with the King from entry. Both Tiverton representatives were among the 130 members[1] excluded. Those who were allowed to enter, almost to a man Independent, formed the 'Rump Parliament'. A High Court of Justice was created by Cromwell for the express purpose of trying the King for high treason, and to the shock of most Englishmen (and nearly all Europeans) on January 30th 1649 Charles I was beheaded. This was, and has remained, the only time a reigning monarch of England has been publicly executed. According to Dunsford[2], the event prompted the Tiverton burgesses to change their scarlet gowns to black. Both the House of Lords and the monarchy were abolished, and the Rump pronounced the British Isles a republic, to be known as the Commonwealth. The executive body of government was to be a Council of State, numbering about 40 men, with Oliver Cromwell at its head.

The Commonwealth promoted a national moral crusade. In Tiverton Triers and Ejectors, who judged the suitability of church ministers, deprived Richard Newte of Tidcombe and Clare in 1650, but granted his wife one fifth of his income for the maintenance of their family[3]. He appears to have temporarily recovered the benefices a few years later, but in April 1654 Cromwell himself appointed his successor, John Rowe[4]. Newte was forced to leave Tiverton, as his life was made unbearable by having 'ten or twelve of the lewdest soldiers quartered with him'. The early 1650s saw further recrimination. A few individuals were intent not only in making names for themselves, but also in destroying the reputation of others. John Tucker accused Thomas Hartnoll of having sent money and arms to the Royalists[5], hoping to receive a fifth of his assessment by way of reward. Tiverton's mayor in 1651, James Clarke, asked to 'be admitted discoverer' of more Royalist sympathisers[6]. He made claims against no less than eight prominent Tivertonians[7], including Roger Giffard of the Castle who was said to have knowingly underestimated the value of his lands. Giffard asked for time to dispute his assessment, arguing that 'his debts are more than he is worth'[8].

---

[1] most were Presbyterians.
[2] 1790, 189.
[3] Walker 1714, 316-8.
[4] *Cromwell, III*, 239.
[5] *CommAdvMoney 1643-56*, 1283.
[6] *CalCommComp 1643-60*, 502.
[7] William London, Peter Atkins, John Deyman, John Goddard, Thomas Prowse, George Waldron, Aquila Skinner and Roger Giffard (ib., 1411-2).
[8] *CommAdvMoney 1643-56*, 1381.

By April 1653 Cromwell considered that the Rump Parliament was taking far too long to implement the Army's policies, so he dissolved it. Two months later, he handpicked 144 'godly men' to form a Parliament charged with bringing about a reformation in religion and manners. Other than those of London, no burgesses or city representatives were present. This Nominated Assembly did too much good work for Cromwell's liking and gave way in turn to Britain's first written constitution, the *Instrument of Government*. Cromwell as Lord Protector of the Commonwealth would rule with a Council of State and a single-chamber Parliament called every three years. The Parliament summoned in the following year did give a voice to Tiverton, although only one member. The deep divisions remaining from the War ensured a very competitive election. There were two contenders for the single seat: Robert Shapcott, member for Tiverton in 1647, and Major John Blackmore, who had been a Militia Commissioner for Devon and Cornwall. He had been rewarded with £200 for discovering malignants[1] (Royalist sympathisers). The amount may be significant, as the *Instrument of Government* had widened the franchise to include all men possessed of personal or real property to that value. The 'well affected inhabitants' of Tiverton later petitioned the Council of State over the election[2], complaining that they had met 'of right' and elected Blackmore, but were 'overpowered by numbers, many of whom had been disabled to vote'. They accused Shapcott of having served in the Royalist army, and on one occasion 'he was at a bowling match till midnight with other Cavaliers having three lanterns, then sitting, drinking and card-playing till four in the morning'. This was all to no avail, however, as Shapcott took his seat when the Parliamentary session began on September 3rd 1654.

Sporadic risings by supporters of Prince Charles, now heir to his father's crown, broke out in 1655 in Devon, Dorset, the Welsh Borders, and Wiltshire. Cromwell's response to this unrest was to divide the country into 11 military districts, each controlled by a Major-General. Devon and the rest of the Southwest were placed under the command of his brother-in-law, John Desborough. In March, he was sent to Tiverton, where 200 local men had been raised to fight the insurgents[3]. Not all the locals were keen to stamp out the Royalist threat, however. Captain Henry Cruwys of Cruwys Morchard was summoned to help secure Tiverton, but responded that 'he would not stir a foot out of his house for the matter'[4]. The Army Council took measures to purge Royalist support from Tiverton and other boroughs, without any regard for custom. Desborough sent orders to dismiss Aquila Skinner, John Deyman, George Waldron, Thomas Prowse and Thomas Hartnoll from the Tiverton Corporation, citing them as 'enemies to the Commonwealth'[5]. They were replaced by William Berry, William Wood, Peter Bere junior, Samuel Foote and Henry Fitzwilliam.

---

[1] *CalCommComp 1643-60*, 1259.   [2] *CSPDom 1653-4*, 279-80.

[3] *CSPDom 1655*, 99.   [4] Cruwys 1952, 8.

[5] (Dunsford 1790, 191-2). All of these men had been reported in 1651 to the Committee for Compounding (see n.7, p.108).

Berry and Wood were from Tiverton families, and Bere from nearby Huntsham, but Samuel Foote and Henry Fitzwilliam were the first of their name found in the area. Three of the five, Bere, Foote and Fitzwilliam, had also been vehement supporters of Blackmore in his unsuccessful attempt to gain Tiverton's seat in Parliament. The town was being manipulated into becoming a tool of the Commonwealth, even if it meant inserting outsiders into its governing body.

Portrait of Protector Cromwell on the Tiverton Market Charter of 1655. This document, in keeping with the prevailing Puritan sentiments, changed the town's market-day from Monday to Tuesday, so that all preparations for the day could be done on Monday and not on the Lord's Day. Probably as a commemoration of this act, a Market Cross was built in Fore Street[1].

Tiverton's clergy were, of course, in the front line of the Puritan Revolution. John Rowe moved on to become a preacher at Westminster Abbey, and his place was taken by Theophilus Polwheele, a learned Independent. Toleration was extended to almost all religious groups. Indeed, Tiverton's Baptists were enjoying greater freedom than they had ever done, and on the 15th and 16th of July 1657 they hosted the ninth meeting of the Western Association of Baptist Churches in Somerset and Devon[2]. Quakers, however, were not made welcome. They were considered by many to be blasphemous as they believed in direct communication with God, and shunned ritual, sacraments and ordained clergy. In 1656, Tiverton received its first travelling Quaker preacher, Thomas Balstone or Boylestone, who held a meeting at the house of Edward Baker[3]. A

---

[1] Dunsford 1790, 192.   [2] White 1971, 69.
[3] DRO 874D/Z1.

few days later, all those who had been present were thrown into the borough gaol[1], described at this time as 'a stinking hole not fit for a man'[2]. Nevertheless, Baker was not deterred; in the following months, he welcomed more preachers, all of whom met with hostility in the town.

On September 3rd 1658 Oliver Cromwell died. He had been persuaded to nominate his son Richard as his successor, but the inexperienced 32-year old commanded neither authority nor allegiance. A military council under Major General John Lambert took control, forcing young Cromwell to dissolve Parliament in April 1659 and to resign as Lord Protector. The Rump Parliament was recalled to give some authority to Lambert's Republicans. Was the nation on the verge of another civil war? Rumours and gossip were rife; many people were in a mind to believe almost anything. On the night of July 14th panic seized Tiverton.

> 'The whole town.. also several families in the parish were raised up out of their beds by a false rumour and alarm, that the ministers of the town, and others fearing God, should be all massacred that night'[3].

People took up arms. The general cry went up that the Baptists and Quakers were going to conduct the killings, with help from an extreme Puritan sect, the Fifth Monarchy Men. Thankfully, especially for Tiverton's Baptists, the more level-headed inhabitants calmed the situation.

The slide to anarchy was being carefully observed by George Monck[4], the commander of the army in Scotland. Refusing to acknowledge the legitimacy of Lambert's regime, he marched south and was welcomed by London in early February. Monck had recognised the sentiments of the English people and the need to return to tradition, to a Rule of Law. He recalled the surviving members of the Long Parliament, thereby tilting the balance back in favour of the Presbyterians. This Parliament dissolved itself, in keeping with the law of 1641, and a new elected Convention was called in 1660. Restoration was the only viable option, and Prince Charles timed his move perfectly. In April, in the Declaration of Breda, he promised to pay the army's arrears, to restore the Anglican Church with its bishops, and to issue a general pardon. There was something in this document for everyone, and it was gladly accepted by the Convention. With his position seemingly assured, he landed in England on May 25th, and four days later entered London. The bells of Saint Peter's rang out[5] and for generations afterwards Tiverton celebrated in its own way. Each year, on this anniversary, a procession meandered through the town, led by an 'Oliver'[6]. This man was dressed completely in black, sometimes naked from the waist upward, with his face

---

[1] DRO QS1/9. [2] DRO 874D/Z1.

[3] *Mercurius Politicus*, 27.7.1659.

[4] whose brother was buried in Tiverton in 1649 (Harding 1845, iv, 14).

[5] Churchwardens' Accounts.

[6] (*Exeter* 1980, 25). Mahood (1952, 70) said the custom was still current in 1952.

111

and hands covered in soot and grease. He was tethered to a rope, and attempted to catch youngsters who threw dirt and stones at him. If caught, they too were smothered with soot and grease. At the end of the procession was a child seated on a throne of oak boughs borne by four men, symbolising the young king.

The restoration of the monarchy was marked by what seems a surge of gratitude at Saint Peter's Church. The Churchwardens' Accounts record the payment of 30s to Lewis Cannington for painting Queen Elizabeth's coat-of-arms, £18 to Francis Pierce for painting the King's arms, £10 to Richard Thorne for the surrounding timber work and 5s for the ringers when the arms were put in place. No parishioner could ignore these colourful proclamations of Royal Supremacy. The rectors in office at the beginning of the Civil War were now restored. Richard Newte regained Clare and Tidcombe from Theophilus Polwheele, George Pierce returned to his portion of Pitt, even agreeing to retain the impostor Chishull as curate for a few months[1]. Polwheele's and Chishull's lives diverged from this point. The former remained in the area, whereas Chishull went back to running his boarding school in Enfield. On April 23rd 1661 the bell ringers of Saint Peter's were again called upon, this time to celebrate Charles II's coronation. It was a joyful day; Tiverton's poor were given 70 dozen loaves of bread, and the few soldiers stationed in the town received two hogsheads of beer, all on the orders of the Mayor[2]. Charles had kept his promise of paying the army their arrears, and most had been disbanded. This led to claims in the Courts of Quarter Sessions from men injured during military service. The Devon J.P.s ordered payments, varying between 30s and £4 10s a year, to Richard Parkhouse, William Gibbs, Robert Bastard and William Hill, all of Tiverton[3].

Tiverton sent two untried members to the new Parliament called after the Coronation – the so-called 'Cavalier Parliament' that would sit for much of the reign. They were Sir Thomas Stukeley of Affeton and Thomas Carew of Haccombe, both from well-established families of the area. Although Charles had promised comprehension for dissenters, Parliament thought otherwise, restricting local political offices to Anglicans. This early legislation seems to have been quite easily circumvented; for example, Henry Fitzwilliam, Tiverton's Town Clerk, was appointed Treasurer for the Devon gaols[4] in 1661, and in the same year, he signed *A Declaration of a Congregational Church in Tiverton*[5]. There was no compromise over the form of worship, however. The Anglican Church and the support of royalty was restored to its traditional role; the revised Prayer Book of 1662 prescribed a national form of worship and clergy who

---

[1] Matthews 1934, 115.
[2] Churchwardens' Accounts.
[3] DRO QS1/9.
[4] *ib.*.
[5] written by Theophilus Polwheele, and signed by many leading citizens (cited in unknown 1964, 60).

failed to take an oath to it were ejected. Tiverton's Pierce and Newte both signed the Bishop of Exeter's Subscribtion Book[1], as did Daniel Cudmore 'minister at Tiverton'[2]. Failure to sign, however, brought swift punishment; the Rector of Loxbeare, Richard Saunders, was sentenced by the Bishop to be removed. In all, about 2,000 ministers, most of them Presbyterians, were deprived of their benefices. Schoolmasters also had to submit, and Henry Batten, the Master at Blundell's, promptly entered his name in the Subscription Book even before the clergy did. Robert Sharpe of Chilcott's School subscribed, as did a John Weekes 'schoolmaster in Tiverton'[3]. Weekes was described by the Mayor as 'carrying on a design of much good and advantage to the youth' and was recommended to teach 'writing, accounts etc'[4].

Many nonconformists were now barred from entering the church, politics, education, and many professions. Trade, commerce, or even emigration were sometimes the only options. A considerable number, as at the beginning of the century, sought refuge on the Continent, especially the Netherlands. One such exile was George Thorne, the son of a Tiverton wool merchant. He had been beneficed at Melcombe Regis in Dorset at the time of the Restoration, but was evicted. He left for Rotterdam 'partly for trade and to get out of the way of ill-meaning neighbours'[5]. Extremists, suspicious of Charles' inclination to Catholicism, his admiration of Louis XIV of France, and his marriage to Catherine, the sister of the King of Portugal, devised plots to overthrow him and revive the Republic. A plan to take Windsor Castle involved Edward Raddon from the Exeter area and Captain. Humphrey Spurway of Tiverton[6]. It was betrayed, and they fled to Holland. Despite mounting opposition Parliament pressed on against dissenters. The Conventicle Act of 1663 forbade them from assembling in groups of five or more, and a year later the Five Mile Act prohibited their ministers from coming within five miles of where they once preached. Breaches in the laws were widely reported. Richard Saunders was accused of holding conventicles 'sometimes lurkeing in Tiverton, sometymes in Loxbeare, and other places for the like ends', and Theophilus Polwheele 'keepes seditious conventicles' at Tiverton[7]. Richard Newte, the archetypal Anglican, was a scholar, much respected, and no persecutor. He was appointed chaplain to the King in 1666, but remained at Saint Peter's, excused attendance at court because of the long distance he would have to travel.

---

[1] DRO Chanter 151.
[2] (DRO Chanter 44). Cudmore is almost certainly the man recorded as Usher of Blundell's in 1648.
[3] DRO Chanter 151.
[4] (DRO PR510/Schoolmasters/Tiverton). But we do not know where he taught.
[5] *CSPDom 1663-4*, 88.   [6] Greaves 1986,116.
[7] cited in Matthews 1934, for Polwheele see pp.393-4, for Saunders p.426.

The Great Fire of London, which destroyed almost 80% of the city, took place in the same year as Newte's appointment. Predictably, the Catholics were accused of causing it, and one of those pointing a finger was the former Rector of Pitt, John Chishull[1]. Much hatred was heaped on the Royal Family's Catholic associations. In August 1666, Peter Crabb wrote to the Privy Council that 'the disaffected in the West are very busy employing men and women to inform up and down that the Queen Mother, Henrietta Maria, intends to bring in popery, and that the King countenances it'[2]. He continued: 'Widow Fasy of Tiverton, whose son is a grand rogue, carries letters for them... saying that the good old cause will be the cause again before a year is over'. There is no evidence for the presence of Catholics in the Tiverton area, and the name of Facey occurs only in William Facey, the pastor of the Tiverton Baptists. Was he fomenting the local population against the King, or was Crabb falsely accusing him to bring about his downfall?

In 1666, Louis XIV of France declared war on England which was already fighting the Dutch. Inevitably, this led to disruption of trade for Tiverton. At least one ship carrying goods destined for the town was seized. This was the *Fortune,* whose cargo of Morlaix linen was jointly owned by thirteen merchants; six from London, two of Exeter and Lyme Regis, and three from Tiverton[3]. In the following year, the Dutch fleet caused panic in London when they destroyed many ships berthed at Chatham. Before England could recover, the Dutch republic, themselves facing a French invasion, agreed to the Treaty of Breda, signed by all three nations[4]. Tiverton people took a keen interest in such international events, especially when there were commercial implications. Shortly before his death in 1670, Henry Newte, the town's (second) Clerk, received a newsletter from Henry Muddiman, the founder of the *London Gazette*. This contained information on the state of shipping to Smyrna (now Izmir in Turkey), news of a Flemish East India merchant ship stranded on the Goodwin Sands, and the restrictions on sugar imports[5]. What is surprising is how far Tiverton's interests extended. One family who had made a fortune from the cloth trade had exotic connections. Nicholas Skinner, who died in 1670, left money to the poor of Tiverton as well as £100 to 'his next relatives in the town'[6]. One of these family members, Thomas, in the following year was seeking a safe passage to the East Indies to enjoy quiet possession of his island of Barella with 'free intercourse of trade' there[7].

---

[1] Matthews 1934, 115.

[2] *CSPDom 1666-7,* 30-1.

[3] *ib.,* 571.

[4] by which the Dutch conceded New Amsterdam and other lands in America along with a handful of African outposts, in return for trading benefits from England, and France granted England some islands in the Caribbean in exchange for Nova Scotia.

[5] *CSPDom 1660,* 540.

[6] *Murray Wills.*

[7] (*CSPDom 1671,* 357). This island is now known as Berhala.

Government appointments were often another avenue to potential riches. One lucrative office that would feature prominently in Tiverton's later history was the Receivership of the Hearth Tax in Devon and Cornwall. It seems that George Clarke in 1670[1] was the first Tivertonian to obtain the post, although the Mr Chilcott who was Receiver in 1668[2] may have been from the local family of that name. The great advantage was that the holder kept a considerable amount of money in his possession until it had to be paid into the Exchequer. Before being appointed, the candidate had to obtain sureties. In Clarke's case, they were provided by Thomas Prowse of Hillersdon, the late Henry Newte's son-in-law Anthony Salter, Thomas Bere of Huntsham, John Doble of Calverleigh, James Calwoodleigh of Uplowman and Henry Worth of Washfield[3]. If the Receiver were careful, the appointment could be used to create an even greater fortune. Careless investment would mean ruin.

Charles II entered into the Treaty of Dover with Louis XIV in 1670, in which he promised support for the French in their war against the Dutch in return for a handsome subsidy which would help make him financially more independent of Parliament. A vital part of the agreement, however, was not made public - Charles' apparent promise to announce his conversion to Catholicism. He declared war against the Dutch, thus gaining the French subsidy, but fell short of announcing his conversion. He had also agreed with France to grant greater toleration to Catholics and Dissenters. Using the royal prerogative, in 1672 he issued a Declaration of Indulgence allowing freedom of worship in newly licensed meeting-houses. Some Tivertonians grasped this opportunity firmly. A 'Church of Christ' at Tiverton sent the King a petition, thanking him for 'his gracious declaration [of Indulgence]', and asking that the Congregationalist Theophilus Polwheele be allowed to preach at the house of Peter Bere[4]. The Presbyterians followed close behind, initially with an application for their minister Richard Saunders to use Blundell's School as a meeting-place[5], and when this request was denied, they asked for him to be permitted to preach in William Wood's house[6]. The Baptist William Facey, received his licence in May to preach in Martin Dunsford's house in Saint Peter Street[7].

For a while at least, the measure of royal toleration shown to Dissenters led to a lighter workload for the ecclesiastical courts. Charges for not attending church or not receiving the sacrament ceased. The Bishop of Exeter's Consistory Court and the Archdeaconry Court had more time to spend on the usual disputes over wills, sexual

---

[1] (*CalTreasB 1669-72*, 576). This direct tax, calculated on the number of hearths in each house, was introduced as an attempt to increase the King's income.
[2] *CalTreasB 1667-8*, 306.   [3] *CalTreasB 1672-5*, 163.
[4] *CSPDom 1671-2*, 272.   [5] *ib.*, 324.
[6] (*ib.*, 458). The occupants of two of these meeting-houses, Bere and Wood, were among the five pro-Parliamentary burgesses imposed on the borough in 1655.
[7] (*CSPDom 1672*, 62). This Martin was an ancestor of the historian.

incontinency, arguments about tithes, and cases of defamation. The latter often followed the same formula; an altercation took place in which a female party was inevitably called a whore. One extreme example occurred in 1672 when Dorothy Hartnoll called Mary Cannington 'whore, theevish whore, shocking whore and old whore'[1]. A similar case was heard concerning the Fowler and Bradford families of Tiverton who, according to the witnesses, were involved in a long-running feud. The court appearance followed an incident when Henry Bradford had accused Edith Fowler of keeping 'a bawdyhouse', adding that she 'bred up servants for Damaris Page'. The interesting point is that Tivertonians should even know of this person and her activities. A few years earlier, 'the poor whores, bawds, pimps and panders' of London had sent a petition to the King's mistress, and the first signature on it was that of Damaris Page[2]. Puritan morals had not survived the Restoration.

---

[1] DRO Chanter 874.   [2] *CSPDom 1667-8*, 306.

9 Church, State and Conscience

By 1673, the Cavalier Parliament had begun to suspect the King of sinister designs. He had committed England to an unpopular war against the Protestant Dutch; his brother, James, Duke of York, the Lord Admiral, had long been suspected of popery; and, at court, Catholicism was becoming fashionable. Locally, the royal policy of indulgence may have been a blessing to dissenters, but nationally it threatened the State Church and the restored Constitution. Parliament's reaction was to force Charles to withdraw his Declaration and re-impose Anglican domination in the Test Act of 1673. By this, all office-holders had to swear oaths of allegiance[1] and receive the sacrament according to the Anglican rite. Tiverton's members in this session of Parliament were Sir Henry Ford[2] and Sir Thomas Carew, whose death at the end of 1673, resulted in the election of the local merchant, Samuel Foote. This interesting man first appears in 1655 and in a very short time had become a much-respected inhabitant of the town. In 1664, he had a new house built for himself in Saint Peter Street on land belonging to the Greenway Charity[3], and he also set up a new rank of eleven seats in Saint Peter's Church[4]. He imported silks from Italy and Holland[5], and, like many others in Tiverton, would have been greatly encouraged by the peace between England and Holland forced on Charles in 1674.

The Test Act had been aimed at Catholics and Dissenters alike. Although Tiverton reveals no evidence of Catholics, the Compton Census of 1676[6] records as many as 500 dissenters[7]. Persecution resumed, and seems to have been harsher than ever. A group of

---

[1] the failure of some members of the Corporation of Tiverton to take these oaths led many people, especially Dissenters, to claim that these burgesses had forfeited the right to sit in judgement in the Borough courts. According to the Deputy Lieutenants of Devon 'eminent lawyers are clear in their opinion that the Corporation of Tiverton is dissolved, and that they have no legal power to act' (*CSPDom 1679-80*, 499-500), and the matter could only be resolved by pardoning the persons 'guilty of offences and neglects', or by granting a new charter. The result was indeed a pardon issued in November 1680 (DRO 5722) absolving those members of the Corporation who had not taken the oaths after the Test and Corporation Acts of 1673 .

[2] during the previous few years Ford had been in Ireland serving as Secretary of State, for which he was knighted in 1672.

[3] Saint Peter's GMH9.

[4] DRO R4/1/Z/PW4.

[5] *CalTreasB 1660-7*, 36.

[6] *Compton*, 269.

[7] Tiverton's Dissenters were the second largest group in Devon, after Plymouth's 900, followed by Dartmouth with 400, Axminster 175, Totnes 150, Modbury, Barnstaple and Northam each with 100, and the constituent parishes of Exeter had over 120 individuals.

Tiverton Baptists faced the J.P.s in August 1673[1], after William Facey had been accused of 'preaching and teaching' to a congregation that included Peter Carthew, Richard and Roger Cock, Thomas Dunsford and Michael Glass, stalwarts in the town's cloth industry. According to one of Thomas Dunsford's descendants, informers would often rush into his house on Sundays,

> 'violently seize the utensils in which the dinner for the family was dressing, throw their contents on the floor, and take away the vessels etc. to be sold to pay the arbitrary fines for nonconformity and attendance at the Meetings or conventicles of the Baptists'[2].

But Dissent was not without its own support. Baldwin Acland, yeoman of Hensleigh, died in 1674 worth a considerable £652. As well as personal bequests to their preachers, he gave £5 each to the town's Presbyterians, Congregationalists and Baptists[3]. He seems to have been making a political statement in favour of Dissent itself, rather than promoting a particular religious belief. A row broke out in 1675 over the election of the wardens for Saint Peter's Church. Two of them were picked annually; one for the country areas chosen by the portions in rotation, and one for the town. The right to choose the town's warden seems to have rested with the parishioners, but trouble arose in this year when the Corporation attempted to impose William Powell, although the parishioners had already chosen Thomas Keene, who happened to be a Congregationalist. The dispute was placed before the Bishop of Exeter's Consistory Court, which upheld the parishioners' rights[4]. Although this was the first such case to be noted, it was by no means to be the last.

There was a flurry of building work in and around the town during 1676, some of it the result of fire. A serious blaze occurred in the summer near Lowman Green, started near the Pound by a careless vagrant with a pipe of tobacco[5]. The full extent of the damage, however, is unclear: the *State Papers* claim 32 houses were destroyed, while Dunsford puts the figure as low as three[6]. The degree of subsequent activity recorded in the Churchwardens' Accounts suggests that the *State Papers* are the more accurate source. Payments were made to 'Thomas Langbridge at two several times, who was scalded in the fire, 2s... paid unto those who took pains in the late fire, £10', and 6d 'paid for beer for the workmen who wrought near the pound'. Money was also laid out for the 'town buckets, ladders and crooks', almost certainly to replace those lost in the blaze. Within a year, building was under way on the sites of the houses destroyed near Lowman Bridge[7].

---

[1] DRO QS74/40/1.
[2] *Memoirs of the Family of Dunsford.*
[3] *Moger Wills.*
[4] cited in Dunsford 1790, 443.
[5] *CSPDom 1676-7*, 233.
[6] 1790, 193.
[7] one of the properties is described as 'part of a tenement... in Barnes Hill' (DRO 2723M/LT63).

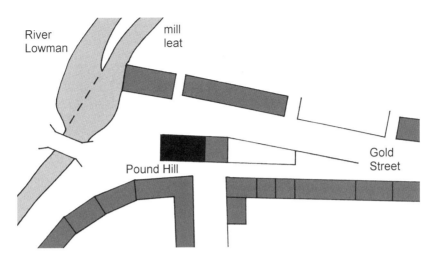

Sketch map of the Lowman Green area c.1790, showing Pound Hill (or Barne's Hill), and the buildings below it, which consisted of the Pound (in black), Westlake's House next to it, and a garden[1].

At the Castle, Gawyn Hill had taken the lease of a plot measuring 128 feet by 102[2], probably sited within the remains of the ancient walls, where he built three small dwelling houses. The Castle had long lost its noble residents, and had become yet another property to be developed. To the north of the town, the Head Weir on the Rive Exe was being renewed by George Hartnoll who paid for the work, after first obtaining permission from the lords of the manor to carry out the work[3].

The primacy of the established Church throughout this period, and long after, was maintained by a remarkable local dynasty, the Newte family. For five generations they provided rectors of the parish, and their status and authority in local affairs was unchallenged. In 1678, Richard Newte, Rector of both Clare and Tidcombe, died of gout. He was buried 'in woollen'[4] in the middle of the chancel of Saint Peter's, under a plain inscribed stone, unlike the very expensive tablet set up in his memory on the south wall. Conscientious to the end, his final few years had been spent in ensuring the future success of his children. Two years before his death he founded a fellowship and scholarship at Balliol for the benefit of scholars from Blundell's. The School's Treasurer records that in 1672 it had received £66 13s 4d from Newte 'in full of his agreement

---

[1] based on plan in DRO R4/1/PP4.   [2] DRO 2723M/Castle 3-5.
[3] KEO Box 8.
[4] one of the first under new regulations requiring all those buried to be clothed in wool, initiated to counteract a fall in the woollen cloth trade.

with the feoffees for his son John's commencement in Balliol College'[1]. Richard Newte's death led to an enquiry into the advowsons of Clare and Tidcombe. The verdict given by the Bishop of Exeter was that both benefices were in the gift of the Newte family. Accordingly, in February 1679, William Mervin, the deceased's son-in-law, was inducted to Clare, and John Newte, having only just obtained his M.A., was made Rector of Tidcombe[2].

This able young man began his incumbency with great vigour. New glebe terriers were drawn up in 1680, and the local method of collecting tithes was also recorded. Tithing had been carried on for hundreds of years and no doubt the procedures had been written down before, but this list[3] is the earliest to survive. The organisation needed to operate such a detailed system was formidable, as almost every agricultural product had to be divided by the landowner before he gave one tenth to the Church. The document shows that crops of wheat, barley, oats, rye and beans were tithed by 'stitches', but peas by rows, with a bough being placed on each share before it was carried away. Grass was to be stood in 'cocks' or 'pooks', and the division made at its first turning. As far as stock was concerned, lambs, piglets, and goslings were taken in kind, whereas a money payment of 4d a cow and 2d a heifer was preferred instead of the tithe on calves and milk. Four pence was to be paid for each hogshead of cider produced, and 2d per orchard and 1d per garden was taken, but the tithes of honey, wax, and hops were paid in kind. A novel arrangement had been devised for the former Courtenay parks of Ashley, New Park, and Godsbeare where the landowners were to provide a fat buck and a fat doe to be shared between the four portions. The order of choosing the joints of meat was made according to precedence; Pitt came first, followed by Clare, Tidcombe and, finally, Priors.

Perhaps Newte's enthusiasm was also driven by fears for the future. Even in Tiverton rumours of an imminent invasion were plentiful. The Churchwardens Accounts for 1678-9 had recorded payments to 'three drummers for beating drums upon the report of the invasion of the French', and 'for two hogsheads of beer that was given to those who met together upon a report of an invasion'. With the French, of course, would come Catholicism. In 1680, £3 was paid to Richard Thorne for 'making and setting up the desk to keep the *Book of Martyrs*[4] in'. There seemed a deep desire to cherish the memory of those persecuted for their Protestant faith during Mary's reign. This was a

---

[1] John Ham of Uplowman died in 1678 and established a fellowship and scholarship at Sidney Sussex and Balliol respectively for boys from Blundell's School (*Moger Wills*), and made the proviso that his youngest son was to be the first to benefit.

[2] (DRO Chanter 25). Later in the year, he also became the Rector of Pitt, on the death of George Pierce.

[3] contained in DRO R4/1/Z/PF2.

[4] a graphic account of those who suffered for the cause of Protestantism under Queen Mary, written by John Foxe and printed in 1559.

period of near hysteria in London, of the short-lived Exclusion Parliaments, and the Popish plot to replace Charles II with his brother James, Duke of York, helped by the French. Many in the Commons were determined to avoid the succession of the Catholic James, but they failed on each occasion. The terms 'Tory' and 'Whig', both derogatory, came into common use. The Whig faction claimed the right of Parliament to dictate the succession of the rightful heir; they appealed to nonconformists and even countenanced rebellion. Tories, on the other hand, were loyal to the Church of England and to the principle of support for the hereditary monarch even were he himself to be Catholic. The effects of political division appear locally in further persecution of conscience.

The full weight of the law was brought down upon Dissenters. In the autumn of 1681, Richard Saunders was arrested. Found guilty of preaching and not taking the Oath of Allegiance, he was sentenced at the County Quarter Sessions to six months in prison[1]. One third of all fines imposed for attending conventicles went to the King, and became known as the 'King's third'. This income could be considerable; cases heard in Tiverton yielded £8 6s 8d in 1681, and £1 1s 8d in the following year, in addition to £6 15s worth of goods taken from William Wood for having a meeting in his barn[2]. As well as the Court of Quarter Sessions, defendants could also be summoned to appear in the ecclesiastical courts, usually for non-attendance at church. It was commonplace for over 30 Tivertonians to be presented at one sitting of the Archdeacon's Court in Exeter. This reflects both the high number of Dissenters in the town and the busy activity of the church courts.

A few took to extremes, believing that only by assassinating both the King and the Duke of York could their cause be achieved. Groups of such men were to be found in several places. There was a 'factious club' numbering about 120 based at the White Hart in Bristol[3], and a similar group at the Salutation in Lombard Street, London, where the patrons included William Raddon, Thomas Parsons and Captain Humphrey Spurway[4]. These men were not Londoners but Devonians. As we have seen (p.113) Raddon and Spurway had plotted the death of the King in 1662, and had escaped soon after, and Parsons was a Baptist from the Membury area[5]. It was claimed they 'remitted most scandalous news to the Dissenters especially the Baptists in Chard, Honiton, Axminster, Colyton, Tiverton, Topsham and Exeter'[6], and gave them details of 'the readiness of the Dissenters in London'[7]. An entry in the *Calendar of State Papers* of 1682[8] implicates two prominent local men in these activities. It was related that a ship 'was loaded beyond sea for Mr Foote, a parliament man, and his son-in-law Mr Burrage, who trade as merchants', the cargo being 'pistols and guns'. Were these

---

[1] DRO QS1/12.
[2] *ib.*
[3] *CSPDom Jul-Sept 1683*, 166.
[4] *CSPDom 1682*, 356.
[5] *CSPDom 1683-4*, 362.
[6] *CSPDom Jul-Sept 1683*, 216-8.
[7] *CSPDom 1683-4*, 362.
[8] *CSPDom 1682*, 69.

weapons intended for use in an armed insurrection? Mr Foote was Samuel Foote, the Tiverton Member of Parliament, whose daughter Margaret had married Robert Burridge[1]. He (Burridge) came from a merchant family known in Tiverton for about 50 years, but originating in Lyme Regis, a town where the inhabitants were 'sufficiently known to his Majesty to be of dangerous and rebellious principles'[2].

After the failed Rye House Plot to murder the King and his brother in 1683, Charles took the opportunity to strike down many of his opponents. Some followed to exile their figurehead, the Duke of Monmouth, and of those who chose to remain, a few Whig magnates were executed, as were many small fry. A warrant was issued early in 1684 for the arrest of Stephen Lobb[3], for his supposed involvement in the Plot. He had appeared before the Devon Justices in 1675 for preaching at a conventicle in Tiverton and had married the daughter of Theophilus Polwheele, the Tiverton Congregationalist. At least one Tiverton Dissenter achieved conspicuous success, however. John Saunders, son of the ejected and persecuted Presbyterian minister Richard once found 'lurkeing' in Tiverton, was appointed Master of Blundell's in May 1684. It can only be supposed that this former pupil, a scholar of Sidney Sussex, had found favour among the feoffees, or else there were Whigs among them.

C̲harles II died early in 1685, but not before he had ensured the succession of his brother and had received the last rites as a Catholic. James II began well, confirming the privileges of the Church of England and calling a Parliament which, as was to be expected, was emphatically Royalist. As usual, Tiverton celebrated; £1 4s was paid 'for beer expended at the King's coming to the crown', and a further 8s 6d for wood 'spent in the bonfire Coronation Day'[4]. In place of Sir Henry Ford and Samuel Foote, and in obedience to the King's instructions that only 'persons of approved loyalty and affection to the Government be chosen'[5], Tiverton's burgesses elected Sir Hugh Acland of Killerton, and William Coleman of Gornhay. They took their seats in May, the same month that orders were despatched to Deputy-Lieutenants and Mayors to disarm 'all dangerous and suspected persons'[6]. The borough of Tiverton, however, seems to have pre-empted this move, for they had already issued warrants to

---

[1] Burridge had received a lease of the Great House in Saint Peter Street, in addition to £2,200 for the marriage portion (deeds in possession of Mid Devon District Council).
[2] CSPDom 1683-4, 179. [3] ib., 393.
[4] Churchwardens' Accounts. [5] cited in Earle 1977, 49.
[6] ib., 54.

apprehend ten persons, of whom two were Robert Carel and Thomas Jones, both known Dissenters[1].

But trouble was on its way from abroad. Charles II's illegitimate son, the Protestant Duke of Monmouth, once Captain-General of the English army, revived the ambitions of Whig exiles and exclusionists. His small band landed at Lyme on June 11th 1685 and gathered more support as it passed through east Devon and south Somerset. The local militia did nothing to engage him, but few gentry declared for his cause. Monmouth, possibly considering Tiverton as a target for recruitment, made for the town. He never arrived, though, perhaps because of the unexplained presence there of George Monck, the Duke of Albemarle. Nevertheless, Tiverton men did join the rebel army, which on June 18th arrived at Taunton where they proclaimed Monmouth the rightful king. Encouraged by these events, the force, now numbering about 5,000, struck out for Bristol where they expected additional recruits. They did not materialise, however, and Monmouth's rather simplistic plan of heading for the main prize, London, was in tatters. He turned his back on his goal and, rather aimlessly, marched westwards.

The royal army, under the command of the Earl of Feversham and John Churchill[2], moved out from Bristol to engage the rebels on the Somerset Levels. As is well known, Monmouth attempted a night attack on a part of this force. What could have been a surprise victory near King's Sedgemoor on July 15th blundered into devastating defeat, leaving 300 rebel corpses, some of which were butchered after the battle. A further 22 rebels were hanged during the following day, and the prisoners, about 500, were herded into the nearby church of Weston Zoyland. News of Monmouth's defeat was marked at Tiverton by the bells of Saint Peter's; there was little to celebrate locally in the repercussions that followed. They bear closer examination.

The captives were dispersed to prisons throughout the Southwest to await trial. In addition, others were arrested as a result of information given to the authorities. James placed the Lord Chief Justice, George Jeffreys, in charge of the criminal proceedings. Cases were heard at an alarming rate; defendants did not get sufficient time to offer a proper defence, but Jeffreys probably did not actually transgress the word of the law. At least 21 Tiverton men can be identified from the trial documents[3], and a further 32 others whose origins are not given, have names that occur in contemporary documents as Tivertonians[4]. Of the identifiable men from the town, Henry Beedle, Philip Collins, Philip Holben, John Mellard and Robert Pitt are simply recorded as having been 'with the late duke of Monmouth', and were probably whipped and fined, or given a short prison sentence. Four others are recorded as being imprisoned: Humphrey Bidgood and Thomas Pitt at Exeter, Thomas Filmore in Wiltshire, and John Theadrock at Wells.

---

[1] DRO QS15/29/20.   [2] later Duke of Marlborough.
[3] *Monmouth.*
[4] including the names of Burridge, Osmond, Alstone, Cornish and Denham.

Filmore died before his trial and possibly the same fate befell Theadrock, said to have been wounded at Sedgemoor. Bidgood was more fortunate; he was pardoned[1], probably after paying a fine. Jeffreys often extorted money from the prisoners in return for their freedom. A large number of the rebels, over 800 in all, were transported to the colonies in the West Indies and sold into slavery. Eight Tivertonians received that punishment, with John Chilcott, James and John Cockram, George Snow and William Wooldridge sent to Barbados, John Finnimore and Henry Rookes to Jamaica, and Thomas Churchouse to Nevis or Saint Kitts[2]. John Marwood was also sentenced at Taunton to be transported but does not appear on any of the ships' lists, probably indicating that he either escaped or bought his freedom. Conditions awaiting the transportees were harsh, and, for two at least, John Cockram and William Wooldridge, a burial in Barbados was to be the end of their story.

Two men from Tiverton were sentenced to death for their part in the rebellion. John Glover alias Tucker was to be hanged on Redcliffe Hill, Bristol, but died before the appointed day. The other, Richard Pearce, met his fate either at Glastonbury or Pensford[3]. The executions were not a quick despatch, for guilty traitors were by law hung, drawn, and quartered. The dismembered body parts were sent far and wide. Tiverton received its share[4]. A Dissenting minister's head was fixed on the Market Cross in Fore Street, the quarters of two men were displayed on poles at the east end of the town near Down's Lane, at the first crossways leading to Bampton, at Waldron's Almshouses, and at the south end of Westexe[5]. These stinking limbs were to serve as a deterrent - but to whom?

For a long time historians have viewed Monmouth's men as a disorganised collection of peasants foolishly following a claimant to the throne. A glance at the individuals who stood trial, however, reveals a different picture. Of the 14 Tiverton men whose occupations are known, only one, Henry Beedle, was closely connected with the land. He held the lease of Plushayes, Norwood and Whiddon[6], so he can hardly be termed a peasant. The remainder comprised the merchant, Humphrey Bidgood, and 12 clothworkers, of whom six were combers, three weavers, one a sergemaker, one a tailor and Henry Rookes, a comber's salter. By taking part in the rebellion they had put their life, livelihood and trade at stake. They certainly had a lot

---

[1] *CalTreasB 1685-9*, 425.

[2] Churchouse may have shared the passage with another man of Tiverton, John Jones. The situation is unclear, however, as there were two men with this name – one of Tiverton, the other from Ilchester - both of whom were ordered to be transported, but one escaped before he reached port.

[3] the uncertainty arising again from the existence of two persons with the same name.

[4] *HMC Pine Coffin*, 373.   [5] Dunsford 1790, 194-6.

[6] DRO 5003M/E1.

to lose. As for the religious affiliations of the rebels they can be determined, although to a lesser extent. Bidgood and Filmore had been censured for attending a conventicle 12 years previously[1]. The Speeds, father and son, well-attested Presbyterians, also took part in the rebellion, but evaded capture[2]. Another Dissenter, and one of the few gentry to give assistance to Monmouth, Sir Edmund Prideaux of Forde Abbey, was imprisoned, but was offered a pardon for £14,760[3]. If, as it seems, the rebels were mainly artisans and, probably, Dissenters, it is surprising that only 20 or 30 men were local. Less than 1,500 men stood trial, whereas Monmouth's army had numbered more than 5,000. What happened to the others? Many of them would have escaped the battlefield and been shielded by sympathisers, especially in places like Tiverton, with comparatively large dissenting and artisan populations. The town's well-established trade links with the Netherlands could also have been put to good use to provide an escape route. A considerable number of Westcountrymen did indeed seek refuge in the Netherlands, and were given incentives to set up cloth manufactories at such places as Leeuwarden, Luneburg and Groningen[4].

After Sedgemoor, James began to believe he could obtain relief for his fellow-Catholics and Dissenters without opposition. Early in 1687 he pardoned many people formerly considered recusants, including Theophilus Polwheele, Peter Bere, George Pile, Matthew Wood, Alexander Johns, George Martin, Thomas Glasse and Peter Carthew, all of Tiverton[5]. In April, he, too, issued a Declaration of Indulgence, granting freedom of worship to Dissenters and Catholics. The various congregations came out into the open again. The Baptists opened a chapel in Newport Street, very near their present site, and appointed an Irishman, Roger Haldanby, as the first Pastor. By the end of the year their congregation consisted of 57 men and 62 women[6], and their income was supplemented by a bequest from Elizabeth Fursdon[7]. The Congregationalists or Independents, under their tireless preacher, Theophilus Polwheele, built a meetinghouse at the Steps, on the west side of Saint Peter Street, below Chilcott's School. A meetinghouse was opened by the Presbyterians in Back Lane in Westexe, where the officiating minister was Richard Saunders. Like Polwheele,

---

[1] DRO QS74/40/1.   [2] *CSPDom 1685*, 405.

[3] in order to raise this fortune he was forced to mortgage his lands, of which his manor of Craze Lowman and the 400 acres of East Chevithorne raised £2,000 (DRO 147Z/T1).

[4] (see Earle 1977, 156-7). The workers were pardoned in the summer of 1686, and many returned home (*ib.*, 159).

[5] *CSPDom 1686-7*, 369.

[6] (DRO 3958D/1). Although, the Minute Book begins in this year, it emphatically states that 'our former book containing matters of this nature being lost in the late times of trouble'.

[7] DRO 3958D add/9.

Saunders had been harshly persecuted in his lifetime but now he, too, led a free congregation.

The apparent benevolence of James soon ended, however. Late in 1687 Tiverton's Mayor, seven capital and five assistant burgesses and the Town Clerk were all dismissed from office, and early in the New Year orders went out for the removal of the Recorder, the Duke of Albemarle, his deputy, and three more burgesses. The much-depleted Corporation nevertheless remained 'obstinately disobeying the royal mandate', but it was dissolved, and a new Borough Charter drawn up[1]. Tiverton, of course, was by no means alone. In Devon, Barnstaple, Totnes, Bradninch, and Exeter had to submit. Indeed, most borough charters were re-modelled under threat of losing self-government. James needed a compliant Parliament. When a male heir was born in June 1688, the dynasty and Catholicism seemed secure. Borough corporations were filled with Catholics or High Churchmen, as were the offices of Lord Lieutenant, Deputy-Lieutenant, and magistrates throughout the country. Tiverton's redrawn charter was issued on September 11th 1688, with changes to personnel rather than powers. The Mayor named in the document was Roger Pomeroy of Sandridge House in Stoke Gabriel, an outsider. Sir John Southcott, a Catholic zealot who had successfully acquired a new charter for Totnes in this year[2], was made a capital burgess. Two more strangers placed on the Corporation were Edward Cary of Torr Abbey and Samuel Sainthill of Bradninch, both formerly strong supporters of Charles I. Roger, Earl of Castlemaine, one of the cabal of Catholics who made up James' inner circle of advisers, was made Recorder. For a town where Catholics had always been extremely rare, Tiverton could now count at least a handful among its burgesses. The picture was similar elsewhere; Catholics were gaining posts and power disproportionate to their number and tradition.

Nevertheless, Dissenters retained a noticeable presence on the new Corporation. Four of the burgesses signed an appeal by the Congregational Church for Samuel Bartlett to assist the ageing Theophilus Polwheele[3]. They were Richard Prowse, who had sought to obtain the new charter, Thomas Keene, Peter Bere senior and Nicholas Hitchcock. Other burgesses considered Dissenters were William Deyman, once charged with non-payment of church rates, and Bernard Goddard, previously found guilty of not receiving the sacrament. John Bere was a High Churchman[4], and John Sibley was likely to have been. As for the rest, neither their political nor religious leanings can be ascertained. They comprised men connected with the cloth industry, and a small, but probably important, group of five whose appearance in this charter marks their first recorded link with the town. They were Mark Robinson, William Lewis, Bartholomew Richards, and James and Nicholas Sheppard. Perhaps, as had

---

[1] Henning 1983, 209.
[2] *CSPDom 1687-9*, 183.
[3] *ExeterAss*, 123.
[4] Henning 1983, 209.

happened in 1655, they had been introduced to the borough because of their religious inclinations.

By the time Tiverton received its new charter in 1688, it was clear that the political nation was again on the verge of upheaval. Seven bishops were tried for seditious libel, having challenged the legality of James' Declaration of Indulgence. The King had never realised how much his position depended on the loyalty of Anglicans until that loyalty was threatened. Those who had been biding their time, waiting for James' daughter, the Protestant Mary, to assume the throne, had been thwarted by the birth of his son which seemed to assure a Catholic succession. They turned in hope to the United Provinces where Princess Mary lived with her husband William, the Prince of Orange. An invitation was sent asking them to intervene in the situation. Meanwhile, James had been offered military aid from Louis XIV, but declined, and Louis went on to ravage the Rhineland. All of Europe seemed set for open conflict. William of Orange, in his attempt to unite the Netherlands, Austria, Spain and some of the German states against France, would rather have England on his side, so, for good political and personal reasons, he began to plan an invasion.

A large force landed in Torbay on November 5th, aided by an easterly 'Protestant' wind which confined the English navy to port. William's men soon reached Exeter and entered the city with great pomp. They met with no resistance. On the contrary, many men, including gentry and Protestant army officers began to flock to William. Troops of horse were soon advanced to ease the progress toward Bristol[1]. One such troop came to Tiverton led by a Captain Cunningham who, on entering the town, could not fail to notice a head and quarters of the Monmouth rebels still on display. He ordered their removal and the remains were buried in Saint Peter's churchyard[2]. An impasse before London was resolved when James, just before Christmas, lost his nerve and fled to France. A Parliament was summoned in February and laid down the main points of the constitutional settlement later enacted, the so-called Revolutionary Settlement. James was declared to have abdicated, and the throne therefore being vacant was offered jointly to William and Mary. A Bill of Rights, passed in October 1689, made it illegal for the monarch to dispense with the law at will, and to suspend laws without Parliament's permission. Parliamentary agreement was necessary before levying taxes and maintaining a standing army during peacetime. The succession to the throne was to remain exclusively Protestant. Earlier in the session, Dissenters were at last rewarded for their loyalty by 'an Act relieving tender consciences', granting them the right to worship freely with their own preachers and teachers. The Declaration of Indulgence finally became law. Nonconformists had to swear oaths of allegiance to the crown and to profess the Christian faith, but they were still denied political offices, and the

---

[1] *HMC Portland vol IV*, 207.   [2] Dunsford 1790, 197-200.

measures did not apply to Catholics or Unitarians.

Sadly, Theophilus Polwheele did not live to see the Bill become law. The leader of Tiverton's Congregationalists was buried at Saint Peter's. Almost immediately, his congregation began to argue amongst themselves. Had differences become important now that persecution was lifted, or, more likely, had Polwheele's strong leadership suppressed matters which, after his death, had come to the surface? A Mr Keene and others were allegedly 'destroying the peace of the church' and refusing to agree to arbitration[1]. The decision was taken to withhold communion from them until they repented. The matter must have been resolved, for a decade later Thomas Keene, in his will, left a piece of land to this meeting at the Steps[2]. The long-suffering Presbyterian minister, Richard Saunders, had good reason to celebrate, as he was chosen in 1691 to be Moderator of the first meeting of the Association of the United Brethren of Devon and Cornwall, which was held at Tiverton[3].

Samuel Foote, M.P. for Tiverton intermittently since 1673, died in March 1691, aged 66. From 1655, when he was first introduced to the Corporation, he had become deeply embroiled in the politics and trade of the town, and had earned the respect and trust of its citizens. His name would die out in the area, as he left only daughters. However, through marriage, the Footes had connections to the Leigh, Cock, Parrett and Cordwent families, as well as to the more prominent Burridges, Cruwys and Newtes. Only three months after Samuel's death his daughter Elizabeth became the wife of Dennis Glynn of Glynn, the owner of the small manor of Farleigh.

In the early 1690s increasing prosperity arising from the cloth trade seems to have imbued Tiverton's Corporation with renewed confidence. Those members living in the town took the opportunity to sort out some long-standing problems. The Borough Charter stated that burgesses had to be resident in the town, although on many occasions this rule had been flouted. Three non-residents, John Forse of Silverton, Anthony Salter of Cullompton and Peter Pierce of Molland, were called to account in 1691[4]. Everything seems to have been agreed amicably; Forse resigned in the following year, Salter in 1693, but the actions of Pierce are not recorded. More important was the issue of Elmore. The land, given in the 14th century (see p.31) for the use of the poor of Tiverton, probably passed to the Crown on the demise of the Courtenays. No records survive to tell us how the gift had been administered, or how the poor had benefited from it, but Elmore was probably looked upon as common land, with stock being allowed to graze there. Over time, it had been encroached upon; buildings had been put up, and small plots enclosed either as gardens or fields. In 1686, a John Sibley had been granted a lease of Elmore, described as

---

[1] *ExeterAss*, 123.
[3] *ExeterAss*, 1-4.

[2] Dunsford 1790, 150-1.
[4] DRO R4/1/C301.

'a plot of barren waste ground containing 12 or 14 acres full of pits and holes, very noisome to the inhabitants and of little or no profit to anyone, and that no-one claimed interest, but that it belonged to the Crown' [1].

Three months later, one Richard Cole filed a petition claiming that Sibley had duped the King as Elmore actually covered 150 acres[2]. The Treasury ordered Cole to sue Sibley as his assertions were found to be true. Although Cole appears not to have taken up the case, the Corporation did. In 1692 the Treasury granted them a lease of the land (stated to be about 150 acres), at a rent of £1 a year. It was to remain in effect for 99 years 'for the use and benefit of the poor of the town', with provisos that the Corporation 'shall assert the Crown title' and shall 'enclose, fence, drain and level' the ground[3]. The Corporation sub-let the land[4] in plots of no more than five acres, apart from one covering 33 acres, to new tenants, all of whom were tradesmen[5].

Tiverton
Rhode Island

Proposed town seal of Tiverton, Rhode Island, USA. The settlement was granted township status in June 1694. It had been founded on land bought from the Wampanoag Indians in 1637. No links have been established between the founders and Tiverton, Devon, but clearly the town held enough significance to provide the name. The motif shown above – a gold fishnet on a blue background – was meant to signify a fishing net; the settlement has always been associated with fishing.

---

[1] recited in *CalTreasB 1689-92*, 1494-5.   [2] *CalTreasB 1685-9*, 1465.
[3] *CalTreasB 1689-92*, 1657.   [4] contained in DRO R4/1/C93.
[5] e.g. William Morrish carpenter, Robert Pingstone and Nicholas Crocker shoemakers, Thomas Johns weaver, Roger Baker fuller.

In the triennial elections of 1695, Tiverton returned Thomas Bere once more, and with him Charles Spencer[1]. Spencer had only just come of age, and was promoted by his father, Robert, the Earl of Sunderland, a notorious political chameleon soon to become Lord Chancellor. Unlike his father, Charles's political views seemed, at this stage, to be distinctly Whiggish, even radical, as he announced that 'he hoped to see the day when there should not be a peer in England'[2]. Tiverton's prosperity was beginning to attract distinguished outsiders, both politically and commercially. Many of the interested people were Londoners, such as Charles Herle, a merchant-tailor, who lent money to Richard Prowse on security of Hayne, Marsh, and other lands[3]. Others included Jerome Clutterbuck, haberdasher, who had property in Fore Street[4], and the merchant Nehemiah Barne who took on a mortgage of lands in Tiverton for £700[5]. Most of these individuals had one thing in common, the cloth industry, which probably indicates how they came to be involved in dealings with the town or its citizens. Perhaps the most significant newcomer was Oliver Peard, of whose family we shall hear a lot more. He first arrived in Tiverton in 1695, coming from a rich trading family with branches in Barnstaple and Plymouth, the latter having strong commercial links with Barbados. Oliver married Elizabeth Blagdon in September, and settled in Tiverton where he would make great use of the undoubted commercial expertise inherited from his family.

Robert Burridge, the late Samuel Foote's son-in-law, secured success at this time. In 1696, he was appointed one of the Receivers-General of both the Land Tax[6] and the Hearth Tax for Devon and Exeter[7]. Such appointments would from this time become the virtual monopoly of a Tiverton merchant[8]. The large amount of money (and temptation) to be accumulated each year had by this time exceeded £10,000. The Whigs had introduced the Land Tax in an attempt to pay for William's expensive and almost perpetual war against France. A more fundamental change had modernised Stuart public finance by this time. The King's debt became a National Debt when the Bank of England raised loans and issued bills in 1694. Two years later, a bank was opened in Exeter, advertising that it would negotiate foreign and domestic bills from places such as Taunton and Tiverton to London[9]. The setting up of a regular postal

---

[1] he had also been elected for Hedon in Yorkshire, but preferred Tiverton.
[2] cited in *DNB*.   [3] KEO Box 15.
[4] Saint Peter's GFS29.   [5] KEO Box 17.
[6] the Land Tax was first introduced in 1691, levied at a rate of 4s in the £.
[7] *CalTreasB 1693-6*, 1308 and *1696-7*, 141 respectively.
[8] although George Clarke's appointment a generation earlier (see p.115) was the first such post gained by a man from the town.
[9] cited in Hoskins 1935, 26.

service between Exeter and Bristol in 1696 made it much easier to send bills of exchange, promissory notes, and ordinary letters[1]. The postmaster at Exeter was required to keep 'account of all the letters and for being a check on all the other postmasters [on this route] and for riding twice a week between Exeter and Tiverton'[2]. Another postmaster would reside at Tiverton; his duties included riding twice a week to Exeter and, in the other direction, to Wellington, for an annual salary of £33. Similarly, his opposite number in Wellington rode to Tiverton and Taunton for £29, and so on through Bridgwater to Bristol.

The organ built by Christian Smith in 1696 for Saint Peter's Church.

A sense of security and prosperity during William's reign led many to make long-term plans. In 1695 the Rev. John Newte bought John Northcote's shares in the farms of Plushayes and Buckhayes, both in the far north of Tiverton parish[3], and he granted half a field at Shrinkhill to the portioners. The annual value of this field, amounting to 30s, was to be used to buy 'devotional books' and to maintain his father's monument in Saint Peter's Church[4]. The field became known as Bible Field. He also gave £20

---

[1] although such services for official correspondence had existed for over two centuries, the idea of a public post was only put into practice shortly before the Civil War.
[2] *CalTreasB 1696-7,* 303.
[3] (DRO 2630M/T/9/6/1a-b). An alternative name for Plushayes was Lower Norwood.
[4] *Saint Peters Benefactions Book.*

towards the cost of an organ in Saint Peter's, a symbolic instrument that he would defend in a sermon preached at its dedication in 1696. It was built by Christian Smith, a German immigrant, and the younger brother of the distinguished Bernard Smith who had been appointed the King's organ maker in 1681. Although Bernard was the more famous, being responsible for the organs at Westminster Abbey, Wells Cathedral, and Saint Paul's, London, Christian was no novice, having himself installed an organ at Norwich Cathedral. During his visit to Tiverton he was accompanied by his family, as the Saint Peter's register records the baptism of his daughter, Edea, in November 1696. Built in the loft over the rood screen, the organ cost more than originally envisaged; additional amounts were necessary for 'the front of the organ loft', for 'making the courtins for the organ', as well as 3s 6d to Humphrey Burton 'for a psalm book for the organ'[1]. The instrument with its magnificent case retains its splendour today.

Commercial success was again the catalyst of charitable benefaction. As John Greenway, John Waldron, and George Slee before him, the clothier John Alstone founded almshouses. In 1696, he gave £500 to be used to build houses in Birchen Lane, Westexe, to accommodate six poor fullers, and to buy land for their benefit[2]. Alstone's foundation, however, seems to have been abused for some time[3], and no sign of it survives. More significant were the bequests of Mary Rice, who died in 1698. She left goods to the value of more than £2,000, and, even after 'her primary engagements' had been met, the residue was still substantial[4]. She stipulated that this money was to be used to buy land, from which the profits were to be paid to her poor relatives. After their deaths, the benefit was to pass to poor persons chosen by her trustees. In 1699 they had purchased Rix near Bolham[5] and a large house near Exe Bridge, which we know better today as the White Ball Inn. Yet more important was a bequest of £50 given to the magistrates of Tiverton by her husband, Thomas Rice, who had predeceased Mary. This was conditional on their beginning to build a hospital for the poor before June 24th 1698[6].

The need had clearly been perceived. A Bill 'for erecting an hospital and workhouse, or house of correction, in Tiverton, and for the better governing thereof, and relief of the poor there'[7] was placed before Parliament on January 28th 1698 by Charles Spencer, one of the town's M.P.s. It was speedily processed, and became law in April[8]. The site chosen for the Hospital or Workhouse was a field known as the Deanes,

---

[1] Burton himself is an interesting figure. Described as a bookseller of Tiverton (DRO Z1/34/2/44), he had received the royal appointment in 1694 as one of the 'distributors of stamped parchment and paper' for Somerset (*CalTreasB 1693-6*, 672.).

[2] cited in Dunsford 1790, 148-9.

[3] see *Charities 1826*, 94-6, for its history.

[4] Harding 1845, iii, 220.

[5] DRO 213M/PF3-4.

[6] Harding 1845, iii, 209.

[7] *JHC 1697-9*, 72.

[8] *ib.*, 191.

belonging to Greenway's Charity. At the time this was a rural location, surrounded by fields. An otherwise-unknown architect, John Abbot[1] designed the building, and an account book of the Hospital[2] records that Edward Hinton made the bricks of clay dug from an adjacent field. Dunsford states[3] that the building took six years to finish and its final cost was in excess of £3,000.

The Hospital or Workhouse built in 1698 on the site now occupied by Belmont Hospital.

The establishment was placed under the control of a Governor, Deputy Governor, and the Guardians of the Poor. The Guardians, comprising the Borough Corporation, the Recorder, the Portreeve and 25 of the 'ablest and discreetest inhabitants', were elected by those citizens who were rated at 1d a week or more. Any man who charitably gave £50, however, could become a Guardian, and those who had contributed £100 toward the building costs would be exempt from paying rates for six years. The Guardians were given the power to levy the poor rate, to correct and punish the paupers in the house, to examine 'what poor are in the town', and apprehend rogues and vagrants 'and set them to work for three years'. The positions held in this establishment, whether Governor, Deputy Governor, Treasurer or one of the Guardians, provided further opportunities for members of the Corporation. The same names appear among the Churchwardens, not all of them even then exclusively Anglican. It could be said that a wider civic apprenticeship had been instigated in Tiverton.

The Hospital was a major construction, but not by any means the only building work going on. Significant repairs were being made at both Slee's and Waldron's

---

[1] according to Little 1953, 116.
[2] DRO R4/1/Z/PO12.
[3] 1790, 360.

Almshouses, and, at the lower end of Bampton Street, the trustees of the Exe Bridge lands[1] built a Corn Market. At the Bridewell prison in Saint Andrew Street, the Mayor had agreed to set up a horse-driven malt mill[2]. The Corporation contributed £145 6s 3d to its construction, and in 1699 it was leased to Roger Chamberlain and Francis Plympton for three years. This establishment, together with the Hospital where, immediately after the completion of the building, wool was being carded and cloth made, sent out a strong message to the criminal, idle and poor of Tiverton. Their sustenance would have to be paid for by work.

The extreme weather of the 1690s heightened concern for the poor. In addition to successive bad harvests, extreme cold, and high winds, Tiverton experienced an earthquake in September 1692, a severe flood just three months later, and in December 1695 a second inundation that saw the waters so high that 'the boys rowed about in tubs and trundles in Mr Peter Blundell's school and green'[3]. The two floods caused a great deal of damage and many people were thrown out of work. The situation was brought into sharp focus in 1697 when the poor rate collected in the parish exceeded £1,000 for the first time[4]. But that was not the full extent of the problem. There was an equally sharp rise in the costs of litigation needed to establish responsibility for providing claimants with relief – no parish wanted to take on more paupers than they were legally obliged to. Although the Justices of Tiverton were empowered to issue settlement orders in their own Sessions, appeals against their decision went before the County Quarter Sessions. One worrying aspect of poor relief at this time was the large migrant population. Their reasons for being on the move were varied. Many tended to leave places experiencing trade difficulties for successful towns, and others escaped from troubled areas. The struggle in Ireland between James II and William of Orange forced many of that country's poor to flee to the West of England in the early 1690s, and several of them obtained work in the woollen trade. By the end of the decade, however, the situation in Ireland had become relatively peaceful and many of them returned and established the trade there. This led the 'merchants, fullers, clothiers etc of Tiverton and parts adjacent'[5] to complain to Parliament in 1698 about the competition from cheap Irish cloth. More emphatically, John Upcott, the Mayor of Tiverton, and 482 other persons (again, of 'Tiverton and adjacent parts') put their names to a petition in support of a Parliamentary Bill to

---

[1] DRO 257M/T16.   [2] DRO R4/1/C93.

[3] Dunsford 1790, 202-3.

[4] this represented a vast increase from 1612 when it stood at a mere £120 (Dunsford 1790, 460).

[5] *JHC 1697-9*, 63-4.

encourage woollen manufacture in England and protecting it from the export of woollen goods from Ireland[1].

Migration to Holland was also causing the same problems, as workers there could undercut the price of Tiverton cloth[2]. We do not know precisely how many local people emigrated, the only clue being the travel passes granted at the time. Thomas Gilbert received one in August 1697[3], but he remains the only person whose home town is specifically given as Tiverton. Passes were issued to Richard Spurway merchant[4], Samuel Dyer weaver, and Thomas Rudd[5], without naming their town of origin, although the names are familiar. All the passes, of course, may have been required for business reasons rather than emigration. No one questions the strong trade links with Holland. There was at Tiverton, as at Exeter and Topsham, a flourishing colony of Dutch merchants as well as a few Germans[6]. Documentary evidence of them is elusive, but a marriage license was sought in August 1700 for Balthazar Vanhulthen of Tiverton[7], a name hardly Devonian.

The end of the War of the Grand Alliance in September 1697 briefly reopened French markets to Tiverton. Nevertheless, local merchants were once more urging active Government protection. In 1699, a petition was sent to the Commons asking it to promote the use of woollen goods which were 'greatly prejudiced by the use of East India silks and calicoes'[8]. Again, a year later they petitioned Parliament, emphasising that 'the sole dependence of the town and adjacent parts is upon the woollen manufacture'[9]. On this occasion their worries centred on Flanders' restriction of English imports in retaliation for the duties imposed on Flemish linen. Cross-channel trade was further hampered by the outbreak of war on the death of Charles II of Spain in 1700. The conflict, known as the War of the Spanish Succession, would see Louis XIV of France promote his grandson Philip to the Spanish throne, whereas most of the rest of Europe supported Charles, the son of the Holy Roman Emperor. One of the French King's first moves was to prohibit exports from England to France and Spain.

Competition also came from within England itself. The cloth industry of East Anglia was affecting that of the West Country; the threat from their 'New Draperies' (see p.96) had not been totally neutralised, and lower labour costs in the eastern region had become a crucial factor. Cloth workers' wages around Norwich were almost 40%

---

[1] (*HMC Lords 1697-9*, 131). Links with Ireland were often strengthened by marriages, with two examples in 1697-8: Christopher Gay of Cork married Sarah Wood of Tiverton, and the widow Joan Howard married an Irishman Derby Kennedy. This situation is hardly surprising with the proximity of Ireland to the prosperous Bristol Channel ports of Bideford, Barnstaple, Ilfracombe, Minehead, Watchet and Bridgwater.

[2] *JHC 1693-7*, 743.
[3] *CalTreasB 1697*, 279.
[4] *CSPDom 1695*, 138.
[5] *CSPDom 1697*, 260 and 234.
[6] Wilson 1965, 189.
[7] DRO Chanter 47.
[8] *JHC 1697-9*, 641.
[9] *JHC 1699-1702*, 156.

lower than in the west. One reason given for the difference is that workers' clubs were keeping wages in Devon and Somerset artificially high[1]. According to Dunsford[2], one such club was established at Tiverton on June 15th 1700. This Society of Woolcombers was formed 'to support their sick, aged and infirm, and to preserve their due claims, rights and privileges'. This raises the question of the fate of those earlier societies, of weavers and fullers, established in the 1550s (see p.72) – had they folded or were they still in existence? Merchants were always suspicious of the activities of such groups, and generally viewed them as breeding-grounds for radicalism and insurrection.

In 1702 Charles Spencer succeeded his father as Earl of Sunderland[3], and vacated his Parliamentary seat for Tiverton. In his place, the Corporation chose Robert Burridge. He had recently laid out over £350 to defend the Corporation in court cases, and he was the person who had paid for the building of the Corporation malt mill at the Bridewell, for which he was given the profits until his money was recouped[4]. On taking a seat in the Commons, he had to relinquish his duties as collector of taxes, but his son Samuel was easily persuaded to succeed him. He provided £25,000 security for collecting the Land Tax and £7,000 for the duties on Marriages and on Houses[5]. Robert Burridge had become conspicuously rich. He owned the Great House, Hensleigh, the White Hart Inn, Coombutler, Smallridge and Firebeacon[6].

---

[1] Wilson 1965, 291.   [2] 1790, 205.
[3] the Earl no doubt attributed his earlier views to youthful indiscretion (see p.130).
[4] DRO R4/1/C93.   [5] CalTreasB 1702, 368 and 383.
[6] DRO 2547M/SS1/8.

10 Tories and Whigs

The bells of Saint Peter's Church solemnly tolled in March 1702 on the death of William of Orange. Soon afterwards, however, they rang joyous peals when his sister-in-law, Anne, the daughter of James II, became Queen. Her coronation and 'proclaiming day' was celebrated in Tiverton with the help of beer to the value of £12 17s 6d[1], but her accession was greeted with some apprehension. She came to the throne at a time when the Grand Alliance seemed to hold the upper hand over Spain and France, but the allies were unsure of her commitment to the War and, looking ahead, were worried about her successor. Tragically, Anne was seemingly incapable of producing an heir; out of no less than 18 pregnancies, only one child survived infancy, and he had died in 1700. Parliament proposed that, on her death, the crown should pass to the Protestant Hanoverian descendants of James I, rejecting the legitimate hereditary claim of James II's son, who had been recognised as heir apparent by Louis XIV of France and by some High Church Tories. This solution was legalised as the Settlement Act; it immediately revived Dutch support, and was reinforced by Anne's appointment of John Churchill as Captain-General of the English forces.

War inevitably increased the hazards of overseas trade. Cloth merchants of Exeter, Tiverton, and Topsham petitioned for convoys of ships to operate between Exeter and Rotterdam[2], in an attempt to reduce the danger of attack. Another way was to shorten the sea journey drastically by sending the bales of cloth overland to London, leaving just the short voyage across the Channel[3]. Yet trade was flourishing, especially between Tiverton and Dutch merchants. In the Dutch National Archive there are letter books containing correspondence between one Amsterdam merchant, David Leeuw, and no fewer than seven Tivertonians; John Andrews[4], George Coles, John Upcott, William and Samuel Lewis, Samuel Bawdon and the ubiquitous Robert Burridge[5]. These same men were probably the 'buyers of serges on commission for foreigners' trying to bring in Irish wool 'to the prejudice of the woollen manufacture and the ruin of all the staple

---

[1] DRO R4/1/Z/PO12. [2] *PC Unbound pt I*, PC1/2/9.

[3] even this crossing suffered in the severe storm that swept across Europe in November 1703. Several vessels were destroyed, and for many days after the coastlines were littered with bodies. The winds were so strong even in Tiverton that Dunsford noted the discovery of a storm petrel in a Barrington Street orchard, and states that Saint Peter's Church 'was uncovered' as were many of the houses in the town (1790, 205-6).

[4] he regularly bought wool, oil, and dyestuffs in Holland to sell to Tiverton's clothiers (PRO C12/1951/11).

[5] cited in Wilson 1941, 37.

ports' deplored in a 1704 petition from the town's merchants and serge makers[1]. Such activity was guaranteed to bring trouble. The cloth workers were so incensed that they rioted, or at least threatened to do so. The events are unclear, but no less a visitor than the great novelist and pamphleteer Daniel Defoe wrote from Tiverton on August 12th that 'here the alarm of the Devonshire justices hurried me too fast'[2]. At the time he was on his travels 'employed in several honourable though secret services'[3]; whether these involved Tiverton directly we do not know.

Ireland again posed a threat to the local cloth industry in 1706. On this occasion, the main bone of contention was a Parliamentary Bill proposing to make New Ross in Wexford a port for shipping Irish wool to England. Petitions were sent from Tiverton complaining patriotically that this would lead to wool being smuggled to France[4], and criticising the import of cheap worsted and woollen yarn from Ireland[5]. One incident illuminates this aspect of Tiverton's trade. At the end of 1706, the *William and Sarah* of Dublin, bound for Minehead, was blown off course, and eventually stranded near Perranporth in Cornwall, where her cargo of wool was looted[6]. The wool belonged to the Tiverton merchants Francis Bere, Thomas Enchmarch and Peter Carthew. Luckily for them, Francis's cousin, George Bere, who was employed in the Arundel household at Lanherne not far from the wreck site, was able to direct operations. Eventually, the wool was recovered and returned to Tiverton[7] and the merchants compensated[8].

Dunsford informs us[9] that in 1706 several 'woolcombers and others' were tried in Tiverton for rioting, and by February 1707 tension ran so high that Tiverton's merchants had become very worried

> *'that the combinations or clubs, into which the labourers in the woollen manufacture have of late formed themselves, is a growing complaint here, and are become so insolent that the masters are obliged to comply with their wishes; and assemble themselves in a riotous manner and daring all authority that opposes them'* [10].

---

[1] *JHC 1702-4*, 470.
[2] (*HMC Portland vol IV*, 270). An earlier letter, dated the 30th July, shows that Defoe had been planning his trip to Tiverton where he would be staying with a merchant called Francis Bere (*ib.*, 214). He would have been an interested observer; a passionate Nonconformist who twenty years before had been in Monmouth's rebel army, and had himself been bankrupted by the War in his profession as an insurer of merchant ships.
[3] *DNB*.
[4] *HMC Lords 1704-6*, 393.
[5] *JHC 1705-8*, 476.
[6] CRO AR15/75.
[7] CRO AR10/290.
[8] CRO AR15/75.
[9] (1790, 206). However, it is uncertain whether this was a fresh outbreak of trouble or simply the legal wheels turning slowly after the disturbances of 1704.
[10] *ib.*, 312.

It seems that the anger subsided during the year, possibly because of the opening of new markets. Despite the continued disruption of the War, Tiverton merchants took the opportunity to build up lucrative links with Hamburg, Cadiz, and Lisbon.

Saint Peter's Church received substantial adornments during 1707. Edward Bryant was paid 14s 10d for writing 40 words in gold on one of the tables of donations, and a new gallery was built over the southern entrance which came to be used by the Master and Scholars of Blundell's. The great ornate candelabra, now hanging in the central aisle, eclipsed all of these. Originally referred to in the Churchwardens' Accounts as 'the candlestick', it weighs over seven hundredweight, and was bought from John Bayley at a total cost of £70, a further 10s was paid for 'guilding again the ironwork thereof'. The wardens recouped some of their outlay, as they received 14s for the box it came in!

Although Saint Peter's Church accounts are detailed, as are those of Blundell's School, it is rare to find similar documents elsewhere. A remarkable exception is a batch of tradesman's bills for work done on behalf of the Hartnoll family[1]. These papers provide glimpses of ordinary life. Mr Shapcot received 9d for a day shaking apples from the trees, and Walter May sent in a bill for 3s to cover the expense of himself and his horse travelling to Topsham for some deal boards. Building in and around the town was continuous. The use of brick had become fashionable, and there was already a substantial brick-making industry in Tiverton. A lease of 1708 allowed Thomas Bigg, a local bricklayer, to 'dig up clay, burn bricks and cut down timber' in Oxen Park for building two houses[2]. The field is probably the site now occupied by Twyford Place, emphasising the usefulness of the area's brick-clay which had already been used for the nearby Hospital. Indeed, the finest example of Queen Anne architecture in Tiverton, Amory House in Saint Peter Street, made extensive use of brick.

Whereas bricks were made locally, many basic necessities had to be brought in from elsewhere, adding to their cost. Large quantities of goods came to Tiverton from the Bridgwater and Taunton districts along routes controlled mainly by the Conservators of the River Tone. In 1707, they announced their wish to add to their charges on handling coal, salt, and lime. Townspeople and villagers from Halberton and Silverton were so alarmed by the imminent increase that they petitioned Parliament; the first signature on the document was that of Peter West of Tiverton Castle. Although he had been chosen as Sheriff of Devon for this year[3], the highest ceremonial office in the county, his position as Lord of the much-reduced Manor of Tiverton now carried little weight. On the other hand, someone like Robert Burridge had great influence. He was almost certainly the town's richest inhabitant, and in a single year earned £10,500 from

---

[1] DRO 2547M/FH205.   [2] DRO 2723M/LT60.
[3] *JHC 1705-8*, 526.

the serge trade[1]. When he chose not to stand in the Parliamentary election of May 1708, his place was taken by a lawyer of the Inner Temple, Richard Mervin. As we may have suspected, the newcomer was not only Burridge's son-in-law, but also the brother of William Mervin, Rector of Clare.

Elections at the end of 1710 did not bode well for the Whig government. The country, and Queen Anne herself, were tiring of them. The oppressive Land Tax necessary to finance the War was a great burden particularly to the landed gentry. They, together with the merchants, whose trade had been severely disrupted, swelled the Tory ranks. John Worth of Washfield, a Tory whose leanings were considered 'doubtful'[2], opposed Tiverton's two Whig M.P.s, Bere and Mervin. The vote resulted in a three-way tie, and, whereas the Parliamentary session opened in November with Tories forming the new government, another election was necessary at Tiverton. The Tory Attorney General, Sir Edward Northey, himself entered the re-run, and he, with Worth, beat the Whigs, thanks only to Mayor George Thorne's casting vote. No doubt, it was this that helped Thorne to obtain the post of Receiver of the Taxes. He had little trouble finding the financial securities necessary to take on the post, amounting to over £20,000[3]. At this time, he was living in Newte's House in Bampton Street, which he leased from the Tory, Sir William Wyndham. As with the Burridge family, the Thornes' success was not restricted to George, for his brother Nathaniel was appointed by the Treasury as the Distributor of Stamps in Tiverton[4].

A Tory government augured well for peace and the Church of England. In 1711 the Occasional Conformity Act tried to re-impose uniformity by preventing Dissenters getting around the Test Act of 1673 and compelling regular attendance at the parish church. Emboldened by the political situation and a resurgent Tory clergy, the Rev. John Newte set to work on Saint Peter's Church. He spent over £80 in 1711 setting up battlements on the roof of the chancel and supplying 'broad glass' for the windows[5]. Moves were also being made to improve the behaviour of some of the congregation. A moral crusade led by the bishops saw the ecclesiastical courts busy once more; The Exeter Archdeaconry Courts in the single year of 1712 dealt with seven instances of fornication from Tiverton, two of bastardy and one of adultery[6]. Although not illegal, one marriage that took place at Saint Peter's during the year probably raised many an eyebrow as the 33-year old Anne Hooper of Cove became the wife of William Allen, aged 83 years!

---

[1] (Dunsford 1790, 450), adding that he generously gave his clerk the £500..
[2] cited in Glassey 1979, 218.   [3] *CalTreasB 1711*, 59.
[4] *ib.*, 269.   [5] *Saint Peter's Benefactions Book*.
[6] DRO AE/I/6.

A Charity School in Tiverton for 60 poor boys was officially opened in1713. The Rev. John Newte was responsible for the venture, having, it appears, been running it himself for a few years. In 1711 he had informed the Society for the Propagation of Christian Knowledge (SPCK) that his support for such a school had resulted in the 'gentlemen of the Corporation' agreeing to raise subscriptions to build and run it[1]. They did not build a new school, however, as the Church House in Saint Peter's Churchyard was used. In 1713 the establishment was placed on a firm basis. The SPCK would appoint the Master; trustees were chosen who were to meet 'at Greenway's coffee house on the last Monday in each month at three in the afternoon', and the subscribers could nominate one boy for each 30s they had given. Some of the boys of the school were allocated seats in Greenway's Chapel during church services[2], no doubt through the manoeuvring of the Rev. Newte. His wish to offer education to girls, a rarity in those times, was fulfilled in June 1714. The Master of the Charity School, William Markham, was allowed £9 a year to rent a house where his wife was appointed mistress in charge of 50 girls[3].

John Newte's improvements to Saint Peter's Church were matched by others made by Oliver Peard, a known Dissenter. He ordered the renewal of the Corporation seats, where the Mayor and Town Councillors still sit, as well as the repainting of the lion and unicorn, on which 3s 3d was spent for 'crocus[4] about the same'[5]. Peard's attempt to ingratiate himself with the Anglican Church, if that was his motive, was perhaps borne of the unease felt by Dissenters. Their fears had been raised by the Occasional Conformity Act, and, far worse, by a proposed Schism Bill, aimed at closing their schools. In Tiverton, as in a great many towns, it was clear that this legislation would probably result in large numbers of Dissenters flooding into the parish church on a weekly basis, more people than Saint Peter's could ever hold. The only answer to this would be the construction of a new building.

It could be said that History in Tiverton began in 1712, with John Blundell's *Memoirs and Antiquities of the Town and Parish of Tiverton, in the County of Devon*. This was not only the first history of Tiverton but, apart from Izacke's work on Exeter, is the earliest known published history of any Devon town, and is nowadays a great rarity. It was written in a small fishing-hut below Collipriest House[6], printed in Exeter by Joseph Bliss and sold by him and a saddler, Nicholas Crocker of Tiverton, for one shilling. The book proudly proclaims that it contains

> *A Brief History of the Succession of the Earls of Devonshire; with the most Memorable Accidents relating thereto. As also an impartial Account of the Benefactors and Benefactions relating to the School-Houses, Alms-Houses and other Pious Uses. Together with the Monuments in Saint Peter's Church. And*

---

[1] cited in Warne 1969, 132.   [2] *Bluecoat School Minute Book.*

[3] *ib.*

[4] red ferric oxide sometimes used to coat metalwork.

[5] DRO R4/1/Z/PW3.   [6] Dunsford 1790, 384.

many other Remarkable Passages for several Hundreds of Years past.
Blundell, equally proudly, describes himself as 'a Gentleman, Native thereof'. Although a slim volume of only 60 pages, its importance was clearly recognised by later historians. Dunsford largely retained the sections into which Blundell divided his book. Although it is full of intriguing details not elsewhere recorded, one section deserves special notice. The author devotes no fewer than six pages out of the 60 to recite in full the rules of a Friendly Society formed in 1704 for the Husbandmen of Tiverton. This is one of the earliest societies formed to help agricultural labourers and shows that the clothworkers of Tiverton were not the only group capable of joint action.

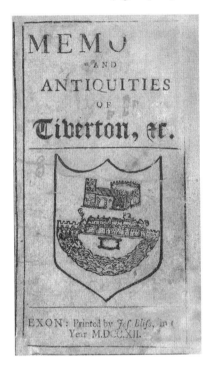

Damaged frontispiece of John Blundell's Memoirs and Antiquities of the Town and Parish of Tiverton, in the County of Devon, published in 1712.

Throughout 1712, some people seem to have taken heart from the imminent end of the War. One was Richard Haydon who, like his father, was a carpenter and what we would now call a property developer. He had often taken leases on vacant plots of land[1], almost invariably with the condition that he build on the property. Now, he

---

[1] e.g. on Barne's Hill in 1693 (DRO 1186M/T18), in Newport Street in 1695 (DRO 3985D adds3-4/1), and in 1698 in Bampton Street (DRO R4/1/Z71).

acquired the two fulling mills on the Lowman called Ham Mills, along with their Rack Field and 'the racks thereon'[1]. Two mills at Bolham also changed hands at this time, being assigned by the dyer Michael Glass to William and Samuel Lewis[2]. The interesting point about this conveyance is that, whereas one of the mills was for fulling, the other is described as a wood mill. This rare type of mill reduced logwood, a Central and South American tree, to a powder that was then used to dye cloth, giving a very dark red or black colour. The example at Bolham is the earliest of its kind recorded in the area. An increase in property transactions involving mills at this time may be seen as a good indicator of renewed faith in the future of the cloth industry. The long-awaited good news finally arrived in April 1713 when the Tory Peace of Utrecht ended England's participation in the War of the Spanish Succession, and Tiverton's trade was once more unfettered.

The Rev. John Newte died three years later. Throughout his life, he had lavished care (and gifts) on his flock. In his will he made provisions for extending education even further throughout the parish. The hamlet of Cove, usually mentioned only for the dilapidated state of either its chapel or bridge, was provided with a charity school funded from his land of Buckhayes. He founded an Exhbition for a Blundell's boy at Balliol College. He gave 250 books from his study at Tidcombe House to form a Parochial Library to be housed 'in the chamber over the vestry' in Saint Peter's Church. This collection formed the nucleus of the present Newte Library[3]. To this he also gave paintings of Charles I, Archbishop Laud, the Earl of Strafford and the Marquess of Montrose, all Cavalier heroes, and obviously those to whom he aspired. Newte's death forced the first changes in Tiverton's clergy since 1679. John Vyvyan, a younger brother of the patron, filled his position as Rector of Pitt, but Tidcombe remained in the family; as he had stipulated[4], his nephew Samuel was presented to the benefice.

During his last years, John Newte had taken a keen interest in the chapel being built in Tiverton to take the expected influx of Dissenters. The site chosen was at the junction of Saint Andrew Street with Fore Street, where an inn called the Cross Keys and an unknown number of houses with their sizeable back plots stood, all of which were bought for about £500[5]. Henry Blagdon and John Upcott, both members of the Corporation, were the principals in the transactions and, according to at least one historian[6], were part of a group with strong Presbyterian connections. Not everyone was in favour of the new church. Peter West at the Castle described it as 'a design on us who are patrons to infringe a power upon our rights'[7]. Despite such objections, subscription lists were drawn up to meet the costs of the new building, and on

---

[1] DRO 213M/T138 and DRO 1186M/L22.
[2] DRO 49/9/6/196.
[3] see Welsford 1979.
[4] *Murray Wills*.
[5] Saint Peter's SG13-15 and 17.
[6] Warne 1969, 55.
[7] DRO 2723M/Eccl1/6.

December 1st 1714 the foundation stone was laid by the aged Rev. John Newte[1]. John James of London, who also designed Saint George's Church, Hanover Square, had submitted the accepted plans. What a coup these Presbyterians had managed to pull off! They had obtained a prime site, so near to the Town Hall as to imply, if not the Corporation's patronage, then their approval, and had begun to build a handsome temple to Dissent in bright yellow Ham stone in the main street of Tiverton. Despite the amount of time and effort already spent in getting this project off the ground, the fundamental reason for the building was rapidly disappearing. The expected strict enforcement of the Occasional Conformity Act had not really materialised, and the much more dangerous Schism Act did not have time to be implemented before the Queen's death in August 1714.

Some Tories had been poised for civil war, and were ready to rally to the legitimate heir, the Catholic James II's son, James Edward Stuart. However, the dying queen handed the white staff of office of Lord Treasurer to the Duke of Shrewsbury, not only a member of the Tory ministry but also an adherent of the House of Hanover. By this action, she split the Tories down the middle, thereby much reducing the Jacobite threat. The reality of the Protestant succession, decided a decade earlier, gave the Whigs their chance. James I's German-speaking great-grandson, Georg Ludwig, was crowned George I. Elections in March 1715 saw the Whigs dominate with a majority in the Commons of more than 100 seats. Thomas Bere was returned for Tiverton after a break of almost five years; his colleague was to be Sir Edward Northey, who had wisely decided to support the Whigs. Nevertheless, despite the political reversal George Thorne continued as local Receiver-General for Taxes[2]. The final months of 1715 saw the anticipated Jacobite uprising restricted to Scotland and northern England, but fighting was over by the following February[3]. Elsewhere, individuals attempted to foment disorder. One of them was Sir William Wyndham, lord of the manor of Pool Anthony and one of the M.P.s for Somerset, who had filled many high Government posts[4]. He was accused of trying to induce the local clothworkers to rebel by giving them money which, however, was 'generally spent in strong liquor'[5], and only narrowly avoided detention in the Tower. Distinctly vulnerable, Wyndham spent the early part of the following year sorting out his local properties. He granted a lease of Newte's House and Warnicombe to the irrepressible George Thorne, Town Tenement and one

---

[1] Dunsford 1790, 207. [2] *CalTreasB 1714-5*, 622 and 670.
[3] the failure of this rising was heralded in Tiverton by the ringing of Saint Peter's bells 'for our deliverance from popery and slavery'.
[4] appointed secretary of war in 1712, Chancellor of the Exchequer a year later, and head of the Treasury in 1714.
[5] *JCTP 1714-8*, 95-6.

third of Pool Anthony Farm went to Oliver Peard[1], and another third of the farm to Henry Blagdon[2], all Tiverton cloth merchants.

The town's future rulers were fortifying themselves. Blagdon did not live many weeks after taking his lease, but his dispositions[3] clearly show that the family had established firm local ties; his sisters had married into the Osmond, Passmore, Glass, and Peard families. Furthermore, he could call on the Rev. William Rayner (Master of Blundell's), George Thorne and Oliver Peard to act as trustees of bequests amounting to over £4,000. Apart from family legacies, he left £10 to be distributed in bread to poor people of South Molton and Tiverton, as well as £30 in cash for those of Tiverton. He gave £400 to his trustees to invest, the proceeds of which would provide a salary for a schoolmaster to teach 'the poor children in the Hospital', and a further £5 was left to a minister of Tiverton to examine the children. By far his largest bequest, however, was £1,000 towards the building costs of Tiverton's new chapel. Later, a fitting memorial to him was erected there, although he is buried in the central aisle of Saint Peter's Church. John Upcott, another of the prime movers for the establishment of this chapel, gave it its first communion plate in 1717[4].

But would it be needed? The building disappears from records for more than a decade. Most people expected that it was only a matter of time before the Whigs repealed the Occasional Conformity and Schism Acts. Once this happened, nonconformist congregations would not be compelled to worship regularly in the parish church. In Tiverton, as many other towns, differing congregations now went their own way. The Presbyterians, the driving force behind the new chapel, said to number a considerable 1,270[5], began building a separate new meetinghouse at the Pitt[6]. The widow Joan Keene gave the reversion of a house at the top of Angel Hill towards the support of the Congregational minister of the Steps Meeting House, and, across the town the Baptists profited from Robert Stone's gift of houses in Water Lane[7].

Tivertonians, angry at unfair taxation and duties, petitioned Parliament during 1717. In May the town's tanners, curriers and other leather workers, along with North Devon tradesmen, complained about the shortage of oak bark in the area[8]. Great quantities of bark, necessary in the leather industry, were being exported to Ireland where no duty was paid on hides. Similarly, the high tax imposed on soap and candles, often used in waxing woollen yarn, was adding to the cost of cloth. A further petition one month later pointed out that if trade in woollen cloth was not supported 'then the

---

[1] DRO 4862M/E1.
[2] SRO DD/WY/Box 159.
[3] DRO 49/9/1/681.
[4] Chanter 1919, 108-9.
[5] DRO 3542D/M1/1.
[6] DRO 213M/T37-8.
[7] DRO 49/9/6/211c.
[8] *JHC 1714-8,* 557.

poor will become too great a burden'[1]. Anger continued to rise, and boiled over into serious rioting in the Tiverton area in October and November. A body of some 900 weavers was moving from town to town, destroying cloth on the looms, and spoiling jars of weaving oil. Some of the clothworkers may well have been those who had been stirred up by Wyndham a couple of years earlier, but on this occasion their main complaint was that they were unable to pay the high wages demanded by their journeymen[2]. The trouble was mainly confined to a trianglular area encompassing Tiverton, Taunton, and Cullompton, the heartland of the local cloth industry. The situation so alarmed Tiverton's merchants that on October 21st the mayor, George Davey, asked for military assistance[3]. Perhaps we should say the request was for additional troops, because it is possible that already there was a garrison in the town. Five months earlier, the Workhouse account book notes a payment of £1 'for beer given the soldiers'[4]. Whereas the riots had been attempts by workers to safeguard their livelihood, the view of the authorities was that

> 'by reason of various societies or clubs of labourers in the woollen industry, the trade has been greatly incommoded, many families impoverished, houses and effects of tradesmen rendered precarious, peace broken, laws eluded, officers of justice assaulted, and money extorted'[5].

It would be easy to paint a picture of early Hanoverian Tiverton that emphasises confrontation and disturbance, as Dunsford does. But there was, of course, another side to the town - one of a thriving social life. For many, the numerous inns and alehouses were a welcome escape from the humdrum of work, but there were other places too. William Hewett kept a coffee-house, in or very near the Town Hall, suitable even as the meeting-place for the Guardians of the Poor[6]. He was also the author of the work often referred to by Dunsford as *Hewett's Manuscript*, now lost. One can only imagine the material contained within it; after all, Hewett had the opportunity to overhear most of the goings-on in the town. Not far away, on the site of the present market area, there was a large bowling green, which was much frequented by the gentlemen of the town. While they played bowls, their wives and daughters could parade around the streets in their finery. And finery there was: Elizabeth Hartnoll's accounts show a payment in 1716 for two rich sable muffs, the price being a staggering £2 16s each[7]. There was plenty of opportunity for some to wine and dine. The Blundell's feoffees often took lavish meals at the Fountain in Fore Street[8], washed down with copious amounts of port, sherry, or brandy. The potential results of socialising on

---

[1] *JHC 1714-8*, 596.
[2] Dobson 1980, 70.
[3] *SPD George I*, 10/25 and 27.
[4] DRO R4/1/Z/PO12.
[5] *JHC 1714-8*, 715.
[6] DRO R4/1/Z/PO12.
[7] DRO 2547M/FH332.
[8] there was another on Angel Hill.

this scale, however, can be seen in the parish register, where the burial of Nicholas Stapling is recorded at the end of October 1717. Alongside the entry, the clerk added that the 'drinking of brandy' was the cause of his death.

Such regular excesses were affordable only to a few Tivertonians, most notably the ruling 25 burgesses and their families. Among this leading group the two George Daveys, father and son, were achieving prominence, with the father being chosen as mayor in 1717 while his son was elected to the Corporation and soon was to become Treasurer of the Hospital. The elder George was a prosperous merchant who, on his death a few years later, was able to leave over £1,000 in money to his wife, and to his son the 'shares of all my ships belonging to Topsham'[1]. The most successful citizen remained George Thorne, still Receiver-General of Taxes after six years[2]. In 1718 he had a house built near Chettiscombe and, 'supplied it with gardens and fishponds'[3]. No doubt an architectural gem, its fate is sadly not recorded. Nevertheless, success did not automatically guarantee a place or promotion on the Corporation; Oliver Peard failed on two occasions in 1719 to be elevated from assistant to capital burgess, losing first to Samuel Burridge by 17 votes to one, and then to William Frost, by 16 to one[4].

Following the death of William Mervin, Rector of Clare, in 1719, Samuel Burridge became embroiled in another contest. Many caveats were filed and enquiries made into the right to present Mervin's successor. Burridge, Nicholas Thomas, and Peter West all submitted claims[5]. By April 1720, another William Mervin, probably the deceased's nephew, had been presented[6], but the patronage was still not legally established, and the matter went up to the Court of Arches at Westminster, the highest ecclesiastical court in the land[7]. While this case was passing through the Courts, John Vyvyan, the Rector of Pitt, furnished Cove Chapel with a new gallery, an act not entirely altruistic as he was recompensed to the amount of £10[8]. The nephew of a former benefactor of Cove, Peter Newte died in 1720. A staunch High Churchman like his uncle, he gave

---

[1] *Murray Wills.*

[2] he already held half of Tidcombe, two-thirds of Warnicombe, one third of Newte's House in Bampton Street (SRO DD/WY/Box 47/3/49) - part of the manor of Pool Anthony.

[3] (Dunsford 1790, 285-6). The site of this building is probably indicated on the tithe apportionment of 1841 by the two fields named Pleasure House at Gatcombe.

[4] (DRO R4/1/C301). Such one-sidedness in elections to the Corporation was common throughout its history. Rather than revealing a lack of support for the losing candidate, it seems to indicate the outcome of prior decisions, for it is not unusual to find examples of a man losing by a large margin in one election, but soon after winning by an equally large majority.

[5] DRO Chanter 48.　　　　　　　　　　　　　[6] DRO Chanter 1530.

[7] DRO PR Basket A/2022.　　　　　　　　　　[8] DRO R4/1/Z/PO12.

500 prayer books 'to be dispersed by careful hands among the poorer sort of the Episcopal Church in Scotland', and left to the two Tiverton charity schools the profits of nine fields in Cullompton, as well as an eighth of Longhayne in Tiverton[1]. A similar share from Plushayes was to be used to pay teachers to instruct the poor children of Chevithorne, Chettiscombe and East and West Mere, who, when they left school were each to receive a bible and prayer book. So the Newte family, through worthy bequests, had, within a decade, added the two charity schools in the town, and those at Cove, Chettiscombe, Chevithorne and Mere to the earlier Tiverton foundations of Blundell's and Chilcott's.

The Whig Parliament repealed the Occasional Conformity and Schism Acts in 1719. Dissenters were given access to local office and permitted to re-open their academies. These institutions, offering a wider curriculum than grammar schools or universities, became of great importance. Joseph Hallett ran one such academy at Exeter and, on its closure in 1720, the Tiverton Presbyterian John Moore set up something similar at the Meeting House in Saint Peter Street, tutoring some 15 students[2]. One prominent Tiverton Baptist family who benefited were the Glasses, who, despite the many religious strictures placed on them, had prospered financially. Until this time they had concerned themselves with minor property transactions - mainly obtaining leases for premises in Westexe where they carried on their dyeing operations - but now they branched out, with Michael Glasse paying £330 for Wayland Farm[3] and Thomas buying lands in Oakford[4].

Parliamentary petitions give some indication of the extent, variety and concerns of Tiverton's cloth trade. In 1719 the town's merchants complained about exports of wool to France and about the growing threat from the lightweight fabrics imported from the East Indies[5]. Concern was also raised[6] over a possible change to the Navigation Acts, which were supposed to prevent British goods being carried on foreign vessels. From this petition it appears that 'vast quantities of serge etc' were being exported to the Italian ports of Livorno and Venice, where it was bought by Persian and other 'Asiatic' merchants. Tiverton cloth, so it appears, was being sold in the markets of the Far East. Irish yarn was again imported in 1720 to ease the problem of supply. The results were predictable; tension again erupted into riot. The Tiverton woolcombers, fearing for their jobs, attacked the houses of the merchants, dragged their Irish worsted outside and ripped it up, ensuring that no one would make money (or cloth) at their expense. Their action had clearly been anticipated, as Dunsford asserts[7] that George Thorne and Thomas Enchmarch had fortified their houses in Bampton Street. Constables were hastily sworn in and some of the woolcombers were taken into custody. They were

---

[1] DRO 2530M/F/3/7.
[2] Brockett 1958, 51.
[3] DRO 49/9/6/204-5.
[4] DRO 5214M/T40-1.
[5] *JHC 1718-21,* 198.
[6] *ib.,* 281.
[7] 1790, 208-9.

freed by others, but soon recaptured with military assistance. Although defeated, the woolcombers had the last word. The Irish yarn was found to be inferior to the local product, and the imports were stopped. Riot was the last resort of popular fears and frustrations which could not be allayed by judicial or legislative means. It constituted a threat to property which local authority sought sometimes to protect by military force. It is doubtful whether, despite Dunsford's opinion, a demand for political representation was ever the real cause. But it was not beyond rival merchants to manipulate popular unrest, as we shall see.

Some of the agitation at this time was due to uncertainty within the local cloth industry. New fabrics, such as sagathies, druggets and drapeens[1], were introduced, in response to the growing desire for lighter fabrics like those coming from the East Indies. The situation was very similar to that of a century before when serge replaced kersey as Tiverton's staple. As then, the changes brought to the fore a new breed of men. Unequalled among the innovators in Tiverton were the Peards, senior and junior, both named Oliver. They had rapidly risen to prominence since the father's arrival from Barnstaple 30 years earlier. In recognition of the prosperity he was bringing to the town, Oliver senior was at last elected as capital burgess in 1721[2], and was voted to be Mayor in the same year. Another up-and-coming family was that of William Heathfield, who had already amassed property in the district. He had purchased houses in Tiverton, as well as the manor of Little Silver[3]. Two rather obscure sources seem to indicate the growing prosperity of some townsmen at this time. One is the annual list of freeholders qualified to serve on juries at the Devon Quarter Sessions[4], and the second is a volume detailing rents paid for pews in Saint Peter's Church[5]. For each of the ten years up to 1721 there had been an average of 26 Tivertonians eligible for jury service, but in that year 38 qualified, and a further three were added in 1722. Pew rents were auctioned each year by the Churchwardens, and the foremost inhabitants liked to display their wealth by outbidding their fellows on these occasions. Many record prices were paid in 1722; (the Baptist) Thomas Glasse paid £8 1s for a pew of nine places, John Waldron £7 3s for one of eight, Philip Blundell paid ten guineas for a rank of seven places 'in front of the north desk' – a prominent place where he could be seen. The highest price in this year was the twenty guineas for five places paid by William Upcott.

The first Parliamentary elections under the terms of the Septennial Act took place in the spring of 1722. Thomas Bere was returned for Tiverton for a ninth time, and was joined by a newcomer. This man, Arthur Arscott, was the brother-in-law of Sir William Yonge, a leading Whig thought to be one of the henchmen of Robert Walpole.

---

[1] these were all lighter, finer fabrics, usually incorporating silk, linen or cotton with the wool.
[2] DRO R4/1/C301.   [3] DRO 49/9/6/207.
[4] DRO QS7/..   [5] DRO R4/1/Z/PW4.

The Rev. E.S. Chalk thought that Yonge had obtained Tiverton for his relation to bolster the Government position there[1]. Serious divisions among Tiverton's burgesses led to a constitutional crisis for the town in 1723. The split was not simply into Tories and Whigs headed by Burridge and John Upcott respectively, but also between those merchants like Burridge and Thorne who had gained a large following through patronage, and those who had to make it on their own and also tried to gain popular support. The days leading up to the mayoral election in August saw both parties using what were for the period conventional means of persuasion. Bribes were commonplace and the amounts offered sometimes substantial, Upcott was said to have tempted William Hewett with £500[2]. Despite these entreaties, Burridge believed that more extreme measures were needed. The Borough Charter stipulated that the election had to take place between nine and midday, and on the morning of the designated day, August 27th, the first of the burgesses began arriving at the Town Hall. Not the mayor, however. With the time rapidly approaching noon, a delegation went to Burridge's home, the Great House, to fetch him, but he was not there. They returned to the Town Hall, but finding it still locked decided to hold the election outside on the steps. Despite the absence of many of Burridge's supporters, a majority of the Corporation was present. They proceeded to elect John Tristram. Yet, all was in vain, for an election without the Mayor's presence was, of course, illegal. The Corporation was dissolved and the borough charter declared void. By his failure to act, whether deliberate or not, Samuel Burridge had reduced a proud town to a mere parish. Authority reverted to the county justices, and considerable responsibility for the administration of Tiverton fell on the churchwardens. It took nearly a year before even a draft Charter was available[3], and a further four months before it could be delivered.

The costs of the new charter were borne by Samuel Burridge, the very same individual responsible for invalidating the old one, and his accomplice, Nathaniel Thorne. Why had they acted as they did in 1723? If it had been purely a response to the growing threat of the Tiverton Whigs then it had backfired on them; many of the burgesses named in the new charter had been in the old Corporation, including the Whig leader, John Upcott. Dunsford suggests[4] that Burridge had used the intervening period to dupe the people of Tiverton into believing a new charter would bring about a wider franchise. All freemen, he proclaimed, would gain the right to vote. This would explain why the arrival of the charter from London was greeted so joyfully. On Christmas Eve, the document was received at Gornhay, where crowds filled the road for a quarter of a mile, and proceeded, to the accompaniment of trumpets, horns, and kettledrums, to Hunt's House at the bottom of Exeter Hill. There, the charter was handed over to the Town Clerk. The crowds then pushed up Gold Street, halted a while

---

[1] 1935, 329.
[2] cited in Chalk 1936, 22.
[3] *PC Unbound pt I*, PC 1/4/1 seq.
[4] 1790, 211-4.

at the Three Tuns, before continuing up Bampton Street where they paused outside Nathaniel Thorne's house. The route then led along Newport Street into Saint Peter Street, with a stop being made in front of Burridge's Great House before the Town Hall was reached. The final part of the official ceremony was the reading of the document. This would have taken at least an hour. Those who stood in the cold December air for so long, eagerly expecting the Charter to endorse a wide, popular franchise, remained in ignorance, for it was read in its original Latin, unintelligible to all but a handful of those present. The powers of Tiverton's ruling oligarchy were in no way reduced.

11 Control of the Corporation

Tiverton was always affected by the death of local worthies. In 1726 Peter West and Thomas Bere both died, depriving the town not only of its lord of the manor for the past quarter of a century but also of its longest-standing Member of Parliament. Following West's death, and that of his son just two years later, the manor descended to his daughters, Christiane, who was to remain a spinster, and Dorothy the wife of Sir Thomas Carew of Haccombe[1]. Thomas Bere had served as M.P. for Tiverton for over 35 years, and was replaced by an outsider, George Deane of Taunton Castle, who held the seat until the elections in July 1727 following the accession of George II. At these, Arthur Arscott was returned, along with his brother-in-law, Sir William Yonge, who was also Recorder of the Borough. Called 'stinking Yonge' by George II, probably for his strong support for Walpole, he relinquished his Tiverton seat as he had also been elected (once again) to sit for Honiton. The Corporation chose James Nelthorpe to fill the vacancy. Another death was that in 1729 of the Rev. William Rayner, Master of Blundell's. He had taught at Tiverton for over 30 years, and in his place the feoffees chose Samuel Smith, who brought with him some of the boys from his former school at Crewkerne. He joined an establishment that had accumulated considerable funds over the previous century, which probably accounts for the building undertaken during his first year at the school. Most of the work was done on the perimeter walls using materials whose origins are quite surprising. The lime used was 'Welch lime' imported through Minehead, 'shelly stones' came from Wiveliscombe, Huish and Treborough (all just over the border in Somerset), and 'cresses'[2] from either North Molton or Barnstaple[3].

Meanwhile, in Newport Street a new Baptist Chapel was under construction. Initially, there had been considerable difficulty in acquiring the site, as the descendants of the former owner of the property, Aquila Skinner, were now resident in America[4]. The Baptists had eventually obtained the property in 1728, and an agreement was reached in the following year with the local builder John Noble to erect a building in brick[5]. Moreover, progress on Tiverton's new church near the Town Hall was at last being made. Work had almost come to a standstill in 1727 because of a lack of funds, but at the end of the year a subscription to complete the building had raised over

---

[1] by this marriage Tiverton returned to a descendant of a Courtenay, as Joane Courtenay in the 15th century had married Sir Nicholas Carew of Haccombe.
[2] ridge stones.   [3] Blundell's Account Book.
[4] (DRO 3958D adds3-4/3-4). Skinner's daughter, Alice, had married a Colonel Henry Ridgley of Anne Arundel, Maryland, whose grandson, also Henry, was a planter there.
[5] DRO 3958D adds3-4/7.

£1,300[1]. The work was finished during 1730, and a pair of chalices was specially made to commemorate the opening[2]. The Bishop of Exeter was asked to allow the performance of Divine Service there prior to the Act of Parliament permitting the use of this second Anglican church. He acceded to this request in November 1730[3].

Then fate dealt two cruel blows. On November 2nd 1730 a bakehouse in Newport Street caught fire, and the conflagration spread towards Bampton Street and Castle Street, destroying 15 houses. The damage to property was contained, but the fire did take at least two lives. The parish register records the burials of Anne, Thomas Mills' wife, and Joan Gibbons, 'killed by the fall of a wall in the fire'[4]. Far worse, just seven months later, on the evening of June 5th 1731, another bakehouse caught fire. This time it was John Tucker's establishment at the bottom of Gold Street. The blaze took hold immediately and, due to an uncommon east wind, it spread into the town. Both sides of Gold Street were gutted and the lower half of Barrington Street was lost in no time at all. The fire was finally brought under control at about four o'clock in the morning. By this time half of Bampton Street had been destroyed, and in Fore Street the flames spread as far west as Coggan's Well. Here the brick or stone-built houses of John Parsons and Oliver Peard, roofed with slates, halted its advance. In ten hours 298 houses had been destroyed, but miraculously there was only one fatality[5]. News of the major disaster spread far; the *Northampton Mercury* related that those items saved from the houses 'were thrown into churches, meeting-houses and adjoining fields where a great many hundred poor persons lay for want of beds'[6]. The 'great many hundred' homeless, it seems, numbered about 2,000 people.

It was estimated that the damage was more than £56,000. This sum, however, did not include £2,200 for the Greenway's Almshouses, the Corn Market and the Shambles, all owned by charities. Of the total value of property lost only about £1,100 was covered by insurance[7]. A year after the fire, the Rev. Samuel Smith published *An Account of the Late Dreadful Fire at Tiverton In The County Of Devon*, which includes a list of donations that deserves mention. It shows us precisely who Tiverton's friends were, and how important the town was commercially. The King himself gave £1,000; this was supplemented by £200 from the Queen, and the Prince of Wales, gave £100. The two sitting M.P.s, Arthur Arscott and James Nelthorpe, both donated £50 each, their patron Sir William Yonge equalled that amount, and Sir Robert Walpole gave £100. The Archbishop of York, Lancelot Blackburn, a former Bishop of Exeter contributed £50. London was particularly generous; many individual parishes made

[1] Harding 1845, iv, 56.   [2] Chanter 1919, 108-9.
[3] DRO Chanter 57.   [4] DRO 2960A/PR4.
[5] Henry Murray, who lived in Greenway's Almshouses.
[6] edition of 14th June 1731.   [7] Dunsford 1790, 216-23.

donations, as did the Cordwainers and Vintry Wards, whereas the Chamber of London raised the significant sum of £1,025, and even 'comedians acting in Southwark' sent £3 10s. Devon's neighbouring counties also gave generously, with £135 4s coming from the Archdeaconry of Cornwall, £121 from Taunton, and amounts of over £50 from Shepton Mallet and Wells, and Bath gave almost £200; and as much as £675 was collected from the port city of Bristol. Normally, Dorset would have been expected to give freely, but an equally devastating fire at Blandford took precedence. A lot of money was collected in Devon itself; over £50 each from Cullompton, Dartmouth, Honiton, and Totnes, while Barnstaple contributed £70. A collection in Tiverton raised a shilling short of £100, whereas Plymouth gave £145 and Exeter £376 5s 11d. By the middle of 1732, when Smith's list was published, over £10,000 had been collected.

Tiverton itself coped well with the aftermath of this fire, unlike previous incidents. Trustees, appointed to distribute the money collected, divided the sufferers into four categories – those who had lost all; those who had lost the best part of their effects; those who had lost a considerable amount, and deserved some assistance; and those who did not wish to receive any compensation at all. The people in the last category had, in fact, sustained over £22,000 worth of damage. Whether they refused help out of altruism or out of the desire not to appear mercenary, we can only speculate. They included landed gentry such as Carew and Coleman alongside the more numerous merchant families of Burridge[1], Davey, Enchmarch, Heathfield, Lewis, Parsons, Peard, Thorne and Upcott.

It was imperative that lessons should be learnt from the disaster. One effect was to extend insurance – less than 2% of the goods lost had been covered. Within months the sergemaker John Besley had insured his premises for £500, John Bowerman his houses and stock for £200, and Clement Govett the same for £400[2]. Many of the surviving policies display all too clearly one of the major causes of the fires; Besley's house was part-thatched, part-tiled; the clothier John Pearse's house was cob and thatched, as were his workshops, outhouses and stable. Thatched roofs virtually ensured a fire would spread, and previous events showed that strong winds sent burning thatch across the town to start further blazes. Everyone knew this, yet only now did they try to remedy the situation, and, even then, only in part. *The Act to Prevent Dangers from Fire in the Town of Tiverton* became law on June 1st 1732[3]. It stipulated that no new building, including outhouses and walls, should be covered with anything other than lead, slates or tiles. Thatch was finally outlawed, or was it? The Act made one exception, thatch on existing buildings could remain. Therefore, despite 1598, 1612 and now, 1731, little had changed in this respect. Tradesmen, like distillers, dyers,

---

[1] perhaps the inclusion of Samuel Burridge's name is somewhat surprising, his outlay to acquire the charter of 1724 had apparently left him short of funds; he had released much of his property to Henry Cruwys in exchange for £2,800 (KEO Box 15).
[2] in Chapman 1978.   [3] *JHC 1727-32,* 938.

brewers, chandlers, soap-boilers, and metalworkers, who needed open fires, were restricted as to where they carried on their businesses. They were prohibited from working out of, or near, 'the principal public parts or streets of the town', and it was ordered that these places should not contain stacks or ricks of combustible materials, such as hay, furze, or wood. If anyone contravened these regulations, they were to forfeit the considerable sum of £5 for each month until the time when the situation was corrected. A Court was set up to oversee the rebuilding of the town, with the power to decide disputes over land ownership and boundaries, and to ensure that anyone failing to rebuild within three years was forced to alienate their property. The Guardians of the Poor were charged to buy fire engines, which would be financed by a parish rate. The Act seems to have been enforced with gusto: the Hospital account book[1] enthuses on a payment of 15s 0½d 'paid to the players of the engine and expenses in searching places dangerous of fire with the Mayor'.

Rebuilding had begun before the Act was passed. As the greater part of Greenway's Almshouses was lost in the fire, the opportunity was now taken to increase the number of dwellings from six to nine. The cost of this and similar work, however, used up the charity's income for several years, with £231 spent in 1731 alone[2]. The Trustees of Exe Bridge and the Market were also in need of a loan to rebuild the Market House. A sum of £400 was secured from Ann Sandford of Ninehead Florey[3], and the work was carried out. Fortunately for us, the building we see today is virtually identical to that of 1731[4]. The Trustees' property in Bampton Street, from the Market House down to the Three Tuns on the corner of Fore Street, had all been destroyed, and now the vacant plots were leased. The terms were favourable, and, interestingly, most of the men who took the leases were involved in the building trade, a group which tended to thrive on disasters. They included John Dunsford, carpenter, Richard Skinner, glazier, and two bricklayers John Noble and Edward Kirby, all local men[5].

In a perverse way, the fire had given people the opportunity to build a new town, or, at least, part of one. The Baptist Church in Newport Street had opened in November, with its new minister, the Rev. Henry Terry. One Thomas Oland was appointed to clean the Church under an agreement 'to pay him 26s a year… and find him brooms'[6]. Finally, on October 11th 1733 the new church in Fore Street, dedicated to Saint George, was consecrated, nineteen years after the foundation stone had been laid. Considered by many to be the finest 18th century town church in Devon, its

---

[1] DRO R4/1/Z/PO12.   [2] DRO R4/1/Z/PF1.
[3] DRO 1589M/T89.
[4] modern restoration has faithfully copied the sturdy wooden Tuscan columns (Cherry & Pevsner, 1989, 816).
[5] cited in Harding 1845, iii, 85-6.   [6] DRO 3958D add/3.

external appearance has altered little. The yellow Ham stone and rusticated quoins are obviously not as bright as they were at first, but the beautifully proportioned building retains a very dignified appearance.

Saint George's Church.

In Hammett's Lane, just off Fore Street, George Davey was having a house built to replace his former home destroyed in the fire. He had contracted a local builder, Thomas Bonner, to construct a substantial structure with features that included 'a front door and frontispiece of the Dorick order'[1]. Bonner's standards, however, were not as high as Davey had required, and a case in the Court of Chancery was the result. Bonner, in his defence, largely blamed a shortage of workmen due 'to the inhabitants [of Tiverton] pressing to get their houses rebuilt'. Nevertheless, the work was eventually completed to everyone's satisfaction, and the result is Gotham House, which in the main retains its original appearance. The financial hardships brought by the fire were also eased. Oliver Peard, elected Mayor in August 1733, petitioned the Treasury for a remission of Tiverton's Land Tax payments. He was not only successful in this issue[2], but also managed to get a waiver on Walpole's unpopular Excise duty payable on beer, cider and candles[3]; in 1734 the arrears due for these payments were also cancelled[4].

[1] PRO C11/519/21.
[3] *ib.*, 414.

[2] *CalTreasB 1731-4*, 459.
[4] *JHC 1732-7*, 282.

Gotham House, built by George Davey after the 1731 fire.

Nathaniel Thorne died just three months after being elected Mayor of the Borough in 1734. He had been Receiver of the Land Tax for North Devon, and in this post he was succeeded by George Osmond, while his place as Mayor was taken by Richard Densham of Peadhill. One of the M.P.s, James Nelthorpe also died in this year. In the national elections called soon after, Arthur Arscott was returned again for Tiverton, and to replace Nelthorpe the Corporation elected another of Sir William Yonge's close associates, Dudley Ryder. No one could have foreseen the long connection this family would have with the borough, but just by looking at Ryder's background it is easy to see that here was a man, and a family, that would fit in well with Tiverton. He was the son of a merchant of West Smithfield, and had been educated at the renowned dissenting academy at Hackney. He had progressed to the universities of Edinburgh and Leyden, where perhaps he had met the Tivertonian Thomas Glasse who was studying medicine there[1]. Soon after his entrance to the Middle Temple, Ryder joined the Anglican Church. He was elected to sit for the Cornish borough of Saint Germans in 1733, and in the same year became Solicitor General.

---

[1] for an appreciation of Thomas Glasse's career, see Cameron 1996.

When John Jones, who had replaced Samuel Smith as Master of Blundell's only in the previous year, died in 1734, the Feoffees made an unusual appointment. They chose Samuel Wesley, a High Churchman, scholar, and poet. Although not as well known as his two brothers, John and Charles, were to become, Samuel was a national figure in his own right. He, too, suffered a fire. The extent of the blaze at the Master's house in 1736 is not known, but the Hospital Account Book records a payment of £5 11s for 'playing the engine at the schoolhouse fire'[1], and Blundell's Account Book includes money expended for 'putting right the damage'. Perhaps the excitement of the fire was almost welcomed by Wesley, for, in a letter to his brother, Charles, he intimated 'I am in a desert, having no conversable creature but my wife, till my mother came last week'[2]. Perhaps life did soon improve for him, however, as Charles returned from Georgia in December, and travelled down to Tiverton to see his brother and mother[3].

Another person in a different sort of desert was William Upcott. Although usually described as a merchant from Exeter, he operated mostly in Tiverton, where he was named as an assistant burgess in the renewed Charter of 1723, and had filled the offices of Mayor and Governor of the Hospital. After the 1731 fire, he was one of those who had refused any financial assistance. Indeed, he even set about rebuilding the Three Tuns and the extravagant folly known as the Market Cross.

The Market Cross in Fore Street, near Coggan's Well.

---

[1] DRO R4/1/Z/PO12.   [2] quoted in Harding 1845, iv, 88.
[3] Harmon 1968, 154.

For many years, however, Upcott had been overstretching his finances. In 1736, his lavish spending finally caught up with him, and in May he was declared bankrupt. The majority of his property was assigned to relatives, Walter Broad and Joan Chishull, for £3,500 to alleviate the situation[1]. His creditors included two Exeter men, William Holwell and Charles Webber, to whom he owed £500 and £1,100 respectively[2], and he was in debt for a £950 mortgage on Pale Barton Mill in Tiverton[3]. We do not know how much his creditors received, but one source[4] mentions a dividend of 5s in the £. He was not alone in having his finances scrutinised, as the Treasury was also investigating those of Samuel Burridge. When he was replaced in 1731 as Receiver of the Land Tax[5], it became clear that he owed a lot of money. The Treasury hoped to recoup some of it from his overseas business[6], sending an agent to estimate the value of his stock in Holland and Flanders[7]. All of his assets were to be administered by George Osmond[8], a man elected Mayor of Tiverton in 1736 and Governor of the Hospital.

The bells of Saint Peter's Church were recast during Osmond's mayoral term. William Evans of Chepstow undertook the task, and the work began at the end of 1736 in the area outside the south churchyard wall. Despite the dangers, which included lighting large fires to melt the bulky bells, crowds of onlookers assembled to watch the work in progress. Evans charged 3d a pound for melting and recasting the tower's six bells which weighed 19,209 pounds, to which was added two new ones, weighing 669 pounds, at 1s 2d a pound[9]. The total cost was nearly £230, of which £139 was raised by subscription. When finished, the bells carried the inscriptions Glory To God In The Highest, And On Earth Peace, Goodwill Towards Men, Prosperity To All Our Benefactors, together with Evans' name, those of the Churchwardens of 1736 and 1737, and Osmond as Mayor[10].

A succession of poor harvests drove up the price of corn during 1737 and led to national unrest[11]. In London, there were riots against the Irish because many of them were taking weaving jobs, and other work, at lower wages. We have already seen (pp.134, 137-8 and 148) how Tiverton workers reacted to imports of Irish yarn, and perhaps events in London had set them on edge again. In May 1738 several clothworkers took offence against an innkeeper called Sam Grimes, who kept the Red Lion Inn at the bottom of Barrington Street[12]. He was in the habit of buying serges that were returned to the manufacturers as substandard, and reselling them to other

---

[1] DRO 1926B/W/T24/1-2.   [2] DRO 257M/T57.
[3] DRO 49/9/6/151.   [4] DRO 49/9/6/67.
[5] *CalTreasB 1731-4*, 83.   [6] *ib.*, 110.
[7] which turned out to be worth just under £5,000 (*CalTreasB 1735-8*, 328).
[8] *ib.*, 195.   [9] DRO R4/1/Z/PW3.
[10] (Pengelly 1876, 767). The inscription on the no. 6 bell is not given here, as it was replaced in 1791.
[11] Gilmour 1992, 93.   [12] Dunsford 1790, 226-7.

merchants at a reduced cost, so bringing down the price of cloth. Other men from Bampton, Uffculme, Silverton, Cullompton, Bradninch, and Culmstock soon joined Tiverton's woolcombers and weavers. Grimes tried unsuccessfully to evade the angry crowd, but he was found and unceremoniously dumped at the Saint Peter Street home of the Mayor, Robert Dunsford. Several hastily recruited constables arrested and imprisoned a number of the rioters. Mayor Dunsford, expecting even more trouble, appealed to Exeter for help. Sixty men of Colonel Montague's regiment were despatched[1]. Meanwhile, in Tiverton a bloody confrontation took place, with the constables forcing the rioters out of the town and up to the top of Exeter Hill. In a scuffle there, the constables knocked a Bradninch man to the ground, and he died. This event brought the disturbance to an immediate end, and the rioters dispersed, well before the arrival of the troops. The consequences of the riot are not known, other than it heralded what seems to have been a relatively long, permanent, military presence in the town. But this was not to be the last episode of its kind by the clothworkers of Tiverton.

On November 6th 1739, the Master of Blundell's, Samuel Wesley died. He was laid to rest in Saint George's Churchyard, where a simple monument was erected in his memory. His two brothers John and Charles came to the town for the funeral, and stayed for a week[2]. There is no record that they preached on that occasion, but they had already both become renowned for their Methodist beliefs and open-air services. Wesley's successor at Blundell's, the Rev. William Daddo, was promptly chosen in January 1740, but could not be officially appointed right away. The delay was because a majority of the feoffees did not attend the meeting, so he had to wait a further eight months for its confirmation[3]. The feoffees were again in the fortunate position of having a surplus of funds, arising mainly from entry fines paid on the School's properties in South Devon. So, as was their custom, they took advice of the Court of Chancery which recommended the best way to dispose of the excess was to 'increase stipends or create exhibitions'[4]. Accordingly, Ham's Exhibitions were inaugurated, with William Bere and Robert Wilcocks the first to benefit. As for stipends, Daddo and the usher, Samuel Dalley, did not receive an increase, but others did. The Treasurer of the Feoffees was allowed £10 a year plus £4 for his duties as clerk, and the porter £2 15s.

In 1740, the Guardians of the Poor began an experiment to produce cloth in the Workhouse. The manufacture was prompted by the need to offset the rising costs of providing for the poor, which, at this time stood at about £1,200 a year. The Guardians sought subscriptions from the townspeople and succeeded in raising over £1,000. The

---

[1] Dobson 1980, 32.   [2] *Wesley I*, 250-2.
[3] Blundell's Order Book.   [4] cited in *Charities* 1826, 82.

money was loaned, however, not given as a donation[1]. Despite the capital outlay the project failed, as had each of the previous attempts. On this occasion, the reason given was the high wastage of materials, which is not surprising as many of the workers were untrained. To make matters worse, admissions to the Hospital rose steeply during the early part of 1741. A severe epidemic of typhus which was to last until the following spring was to blame. Martin Dunsford states that about 400 townsfolk succumbed to the disease, and on some days as many as a dozen funerals took place at Saint Peter's[2]. Even the tolling of the church bell was suspended to prevent a general alarm. In twelve months as many as one in twelve of the town's population died. The register of Saint Peter's enlarges Dunsford's estimate of the calamity: during the period from February 1741 to April 1742 there were 758 burials, although not all of them, of course, due to the disease. Toward the end of the outbreak, a pregnant Mrs Cosway of Coombewillis Farm, went to stay at Oakford in an attempt to avoid the contagion. There, in November, she gave birth to a son, Richard, who was to become one of Britain's greatest miniature painters[3]. Another birth would also prove significant. In the spring of 1742, a bookseller of the town, Philip Parkhouse, had married Hannah Richards, and on Valentine's Day in the following year, their first child, Hannah, was born. Who could have guessed that she would prove to be a renowned playwright?[4].

Britain had avoided war for almost a quarter of a century, mainly through Walpole's *laissez-faire* attitude. In 1739, however, Parliament demanded action against Spain, following reaction to the loss of Captain Jenkins' ear, and, more importantly, the War of the Austrian Succession again raised the price of involvement on the continent. Faced with an increasingly capable opposition headed by the Prince of Wales and the dwindling support of his own Whig party, Walpole resigned in 1742. Any optimism felt in Tiverton a decade earlier had largely vanished by this time. Bad harvests, inclement weather, an outbreak of typhus, and, now war, had all contributed to dissipate the feeling of well-being. Trade was hit; Spanish and French markets were lost, and shipping once more came under attack. Consequently, Tiverton and other Devon cloth towns were again forced to transport much of their produce overland to London, from where it was sent to the German and Dutch markets. On the other hand, the situation favoured cloth manufactured nearer the North Sea, notably the

---

[1] the Hospital accounts a few years later record the payment of interest due to the subscribers.
[2] Dunsford 1790, 228 and 463.
[3] Barnett 1995 is a recent biography of both Richard Cosway and his wife, Maria.
[4] for a full account of her life and work, see de la Mahotière 1997.

lighter 'Norwich stuffs', which had long been gaining in popularity.

The slump in trade in the Southwest had evident results. The *Gentleman's Magazine* of 1743[1] claimed that because of debt, 'great numbers filled the gaols and prisons so as to create a pestilence'. The same article stated that 'many landlords and tenants, as well as merchants and tradesmen about Exeter, Taunton and Tiverton have of late broke beyond number or example'. The *Magazine's* assertions can be substantiated by many sources, including the Devon Quarter Sessions order books. In 1743 alone, the Justices appointed custodians of the goods of Edmund Cleverdon, husbandman, William Marshall, perukemaker[2], and the butcher John Whitefield, all bankrupts of Tiverton[3]. Thomas Burnell, one of the town's blacksmiths, had 'run away for debt', leaving an apprentice still legally bound. The boy's father had to apply for the termination of his son's contract[4]. In trying times, masters cut their overheads wherever possible. This probably explains the rise in instances of dismissal, whether for alleged theft or, as in the case of Elizabeth Prouse, for her idle and disorderly behaviour[5].

Nevertheless, money was still to be made in Tiverton, although possibly by fewer individuals. The goldsmith Nicholas Marder was able to pay £1,400 in 1744 for the Half Moon Inn[6], and Walter Broad and Joan Chishull paid £1,800 for Pale Barton, but immediately used it as security for a £1,700 loan[7]. George Osmond remained the richest person . His appointment as Receiver of Taxes had catapulted him straight to the top of the financial and business tree. One measure of his prosperity is revealed in his dealings with the Sun Life Insurance Company. In a study of the policies issued in the period from 1731 to 1784, the amount insured by Osmond in the spring of 1740 is unsurpassed for Tiverton. The policy details goods to the value of £6,100[8] made up of the 'stock in trade in the dwelling house and workshop' of no less than nine individuals, ranging from £500 for the goods held by Thomas Davey to £1,000 held by John Harris. Osmond clearly had these nine fully in his employ and, no doubt, a whole host of others worked on less strict arrangements. His position was not without criticism, however. One reason given for the decline in Tiverton's trade was that his Receivership enabled him to 'forestall the markets and afford to undersell abroad his brother tradesmen'[9]. Osmond died in the summer of 1744, leaving £4,000 to his wife, £1,000 to his sister, and the considerable sum of £500 to a very fortunate apprentice and servant, Edward Chave[10]. Captain Daniel Ewings received Osmond's share in the 100-ton *Mermaid* 'now at Topsham Key'.

Osmond's death, of course, meant that there was a vacancy for the post of Receiver-

---

[1] p. 141.
[2] wigmaker.
[3] DRO QS1/18.
[4] *ib.*
[5] DRO R4/1/C338.
[6] KEO Black Chest 2.
[7] DRO 49/9/6/152-3.
[8] Chapman 1978.
[9] *Gentleman's Magazine 1744*, 140.
[10] DRO 1936M/FW38.

General of the Taxes. A petition was sent to the Treasury by Samuel Lewis senior and junior, Thomas and Richard Enchmarch and George Lewis, describing themselves as 'makers and exporters of woollen goods of Tiverton', stating

> *'that by the receipt of the land tax for that part of the county being in the hands of one of the merchants there, has occasioned their trade to decay for some years past, and praying that the receiver of the land tax for Devon may not be of the town of Tiverton or any way concerned in this trade there'* [1].

Their pleas went unheeded; the newly elected Mayor of Tiverton, Oliver Peard, was appointed [2]. This single action meant that Peard's financial status, like that of Osmond, placed him far above any other Tiverton merchant. In the single year of 1748, Peard received almost £550 in fees alone for undertaking the Receivership, and, more importantly, the House and Window Tax and the Land Tax brought in over £44,000 [3]. All of this was at his disposal until paid into the Treasury. He was now largely immune to the trading difficulties experienced by other clothiers. Nathaniel Ryder later wrote [4] that out of Tiverton's Corporation of 25 men, Peard had

> *'15 or 16 of them who are either truly under him as being employed in his house, or else beige makers, hot pressers, tuckers, etc., and depend upon him wholly for their business which is considerable.'*

Financially secure, Peard now expanded his landed property. He bought a large share of Cowley Moor Farm, as well as premises in Gold Street, Saint Peter Street, Westexe, and Town's End [5]. Bolham was to be his particular domain. He had a mansion built there in 1750, probably that now known as Bolham House. The location was accentuated by the construction of a canal leading to his house, flanked by two long rows of lime trees, many of which still survive alongside the stretch of road that passes the entrance to Rix Farm. From his home Peard could keep an eye on some of his commercial business, as he also owned the dyestuff and fulling mills at Bolham operated by the Webbers.

Many questions concerning dyeing operations in Tiverton remain unanswered. Regarding the dyestuff mills, did any dyeing actually take place there, or were they just grinding the logwood? In property deeds, the Webbers are designated 'dyestuff grinders' or 'raspers', or even 'fullers', but never 'dyers'. Who was responsible for importing the logwood? Webber or Peard? We simply do not know. Of the little information we have regarding dyeing methods in Tiverton, most comes from just a couple of documents, especially an inventory of the goods of Spurway Patey. He was a dyer, who carried on

---

[1] *CalTreasB 1742-5,* 512.
[2] *ib.,* 654.
[3] DRO 1926B/D/F6/29.
[4] cited in Bourne 1986, xvii.
[5] KEO Box 8.

his trade behind his house in the lower part of Gold Street, although he had storage space elsewhere in the town. In a house in Castle Street he kept 56 weys[1] of 'woold' (woad) and 37 weys of woodwax. At home in Gold Street he kept a further 67 weys of woodwax, and 'in the stuff chamber' varying quantities of potash, logwood, red sandalwood, brazilwood, copperas, old fustick, redwood and 'old lead', and in the 'ware shop' indigo, peachwood, more redwood, galls, argol and archall[2]. The raw materials for these dyes were mostly imported from Central and South America, but we know little about this trade. They were obviously for local use as, when they were sold, the purchasers were to a man Tiverton sergemakers[3]. Such a large variety of dyes enabled them to produce cloth ranging in colour from the green of copperas, yellow of fustic, blue of indigo and woad, violet of archil, red and purple of brazilwood, to the black of logwood.

Trouble broke out in the town again in the spring of 1749. It seems its clothworkers needed little excuse to take to the streets to protect their livelihood. As in 1738 substandard cloth was being resold, this time by one Thomas Beedle. A crowd of woolcombers and weavers assembled near the Castle and, fortified by a hogshead of cider, marched on Beedle's house, the Crown and Comb Inn at the end of Water Lane. Once there, they ransacked the premises[4] and discovered one of Beedle's combers, Moses Quick, hiding in a vat of urine[5]. He was taken out and led through the town to the mill leat in Westexe, where he was ducked and almost drowned. The unfortunate man was revived with alcohol and sent staggering on his way. Believing the lesson to have been taught, the crowd dispersed. There is no record of criminal proceedings, but the Baptist Church Minute Book notes that two of its members, William Simmons and John Rippon, 'had been concerned in a late riot in judging condemning and punishing of a man in a most cruel and barbarous manner'[6].

Towards the end of 1749, the actions of Tiverton's clothiers resulted in further unrest. Ignoring previous experience, they resolved to bring in increasing quantities of Irish worsted. The combers returned all their work to the merchants and took the woolpads, used for carding, from the combshops, announcing they would not resume work until the merchants stopped importing Irish materials. The Woolcombers' Club, in its 50th year, met at their headquarters in the Half Moon, and finally decided they would live off the club's funds until either 'the weavers starve or the merchants comply'[7]. Tiverton remained on edge as the combers' funds ran low. Threats persuaded

---

[1] an obsolete unit of weight, usually taken to be 182lbs.
[2] DRO 52/13/11/11.   [3] DRO 52/13/11/12.
[4] Dunsford 1790, 228-9.
[5] collected at inns, and widely used for de-greasing wool.
[6] DRO 3958D/1.   [7] Dunsford 1790, 230-2.

the merchants to summon troops. In an attempt at reconciliation they then proposed to limit the Irish worsted to just enough for 20 cloths a week. The combers rejected their offer, and many of them left Tiverton to find other work. Gradually, however, they returned. These events received national notice through the pages of the *Gentleman's Magazine* which, in January 1750[1], apportioned the blame firmly on the introduction of Irish worsted. The plight of the combers also gained support from the anonymous publication of *The Tiverton Woolcombers' Defence*, probably the work of William Daddo, the Master of Blundell's.

Tiverton's cloth production was forced to adapt during the 1750s. Competition from the lightweight Norwich stuffs was increased by legislation that restricted the importation of cotton goods from the East Indies. Local clothiers resorted to industrial espionage. One of their number, Francis Enchmarch, together with a weaver travelled to Norwich, where they made 'themselves fully acquainted with the plans of these woollen manufactures', before being discovered and escaping back to Devon. The result was the addition to Tiverton's range of products of the exotic-sounding 'camblets, tarborates, barragons, lutestrings etc'[2], as well as brocade damasks and sagathies[3]. About twenty houses on the west side of Bampton Street were given over to producing the new fabrics. About this time scarlet was added to the range of colours of cloth produced in the town, almost certainly using cochineal. Where did this leave the woolcombers? While merchants could change their product almost at will, and weavers could weave with whatever they were given, combers had to work with wool or abandon their trade altogether. It is no wonder that this group became the most militant.

John Wesley visited Tiverton in August 1750 for the first time since his brother's funeral 11 years before. He preached to 'an abundance of people' and enthused, in his diary, 'Surely good will be done in this place'[4]. A month later he returned to an even more impressive reception, when, prophetically, 'it rained in the day several times, but not a drop fell while I was preaching'. Wesley was aware of the opportunity presented in the town. 'Here is an open door indeed! May no man be able to shut it!'[5]. He hastily proceeded to place a foot in that door by appointing one William Robarts to serve the area. Unfortunately for Wesley, his euphoria was not to be long-lived. In the following year, he made a very successful visit in August, but his return in October was completely different. He himself wrote that, in addition to a large crowd of believers assembled to hear him preach in the Market Place, there was a noisy band of the 'sons

---

[1] p.41.
[2] Dunsford 1790, 235-6.
[3] Kerridge 1985, 88.
[4] *Wesley vol II*, 202-3.
[5] *ib.*, 206.
[6] (*ib.*, 244). Probably referring to this incident, Dunsford says these 'sons of Belial', were 'servants of men attending Blundell's School's annual meeting' (1790, 233-5).

of Belial' with 'a drummer at their head'[6]. He was heckled throughout his sermon, and was escorted from the place for his own safety. There is no doubt that there was opposition to Methodism in Tiverton. The Mayor[1], when asked whether Methodists should be banished from the town, replied that with Saint Peter's, Saint George's, the meeting houses, and open-air preaching, there was already enough religion in Tiverton. He added

> *'if people were not able to go to heaven by one of these ways then, by God, they would not go there at all as long as he was mayor'* [2].

More seriously, in 1752 William Robarts was the victim of an assault by Thomas Hall who threw stones and dirt at him[3]. Nevertheless, in 1752, the Methodists opened a meetinghouse in a room behind some cottages on the east side of Saint Peter Street, and Tiverton became the centre of a circuit that encompassed the whole of Devon.

Beyond the town, changes were taking place in the countryside where more methodical and scientific approaches were being applied to agriculture. Clauses, known as conditions of husbandry, relating to the amounts of lime or dung to be spread on the land had first appeared in a Tiverton lease as early as 1686[4], but only become commonplace from the middle of the 18th century. As an example, each acre of a part of Gogwell had to be dressed with '10 hogsheads of lime or 150 seams of dung'[5]. The effect of such conditions was to make the tenant maintain the fertility of his land, instead of letting it deteriorate towards the end of his tenancy. They became increasingly specialised. A later lease on the Gogwell land stipulated

> *'no more than three successive corn crops, always seeding out the last crop with 10lbs of clover seed and two pecks of eaver seed per acre, crops in the last year not to be sown with pease as no grass seeds can be sown therewith, not to sow with hemp, flax or rape seed, no more than two successive wheat crops'* [6].

Conversely, many vestiges of the old manorial system remained. The manor of Saint James at Manley in 1749 could still exact two oxen as heriots on the death of the tenant of Copplestone[7]. Some manors remained with their ancient lords; the Carews held a quarter share of much of the original medieval manor of Tiverton; similarly, the Worths retained great swathes of land locally, and the Gwyns held Lowman Clavile and East Chevithorne. Other manors had passed from the gentry to professional families, such as Frogwell, which was in the possession of Caleb Pierce, an apothecary[8].

Parliament was dissolved in April 1754, and the Corporation of Tiverton went about its preparations to choose new members. The town's clothworkers with other

---

[1] Thomas Heathfield or Henry Hodge, depending on the time the event occurred.
[2] cited by Hoskins 1959, 128.   [3] DRO QS9/44.
[4] (DRO 1292M/Leases/Tiverton 3), relating to Manley.
[5] DRO 1160M/Leases/Tiverton 6.   [6] DRO 1160M/Leases/Tiverton 8.
[7] DRO 411Z/M1.   [8] DRO 49/9/48/11.

groups now demanded a right to vote. The Mayor, Oliver Peard, became so concerned that he called for a military presence. Lieutenant James Suttie and a detachment of Enniskillen Dragoons, promptly arrived in the town 'with swords drawn'[1]. Excitement rose to fever pitch on April 17th, thought to be the election day, when a large crowd took to the streets. Led by the banners of various friendly societies they marched down Saint Peter Street as far as Peard's townhouse in Fore Street. There, the Town Clerk read the Riot Act. The crowd resumed their procession as far as the Three Tuns, where the Dragoons blocked the way. When they did not respond to a second reading of the Riot Act, the soldiers mounted their horses. Tension was diffused only with the announcement that this was not in fact the election day. The townspeople returned to the area around the Castle and Saint Peter's to plan their next move. When perhaps it would have been better to let matters rest, the Town Clerk provocatively read the Riot Act for the third time. The mob stood its ground, refusing to disperse, so the soldiers descended on the churchyard in an attempt to arrest some of the ringleaders. The crowd moved back into Fore Street where they were faced by mounted soldiers with swords drawn, and others on foot with bayonets fixed, all under orders to attack. A ferocious skirmish took place, leading to many injuries. Humiliation followed for the Dragoons, as Lieutenant Suttie's sword was seized by some women and never returned. Was it kept as a trophy by one of the clubs? We can only guess.

The way was now clear for the election by the Corporation. Sir William Yonge was chosen to be one of the Members of Parliament, the other seat going to Henry Pelham, a cousin of the recently deceased Prime Minister. Probably in an attempt to draw a line under the violent events that had taken place, Yonge paid out large sums of money to many of those who had been injured. He died towards the end of 1755, however, and Thomas Ryder, the brother of Dudley, who had been elected for Tiverton in 1734, took his seat in the Commons. This was purely a temporary measure until Dudley Ryder's son, Nathaniel, reached his majority. Eighteenth century politics would be characterised by patronage, and Tiverton would become the archetypal pocket borough under the Ryder family. It is likely that such a system had been in operation for a long time, probably from the arrival of Yonge in the 1720s. The first certain example occurs in a letter from Oliver Peard written in 1756 to Thomas Ryder soliciting a military post for his brother-in-law, Major John Leman[2]. Having kept the seat warm, at the end of 1756 Thomas duly resigned. Young Nathaniel was no doubt encouraged by a letter from 21 of Tiverton's 25 burgesses expressing the 'hopes and expectations we entertain

---

[1] Dunsford 1790, 238-42.   [2] *Harrowby MSS vol I*, 3.
[3] cited in Chalk 1935, 322.

of your regard and attachment to our future interest'[3].

He was soon at work in the Commons taking care of this 'future interest'; in particular, regarding the local roads. Privatisation was the rage of the 1750s. Beginning with London, trusts were established by Act of Parliament to take tolls from road-users in order to build better roads and maintain them more effectively than parishes ever could. Tiverton did not lag behind. The Mayor and many others presented a petition to the House of Commons in January 1758. They pointed out that the roads in the vicinity of the town had became so ruinous that an Act was necessary to have them 'widened, enlarged and repaired'[1]. Nathaniel Ryder reported early in February that a surveyor had confirmed their poor condition, and a Bill was given its first reading on the 10th of that month[2]. The Earl of Portsmouth, who lived at Eggesford, raised some opposition. He petitioned, unsuccessfully in the end, to have one of the roads extended to Witheridge[3], no doubt better to serve his lands at Chawleigh, Chulmleigh and in the Taw valley. Following the insistence of 'the gentlemen between Tiverton and Crediton', the turnpike road originally projected to run from Tiverton to Cadbury Cross, was extended all the way to Crediton Forches[4]. The Bill received its third reading on March 9th, was agreed by the Lords a week later, and on the 23rd received royal assent as the *Act for Amending Several Roads Leading from the Town of Tiverton*[5]. The Act empowered the Trustees, over 130 in number, to make bridges and drains, to widen roads, and to determine the amount of statute labour to be performed[6]. Certain categories of traffic were exempted from paying tolls, and the list reveals both national and local concerns. It included all traffic on His Majesty's service, those employed in passing on vagrants, going to or from church on Sundays and attending funerals, those transporting manure, hay and straw which was unsold, horses that were coming from or going to pasture or shoeing, and, very important to Tiverton, all traffic transporting woollen goods to the mills or tenters and dyewoods to and from mills. Although the tolls were meant to make a profit, the cloth industry was not to be endangered. Quite the opposite; the cloth producers' lot would, it was hoped, be improved by a more efficient and speedy road network.

The Tiverton Turnpike Trustees held their first meeting in the Town Hall on April 13th 1758. They decided to erect toll-gates near Hunt's House at the foot of Exeter Hill, at Ashley Gate, Cottey House, Bonny Pit Gate (near the present cemetery), and Red Ball on the border of Holcombe Rogus and Culmstock parishes[7]. Advertisements were

---

[1] *JHC 1757-61*, 47.
[2] *ib.*, 68.
[3] DRO R4/1/Z32/3.
[4] DRO R4/1/Z32/4.
[5] *JHC 1757-61*, 168.
[6] each farm had to provide men and horses according to its value. In the parish of Tiverton, this burden fell most heavily on Chevithorne, which had to provide four teams, with Gornhay and Collipriest each furnishing three teams (DRO R4/1/Z32/9).
[7] (DRO R4/1/Z1). That at Red Ball was moved to White Ball within a month.

posted inviting tenders for building new toll-houses which were to be 14 feet square with 'a chamber over'[1], but existing houses were used at Ashley and Cottey House[2]. Almost immediately, money was borrowed on security of the tolls - £600 in May and a similar sum in October[3] – by selling £50 deeds poll. In this investment, Oliver Peard led the way, taking the first six deeds[4].

There were problems from the outset. Many individuals disagreed with the turnpike system and others simply did not want to hand over money. Before long, incidents were reported to the Trustees or the courts. In March 1759 Thomas Coles, a Washfield waggoner, was fined for paying only 9d to take a wagon with four horses through Bonny Pit Gate, but a little further along the road he added another horse, so defrauding the Trust of 3d[5]. John Upham of Rewe not only refused to pay the toll altogether, but also assaulted the collector and his wife[6]. The road from Tiverton through Silverton to Topsham, used for transporting cloth destined for export, presented difficulties due to the terrain. Special licences were necessary to use large teams of horses, such as that issued by the Justices to Francis Enchmarch allowing him to use five horses to pull his wagons up the steep ascent from Silverton to Christ Cross and on the hills either side of Butterleigh Water[7]. For people travelling to or from Exeter and Crediton matters were soon improved greatly by driving a road, 20 feet wide, along the western side of the valley from Ashley to the Bartons, the present section of the A396[8]. Tiverton had sound commercial reasons for obtaining the Turnpike Act. A more efficient road system would lead to quicker, therefore cheaper, deliveries of cloth and other goods, which would in turn, hopefully, encourage investment in the area.

Again, war hampered enterprise. The Seven Years War had broken out in 1756, and most European states were drawn into it. Britain became allied with Prussia and Hanover against France, Austria, Saxony, Sweden, Russia and, later, Spain. Despite continued British success in India and Canada, especially during 1759, there was widespread disruption to trade. Indeed, according to Dunsford[9], Tiverton's prosperity ended on October 25th 1760 with the death of George II. Production of the Norwich stuffs in Tiverton ceased in the following year[10], less than a decade after their

---

[1] DRO R4/1/Z32/4.
[2] DRO R4/1/Z1.
[3] DRO R4/1/Z283.
[4] DRO R4/1/Z12.
[5] DRO R4/1/Z1.
[6] he must have escaped from the scene, for he is next encountered at Plymouth Dock Barracks asking for pardon (DRO R4/1/Z32/3-4).
[7] DRO QS1/20.
[8] the land used for this new stretch was owned by Joanna Lewis and Dame Dorothy Carew, and was exchanged for the section of the old road that ran parallel to the river but higher up the slope (DRO R4/1/Z27).
[9] Dunsford 1790, 56..
[10] ib., 244.

introduction, and, to make matters much, much worse, a mixed serge manufacture was established at Wellington[1] that attracted many skilled workers. The Seven Years' War ended in February 1763, but would Tiverton's trade recover? Much would rely on Oliver Peard.

Peard's financial position had rendered him largely immune to fluctuations in trade. The £45,000 or more a year he collected from the Land and Window Taxes[2] was often used to make loans to other merchants. Ryder said of his character

> 'he seems a man of very generous open disposition and one who by his general conversation one would not suspect to have much design. But yet when any matters of importance come upon the carpet, it is easy to discern by his expressions that both they and his conduct is as cautious and guarded as possible'[3].

He could be genuinely altruistic, and was instrumental in the early career of the young Tiverton artist, Richard Cosway. He was also hard-headed and controlled much of the local cloth production. In a letter written to Nathaniel Ryder in 1763 he proclaimed that he was using over £60,000 of his own money in Tiverton[4]. When Charles Gore, one of the M.P.s for the Borough, was going abroad, he asked his colleague, Ryder, whether the best way to inform the town of his absence was a letter to the Mayor and Corporation, or one to 'our good friend' Oliver Peard[5]. It is plain to see who was really in control of the borough.

All was to change, however, when the sound of a shot echoed through Fore Street on the morning of Monday, December 18th 1764. Oliver Peard had blown away half of his face with a blunderbuss. Many people sought a reason for his suicide. The mystery had not been solved by the time his body was interred beside that of his wife at Holcombe Rogus on December 21st, nor by the time a memorial was raised in Saint George's Churchyard, nor indeed to this very day. Why did the richest man in Tiverton, and one of the richest in the county, take his own life? Were financial troubles to blame? Nothing has so far been discovered to support such a presumption. Indeed, his successor as Receiver-General of Taxes handed over the correct amount for the year 1765-6[6]. Was there a scandal? The fact that none emerged may simply quash this idea, equally the large amounts of money at hand could have been used to keep the secret under cover. The medical history of the Peards provides a possible explanation. An unusually high percentage of the family's males did not survive their 30th birthday. Oliver, on the other hand, lived into his 60s, but left no heir[7]. His father had died in 1724 shortly after consulting Dr Henry Cheyney at Bath, a man renowned for being

---

[1] Dunsford 1790, 56.
[3] Bourne 1986, xvi.
[5] Chalk 1935, 333-4.
[2] DRO 1926B/D/F6/33.
[4] *Harrowby MSS vol I*, 15.
[6] DRO 1926B/D/F6/35.
[7] he was married in 1733, but was obliged to make a settlement of some of his lands on his wife in 1748, there being no heir.

adept at treating 'melancholy'.

Was there some degenerative condition running through the family? Such medical clues are tenuous and, of necessity, speculative. A letter from Henry Osmond to Nathaniel Ryder, dated January 7th 1765[1], provides a sinister twist to the mystery. Osmond had expected to receive a large bequest from Peard, but was devastated when he discovered that the great man had died intestate. Intestate, only because 'he was prevailed upon to burn' the will he had made just two days before his death. Who had persuaded him to do this?

---

[1] *Harrowby MSS vol I*, 25.

12 The Georgian Borough

Peard's death caused a political crisis for the town and for the Ryder interest in the constituency. He had been Tiverton's chief merchant as well as agent for its patrons. His office as Receiver-General of the Land and Window Tax passed briefly to a former Major, Daniel Hamilton. In many circles, this was a popular choice because it broke the monopoly of the Tiverton merchants, but Hamilton's close association with the Ryders was less well received[1]. He refused to consolidate his position with a place on the Corporation, and soon moved to Exeter[2]. Apart from Peard, two other burgesses had died in 1764, and it was clear that the election of their replacements would be fiercely contested. Two of Peard's cousins, yet another Oliver Peard and John Dickinson, proposed George Lewis, Richard Enchmarch and John Duntze[3]. Whereas Lewis and Enchmarch were acceptable to the other burgesses, Duntze had his critics. Descended from German immigrants, he could claim a close connection with Tiverton as he was married to a Lewis heiress of the town. Nathaniel Ryder was soon warned of danger by Henry Osmond; an Exeter merchant called John Baring was 'coming here to settle a fortune'[4]. Also of German origin, he had arrived in Devon in 1717, and rapidly accumulated great wealth. He soon won over the support of many of Tiverton's clothworkers by promising to bring much-needed trade to the town. The battle lines between Duntze and Baring were drawn. The election was deemed sufficiently important for George Grenville, the Prime Minister, to offer Ryder help to secure the right candidates, claiming he had influence among some of the inhabitants[5].

Unrest seemed inevitable. Henry Osmond and the Mayor, John Webber, both pointed out to Ryder that troops might be necessary[6]. Baring's followers, firmly believing that their man had the support of the majority of the Corporation, insisted that Webber call an election immediately. At first he refused, but on June 12th 'one hundred of ye poor starving creatures surrounded the Angel Inn where the Mayor was and thro' fear got him to sign that he would call a Hall [for an election] and they left in peace'[7]. He duly advertised this for Monday, June 17th, a date recorded in the Hall Book[8]. Daniel Hamilton did all he could to delay the election, fearing that if Baring

---

[1] (Ward 1953, 171-2). He was to be 'allowed' to hold the position on payment to the Corporation of £60 and a pipe of wine each year.

[2] DRO R4/1/Z79.

[3] *Grenville 1763-5*, 279.

[4] *Harrowby MSS vol I*, 25.

[5] *Grenville 1763-5*, 279.

[6] (*Harrowby MSS vol I*, 53-4). The town had been home to Colonel James Oughton's regiment since the end of 1763, but clearly reinforcements were meant.

[7] DRO R4/1/Z79.

[8] DRO R4/1/C1.

were elected he would lose the Receivership. Just two days before the vote, he persuaded Webber to announce his intended absence on the day, so it would have to be postponed. Despite this, most of the 24 burgesses turned up at the Town Hall on the 17th. Of these, no fewer than 14 declared publicly for Baring[1]. The crowds waiting for a result were understandably incensed. Fortified by two hogsheads of cider, according to Osmond[2] bought by Baring, they decided to march on the Mayor's house at Bolham. This was attacked and severely damaged, as were Webber's mills. His cloth racks were destroyed and the sluices on the mill leat wrecked[3]. The incident was considered so serious that the King himself was immediately informed of the 'outrages' committed by a crowd said to have numbered '300 and upwards'[4]. He even offered a pardon to anyone who could bring in two of the ringleaders, Thomas Cocker and Francis Lock, or any of the others involved. No one, it seems, was induced to accept.

The election took place eventually on July 1st. When votes were cast, the result was uncomfortably close; Lewis, Enchmarch and Duntze, were each elected with 11 votes, but John Baring failed, with 10. The manoeuvring by the Ryders and their so-called lackeys had kept out a man who promised work for a great many people in the town. Predictably, Baring's supporters took to the streets and violence followed. The windows of the Town Hall were smashed, Peard 'had his hat knocked about his head'[5], and a vocal majority of the women in the crowd chanted defiantly 'Baring for ever, no piss for Webber'[6], referring, of course, to the fullers' practice of using urine to wash cloth. Soldiers stationed in the town attempted to quell the troubles, and arrested three rioters. The prisoners were taken off towards Exeter, but the soldiers were told that there was a 500-strong crowd on Stoke Hill waiting to rescue the three. Yet again, we do not know what happened there. When the violence ceased, the accusations began. Hamilton was accused of having had one of the burgesses kidnapped and kept under guard to prevent him from voting, and that Webber had tried to extort £200 from Baring. The prospect of further trouble persisted. At the end of July, one of the town's merchants, George Cruwys, received a letter threatening to burn down his house and murder him[7]. A similar letter was sent to a certain James How's father. It said menacingly 'as shore as thee hast a soul in thy body thou shalt be rested in thy bed before the winter is over, and as for thy son, we will fold him up one night or other, we have sworn and will perform'[8]. It is impossible to tell whether these were political in aim or simply personal vendettas.

---

[1] DRO R4/1/Z79.
[2] *Harrowby MSS vol I*, 67.
[3] *ib.*, 70.
[4] *HOPG3 1760-5*, 568.
[5] *Harrowby MSS vol I*, 74.
[6] *ib.*, 75.
[7] DRO R4/1/Z/PO13.
[8] *Harrowby MSS vol I*, 178.

Oliver Peard's personal fortune was bequeathed to his sister, Mary. She was his next-of-kin[1], for his wife predeceased him, and the marriage had remained childless. Mary had immediately moved out of her house near Saint Peter's Church into her brother's Fore Street mansion. She showed herself an uncompromising woman, not prepared to underpin Tiverton trade with her new-found fortune. She advised one clothier who had been kept by Oliver, to 'take care of himself', as no trade would be carried on with her money[2]. The dead man's two cousins, Peard and Dickinson, took over his business interests, which were also attracting the attention of the Barings[3]. Their enterprise was concentrated in Westexe, where the partnership had just bought those mills termed Six-Mill and Four-Mill[4]. Just as they were beginning to realise some success, Peard died in April 1767. His will names his young son, yet another Oliver, as heir. Apart from this boy, it mentions no single personal bequest over £50, other than a sum of £300 to 'Jane Woodlake my servant maid who has several times preserved my life and saved me from burning by falling into the fire'[5]. Is this another clue to a hereditary medical condition, which perhaps had driven his uncle to suicide in 1764?

George Davey had forfeited his post of Town Clerk because of his support for Baring. Beavis Wood, a native of Norwich, another important centre of cloth production, took his place. Wood, therefore, already had a good understanding of the industry and how important it was for Tiverton. He was a lawyer and brought his professional expertise to the clerkship, along with a strong sense of loyalty to the King's government, the Established Church, and to the Ryder family[6]. He is best known to us now as the author of a huge number of letters to the Ryders, mainly in their capacity as Parliamentary representatives of Tiverton. This corpus of work is contained in the Harrowby Papers and part of it has recently been made widely accessible by John Bourne's volume, *Georgian Tiverton*. The correspondence shows that he had little time for Dissenters or those who proposed reform in any guise, for as Bourne says, he 'saw no hope in change'[7]. Little happened that went unnoticed by Wood, and all was communicated to the Ryders in London or at Sandon Hall in Staffordshire.

Trade in Tiverton was hardly flourishing when Beavis Wood arrived. Indeed, Daniel Hamilton, the man Wood replaced as 'informer', would write to Nathaniel Ryder about the Baring family's financial position in 1766. He gloated over the failure of their Spanish business interests, which had left them with debts of £12,000[8]. The setback does not seem to have been as serious as Hamilton hoped, however, as John and

---

[1] DRO 1936M/FW50.
[2] *Harrowby MSS vol I*, 148.
[3] *ib.*, 182.
[4] (KEO Chest 1). So named for the pairs of fulling stocks they contained.
[5] *Murray Wills*.
[6] Bourne 1986, xi-xii.
[7] *ib.*, xiii.
[8] *Harrowby MSS vol I*, 183 and 186.

Charles Baring actually expanded their interests in Tiverton in the following year. They abandoned their attempt to woo Peard and Dickinson, preferring to forge a partnership with one William Smale. He had prospered as a merchant through the 1750s, and used much of his money to buy property, including the Market Cross in Fore Street[1]. Together, Smale and the two Baring brothers insured their interests for £5,900 in August 1767. Of this sum, the utensils and stock kept in the Cross (called the Folly in the policy) accounted for £3,000, and the building itself a further £300, while six houses and offices in Fore Street and their contents took care of another £1,500[2]. The remaining premises were widespread, and included property in Bampton Street, Saint Andrew Street, and, outside the town, at Collipriest, Lythecourt, Middle Marsh and Bolham, as well as buildings at Witheridge and further afield at Winkleigh. Many of the buildings are listed simply as barns or linhays, implying they were used for storage of items used in producing cloth or even as places to dry the cloth itself.

Some enterprising Tivertonians continued to look to improve communications as a means of boosting trade. The Tiverton Turnpike Act (see p.168) was amended in 1767, permitting the Trustees to build a new stretch of road linking Bickleigh Bridge to Silverton by way of the valley. This new route would avoid the steep gradients of the road from Tiverton through Butterleigh to Silverton. An even more ambitious scheme was proposed in the following October. Money was collected to pay for a survey for a projected canal to run 'by way of Taunton and Tiverton to Exeter'[3]. If successful, this waterway would link the Bristol and English Channels, making the long, arduous, and dangerous journey around Land's End unnecessary. The idea had been mooted; it would take all too long to be attempted.

A few individuals took it upon themselves to search for new markets. Martin Dunsford travelled to London in 1768, and then to Holland, in an attempt to restore business. Although he was unsuccessful in Holland, he made some good contacts with American merchants in London, which proved beneficial, at least for a short time. Meanwhile, John Thorne held a meeting with some of Tiverton's clothiers to discuss a plan to 'enlarge the Asian commerce'[4]. The islands of the West Indies also held potential as markets, and Tiverton already had links with some of them. Blundell's admissions registers, begun in 1770, reveal two boys, John Audain junior and John Esdaile[5], from Saint Christopher. In December 1773, James Nibbs, the owner of a sugar plantation in Antigua, visited the Mayor of Tiverton. He brought news that a 'Mr Alderman Oliver' might place orders to have the clothing of 'his negroes' made in

---

[1] DRO 257M/T64.
[2] Chapman 1978.
[3] *Harrowby MSS vol II*, 10.
[4] *ib.*, 9.
[5] the son of Archibald Esdaile, soon to become governor of Saint Christopher.

Tiverton and that this would bring much employment. Beavis Wood, the source of this information, added

> *'I fancy the Tiverton combers and weavers have always been such free fellows that they will not choose to go to work for slaves, as the wages must certainly be very low on such a mean fabrick as they are clothed with'* [1].

The inmates of Tiverton's Workhouse were now required to support the town's traditional industry. Cloth production, or various processes of it, is often mentioned in relation to the institution, but usually on an *ad hoc* basis. From 1772, however, there seems to have been a more organised approach. When the position of Master was advertised in the *Exeter Flying Post*, it called for a single man 'thoroughly acquainted with the woollen manufacture'. The wool was sorted by the inmates and sent out to those combers who were applying for poor relief. They received 2d for each pound combed, but should they refuse the work their relief was terminated [2]. The wool was then returned to the Workhouse, spun, generally by the children, and finally woven into cloth. In 1774 these operations earned £161 5s 1d [3], just 6% of the money needed to support Tiverton's poor. A report submitted to Parliament shows that in the same year £2,546 15s 6d was raised in Tiverton by the poor rate. Of this total, over half was spent on food and fuel, and a third was paid as occasional outdoor relief.

The lists of contributors to the poor rate show that many of Tiverton's richest inhabitants were still closely associated with the great Oliver Peard, although he had died a decade earlier. His sister Mary, and her nephew Benjamin Dickinson, had the highest assessments, along with the merchant and Mayor of that year, George Lewis, and 'Madam' Lewis [4]. They were closely followed by Henry Osmond [5]. Mary Peard had put a lot of her inherited capital to good uses. She bought Middleway Farm, Cruwys Morchard, from which the profits were to be used by the Tiverton Charity Schools [6], to which she gave a further sum of £1,000. Similarly, she purchased the estate of Marlecombe in the parish of Awliscombe [7]. Its revenues were to keep Saint George's Church in good repair and, when the time came, to maintain her tomb there. Although being female excluded her from the Corporation, she still had power over some of the burgesses. She threatened Henry Osmond in 1769 that if he did not vote for her nephew, Benjamin Dickinson, in the mayoral election, 'she would convert the £10,000 which she was going to leave to his son into a shilling' [8].

---

[1] *Harrowby MSS vol II*, 66.   [2] DRO R4/1/Z/PV1.

[3] in *HC18th vol 31*.

[4] the widow Joanna Lewis, mother-in-law of John Duntze.

[5] DRO R4/1/Z/PO3.   [6] DRO 2685B add/PF2.

[7] DRO 2685B add2/PF1.

[8] (*Harrowby MSS vol II*, 27). This seems to have been 'the fortune' that Henry Osmond expected to receive from Oliver Peard's will.

Events in the American colonies captured national attention in 1776. The colonists' resistance to taxation without political representation developed into the Declaration of Independence and armed conflict. There was considerable sympathy in Tiverton for the cause of the colonists, especially among Dissenters. Many merchants mourned the loss of trade, not least Martin Dunsford, who decried the consequences of

> 'the unhappy war, which the arbitrary English ministry unjustly commenced
> and cruelly prosecuted, to the utter ruin of our trade and connection with the
> 13 American Colonies which was peculiarly injurious and distressing to me
> by stopping the course of my best trade, and leaving large quantities of goods
> on hand which were not all sold in the course of many years, and then with
> considerable loss' [1].

The situation forced him to make three further journeys to the Low Countries, in a desperate attempt to find outlets for his serges[2]. But his efforts were largely for nothing, as the situation worsened. France sided with the Americans in 1778, and Holland followed suit soon after. Britain stood virtually alone. Men from Tiverton were not merely observers; some actually fought in the conflict, in the navy as well as the army. Saint Peter's Vestry met to consider how to relieve their families[3]. Dorothy Drewe, in her claim for poor relief, said that her husband was a marine serving on *HMS Cumberland*[4]. By 1780, the war had become thoroughly unpopular in Britain. Taxes were high, and the nation's debt was mounting. The Commons demanded a reduction of the influence of the Crown, and there was a surge of support for parliamentary reform led by the Corresponding Societies. Yet, it was to be an age-old problem that led to extreme violence and bloodshed. A group of radical Protestant associations, headed by Lord George Gordon, incensed with the concessions granted by the Roman Catholic Relief Act (1778), marched on Parliament demanding its repeal. The rioting that followed in London lasted for eight days, during which more than 300 people died. Parliamentary elections followed, and raised the hopes of many of the Government's critics. Rather than a change, however, the results in effect handed the Government a new lease of life.

There was little to celebrate in Tiverton during these years. Even the unique success of Hannah Cowley was afflicted by fate. The daughter of Philip Parkhouse the Tiverton bookseller had achieved fame in 1776 when her first play *The Runaway* was embraced warmly by the London theatres. Her subsequent efforts were not so well received, however. In December 1780 her father was obliged to ask Nathaniel Ryder for a

---

[1] Dunsford 1904, 220.
[2] *ib.*
[3] DRO R4/1/Z/PV1.
[4] DRO QS1/21.

pension for his daughter or a better position for her husband, as the couple were having to rely on the profits of her plays to survive[1]. The year ended with the death of the town's principal inhabitant, Mary Peard, who passed away on its final day. Her vast fortune, almost £70,000, was left largely to the Dickinsons – Mary, James, Henry, and her favourite, Benjamin, whom she made sole executor. She bequeathed her lands in Halberton to Henry Peard Osmond 'her kinsman', and her young cousin Oliver Peard junior received property and £6,000. William Tucker later wrote to Nathaniel Ryder commenting that all her relations, 'except Mr Dickinson, are much disappointed at the will'[2]. Indeed, Benjamin was given most of the Tiverton property, including the Great House in Fore Street[3] which he had shared with his aunt.

Dickinson's business rival, William Smale, continued to buy up land. He acquired the mills at the bottom of Hammetts Lane[4], as well as premises in Wellbrook Street, Broad Lane, and Bolham[5]. His trading partner, Charles Baring, was probably responsible for introducing one of his own relatives, Nicholas Dennys, to Tiverton. In a property deed of 1772[6], he is termed 'merchant of Tiverton', although from later evidence, he appears to have been a linen-draper of London. Was Baring using Dennys as an excuse to withdraw from his alliance with Smale, or to disassociate himself from Tiverton altogether? Such a reason is tempting to propose, as Dennys, too, was, by 1779, in partnership with Smale. Together, they bought various shares of Frost's Meadow[7] in an attempt to secure this important field, now part of the Heathcoat's Factory site, under single ownership.

Falling demand for cloth was inevitably having an effect on some of Tiverton's mills. In 1782 Nicholas Dennys, William Smale, and his son, also William, acquired two of the Westexe mills, the fulling mill known as Govier's, and Pale Barton Mill. Whereas both of those were still operating as fulling mills others had undergone a change of use. The dyestuff mills at Bolham[8] at this date are described as 'former wood now fulling mills', implying an adaptation as a result of the severe disruption to the Atlantic logwood trade. More serious, however, were the alterations to three in Elmore known as Bury's Mills. The owners, John Rossiter and his relative Bartholomew Branscombe,

---

[1] (*Harrowby MSS vol III*, 95). These proceeds were often meagre, for an earlier letter asserts that she 'treats with contempt all the abuse lately heaped on her; she has only received £30 for her Tragedy but is preparing another comedy'.

[2] *Harrowby MSS vol III*, 123. [3] DRO 1926B/W/W15(1).

[4] DRO 74/3/608.

[5] the Barnstaple Inn in Wellbrook (KEO Box 5), Greenway Charity property in Birchen Lane (Saint Peter's GBL14), and Blagdon's Means at Bolham (DRO 52/13/3/15a-b), respectively.

[6] DRO 213M/T108-9. [7] DRO 213M/T23-8.

[8] KEO Chest 49.

had converted them to grinding corn[1].

Despite its decline in trade, Tiverton could still attract newcomers. We have already mentioned one, Nicholas Dennys; another was Thomas Winsloe, who bought Collipriest. He quickly ingratiated himself with the townspeople by having the bridge at the bottom of Saint Andrew Street rebuilt in 1773, to which the parish contributed a modest £20. He was one of the few people who actually benefited from the War, as in 1779 he secured a contract to provide Portsmouth Dockyard with 'painters' works'[2]. In Tiverton his name should be remembered for what the *Exeter Flying Post* described as the 'newly-built modern brick and tiled mansion house'[3] at Collipriest. It is surely the finest surviving Georgian residence in the town. The main front with its elegant parapet, facing down the Exe valley, consists of five bays and three storeys, and was built about 1778 by Winsloe. The south front, now hidden from view of the passer-by, is earlier and originally had nine bays. It dates back to the early 18th century, and could well have been part of the house originally built by John Blundell, our first historian.

Collipriest, the house built by Thomas Winsloe c.1778.

The appearance of late 18th century Tiverton can be glimpsed from the small number of buildings of that time which have survived. Starting from Winsloe's mansion at Collipriest, the way up to the town was via Saint Andrew Street. When crossing the bridge over the Lowman, a glance upstream would have revealed a busy stretch of water in the 18th century, for as many as five mills were working between this

---

[1] KEO Chest 1.
[2] *PortsDock*, 117.
[3] edition of 22.11.1770.

bridge and that at Lowman Green. At the bottom of Saint Andrew Street the building until recently known as the Country House Inn is Georgian, as are numbers 26-29, which form part of a terrace. Around what would still have been the shining magnificence of Saint George's, the buildings standing on either side of Saint Peter Street had survived the ravages of Tiverton's worst fires - Slee's Almshouses, the Great House, and the Chilcott School with its Master's House. Further along Saint Peter Street, past the earlier Amory House, we would see a mixture of substantial Georgian houses with stuccoed and brick frontages, such as 'Mr Owen's House', pictured in 1777. Across from the ancient Church and Castle, not much in Newport Street now remains of its 18th century appearance. To the north, however, the house called Rosebank, in Bartow's Causeway, does appear to be late Georgian in style. A little further out of town, not far from Henry Osmond's house at Pinnex Moor, Martin Dunsford had purchased a field, where he converted a stable into a cottage that he called Villa Franca. Dunsford's walk from there down to the town would have taken him past the handsome door of the Old Brewery, now number 57 Bampton Street, a building which had survived from the previous century. A noticeable feature of modern Bampton Street is the 17th century red sandstone archway at number 27, taken from Upcott's Market Cross. On the opposite side of the street the Market Chambers have been tastefully restored to their original appearance. Little is now visible of 18th century Gold Street, even the Greenway Almshouses are now of stone, whereas they had been rebuilt in brick after the 1731 fire. Towards the bridge, the Lowman Restaurant is another rare Tiverton example of a Queen Anne-style building. Fore Street has some fine examples of Georgian architecture, although they are not always apparent. Eyes must be raised upwards from the modern shop fronts to see what Cherry and Pevsner[1] describe as remnants from 'the dignified terrace houses' built after the fire of 1731. On the north side of the street, opposite Coggan's Well, is a building where the upper storey of red and blue brick contains segment-headed windows and keystones. Two further impressive buildings are to be found just off Fore Street, in Phoenix Lane. Raymond Penny House is a possible conversion of an older building, with a late 18th century pedimented porch. Gotham House, originally the aplendid home of the merchant George Davey, was recently restored by its owners, Bevan Ashford.

Intermingled with residences and business premises were inns and public houses. In 1779 the Land Tax assessment lists no fewer than 35:

north side of Fore Street	Half Moon;
south side of Fore Street	New Inn, Phoenix Inn, South Molton Inn, late Fox and

---

[1] 1999, 814.

	Goose Inn, Three Crowns;
north side of Bampton Street	Vine Tavern, Cross keys;
east side of Bampton Street	Boars Head, Plough Inn,
	Black Horse;
west side of Bampton Street	Sun Inn, late Hare and
	Hounds, Black Horse Inn;
Town's End	Blue Bottle Inn, Bampton Inn;
Water Lane	Flower Pott Inn;
east side of Barrington Street	Woolpack;
Lowman Green	King's Head Inn, Coach and
	Horses Inn, Prince's Head Inn;
Elmore	Bell Inn;
Newport Street	Green Dragon, Eight Bells
	Inn;
east side of Saint Peter Street	Old Bow and Quiver;
west side of Saint Andrew Street	Angel Inn, Bridewell Inn;
Westexe from lower end	
to Wellbrook Bridge	King's Head Inn, King of
	Prussia Inn, Lower Boot Inn;
Birchen Lane	White Hart, Barnstaple Inn;
Westexe from Wellbrook to	
higher end of Leat	Green Dragon Inn;
Westexe from Greenland to	
Exe Bridge	Swan Inn, Seven Stars Inn.

Of these, just three have survived in name; the Half Moon, the Cross Keys, and the Seven Stars. Many of the inns were home to clubs and societies. The Vine in Gold Street was the meeting-place of a Freemasons' Lodge established in 1767, but most important, and politically notorious, was the Half Moon where the combers and weavers met.

A public meeting was called in Tiverton for November 28th 1782, to decide on the form of a petition to be sent to the Commons urging a much wider electoral franchise for the Borough. Several hundred people attended the gathering, most of whom voted for Martin Dunsford to act as chairman. The meeting was passionate, especially after the proposed petition was circulated. The document had been drawn up by George Owens, an attorney, recently arrived in the town, and asserted that the exclusive advantage given to the Corporation 'is injurious to the rest of the inhabitants and a national grievance and unlikely to speak the voice of the people'[1]. The only objection to its contents came from the Rev. William Wood, who

---

[1] *JHC 1782-4*, 127.

was soon silenced by Nicholas Dennys and George Dunsford. The document was passed around the meeting for signing, and on the following day it was carried through the town and endorsed, according to Dunsford[1], 'by all ranks'. Seven men were chosen to promote and deliver it to Parliament: Martin and George Dunsford, George Owens, James Pulling a sergemaker, the farmer William Stone, and the two prominent merchants, Nicholas Dennys and William Smale. It was presented to the Commons on the last day of January 1783, when it was read, and, not surprisingly, strongly opposed by both Tiverton M.P.s. Its fate, together with many similar documents from all over the country, was 'to lie on the table'. The Tiverton Corporation, like many another privileged oligarchy, was being challenged by an articulate opposition whose main bone of contention was the closed nature of most town governments. Yet the burgesses were determined to keep it so, as Tiverton's Hall Book records: it was 'resolved and agreed they [the petitioners] are unworthy of being allowed into the Corporation'[2].

The signing of the Treaty of Versailles in September 1783 heralded joy and relief. The conflict between Britain, France, Spain and the American colonies ended with the loss of lucrative possessions and the birth of the United States of America. The peace, however, could not cure all local ills. A severe winter in 1784 led many of Tiverton's poor to apply for relief. The situation was so dire that John Besley, one of the Corporation, felt obliged to distribute 250 pounds of beef and a large quantity of peas, but 'could not give to a quarter of those that applied'[3]. Besley's name was linked with that of Benjamin Dickinson in a complaint sent to Nathaniel Ryder in 1785. Thomas Enchmarch, again pleading poverty, explained that he paid large property rents to both Besley and Dickinson 'who seem indifferent how we go on'[4]. The Enchmarch family had long enjoyed the financial and commercial protection of Oliver Peard, but the 20 years since his death saw them reduced to poverty.

Despite personal tragedy[5], Martin Dunsford at this time was enjoying particular success as a Churchwarden of Saint Peter's. He was elected by the Parish Vestry four years in succession, from 1783 to 1786, prompting Beavis Wood to sneer 'notwithstanding his doctrine that all offices and parliaments should be annual'[6]. During his second term, a former inhabitant of Tiverton, Richard Cosway, presented the Church with the large painting of the Angel delivering Saint Peter from Prison[7]. By this time, Cosway was considered one of the leading miniaturists of his time. Dunsford's election as churchwarden in 1785 would be opposed. The clergy with the

---

[1] 1790, 238.
[2] DRO R4/1/C1
[3] *Harrowby MSS vol V*, 1.
[4] *ib.*, 95.
[5] in the previous year he had lost both his young wife and infant daughter.
[6] *Harrowby MSS vol V*, 76.
[7] although he had made the initial offer four years earlier (DRO R4/1/Z/PV2). It now hangs over the vestry door in the north aisle.

support of some of the local farmers attempted to introduce their own candidate. Such was the strength of local feeling that the Vestry meeting was attended by more than 2,500 people, who filled the Church House and spilled into the churchyard. The Parish Vestry, of course, was a powerful body with all male ratepayers wielding a vote – the nearest Tiverton had to democracy. Once re-elected, Dunsford successfully (but belatedly) applied to the Bishop of Exeter for permission to erect the burial monument that had been in place for many years and stands today outside the entrance to Saint Peter's Church. There had been complaints about the pillar, which, according to Dunsford himself, had been 'made more out of enmity than to enforce proceedings'[1].

The pillar standing outside the south porch of Saint Peter's Church, recording some of the descendants of the Dunsford family.

---

[1] DRO Faculty Causes/Tiverton 4.

In June 1785 he championed the cause in the Borough Court of seven labourers charged with taking wood from Custom or Bickley Wood, to the north of the town. The men claimed that to do so was an ancient custom and right of the poor, but were found guilty and, unable to pay their fines, were imprisoned. Dunsford asserted that such a right had probably been granted after the fire of 1612, and thought it also included permission to take timber for building purposes. The Justices apparently reconsidered the sentences; the men were released, and their unpaid fines were never demanded[1].

Another of Martin Dunsford's achievements as Churchwarden in 1785 was to set up Sunday Schools in Tiverton[2]. The Parish Vestry with great enthusiasm adopted the scheme, and before long nine schools were established. More than 240 children, of all denominations, were taught at schools in Saint Peter Street, Bampton Street, Elmore, Bolham, Saint Andrew Street, Town's End, Wellbrook and two others in Westexe[3]. A few years later, in 1788, the Vestry faced another problem of basic education: what to do with the children in the Workhouse. The decision was for each child to spend four hours a day in the school there, and it was further proposed to set up 'proper schools of industry for the better relief and employment of the poor'. Not everyone was so enlightened, however. Samuel Clarke, a ropemaker by trade, had offered his services as Governor of the Workhouse, stating that 'my present business furnishes me with an opportunity of deriving more advantage than others by employing the children at an earlier age than any other profession can do'[4].

A most spectacular event took place in and above Tiverton on May 16th 1788. A Mr West took off from the Bowling Green behind Fore Street in a gas-filled paper balloon. Carried by a northerly wind, he travelled three miles before landing near Bickleigh[5]. What is remarkable is that this feat took place just six years after the very first ascent by the Montgolfier brothers. Further celebrations took place in the following month when the Combers and Weavers Clubs held the 'gayest procession thro the streets'[6]. This annual event saw the artisans following an effigy of their patron saint, Bishop Blaise. 1788 was also Perambulation Year, when the course of the Leat was walked. On this occasion the Hundred Bailiff carried a bushel of cakes for the enjoyment of the

---

[1] (Dunsford 1790, 124). However, a much earlier date is suggested by a copy of an 11th century deed from Baldwin de Redvers to Robert de Worth which records the grant of land at Fairby and 'the common of Byccliff' (DRO 49/9/1/1). Perhaps this alludes to a right to the contents of the wood rather than land shared by tenants.

[2] the move had no doubt been prompted by the foundation of the national Sunday School Society by Robert Raikes earlier in the year. Tiverton's response was remarkably rapid.

[3] DRO 2655C/EFA23.

[4] DRO R4/1/Z/PV3.

[5] Dunsford 1790, 263.

[6] *Harrowby MSS vol VII*, 86.

boys who accompanied him[1].

Throughout the summer, news had been filtering back to Tiverton of one of its more colourful inhabitants, Thomas Davey. Two years earlier, Davey's father had successfully begged a commission in the Navy for his son, who was based at Chatham Barracks. The young man was waiting to embark on a truly historic voyage. His ship was bound for Botany Bay in the land later known as Australia, carrying 800 convicts, the first batch of transportees heading for a newly established penal colony there. Davey was to help set up a garrison and cultivate the land. He had volunteered for this journey whereas 'the major part of the officers of the marines hath declined going on an expedition so very disagreeable'[2]. The ship eventually berthed on 26th January 1788 at a spot which became known as Port Jackson. According to Davey's wife, he was the first man to step ashore[3]. Another man who had connections with both Tiverton and prisoners was Thomas Hodge. In his case, he was the agent for the sale of British convicts in Westmorland County, Virginia, where he was also a successful planter. His grandfather, Sampson Hodge, had been a pewterer in Tiverton, and some of the family had emigrated to America. Thomas visited Tiverton in 1789, and contracted a lease of the houses he owned on the north side of Fore Street[4]. He paid a visit to Hensleigh, where another man familiar with foreign lands, John Gabriel Stedman, lived with his wife and two sons[5]. Stedman was a Scotsman who had served as an officer in the Dutch army[6], and had been prominent in the administration of Surinam. Almost certainly through Tiverton's Dutch trade links, he had become acquainted with William Smale. After the peace of 1784 he began to look for somewhere in Devon to retire, and Smale told him that Hensleigh was vacant. The Stedmans intended to 'quietly pass our days with company'[7]; they seem to have settled into their new home and soon became an accepted and welcome part of Tiverton society. One of their sons, Johnny, had been born in Surinam to Stedman's first wife, a half-caste, and this lad of mixed blood attended Francis Gloyns' school in Saint Peter Street[8].

Whereas the sight of a black boy in Tiverton was not so unusual[9], it was topical. Nationally, the subject of the slave trade was being widely debated at that time, and in Tiverton Martin Dunsford had already helped to convene a meeting to discuss its abolition. Dudley Ryder was quickly informed of this by Beavis Wood, who said the

---

[1] *Harrowby MSS vol VII*, 100. [2] *Harrowby MSS vol VI*, 81.
[3] *ADB.* [4] TivLib D44.
[5] *Stedman*, 326. [6] *ib.*, 237.
[7] *ib.*, 252. [8] *ib*, 256.
[9] the parish register had recorded the baptism in 1780 of Thomas Gallen 'a black boy'. The entry states that he was living with Mrs Hamilton of Bristol, who had inherited Gotham House from her father, George Davey, so it is possible that Thomas was actually living in the town.

subject was one 'which Messrs Dunsford and the patriots and sons of liberty say much about'[1]. He was always eager to decry them.

Remarkably, the tireless Martin Dunsford was all the while engaged on the work which has made him famous. For four years, he tells us, his 'leisure hours were employed in collecting materials, digesting, arranging and writing', and, on April 5th 1792, his *Historical Memoirs of the Town and Parish of Tiverton* was finally published. The launch was two years later than anticipated. The announcement of its publication in the *Exeter Flying Post* states that the author in 1790 had originally intended to produce a book of no more than 200 pages, costing 6s. However, such was his desire to omit no detail, that the final work ran to 498 pages and the writer 'trusts that his subscribers will be actuated by the same liberal spirit (as his) by taking the book at 11s'. Dunsford achieved an amazing feat by compiling this work, using material 'collected from the best authorities'[2].

His purpose for writing the book appears in the dedication:

> 'To all the Virtuous and Industrious Poor of Tiverton. To you, my friends, this
> work is dedicated; because it was at first undertaken to advance your interests,
> by opening to your view, and depositing in your hands, a chronological list of
> the public charitable donations.. and the names of the present dispensers of
> them; that you might know where and to whom to apply'.

But it was more than this: he believed in Reform, Natural Rights and Liberty, and directed the *Memoirs* accordingly. The Chronological List of the Public Donations was supplemented by sections on General History; Concise History of the Lords of the Hundred, Manor and Borough of Tiverton; A Chronological List of the Most Remarkable Occurrences; Descriptions of the Parish and Town of Tiverton, Antiquities, Public Buildings, Etc.; and an Appendix Containing Copies and Extracts of Original Papers and Records.

In wealth of detail it is a local history without comparison, and is even more astonishing when we consider the paucity of sources available at the time. The two maps, one of the whole parish, the other of the town, are intriguing documents in their own right. The attention to detail was such that the latter not only pinpoints the locations of gardens and orchards, but also shows where the cloth racks were situated. When possible, the accuracy of Dunsford's material can, in almost every case, be substantiated, but this is not to say that the volume is completely free of error[3]. Nor is the writing entirely without bias. His sympathies clearly lay with Reform, the Whig

---

[1] *Harrowby MSS vol VII*, 10.

[2] although many of his sources, such as *Hewett's Manuscript* and *Farmer Roberts' Diary*, are now lost.

[3] e.g. pp.392-4, where the extract from the Domesday Book. refers not to Tiverton, but to North Tawton.

interest and Dissent, and his stance against the closed Corporation is obvious. In style and outlook, the contrast with Beavis Wood could hardly be greater.

Dunsford's sincere admiration and respect for his native town and its inhabitants can nowhere be better seen than in his eulogy:

> 'The inhabitants of Tiverton have long been characterised for a general disposition to social intercourse and conversation. The fine bowling-green in the centre of the town, invites the gentlemen to associate there in dry summer evenings, for salutary exercise; and tea parties, &c. of ladies and gentlemen, are much encouraged in the same season of the year, by the many variegated walks near the town, and hospitable farm-houses in the parish. The adjacent hills and woods afford the means of much diversion to the lovers of the chace, in and about Tiverton. Regular assemblies, concerts, and card parties, are frequented in the winter. Many evening clubs and friendly societies have been likewise formed here, for mutual enjoyment and recreation after the business of the day; where the temperately circulating glass, and friendly offerings of tobacco, have, perhaps, had a happy tendency to promote good humour and good will. Let us hope, that no frivolity of manners, no pride of wealth, of ancestry and arms, or difference of opinion, will hereafter lessen those reasonable enjoyments'[1].

One part of the volume often overlooked is the list of its 412 subscribers – those who realised its significance, together, no doubt, with some who simply desired to see their name in print. Most of the prominent inhabitants of Tiverton are included, as are nearly all the feoffees of Blundell's School. Clergymen and historians abound, such as the Rev. Richard Polwhele, who began to produce his *History of Devonshire* in the same year; John Watkins, the author of a history of Bideford in eight volumes, and national figures such as Richard Gough, who was director of the Society of Antiquaries of London at this time. Significantly, out of the 412 names, no fewer than 40 have entries in the *Dictionary of National Biography*. Probably most of the subscribers took prompt delivery of the volume, but not Nathaniel Ryder. Beavis Wood informed him that he would get his copies

> 'when I come up [to London] in the next term... as I think you know as much of Tiverton as this author I presume you will not be impatient to read this history written by an anti-Corporator'.

Eager as Wood was to condemn those who opposed the Corporation was it really endeavouring to serve the town? Or was it simply looking after the interests of its members? To take Benjamin Dickinson as just one example, although described as trading 'in Great Britain, Holland and elsewhere', he did not seem to care much about

---

[1] 1790, 57-60.

Tiverton's welfare. He was firmly seated at the top of the town's social pile and had no intention of moving. He was building a mansion at Knightshayes, and in January 1787, in partnership with William Lewis, and William and John Besley, opened Tiverton's first bank 'in the underpart' of the Town Hall. He also made provision for his next generation. His two sons, John and Benjamin Peard Dickinson, became full partners in their father's commercial enterprises on reaching the age of 21[1], and soon contracted good marriages. John's wife was to be Harriet Bowden, the daughter of a rich Bampton landowner, and Benjamin was about to be betrothed to Elizabeth Adney the daughter of the Rector of Uplowman. By the end of 1791, Dickinson had acquired all the trappings of a self-sufficient landed gentleman, including a portrait painted by the artist John Fulton[2].

The volume of Tiverton's external trade at this time is almost impossible to gauge, but one source is in its own way revealing. In the *South Molton Gazette* of June 2nd 1894 extracts appeared from an account book of a Tiverton cloth merchant beginning in 1788. Unfortunately, the merchant's name is not given, but it is evident that he regularly exported woollen cloth to the Continent, including Italy. Whereas most of the entries simply refer to 'pieces of cloth', occasionally more elaborate work is mentioned, such as the 'carpet for table, 72 inches long and 63 inches wide', bound for Ancona. The number of cloths exported reflects the fortunes of Tiverton. The anonymous merchant sent 1,143 pieces in the final nine months of 1788, but only 585 during the whole of 1789. This trend continued, and in 1791, only 63 pieces were sent.

Nevertheless, a glimmer of hope was on the horizon. Beavis Wood wrote in the autumn of 1791 'that something in trade is going to be introduced for the benefit of this town'[3]. Nicholas Dennys and William Smale announced their plan to build a large cotton mill in Tiverton. The implications were enormous. It was a momentous change for an area so long dependent on wool, and no doubt was seen by many as almost a betrayal of the past. By this time, the two men were already handling more cloth than any other business in Tiverton, and even had their own ship, a five-year old 'hagboat sterned brigantine', the *Juliana*[4]. Before the building of the factory had begun, however, William Smale died, and it seems that his sons did not share his enthusiasm for a daring new venture. Nicholas Dennys was joined by Thomas Heathfield, formerly of Tiverton but now living at Nutwell in Woodbury parish and the owner of a mill at Sheffield, and a Mr Middleton of Staffordshire, and (according to Wood) 'an unnamed Exeter gentleman'[5]. The mill was to operate under the name of Heathfield and Dennys, but where was it to be built? Much of the site had already been acquired. As we have seen

---

[1] DRO 1926B/D/B1-5.
[2] *Stedman*, 336.
[3] *Harrowby MSS vol VIII*, 142.
[4] DRO 3289S/1.
[5] possibly a man named William Tompkins.

(p.178), Dennys with William Smale in 1779 had bought Frost's Meadow, beside the Exe, and to this was later added 'land on the north side of Exe Bridge', Boysham and a house called Greenland, as well as 60 acres containing the Hams, Tomswell Close and Six Pound Meadow - making, in all, a strip from Exe Bridge to Head Weir[1]. Contracts were drawn up for the building work in the autumn of 1791. William Gream of Ottery Saint Mary was to be the mason in charge, Edward Boyce was given responsibility for the carpentry work, and Matthew Marshall and James Beck the lathing and plastering[2].

The mill promised radical change to traditional practices. The Sun Fire Office insurance policies clearly show that cloth was still being produced almost entirely under a domestic system. The various processes were carried on in cottages, sheds, small buildings, linhays, and barns, spread all over the town, and beyond. Such methods hampered large-scale capital investment, and made the passing of materials between processes both time-consuming and inefficient. Control of the product and the workforce was difficult, and widespread mechanisation was impossible. All could be overcome, however, with a purpose-built mill, which could make use of the technical advances that were quickening a revolution in manufacturing. The invention of the flying shuttle and the development of power-driven looms had led to an urgent need for an increase in the speed of spinning. The solutions were Hargreaves' spinning jenny and Samuel Crompton's 'mule', which made it possible for one person to work 1,000 spindles at once. All of these advances, initially made for the woollen trade, could in practice be brought together only in the environment of a large mill. Some such buildings already existed in the North of England. Indeed, much of the machinery installed in the Tiverton mill was brought down from Heathfield's establishment at Sheffield. Tiverton was to take part in what we now call the Industrial Revolution. Its brand-new monument to industry and production was rising five-storeys high above the small thatched cottages and dominating the Westexe landscape just as its successor does today.

---

[1] KEO Chest 1.

[2] Harding 1845, i, 201.

13 The Wars Against France

By the summer of 1789 support of America had brought bankruptcy to France. Reforms were demanded. Feudalism was abolished and the heady doctrines of the Rights of Man were proclaimed. In England Whigs and radicals embraced the revolutionary slogan 'Liberty, Equality and Fraternity', but the bloody excesses that followed changed many minds. Louis XVI was executed in January 1793, and on February 1st the National Convention of France declared war on England, and invaded the Netherlands. By the closing of the Scheldt, England, and Tiverton, were denied their traditional markets. At first, the outbreak of Revolution did not immediately cause much of a local stir. Sympathy with the Revolutionaries had been shown in December 1792, when an angry crowd had gathered to search for a number of French aristos who, they thought, were being sheltered by Mr Nagle of Calverleigh, a known Catholic, and even Beavis Wood[1]. In the spring of 1793 a partner in the new mill, Joseph Hogg, a supporter of the French Revolution, was forced to apologise to John Stedman for insulting the Army[2].

The mill itself became the focus of anger during 1793. Many clothworkers were fearful of losing their jobs to machines. Several girls and boys had already been sent to Sheffield to learn how to use the machinery at Thomas Heathfield's mill[3]. In May, William Tucker[4], the Mayor of Tiverton, thought it wise to call a meeting of representatives of Heathfield and Dennys and some weavers and combers to discuss the introduction of a combing machine. The combers were assured that, rather than jeopardise their jobs, this invention would actually herald an increase in work[5]. Nevertheless, a month later the Worcestershire Militia were called, as the impending arrival of the machine had caused 'a dangerous and uneasy spirit amongst the manufacturers'[6]. The situation remained unresolved. In 1794 the combers and weavers petitioned the Commons for the suppression of woolcombing machinery. They claimed that a single machine, operated by one person assisted by four or five children, would perform the work of 30 men working manually[7]. In the light of these events, what sort of work was being done at the mill? When the enterprise was first planned, it was clearly intended as a cotton mill. The trouble, however, was clearly connected with processing wool. This is one instance where there does not seem to be any reliable

---

[1] *Harrowby MSS vol IX*, 85.   [2] *ib.*, 123.
[3] Harding 1845 i, 198.
[4] he was probably well-suited to peace-making, as he was the father of 22 children and uncle to 75 nephews and nieces. Furthermore, his two servants who were to act as his mace-bearers had fathered 39 children between them (*EFP* 25.10.1792).
[5] *Harrowby MSS vol IX*, 123.   [6] *ib.*, 119.
[7] *JHC 1794*, 144-5.

source which could answer the question.

It did not take long for the war against France to affect Tiverton's trade, which was already at a low point. In 1794, the 'anonymous merchant' exported just 28 pieces of cloth, representing six complete orders. Whereas he had previously been in the habit of attaching fabric samples to the pages of his order book, this now ceased. It was as if he was now too heavy of heart to follow his usual practice[1]. John Stedman wrote in 1795 that 'the trade of Tiverton is totally ruined', and that Nicholas Dennys and Joseph Hogg's ship, the *Juliana*, had been lost at sea[2]. In a letter to Beavis Wood in March of the same year, Thomas Heathfield stated that the French had cornered the trade in cotton wool which meant that the Tiverton production would be 'cut to the quick'[3].

The loss of Dutch exports cost Benjamin Dickinson £6,000[4], and he suffered further setbacks in 1795 to his mills at Bolham. In late January, a wicker weir that directed water to the mills was destroyed by a sudden surge of meltwater in the Exe. A few weeks later, the mills were burnt, and the miller, William Webber, and his family were fortunate to escape[5]. After this, the Dickinsons gave up 'all business'[6]. Benjamin concentrated on his role as a country gentleman in his mansion at Knightshayes, and his son Benjamin Bowden Dickinson, devoted his time to purchasing property[7]. Some, however, could see no escape. Richard Enchmarch had already taken to relief from the bottle, and in May 1795, he ate some hemlock in a salad, according to Beavis Wood, mistaking it for parsley[8]. Whether it was deliberate or an accident, the unfortunate man was dead by July[9].

The collapse of Tiverton's cloth industry seems responsible for a change in the very basis of the town's economy. After three centuries, the cloth merchants were no longer the dominant social or political force. The *British Universal Directory*, published between 1793-8, gives a list of the 'principal inhabitants' of the town, numberng some 101 individuals. Their occupations were many and various:

---

[1] *South Molton Gazette* 2.6.1894.   [2] *Stedman*, 369-70.

[3] *Harrowby MSS vol X,* 140a.   [4] *Stedman*, 369-70.

[5] (*Harrowby MSS vol X,* 77 and 97). Not long after this, Webber left Tiverton and took up an appointment as tidewaiter at Topsham (KEO Chest 49), a post procured for him by the Ryders.

[6] *Harrowby MSS vol XI,* 104.

[7] for example. paying over £3,000 for Wood, Honeyland and Gotham (DRO 1926B/W/E20/22/1).

[8] *Harrowby MSS vol XI,* 20.

[9] his brother, Thomas, devastated by the death, left Tiverton for a position in the India House, which had been procured for him by his 'Aunt Coade' (*Harrowby MSS vol XI,* 104).

attorneys - 7
auctioneer - 1
bookseller - 1
builders - 4
cabinet-makers - 2
chandler - 1
chemist - 1
clergy - 9
currier - 1
cutler - 1
druggist - 1
dyer - 1
fellmonger - 1
fullers - 2
gentry - 13

harness-maker - 1
hatters - 2
ironmonger - 1
linen/woollen drapers - 5
maltsters - 2
merchants - 5
painter - 1
plumber/glazier - 1
postmistress - 1
printer - 1
ropemaker - 1
saddler - 1
sergemakers - 8
shoemaker - 1
silversmith - 1

stationer - 1
staymaker - 1
surgeons - 5
tailor - 1
tanner - 1
tinman - 2
tobacconist - 1
watchmaker - 2
wheelwright - 2
whitesmith - 2
wine-merchant - 2
woolstapler - 1
writing-masters - 2

Of these 101, only 17 were directly involved in the cloth trade and a further five are listed simply as merchants. On the other hand, the considerable number of attornies, gentry, and surgeons would have been attracted by the wealth created from cloth, but would not, of course, have contributed to it. Native textile manufacturers no longer led the Borough of the 1790s. Indeed, those still making a living from the cloth trade were, in the main, against such closed Corporations. Oldfield, in his *History of the Boroughs of Great Britain*[1], has good words to say about just three members of Tiverton's Corporation. The farmer, William Martin, he says, 'eats his mutton, and does as he is bid without grumbling', and of John Webber he notes that 'in this good man's case there is something like a display of justice', and George Cruwys is described as 'the sapient vestry-clerk of the parish'. Of the rest, many were closely connected to the town's M.P., Sir John Duntze, who died in 1795: Henry Osmond junior and William Horabin both worked for him at Exeter; William Lewis was a close relative, and the Rev William Walker was Duntze's cousin. Oldfield adds that Walker had obtained through Duntze a Government living at Bath 'which he scarcely ever visits, except to receive the fruits of Christ's vineyard'! What is most clear from Oldfield's *dramatis personae* is the number of Government posts that patronage had brought to Tivertonians: Benjamin Dickinson's brother was a Supervisor of Excise, and his brother-in-law worked in the Customs; William Wood was an extra-officer in the Stamp Office; Beavis Wood, as well as being Tiverton's Town Clerk was also the Receiver of Crown Rents in Devon, Cornwall and Somerset; Bernard Besley was

---

[1] 1794, 213-4.

Comptroller of Customs at Exeter, and Philip Parkhouse, the bookseller, was a Distributor of Stamps. Patronage was also responsible for bringing a very odd visitor to Tiverton. Lieutenant Thomas Davey (see p.185) had returned from Botany Bay by June 1793, and informed his patron, Nathaniel Ryder, that he had brought back some gifts for him. Two of these, some seeds and the skin of a Maori, Ryder accepted. He graciously declined two further offerings, a dog and a kangaroo, saying that if he 'had resided chiefly at my own house in Staffordshire I should have been happy to have had these curious animals'[1]. Whatever became of the kangaroo? Perhaps, its remains are lying somewhere in Tiverton waiting to confuse future archaeologists?

If concern for cloth was apparently no longer foremost in the minds of the burgesses, what was? Improvement. Transport was one thing that had captured their imagination. A scheme to bring a canal to Tiverton had, as we have noted, first been suggested in 1768, with no result. The benefits seemed clear. Goods such as coal could be carried to the existing markets at a much lower price than by road, and the product of 'the great limeworks at Canonsleigh', selling some 20,000 tons a year[2], could be distributed much more easily. Following a meeting at Cullompton in October 1792, however, progress was made. A survey showed, optimistically, that the cost of constructing a canal from Taunton to Topsham would be £166,724, of which £22,229 would be necessary for the intended branches to Tiverton and Cullompton[3]. It also highlighted the many difficult gradients that would have to be faced. One particular problem would be the fall of 56 feet from West Manley to the basin at Tiverton. Such a drop, however, was due only to the fact that at this time the canal was intended to terminate near Old Blundells[4].

As with the canal, a scheme to improve Tiverton's streets was revived at this time. An Act of Parliament had been proposed in 1790, but the strength of opposition had deterred the Corporation. On that occasion, a satirical broadsheet, signed Richard O'Blunder, was circulated, stating

> *that cross deep gutters and irregular pavements, as left to us by our fore-*
> *fathers, are highly ornamental; that it has been customary from time*
> *immemorial, for horses to fall and break their knees in Tiverton streets, which*
> *make them more careful, and travel safer ever afterwards'* [5].

In February 1794, a petition was sent to the Commons describing the conditions of the streets more seriously as

> *ill-paved, unsafe, dangerous and greatly incumbered by various*
> *encroachments and buildings, and obstructed by spouts and gutters by which*
> *they are also rendered incommodious and in many parts dangerous to the*

---

[1] *Harrowby MSS vol IX*, 117.
[2] Hadfield 1967, 97.
[3] *ib*, 96.
[4] DRO 949M/P12.
[5] DRO 1092 addA/PZ7.

inhabitants and visitors; and if powers were given to pave and improve these streets it would tend greatly to the health, convenience, safety and emolument of everyone[1].

A counter-petition was submitted, stressing that the people of Tiverton were 'already groaning under a load of taxes, from a sinking trade, and a numerous poor'[2]. Nevertheless, the Bill progressed and became law on April 4th. The *Act for Paving and Otherwise Improving the Town of Tiverton* appointed Commissioners, empowered to levy a paving rate on all properties within a half-mile radius of Coggan's Well[3].

Money was needed by the Commissioners to buy properties in order to create some semblance of neatness and order in Tiverton's streets. As well as a paving rate, deeds poll, mostly at £50 each, were issued and sold. The first batch of properties bought lay in Westexe, near Exe Bridge, on Angel Hill, in Gold Street near the Pound, and in Bell Lane near Saint Peter's Church[4]. An unexpected opportunity soon arose for the Commissioners to realign some of these properties when, on June 30th, a fire destroyed all the houses on both sides of Westexe from Birchen Lane to Wellbrook. From there, it spread across the Exe and consumed premises on Angel Hill, and at the lower end of Saint Peter Street as far as the Old Bow Inn adjoining Slee's Almshouses. It went on up Fore Street, where it was halted only by pulling down part of William Dicken's ironmonger's shop[5]. In total, 130 houses were destroyed. Work began immediately to rebuild the properties with street frontages in alignment Surfacing work was also under way by July on a short stretch of the 2½ miles of streets under the Commissioners' control. The first section tackled was in lower Gold Street near the Pound[6]. John Veatch was contracted 'to procure 2,000 feet of Langport stones for paving the footpaths at 9d per foot and 1,000 feet of kerb stone at 1s per foot'. He was also to get material from the rivers near Tiverton as well as flint from the Blackdowns. This work, as well as fulfilling a genuine desire for civic improvement, provided sporadic employment for a large number of local men and boys.

Soldiers were often stationed in Tiverton in these times of war. Friendships and long-lasting relationships sometimes developed between them and their hosts. Indeed, in 1796 during the nine months' stay of the 11th Regiment of Foot, no fewer than 27 of the men were married in Saint Peter's Church[7]. Not all sought such permanent arrangements, however. On one occasion, two soldiers along with a local lad

---

[1] *JHC 1794*, 144.
[2] *ib.*, 202.
[3] DRO R4/1/C349.
[4] *ib.*
[5] DRO 2960A/PR6.
[6] DRO R4/1/C360.
[7] DRO 2960A/PR14.

'made a midnight ramble', and broke into a house in Elmore 'in order to play with some of the ready girls there'[1]. Other, more demure young ladies were frequently treated to evening entertainment as the regimental bands paraded through the streets. In a rare autobiography, Elizabeth Ham recorded her days at a boarding school in Saint Peter Street run by the Misses West[2]. After a supper of bread, cheese, and a little cider, the girls watched the soldiers marching below their bedroom window[3]. More amusement, although not always intended, was on offer on Blundell's schoolhouse green, where the local troop of Volunteers carried out their drills. Formed by John Worth of Worth in 1797, at first they were equipped with short sticks in place of swords[4]. In this same year, the Mayor of Tiverton, William Jenkins, received an unexpected letter from the Government. The Transport Commissioners had decided that the French prisoners-of-war held at Ashburton were to be moved inland, and Tiverton had been chosen to take them[5]. Accordingly, 176 Frenchmen arrived in September and, from this point until the end of 1798, 329 passed through the town[6]. They caused no trouble during their stay, indeed their help was greatly appreciated when another fire broke out on November 24th, 1797. Although 12 houses were consumed, the incident could have been much worse if not for the aid given by the prisoners. The Mayor offered them 15 guineas to repair their damaged clothes, but they refused[7]. The first group left Tiverton at the beginning of December for Bristol[8], shortly to be replaced by more.

Rumours of plots and conspiracies flourished during the War. Jacobins, the name given to those radicals who supported Revolutionary France, were thought to be active everywhere. Tiverton was no exception, and Beavis Wood wrote to the Ryders about the Jacobin newspapers circulating in the town. His information was that *The Courier* was taken by the Blundell's Usher, Mr Ley, and Mr Alier, an 'alien' in Saint Peter Street, while *Bell's Messenger* was delivered to the Phoenix Tavern, the meeting place of many clubs[9]. It was feared that these sympathisers would somehow support a French incursion which, after the attempted invasions of Ireland in 1796 and 1798, and Pembrokeshire in 1797, gained increasing credibility[10]. Strong measures were taken to prepare for the expected event; Martello towers were built around the coast, and Volunteers were made ready. John Worth's men were under orders to assemble at

---

[1] *Harrowby MSS vol XI*, 114.
[2] Gillett 1945.
[3] *ib*, 58-9.
[4] Harding 1845, i, 158.
[5] (cited in Reed 1988, 10). This article is the most thorough treatment of the subject of French prisoners-of-war at Tiverton.
[6] Skinner 1906, 257-60.
[7] *Harrowby MSS vol XI*, 160.
[8] Harding 1845 i, 159.
[9] *Harrowby MSS vol XII*, 59.
[10] Britain's vulnerability was acute in the early part of 1797 when mutinies virtually immobilised the navy.

Bickleigh Bridge, as were the Volunteers of Bampton and Halberton Hundreds. The Tiverton contingent, numbering 62 infantry and 45 cavalry[1], were to take three days' provisions for each man and three days corn for each horse.

The longer the War lasted, the more serious was the effect on Tiverton's export trade. Letters written to Dudley Ryder in the autumn of 1798 bemoaned the loss of the Italian, Spanish, Flemish and Dutch markets, which had left the 'mill streams, fulling mills and tenter grounds quite unoccupied'[2]. To make matters worse, in 1797 the Government had been forced to treble the assessed taxes to pay for the War. Many landowners were compelled to sell their property. Elizabeth Tuckfield sold premises in Fore Street and land near Chettiscombe Moor to Henry Dunsford for £840[3] to lessen the burden. A scheme was devised to allow the redemption of Land Tax in return for buying government stock; in essence, a forced war loan. The Tuckfield's Devon lands were contracted for £13,504[4], whereas Edmund Glynn's agreement for the Manor of Farleigh was worth over £3,000[5]. Government revenues were still not sufficient to cover the cost of the War, so in 1799 Pitt introduced an income tax. It was fixed at a rate of 2s in the £ for incomes over £200 a year, with total exemption for those who earned less than £60.

Trouble, not from France but from within, erupted during the winter of 1800-1. The high price of provisions was to blame. In the Southwest, several companies of Volunteers mutinied, leading the regional commander General Simcoe to confess that 'the law of the country was totally overthrown'. About 1,000 people, mainly from Tiverton's clothworkers' clubs, gathered in the Works near the Castle in the last week of March 1801 to discuss a plan of action. They summoned before them the local millers, bakers and food suppliers, with whom they came to an agreement on the prices of commodities. Following this, some of the men went into the countryside and made the farmers account for their food stocks, persuading them to supply the Borough Relief Committee with corn[6]. Because of concern for public order, two companies of the 24th Regiment were ordered to the town[7], but were not engaged, as the trouble soon subsided.

Social unrest due to rising food prices was always the fear of the ruling classes. So, too, was the ever-increasing cost of poor relief and the rate at which the population was growing. Imagine then the effect of the work entitled *An Essay on the Principles of Population as it affects the Future Improvements of Society*, written by Thomas Robert Malthus in 1798. This short publication stated that the growth of population tends to be faster than the growth of production, so that poverty is inevitable and must increase.

---

[1] DRO 49/9/1/730.
[2] *Harrowby MSS vol XII*, 36.
[3] DRO 49/9/3/130.
[4] DRO Z1/50/9/3.
[5] DRO 2685B add/T/Tiverton/1.
[6] PRO HO 42/61.
[7] *Harrowby MSS vol XIII*, 20.

The Government's first response to Malthus' theories was to produce dependable population statistics. Hence the first general census of Britain, taken in 1801. The results showed that in England and Wales there were almost nine million inhabitants, compared with an estimate of 5½ million just over a century earlier. The population of the parish of Tiverton turned out to be 6,505, placing it third in the county, behind Plymouth (43,194) and Exeter (16,827). It is clear that this figure for Tiverton was lower, considerably lower, than it had been at the beginning of the 18th century: Dunsford estimated the population in 1705 to have been 8,693, and even in 1665 it supposedly stood at about 6,742[1].

Tiverton differed in one important demographic aspect from most Devon parishes. The Census revealed that its agricultural labourers did not form the majority of the working population; 1,089 people were employed in farming, whereas 1,617 worked in trade, manufacturing, or handicrafts. Many of this larger group had found employment at the Heathfield, Dennys and Company's mill. The partnership had been re-ordered in 1798; of the total capital of £24,000 Thomas Heathfield and Joseph Wells of London[2] together held £7,000, Nicholas Dennys £5,000, William Jackson of Cowley Place, Exeter, £5,000, Richard Lardner of Tiverton £4,000, and Samuel Young of London, £3,000. Two other men were parties to the agreement, one being Henry Dunsford to whom the company's premises were entrusted, and the other, Joseph Armitage, was made manager[3]. However, in 1801, Wells withdrew from the firm and Nicholas Dennys retired, and within a year was bankrupt. From this point, the business was renamed Heathfield, Lardner and Company[4]. But the firm, as almost every other enterprise in Tiverton, was hardly thriving. It becomes evident that the Factory itself began to depend on loans. The trustees of George Welsh Owens recorded interest paid on sums loaned to the Company beginning in 1803 with £600, and rising to £2,000 by 1806[5]. Some of this money was probably spent on the outright purchase from Blundell's School of the 8¼ acre field known as Boysham, which contained the factory buildings[6].

Key businesses failed at this time, among them that of Martin Dunsford, the merchant and historian. Despite a desperate effort to reduce his debts by mortgaging his house in Bampton Street[7], he was declared bankrupt in 1802. The *Flying Post* of January 20th 1803 carried a notice of the sale of his properties, which included many houses in Moretonhampstead as well as those in Bampton Street and Barrington Street in Tiverton, and lands in Bampton. His debts must have been considerable, as his

---

[1] 1790, 464.
[2] a partner in Heathfield's Sheffield firm.
[3] (DRO 2292M/99b). He was paid £150 a year for 'rent of house, coal and candles'.
[4] Harding 1845, i, 202.
[5] DRO 49/9/2/265.
[6] Harding 1845, iii, 116.
[7] DRO 52/3/3.

creditors received only 1s 10d in the £[1]. Another person in distress was Elizabeth Lewis, whose husband, William, a partner in the Tiverton bank, had committed suicide in 1798. Benjamin Dickinson, also a partner, was blamed for the death, as he had not assisted 'in the embarrassment of the bank'[2]. In 1803, Elizabeth, threatened by legal proceedings, was forced to sell to pay off the debts. The main creditors were Francis Colman of Gornhay, and his partners in the Tiverton Bank, Dickinson, and William Besley[3]. A total of £1,746 was raised from his property, but even after paying Colman and the partners of the Bank, there was over £9,000 still owing[4]. In stark contrast, Dickinson himself was doing well. In June, he added a codicil to his will, promising £20,000 for the use of his grandchildren[5].

Although the Treaty of Amiens brought a year of peace, Britain and France resumed hostilities in May 1803. Shortly afterwards, in the summer, another group of French prisoners was sent to Tiverton. For some, the stay was to be short; Saint Peter's register records the burial of two of them in September. Other lives would begin in Tiverton, however. A month after the burials, James Antoine, the son of Jean-Baptiste and Louisa Harriett Dupont was baptised in the church[6]. After the Battle of Trafalgar in October 1805, the town received more prisoners of war. A few were figures of international standing, such as Admiral Dumanoir, the chief commander of the combined French and Spanish fleets, and Admiral Pierre de Villeneuve, who had actually been in charge at Trafalgar. Dumanoir lodged at the Angel, where the landlady offended him so much that he quipped 'the house is high, the walls are thin, there's an 'Angel' without, but a devil within'[7].

Useful information on contemporary Tiverton is revealed in the diaries of Henry Ellis[8]. As a young man, he was apprenticed in 1804 to John Tucker, an Exeter watchmaker who, in the following year, took over his father's business in Tiverton. Ellis lodged at his master's house in Fore Street, along with a varied crowd of people. In his words there were 'the actress, a little woman, long past her meridian, also an artist who had provided sketches for *The Beauties of England and Wales*, but now down on his luck'[9], and a certain Monsieur Doulay, one of the French prisoners on parole. Ellis often attended concerts at the Angel Inn, where he sometimes saw Dumanoir and

[1] DRO 3958D add/3.
[2] (*Harrowby MSS vol XII*, 26). Such was the desperation for a salary and a Government post, that shortly after Lewis's suicide Dudley Ryder received two letters seeking the spoils of Lewis' misfortune. William Tucker, after mentioning the 'sad loss', added that 'his death must have occasioned a vacancy in some employment or agency under Government, please think of me', and William Jenkins asked after Lewis' position as agent for the island of Antigua (*ib.*, 14 and 17 respectively).
[3] DRO 74/3/622.   [4] DRO 1926B/D/F1/8.
[5] SRO DD/CN/Box 16/2.   [6] DRO 2960A/PR7.
[7] Skinner 1906, 258.
[8] (DRO 76/20/1-8). The first four volumes are concerned with his time in Tiverton.
[9] DRO 76/20/1, p.46.

Villeneuve. The apprentice watchmaker was one of the founders of the Tiverton Juvenile Debating Society, one of whose first meetings discussed the motion 'Whether Bonaparte carries his conquests by intrigue or valour', and it was decided that he did so by intrigue![1]. The group's secretary was Robert Loosemore, a close friend of Ellis, who came from a Knowstone farming family. He could not continue in farming because of a broken thigh, so he had been placed in Francis Gloyns' Commercial School in Saint Peter Street. A few years later, Loosemore withdrew from the Society, firmly expecting to be appointed under-secretary to the Governor of Van Diemen's Land (Tasmania)[2]. Ellis does not enlighten us further, only to remark later that 'Loosemore had been greatly deceived as to the appointment'[3].

Beavis Wood, half-blind, retired as Town Clerk in 1806. In one of his last letters to his patron, in typical style he wrote that 'Father Dickinson and his crabbed son are still amused and played with by the young captains'[4]. However, the 'Father' died a few months later. He had succeeded in accumulating a great fortune of over £65,000, and his will lists almost £37,000 in legacies (as well as £6,500 in debts)[5]. His interests in the Tiverton Bank passed to his son, John, Henry Dunsford junior, and George Barne, who were each to hold 30% of the bank's stock, with the remaining 10% in the hands of Arthur Boase, an accountant[6].

In 1809 the nation celebrated the 50th anniversary of the accession of the popular, if allegedly mad King George III[7]. Processions and feasts were the order of the day, but not all Tivertonians celebrated in the same style. The Corporation had initially intended only to organise a meal for which participants had to pay, but were advised by one of the town's M.Ps, William Fitzhugh, to give a dinner to the poor as well[8]. They acceded to this wish; a bullock was roasted in a field near the Bampton Turnpike Gate, and paupers were given beef and pudding[9]. Ellis, in his diary, concurs that there were two separate meals, adding that those who attended the ox-roast behaved

> 'like a set of cannibals celebrating their horrid rites... how much better would it have been had the animal been cut up undressed and the joints distributed among the families of the poor'[10].

The poor had suffered from a run of bad harvests. A Bill before Parliament to regulate the price of corn was causing great concern in 1810. Many bakers in Tiverton

[1] DRO 76/20/1, p.58.
[2] the Governorship had been solicited by Thomas Davey of Tiverton.
[3] DRO 76/20/1, p.141.
[4] *Harrowby MSS vol XIII*, 141.
[5] DRO 1926B/W/F2/2/1.
[6] DRO 1926B/D/B8.
[7] DRO 70/26/9.
[8] Chalk 1935, 340.
[9] Harding 1845, i, 172-3.
[10] DRO 70/26/9, p.61.

and elsewhere in Devon submitted a joint petition to the Commons, criticising the proposal[1]. Much worse was to follow. The harvest of 1811 produced so little that over 3,500 bushels of wheat were bought by the Parish Vestry and sold at a reduced rate to the poor of Tiverton[2]. In previous years, this would have provoked noisy protests. Although no such action is recorded, new banners were given to the Combers and Weavers Clubs in the year[3]. Elsewhere there was unrest; not against the price of goods, but against the introduction of textile machinery. Luddites broke machines first at Nottingham, then in Yorkshire, Lancashire, Derbyshire, and Leicestershire.

Whatever the state of trade may have been, attempts to improve the town continued. John Wood had succeeded his cousin Beavis as Town Clerk, a post that was central to much of the work carried out in the town. One of his first tasks was to draw up a contract to 'clear the road of houses from the top of Angel Hill into Saint Peter Street'[4].

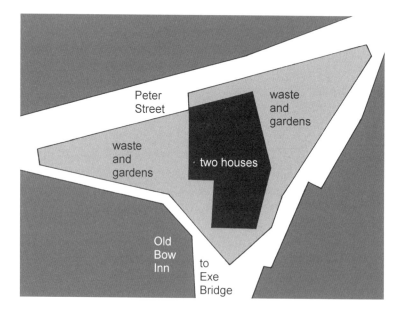

Plan showing houses and gardens on Angel Hill before they were removed c.1806 [5].

---

[1] *JHC 1810*, 220.   [2] Harding 1845, i, 186.

[3] in February, Matthew Wood gave the Combers their flag, a splendid item with a blue silk background showing the patron saint of clothworkers, Bishop Blaise, on one side, a shepherd, shepherdess, a lamb and a dog on the other. A former weaver of the town, Captain George Darby, presented the Weavers with their banner in June (Harding 1845, i, 173-4).

[4] *ib.*, i 169.   [5] taken from DRO R4/1/PP3.

This work provided an opportunity to build a common sewer there in 1810[1]. For centuries, much of Tiverton's waste had been channelled through the town by underground drains until it emptied into the rivers[2]. The more solid matter had another, equally unsavoury way of being treated. A team of packhorses carried the abundant 'night soil' clear of the town, and across the fields near Ashley[3]. Whether it was spread on the fields there, or emptied into the Exe near Bickleigh, we do not know. The Corporation also appointed a Committee at this time to look into how the Town Leat was routed through the town, and who benefited from the supply[4]. These allied problems of sewerage and an inadequate water supply were, literally, to plague Tiverton for a very long time. In fact, many would say they have never been resolved.

The United States declared war on Britain in June 1812. What direct effect this had on Tiverton we simply do not know. The extent of its commercial links with America has not been established, but the 'anonymous merchant' had been sending small amounts of cloth to New York and Philadelphia in the late 1790s[5]. Cloth was also being sent in the opposite direction, according to a petition sent to the House of Commons by the inhabitants of Tiverton. The town, they said,

> 'during some years past, has had very little of other employ for its numerous labourers but the manufacturing of an article called long ells for the East India Company; and that previous to the [Napoleonic] War, there was a considerable commerce from Tiverton to different parts of Europe, which consumed the wool grown within many miles of it and gave full employ to the labourers, but since that time there has been no demand and, but for the orders of the East India Company for long ells, the labourers and their families would have been reduced to depend on poor relief'[6].

Tiverton's links with the Far East and the East India Company stretched back for some 200 years (see p.93). Indeed, William Fitzhugh, one of the borough's M.P.s, was a factor in the East India Company and, as such, would have promoted the town's interests in that trade.

Napoleon's disastrous retreat from Moscow in 1812 lost him half a million men, the confidence of his allies as well as the awe of his enemies. Meanwhile, in Tiverton the

---

[1] (DRO R4/1/C356). This was to be of generous proportions, 30 inches wide by 42 inches high.
[2] those from the higher part of Fore Street and the Hammett's Lane area ran south into the Lowman, those of Newport Street joined those of Bampton Street and ran into the Gold Street sewer which, once that from Barrington Street had been added, emptied into the Lowman. The sewers of Saint Peter Street and Angel Hill emptied into the Exe near the bridge, and those in Westexe ran either directly into the river or into the Leat (DRO R4/1/C355).
[3] DRO 49/9/3/132.
[4] Harding 1845, i, 171-2.
[5] *South Molton Gazette* 2.6.1894.
[6] *JHC 1812-3*, 124.

French prisoners on parole had largely won the trust of the locals. Events showed that not all deserved it, however. Fourteen escaped from the town during the year, and another four attempted to follow but were found in Blundell's Schoolhouse Meadow. This caused a great deal of embarrassment, especially to the Corporation who were blamed for being far too lax. One of those who had escaped was a Captain Boulangé, who had been teaching French to young Henry Ellis. On the other hand, Alexandre De La Motte (later shortened to Lamotte) had found employment as a teacher of French at Blundell's, and appears in the Land Tax Assessment as the owner of a house on the north side of Gold Street[1]. The large numbers of French prisoners-of-war in the Southwest had led to the building of Dartmoor Prison. Many of the labourers employed there afterwards moved elsewhere to similar projects. At least one of them, John Rawlings, found work[2] as one of the hundreds of canal-cutters and navigators (hence 'navvies') working on the Grand Western Canal.

Progress on the Canal had been suspended in 1811, as the cost of cutting through so much rock was proving far too expensive. Work was resumed after it was agreed to complete only the stretch from Holcombe Rogus to Tiverton, abandoning the branch to Cullompton, and to terminate the Canal at its present basin, not to a point near Collipriest Dairy or near Old Blundells. Although the initial scheme had been severely curtailed, it was predicted that about £10,000 a year would be obtained from the lime trade on the short stretch to be built[3]. Negotiations for the land needed by the Canal Company were quickly underway. The section within the parish of Tiverton, from West Manley to the Basin, although just a narrow strip, came to almost 25 acres, and cost the Company about £3,000. Philip Blundell received just under £1,200 for his ground, which included part of Town Tenement, and some of the lands near his home, the Lodge or Zephyr Lodge[4].

Blundell invested some of that money in deeds poll of the Tiverton Turnpike Trust. In fact, in the years 1811 to 1813 he bought no fewer than 52 deeds, costing £2,600[5]. It is surprising that the Trust succeeded in borrowing this money on security of the tolls, as a new Roads Act, passed in 1811, was necessary only because not enough funds could be raised to pay previous investors or to maintain existing roads. Nevertheless, the Trustees solicited yet another Act in 1813. This time, the intention was to build new roads. Although they had obtained authority under the Act of 1767 to build a new road towards Exeter, this was now extended to form the route of the present A396. Silverton and Thorverton would be avoided, the road would go as far as Stoke Canon,

---

[1] he chose to remain in Tiverton after the War.   [2] DRO R4/1/Z/PO15.
[3] Hadfield 1955, 197-8.   [4] DRO Z9/Box 94/8.
[5] DRO R4/1/Z14.

and then climb up through Stoke Woods to enter the city along Pennsylvania Road[1]. To the north of Tiverton, a new road would be built along the Exe Valley as far as Holmingham, before heading off toward Bampton[2]. These routes are instantly recognisable to us today. Indeed, much of our present road system was laid during the Napoleonic War.

The Wesleyan Chapel, now the Methodist Church, in Saint Peter Street, was rebuilt in 1814 on the site of an older meeting-house.

In April 1814 Napoleon was banished to the island of Elba. Tiverton could celebrate what was thought to be the end of the War. Festivities in the town began on May 16th and lasted four days[3]. There was further cause for rejoicing on August 25th, when the first barge full of coal entered Tiverton along the Canal[4]. Another commodity, lime, was to dominate activity at the Basin. Henry Dunsford and Browne (presumably, John of Canonsleigh House) were soon advertising in the *Exeter Flying*

---

[1] DRO DP18.
[3] Harding 1845, i, 190.
[2] DRO DP16.
[4] *ib.*, 191.

Post that they could supply it at 5s 6d per hogshead[1]. The Turnpike Commissioners did not take long to seize the opportunity to profit from the increased traffic that soon sprang up around the Canal Basin. Turnpike gates were set up at the foot of Exeter Hill and near Hill's House[2]. The vital task of maintaining the waterway was entrusted to one man, William Wawman of Sampford Peverell. He agreed to repair for three years the 11½ miles from Holcombe Rogus to the Basin, including the fences, bridges and hedges and to close all stop gates at nine o'clock on summer evenings and six o'clock at other times - all for £300[3].

The improvement of roads and the coming of the canal in themselves did not signify a recovery in Tiverton's fortunes. There were still failures, some unexpected. At the beginning of February 1814, the 80-year old Beavis Wood died. During his latter years, he had distanced himself from local affairs. The reason for this became apparent once his executors began sifting through his papers. People like his cousins, the Enchmarches, were expecting considerable legacies, but Wood left nothing but debts in spite of having once been not only Tiverton's Town Clerk, but also steward of King's College's manor of Manley, receiver of the Crown rents[4], steward of the manor of Fairby and of Thomas Carew's Tiverton and Bickleigh estates[5]. Neither office nor connections could guarantee personal prosperity. An auction was held at the Parsonage House in Saint Andrew Street in an attempt to recoup some of the money. His personal possessions included a library of about 700 books, with 'some scarce law books and the Statutes at Large', as well as a 'pair of globes and philosophical instruments'[6].

In the following year, Joseph Armitage, the manager of Heathfield and Company died. Subsequent inspection of the firm's accounts revealed that the business was not viable, so production was stopped immediately. Just nine days after Armitage's death, the auction of the property was advertised in the *Exeter Flying Post*, where it was described as a

> spinning and weaving factory, in a populous town full of hands, who in a great measure depend on the concern for their livelihood; brick building 94ft long x 33ft wide, five stories high; three underrooms full of combing, drawing, roving and spinning worsted, two upper stories full of machines for spinning abb[7], shute or weft[8]; large buildings containing spinning jennies; fulling-mill driven by the same stream after it has passed the spinning mill. The above concern is one of the most desirable in the kingdom for carrying on the

---

[1] *EFP* 2.1.1815.
[2] DRO R4/1/Z3.
[3] DRO 2062B/E1.
[4] *Harrowby MSS vol XIV*, 100 and 127.
[5] TivLib folio 1/39.
[6] *EFP* 18.8.1814.
[7] coarse yarn.
[8] or shoot, the filling thread in a loom.

spinning and weaving branches upon a large scale from having the whole of the Exe to drive the wheel, the low price of labour, the ready market for sale of the worsted, yarn and pieces[1].

The main source of employment in Tiverton was now a relic. Even Britain's final victory at Waterloo in June 1815, Napoleon's banishment to Saint Helena, and the Treaty of Vienna together could not assure the future of the town.

---

[1] *EFP* 30.3.1815.

14 Heathcoat and Reform

In the fraught times after the Napoleonic Wars a young man from the Midlands with a genius for invention and the business acumen to exploit it came to Tiverton. He bought Heathfield and Company's redundant mill and established a lace manufactory there. In Tiverton's long history there have been few decisions of greater consequence. The young man was the 32-year old John Heathcoat[1], who had begun his working life as an apprentice framework knitter but soon left to work for William Shepherd, a knitting master and framesmith[2]. When only 18 years old he married Ann Chamberlain, a widow six years his senior, and entered into a business partnership with her brother, Samuel Caldwell. In 1804 the two men[3] applied for a patent for 'some new machinery to be attached to frames called warp frames whereby they will make all kinds of thread lace'[4]. Heathcoat experimented further, and in 1808 patented a machine for 'the making and manufacturing of bobbin lace or lace nearly resembling foreign lace'[5]. This would be the making of John Heathcoat's fortune. By 1815 his machines were being licensed to other manufacturers throughout the Midlands. Although the royalties from the licences were earning him as much as £16,000 a year, they also attracted a great deal of resentment from his competitors[6]. Anger rose when it was rumoured that he was developing a powered version of the bobbin-lace machine which would put other manufacturers at a great disadvantage[7].

He was either setting up or already in production at Tiverton by May 1816 when terrible news reached him. Lace-frames, mostly of his design, had been destroyed in Nottingham, and later at New Radford. Realising that an attack on their three-storey factory at Loughborough was imminent, Heathcoat's partner, John Boden, armed a handful of nightwatchmen with pistols and bayonets. This did not deter the assault that took place on the night of June 28th. All the machines were either destroyed or rendered useless, and one of the defenders was shot. On the following day, Boden

---

[1] there are two biographies of Heathcoat, which vary considerably in their facts and view of the man. Gore Allan's *John Heathcoat and His Heritage*, sees him almost as a saint and the saviour of Tiverton, whereas Varley's article 'John Heathcoat (1783-1861), Founder of the Machine Made Lace Industry', provides a much more balanced view, placing him in a wider context.

[2] Varley 1971, 3.

[3] in the names of Samuel Caldwell of Hathern, Leicestershire, frame-smith, and John Heathcoat, late of Nottingham, now of Hathern, frame setter-up.

[4] DRO 4302B/P2.

[5] DRO 4302B/P1.

[6] Varley 1971, 18.

[7] Henson 1970, x.

informed the local magistrates of the Company's intention to claim damages[1]. Just a couple of days later, Heathcoat wrote a letter to the Mayor of Tiverton requesting him 'to take such steps as you may think best to prevent or defeat any attempt to destroy our manufactory'. The long-held myth that Heathcoat was driven down to Tiverton as a result of a Luddite attack is best forgotten. Indeed, were the attackers Luddites? At the trial of those apprehended, it was revealed that some of them had also 'done the Radford job', and were paid well for their 'work' at Loughborough – seven of them were hanged[2]. The incident smacks of industrial sabotage committed by men in the pay of the firm's rivals. Heathcoat himself, in his letter to the Mayor of Tiverton, says the violence had arisen 'principally, if not wholly, owing to the offence of removing here, and... the Nottingham Lace Makers have sworn my entire destruction'.

Early engraving of the Heathcoat Lace Factory.

No such attack disrupted Heathcoat's endeavours in Tiverton where a labour force was being engaged and contracts drawn up. The workers agreed to undertake whatever job they were given, for 13 hours a day, and six days a week. Wages were paid according to age and experience: a 16-year old labourer could receive 4s a week, rising to as much as 8s at the age of 21. Somewhat surprising perhaps, this was less than the 6s young

---

[1] LRO 12036/2.   [2] *Leicester Journal* 4.4.1817.

agricultural labourers could expect[1], but it was a regular job, out of the rain and snow, and would have been more attractive. Furthermore, a qualified worker at the Factory could get a guinea or even 25s a week. To begin with, the better rates were paid invariably to the skilled men who had travelled down from the Midlands, such as the lacemakers, frame-smiths and weavers, of whom 20 are recorded before the end of 1816[2]. Local smiths, however, were in demand and could expect 12s a week. Most important, an annual bonus of five guineas was promised to each worker 'if devoted'. In November, Heathcoat started to recruit women at rates from 2s 6d to 4s 6d a week, slightly higher than the lowest male wage. From notes written on some of the surviving agreements, it can be seen that the work was not suited to all of the women. Several were given notice to quit or left of their own accord. In some cases, opposition from the family is expressed; for example, Elizabeth Fear, 'her grandmother objects', and Elizabeth Capern, 'her husband is not quite agreeable but rather than leave she will engage'. By working at the Factory, many women and girls could achieve a high level of financial independence. This would have been strange for some of them, and possibly seen as a threat by the menfolk. Children were also employed, and often their earnings were taken into account when applications were made for poor relief. Vestry minutes show a nine-year old boy, called Gloyns, 'earns something at the factory', and of Esther Moggridge's three children, the eldest of whom was only 8½ years old, one earned 1s 6d a week there[3].

Not everything ran smoothly. Heathcoat and Boden had anticipated using the compensation from the damage at Loughborough on their Tiverton enterprise. The Leicestershire authorities, however, refused to hand over the £10,000 award, stipulating that the money had to be spent locally[4]. Although none of the trouble the Company had experienced in the Midlands seems to have followed it, at times suspicions were aroused. It has been claimed that in 1817 some of the immigrant Loughborough workers argued with Heathcoat, and set up their own business aided by a local doctor[5]. There seems to be no evidence for this statement, and it is difficult to suggest the name of a doctor who would have become involved. Some time later, Thomas Osgood was brought before the Quarter Sessions charged with stealing models of machinery from the Factory. Whether this was industrial espionage or simple theft we do not know, but Osgood was sentenced to three months' imprisonment[6]. Nevertheless, these seem to be irritations rather than serious worries. Indeed, most aspects of business life must have been pleasing for Heathcoat, who was living in a house on the west side of Saint Peter Street near the church. His son, John Francis Heathcoat, was baptised in March 1817, but did not survive the year, and a daughter Caroline, was christened in September of

---

[1] Clark 2001, 9.
[2] DRO 4302B/A9.
[3] DRO R4/1/Z/PV6.
[4] Darvall 1934, 210.
[5] Varley 1971, 19.
[6] Harding 1845, i, 231.

that year. A new partner, Thomas Barfoot Oliver joined Heathcoat and Boden at the Factory, where full production was reached following the removal and sale of the old Heathfield machinery[1]. This coincided with the arrival of more men from the Midlands, a number of whom were described as sinker makers and letters-up[2]. Confidence in the firm was bolstered in 1818 when news spread that it was about to establish production in Paris[3].

The effects of the Heathcoat Factory on Tiverton and the surrounding area were immediate and immense. Although Heathfield's business had operated from 1792, we do not know how many people were employed there. In any case, that had depended on the traditional manufacture of cloth, whereas the product of the new factory, lace, was highly marketable as long as demand was sustained. As well as the large number of local people employed, Heathcoat's contracts show that people from as far afield as South Molton, Bampton, Crediton, Wellington, Culmstock, as well as the parishes adjacent to Tiverton were taken on. Many were clothworkers who, with little or no work at this time, were probably dependent on poor relief. It is likely that this was the reason for the drop in annual expenditure on the parish poor that occurred. From £7,500 in 1816, it fell to less than £6,500 for the following four years[4].

Long-held economic, political, and social grievances surfaced once the Napoleonic Wars had ended in 1815. Landowners had benefited from the conflict through increased production and rising rents. Agricultural labourers, on the other hand, had been particularly badly hit by the corresponding rise in the cost of basic commodities. Following the decision by the farmers and landholders to reduce wages, in spite of escalating prices, artisans in Tiverton called a meeting in January 1816. They reeled off a list of items that had doubled in price during the previous 20 years; the rent of a house had risen from £2 10s to £5 5s, faggot wood had soared from 18s to £1 16s per hundred, wheat from 4s to 8s a bushel - and on and on it went[5]. The artisans decided to agree to a drop in wages only when these items had been reduced to their former price[6]. The situation remained tense until improved harvests in 1816 and 1817, and the presence of the Enniskillen Dragoons, diffused the anger. Elsewhere in England, there was serious unrest. The reasons were varied. In many rural areas, the enclosure of strip-fields had taken away the independence of labourers and smallholders, reducing them to mere wage earners dependent on the whims of their masters and the price of

---

[1] which included 32 spinning frames and 60 broadcloth looms (*EFP* 10.4.1817).
[2] DRO 4302B/A10.   [3] DRO 4302B/F22.
[4] *Poor 1822.*
[5] butter from 6d to 1s 2d per pound; beef and mutton from 2d to 5½d; potatoes from 2s to 4s 6d; shoes from 5s to 10s a pair; shirts from 3s to 8s 6d each; stockings 1s 6d to 4s a pair; and working tools were costing up to 50% more than ever known before.
[6] DRO 805A add2/PZ21.

basic goods. In the towns, an ever-increasing labour force began again to demand political representation. Violence was seen sometimes as the only resort. Parliament's reaction was the Seditious Meetings Act (1817) and the so-called Gag Acts, forbidding all public meetings not licensed by magistrates. Nevertheless, a meeting in Manchester to support Parliamentary reform on August 16th 1819 was attended by about 60,000 people. The magistrates over-reacted to some jostling of the local militia, and ordered regular troops to charge the crowd. The result was 11 deaths and many hundreds injured – the notorious Peterloo Massacre. Even more outrageous was the Grosvenor House Plot, when a dinner at the Earl of Harrowby's house was to be the scene for the murder of the entire Cabinet. The perpetrators were captured before the attempt and five of them were subsequently hanged for treason.

In 1818, the Government set up a national enquiry into the activities of charitable trusts[1]. This action was prompted by the pressing concern of how to meet the rising cost of poor relief; the greater the amount provided by charities, the less would have to be found elsewhere. The Charity Commission, as it was called, set out to investigate every parish in England and Wales. In advance of the Commissioners, letters were sent to the clergy, asking for details of local charities and for someone knowledgeable to be present at any enquiry. Armed with published local histories, property deeds, and wills of benefactors, investigations took place all over the country. The Commissioners sat in Tiverton during August and September 1819, and looked into every known charity in operation, and even a few that had been lost in the troubles of the 17th century. The results were, in time, published. The report for Devon appeared between 1826 and 1830, filling 1,499 pages, surpassed in number only by London's 2,077. As well as giving details of the original gift, when known, the Commissioners collected a lot of information on the lands owned by the charities, including names of lessees and occupiers – all providing invaluable material for future historians.

George III died in January 1820, and was succeeded by the Prince Regent, George IV. In Tiverton, to celebrate his Coronation 300 'respectable persons' had been invited to enjoy a 'cold collation' on Blundell's School Green[2]. For the Pastor of the Steps Meeting House, the Rev. Matthew Noble, the occasion was perhaps too much, as he was 'overcome with wine'. His impropriety was not to be overlooked as, shortly afterwards, he was asked to quit his ministry[3]. The King's estranged wife, Queen Caroline, had always been surrounded by controversy; rumours of affairs were constant, and she had been barred from attending her husband's Coronation. Even her death in August 1821 caused a dispute in Tiverton. The officiating Anglican

---

[1] Clark, 1995.
[3] TivLib folio 4/661

[2] Harding 1845, i, 232.

clergyman, probably the Rev. William Rayer of Tidcombe, refused to preach a commemorative service for her, or allow anyone else to do so, leaving the Nonconformist chapels alone to serve the community on that Sunday[1].

From 1819, access to Saint Peter's Church had been restricted because of alterations. The seating, described as being 'in an irregular and dilapidated state', was being renewed[2], the floor levelled, the organ moved to the west end of the church, and the centre aisle given a new ceiling[3]. Work began in November, but the extent of the refurbishment meant it was not completed for almost two years. More alterations were undertaken in 1824. The porch was taken down and rebuilt. Although most of the original carving was preserved, by comparing later illustrations with that in Dunsford's *Historical Memoirs* it appears that the battlements and frieze were added. At the same time, the screen that separated the Greenway Chapel from the south aisle was removed, leaving just the solid base. Building projects were not just confined to the Church. A meeting was held at the beginning of 1818 to discuss improving Exe Bridge. Rather than just repair the structure, it was decided to widen the whole bridge and reset the foundations. At first, the costs were estimated at £700, of which the parish rates would supply £300, the Exe Bridge Trustees £200, and the rest would be raised by subscription[4]. The finished cost of the work, however, £1,500, was more than double the original estimate, to which the parish rates contributed £900[5]. Meanwhile, on the west side of upper Saint Andrew Street a new building was going up. This was to be used as a National (Church of England) School[6], designed to take about 350 children.

How much were such projects influenced by the prosperity of the Factory? The business was clearly thriving; in 1821 £10,700 was paid for 'mills and premises bought at auction'[7]. This almost certainly refers, in part, to the site at Pilton, Barnstaple, where the remains of the Raleigh woollen mills were bought and a bobbin-net factory established. This development was put in the hands of John Boden and John Heathcoat's elder brother, Thomas[8]. At Tiverton, both Boden and Oliver withdrew from the partnership, but the business expanded, adding a gasworks and foundry[9]. As well as light for the Factory, the gasworks were soon providing illumination for parts of the town. The Tiverton Paving Commissioners, as part of their programme for improvements, called two public meetings at the end of 1821 to gauge opinion on the

---

[1] DRO 65/15/21.

[2] one condition of the grant was that no changes would be made to the seats of Sir Henry Carew without his permission (DRO Chanter 710).

[3] Harding 1845, i, 229-30.   [4] *ib.*, 227.

[5] *ib.*, iii, 75-6.

[6] now the site of the Mid Devon Christian Centre.

[7] DRO 4302B/A1.   [8] Reed 1978, 97.

[9] Harding 1845, i, 214.

introduction of street lighting. Support was unanimous, and an Act of Parliament was obtained in May 1822[1]. The dating is not clear, but it would be of some interest to discover which came first, the Act or the gasworks. Unlike the latter, the foundry took a while to set up. The first casting was not produced until June 1824[2]. The earliest records of the foundry do not exist, but an account book beginning in 1831 shows that, in addition to work for the Factory, objects such as plough shares were being made for customers from Crediton, Morchard Bishop, Cullompton, Bradninch and other places in the area[3].

In the summer of 1822, John Heathcoat travelled to France, presumably to further his Paris enterprise[4]. On his return in the following year, a welcoming dinner was held in the Factory yard for over 1,000 people, and a procession took place, at the head of which was carried a large flag made entirely of lace and measuring six yards by three[5]. He returned with even more enthusiasm, if that were possible. He obtained five patents in 1824, one of which was concerned with drawing silk from cocoons[6]. This was highly relevant to his Tiverton enterprise, for he bought 2,000 mulberry trees for planting on land he had just bought at Shillands. He clearly intended to produce his silk locally. But, from the absence of further references, one must assume that this was a rare failure. Just like many successful contemporary industrialists, Heathcoat was investing in land. Indeed, Westexe was fast becoming his kingdom; in 1822, he bought the former Jackson and Vickery mills and those of Rossiter, as well as a nearby field, costing in total more than £3,000. He also acquired three houses in Leat Street from William Salter, along with a plot of land beside the Leat adjoining an area already known as Loughborough. Not long afterwards he added Pinkstone's Corner and the Cucking Stool Mills in Westexe, as well as the out-of-town properties of Fordlands at Mere, and mills at Bolham[7].

The issue of Parliamentary reform resurfaced in 1823. Locally, the Corporation was the subject of a book, *Cursory Observations on the Charters Granted to the Inhabitants of Tiverton in the County of Devon*, penned anonymously by 'a friend to local jurisdictions'. From later evidence, it is almost certain that the author was George

---

[1] *JHC 1822*, 292.

[2] (Harding 1845, i, 214). A Cornelius Varley helped in the early stages as a consulting engineer, but he is best remembered as an artist, and merits an entry in the *Dictionary of National Biography*. During his stay at Tiverton, he produced a number of drawings, including some of the factory buildings (Smiles & Pidgley 1995, 107).

[3] in private hands.

[4] before leaving, he gave William Lockett of Derby and Samuel Amory of Throckmorton Street, London, power of attorney over his lands, and appointed them trustees for his wife and three daughters (DRO 4302B/T4).

[5] *EFP* 25.9.1823.   [6] DRO 4302B/P5-9.

[7] DRO 4302B/A1.

Coles[1], a Tiverton Justice. The small volume highlighted the fact that the vast majority of the population of the borough had no political representation, and pointed out the vested interests of the Corporators. Of the 25 burgesses, the author revealed that ten were non-resident[2], therefore ineligible under the terms of the Borough Charter. Of the rest, he considered John Govett (the Recorder), John Wood (Town Clerk), and the Rev. John Pitman (a former Recorder), as holding offices incompatible with being burgesses. The fact that there were four examples of father and son, and two of brothers was highlighted. The extreme case of family ties was that of John Duntze; also on the Corporation were his brother James[3], a brother-in-law, John Burridge Cholwich, and another relative, Samuel Walker. Intermarriage among the corporators was, of course, nothing new, but previously the families had been Tivertonians involved in the cloth trade with the commercial fortune of the town close to their hearts and pockets. Now, it seems, the burgesses' interests were mainly elsewhere; they gained little from Tiverton and gave little back. Coles' outspokenness seems to have had partial success, as two capital burgesses, Sir John Duntze and John Govett, resigned in 1824[4]. Soon after, it was revealed that Duntze had been paying the Corporation for his post as Receiver of the Land Tax. Coles was not sated. He encouraged publicans to refuse to pay both the Corporation Malt Tax and the freeman's admission fee of between £2 and £5 which enabled traders to work within the borough. In the following year a printed pamphlet appeared entitled *Parliamentary Election Franchise Questioned, As Exercised in the Borough of Tiverton*[5], again anonymous, but, without a doubt, the work of Coles. Although the Corporation faced the greater tirade from the reformers, Blundell's School also came under fire. Questions were being asked about admissions, in particular the interpretation of Peter Blundell's will regarding 'natives' and 'foreigners'. The Feoffees rightly defined natives as being those born or mostly brought up under six years of age in the town of Tiverton[6], but they sought legal opinion as to the consent of ten householders of the town needed to admit foreigners now there was no subsidy[7].

Any feelings of disenchantment seem to have been temporarily put aside once it was time for the Races. Horse racing was held, apparently for the first time, in 1823 and

---

[1] Coles in 1827 wrote to the Secretary of State about 'close' boroughs, pointing out that 'want of education, intelligence etc, too frequently places the Corporate leader in the hands of a crafty town clerk' (cited in Webb & Webb 1908, vol II, 697).

[2] the Mayor (and Receiver of the Land Tax) Sir John Duntze, the Earl of Harrowby, John Worth, John Burridge Cholwich, Samuel Walker, Richard Ryder, John Pitman jr, Perry Dicken, William Besley and John Dickinson.

[3] a former Deputy Paymaster-General in the Mediterranean

[4] DRO R4/1/C301.   [5] *Harrowby MSS vol XVI*, 95a.

[6] Blundell's Order Book.   [7] DRO 2065M/SS3/6.

proved so successful that the Race Committee wrote to the Ryders desiring that the event should be 'established'[1]. These were held at the end of August or beginning of September, and the *Exeter Flying Post* recorded that on the first day of the 1824 meeting upwards of 10,000 people attended[2]. The Races took place in a large field now occupied by the East Devon College and Tiverton High School. A spacious grandstand was provided, entry to which cost 2s 6d, and was the only spot from where a view of the complete course was possible. Tiverton's innkeepers, who erected booths near the grandstand, provided refreshments. The Tiverton Races became a popular and eagerly anticipated feature of the sporting calendar, and brought a great many people into the town. Wrestling was another sport greatly enjoyed locally, and drew audiences of many hundreds. One match in the 1820s lasted for two hours 12 minutes, and was so appreciated by the spectators that 'a liberal subscription was opened for the beaten man'[3]. For those who could afford it, indoor entertainment during the winter months centred on the Theatre, which stood on the west side of Saint Peter Street. Henry Lee had it enlarged in 1824, and a few years later, during November and December, the aficionados enjoyed such productions as 'She Stoops to Conquer', 'Pizarro in Peru', 'Romeo and Juliet' and 'The Rivals'[4].

John Heathcoat, meanwhile, continued to work tirelessly. In the single year of 1825, he toured Italy, sent an agent to Bengal to investigate the silk industry there, and persuaded a French woman to travel to Tiverton to instruct a group of girls in silk reeling[5]. He also submitted three patent applications, the last being an improved method of producing ornament on net[6]. Business was going so well that in April the *Exeter Flying Post* announced 'another factory.. on an extensive scale is commenced in the Factory Ham'[7]. The gasworks and foundry have already been mentioned, but the Heathcoat and Company's brickworks are almost completely unknown. Like all the firm's enterprises they were substantial. Batches of up to 50,000 bricks were fired at one time, and in June and July 1825 enough clay for about 270,000 bricks was dug[8]. Surprisingly, we know neither where the brickworks were situated, nor where the clay came from.

The lace industry then took a turn for the worse. In 1826, according to Varley, John Heathcoat was forced to bring in Joseph Buckley, who injected £20,000 into the company[9]. There was a shortage of work in Tiverton during the year, which led many women to apply for poor relief as their menfolk had 'gone looking for work'. Many of them had journeyed to Chard where a lace industry had begun in 1821, also by workers

---

[1] *Harrowby MSS vol XVI*, 27.
[2] *EFP* 2.9.1824.
[3] cited in Porter 1989, 200.
[4] TivLib folio 1.
[5] Varley 1971, 28.
[6] DRO 4302B/P10-12.
[7] 14.4.1825.
[8] DRO 4302B/A1.
[9] 1971, 24-5.

from Nottingham. Nevertheless, Varley's assertion should be treated with some caution. It is true that Heathcoat's annual profits dropped from £48,500 to just under £19,000[1], but the relocation of the Paris factory to Saint Quentin in this year would have eaten into the year's profits considerably. On the marriage of his daughter Ann to the London solicitor, Samuel Amory, Heathcoat fêted over 1,500 people in Tiverton with 'a quantity of cyder, bread and cheese'[2]. Furthermore, 1826 is the year given by Harding[3], when a new waterwheel, 25 foot in diameter and 20 foot wide, was erected for the Factory. These were hardly the actions of a man in severe financial difficulty.

Crime was always a temptation for people out of work, even if conditions in the Tiverton Gaol should have been a sufficient deterrent. The institution was sternly criticised by the surgeon, J.E. Coward, in May 1826. He certified that one of the prisoners, a debtor named William Beer, needed 'free and open air for the benefit of his health', but Coward concluded that the prison was 'unwholesome and quite unfit for the reception of any prisoner'[4]. Nevertheless, for some people these conditions were not severe enough. The Vestry in January 1828 applied to send some Tiverton miscreants to the County Prison, where 'the treadwheel... [is] much more disgraceful and degrading to the offender than any punishment that can be inflicted in the house of correction for this borough'[5]. Their wishes were granted; by June 13th an agreement was made to take up to ten Tiverton prisoners a year at a charge of 10s a week each[6]. Tiverton seems to have relished the opportunities afforded by this punishment. One week after the agreement, Mary Catford appeared before the borough Justices for having an illegitimate child, and they decided 'to commit her to the treadmill'[7]. Those spared the Exeter device were provided with suitable work at Tiverton. For obtaining by false pretences one duck, a few sausages, and half a dozen eggs, Philip Chave received three months hard labour. Daily tasks, lasting 12 hours in summer, 10 hours in winter[8], were either to beat hemp or break stones for the streets. Transportation, usually to Australia, was often the fate of people who committed more serious offences. Such was the sentence passed on the Tivertonians William Crudge, guilty of receiving a silver pencil case, John Osmond, for four charges of theft, and Samuel Tucker for stealing and embezzlement[9]. At least the inmates of the Gaol and the Workhouse had access to medical attention, unlike the great majority of people who had to pay for what

---

[1] DRO 4302B/B5.
[2] *EFP* 24.8.1826.
[3] 1845, i, 224.
[4] DRO R4/1/C334.
[5] DRO R4/1/C341.
[6] DRO R4/1/C97.
[7] DRO R4/1/Z/PV8.
[8] broken by a half-hour's break in the morning and in the afternoon, and an hour for lunch.
[9] DRO R4/1/C309.

passed for treatment. This situation did not go unnoticed by Anna-Maria Turner. As well as gifts to both Slee's and Waldron's Almshouses, she left £500 to be invested to buy drugs and medicine for those not getting parish relief[1]. Her bequest seems to have jolted some people into action, for at the end of the year the Parish Vestry suggested that doctors should vaccinate as many of the poor as they could against smallpox[2].

For centuries, the markets in the streets of Tiverton had been regular, if ramshackle affairs, and although there were rules, enforcing them was difficult. Meat, fish, poultry and vegetables were sold in Fore Street, Gold Street, Bampton Street, and on Angel Hill on Tuesdays and Saturdays; the livestock market was held in and about Newport Street and Saint Peter Street; and sheep were sold in the Works opposite the Castle. In keeping with a national trend, the Corporation and most of the Market Trustees sought a Parliamentary Act to provide a market place away from the streets. Despite a counter-petition from some local farmers and butchers, a Bill was brought in and passed in June 1825[3]. The Act decreed that no goods were to be auctioned either in the streets, or in the market on non-market days, and that the Corporation was permitted to hold fairs in the market place. Obtaining the Act, however, proved the easiest part of the scheme. Much more difficult was clearing the area in the centre of the town on which the Market Building was to be erected, and where the livestock pens would stand. The list of lands to be bought included 19 cottages, 10 houses and the Half Moon Inn, a smith's shop, dyehouse, stables and many other outhouses, and at least 14 gardens including the Bowling Green[4]. Negotiations were still going on in 1828[5]. The amount spent on purchasing a central site was £4,300, just over half the cost of the entire project[6]. The Market Building, on the other hand, was funded by subscription, with the largest contributions being the £2,000 from the Ryders and the £1,000 given by John Heathcoat[7].

The New Market was finally opened on 8th June 1830. The scenes both within and without the Market Building can be imagined from a surviving list of tolls[8]. The vendors had to pay

for every unenclosed stall 6ft square	6s
for every foot in length of the tables in the centre building under 8ft	5d
for every wheelbarrow containing goods	6d
for every handcart	1s

---

[1] DRO 49/9/3/97.　　　　　　　　　　[2] DRO R4/1/Z/PV8.

[3] *JHC 1825*, 519.　　　　　　　　　　[4] DRO 2070B/M/M2-3.

[5] Henry Marder refused £350 for his premises fronting Fore Street and sought the decision of the Commissioners, but the sum was confirmed (*EFP* 27.8.1829).

[6] Harding 1845, i, 237.　　　　　　　　[7] DRO 257M/B7.

[8] DRO R4/1/C381.

for a cart drawn by a beast	2s
for every score of sheep penned	1s
and in addition when sold	6d
for every ram	4d

The toll collector's account book, beginning on the Tuesday after the opening, records

- 56 butchers stalls
- 3 earthenware stalls
- 62 persons with baskets in the lower building
- 83 persons with baskets in the upper building
- 73 bags of potatoes in the stands on the ground
- 7 stands with earthenware on the ground
- 2 stands with baskets
- 18 old stalls used for various purposes.

Later entries show charges for '14 pots with herrings' and 'three clothiers' stalls', 'eight tables with seeds' and 'six pots of mazards'[1]. The Market was the commercial centre of Tiverton, a place to sell local produce and attract buyers from further afield. As such it remains to this day.

Tiverton's new Market Place, which opened in 1830, replacing the markets which had previously been held in the streets

---

[1] DRO 2070B/M/M4.

Early in 1831, a group of prominent Tiverton citizens approached the Market Trustees with a view to buying some of their property. They wanted the premises at, and over, the Fore Street entrance to the Market, to establish public rooms for billiards and reading, as well as dancing. The cost of £2,175 was raised by subscription and a further £750 was borrowed from John Heathcoat's daughter, Eloise[1]. The people of Tiverton, however, would have to wait a further three years before these Subscriptions Rooms, as they were to be known, were opened.

Following George IV's death in June 1830, the proclamation of his brother, William IV, saw a procession in Tiverton, 3,000 strong, headed by the banners and members of no less than 17 benefit societies[2]. Later in the year, William's wife, Queen Adelaide, was presented with a lace dress and shawl made at John Heathcoat's Tiverton factory[3]. This is the first record of a gift from the Factory to a member of the Royal Family, beginning an association that still continues. John Heathcoat had come a long way from his humble beginnings as the son of a smallholder; sheer hard work and determination, combined with his innate business sense and a keen inventor's eye, had given him, or at least his product, royal recognition. Heathcoat himself in October 1831 was preparing to move from Saint Peter Street to Bolham House[4] when a serious situation arose at the Factory. About 150 of the men went on strike following a drop in wages[5]. Sympathisers joined the strikers, and soon a crowd numbering over 1,000 was parading around the town. They marched into Westexe where effigies were burnt in front of the house of a Factory foreman, and the menacing sound of firearms was heard[6]. Like old days, 300 soldiers arrived in the town, and further trouble was prevented. A group of the strikers approached Heathcoat with an offer. They would contact their fellow lace workers at Barnstaple, Taunton, Chard, Nottingham, and other towns to determine the average wages, and would return to work for an equal rate. Their plan backfired, however, as they discovered that elsewhere lace workers received less than in Tiverton. To their credit, they kept their word and resumed work[7]. Any relief that Heathcoat may have felt, however, was soon tragically overwhelmed by the death of his wife, Ann.

Whereas the unrest at Tiverton was an isolated incident, widespread disturbances took place in other parts of southern England. Farm workers, often urged on by radical reformers, attacked landlords and property. The northern and Midland towns, while they did not experience such violence, did see a growing support for reform movements. In Tiverton, the Corporation seems almost to have been reforming itself;

---

[1] DRO R4/1/Z/PP9.   [2] cited in *DSN* 19.6.1930.

[3] *EFP* 25.11.1830.

[4] where, in August, 'two men and a lad' had been working for John Radford 'preparing for papering' (DRO R4/1/PP16).

[5] Freeman 1927, 44.   [6] TivLib folio 9/1237.

[7] Harding 1845, i, 243-4.

two capital burgesses, John Wood and John Pitman of Broadhempston both resigned in 1830[1], following the example of the Rev. Perry Dicken and John Burridge Cholwich a few years previously. Each had been severely criticised by George Coles in 1823, as we have seen (see p.213).

Continuing unrest between 1830 and 1832 ensured that Parliamentary reform remained uppermost in people's minds. The repeal of the Test and Corporations Acts in 1828, and the Roman Catholic Emancipation Act a year later, had paved the way for political change. A Reform Bill was introduced in March 1831, but was balked a month later, and the King was pressed to dissolve Parliament. In the election that followed, the Tories, Granville Dudley Ryder and Spencer Perceval, won the Tiverton seats for the anti-Reform faction, defeating another Ryder, Viscount Sandon, a Reform Tory, and the Radical 'handsome Irish barrister' James Kennedy. Nationally, the opposite was the case; supporters of the Bill gained a strong majority behind the Whigs Lord Grey and Lord John Russell. Yet, almost inevitably it was defeated in the Lords, as was its successor in May 1832. The Whig Government obtained a royal pledge that, if necessary, extra peers would be created to ensure the passing of the Bill. The threat was sufficient. The legislation received Royal assent on June 7th, and the poor at the Tiverton Hospital received an extra allowance to celebrate the occasion[2]. Benefit societies, with the Factory workers and children, walked and danced in procession around the town, and the day ended with over 1,000 people feasting in the Market[3]. Did they really have anything to celebrate? Certainly, the middle classes did; but the labouring population remained unrepresented in Parliament. The redistribution of seats had greater impact, as it was a better reflection of the demographic situation. Sparsely-populated Cornwall, previously boasting 44 M.P.s, now returned 16, whereas the industrial North, especially Lancashire, Cheshire and Durham gained considerably. Tiverton retained its two members, now chosen by 462 electors, not, as had been the case since 1615, solely by the 25 burgesses.

The country's 200,000 extra voters had to wait six months, however, before they could exercise their right. The interval saw more political activity in the constituencies than ever before; electors now had to be canvassed. In Tiverton by the end of June two contenders had already declared their intention to stand. James Kennedy, the 'barrister of great eloquence but scanty means' had captured the hearts of the Tiverton Reformers and was seeking to reverse the defeat of the previous year. He was joined in the fray by the town's entrepreneur *par excellence*, John Heathcoat. The Rev. E.S. Chalk was probably correct when he suggested that Heathcoat had earlier been approached to join

---

[1] DRO R4/1/C301. [2] DRO R4/1/Z/PO15.
[3] Harding 1845, i, 247.

the Corporation but preferred to bide his time[1]. Two further candidates entered this election: Benjamin Wood, whose house at Westexe had been attacked by the strikers in the previous year, and Charles Chichester of Calverleigh. An election without a Ryder! In fact, according to the Town Clerk, the safety of any member of that family in Tiverton could not be guaranteed[2]. It remained for Dudley to reflect from afar on the family's long Parliamentary association with Tiverton, claiming

> 'during the whole of this period, neither myself nor any member of my family, has owned a house or an acre of land within 100 miles; nor is there a single elector who owes me a single shilling, or whose vote I can in any sense command. Indeed, money is quite out of the question'[3].

In the midst of growing election excitement, Devon was hit by a serious outbreak of cholera. It was announced at the end of August that, owing to the disease, Barnstaple Fair would be restricted to the sale of livestock, 'no public exhibitions or amusements will be allowed', and vagrants would be 'treated severely'. The Michaelmas Fair at Tiverton was cancelled because of the risk of infection[4], and in October a temporary cholera hospital was set up at the Workhouse[5]. Nevertheless, election day finally came in December. Each of Tiverton's 462 electors had two votes, but only 736 were cast. The result was no surprise; Heathcoat obtained 376 votes, Kennedy 265, and a long way behind were Wood with 55, and Chichester 40[6]. The town celebrated in traditional fashion. A victory procession meandered around the town, led by four men on horseback, followed by drums and fifes, and the clubs four-abreast with their banners flying. Then came Heathcoat's women and girls four-abreast, the band, Heathcoat's electoral committee, and John Heathcoat himself in a carriage drawn by four horses with postilions and pages. Next was Kennedy's committee, then the Irishman himself in a carriage followed by the friends of both members[7]. Kennedy did not immediately take his seat in the Commons, as his qualifications to stand as a candidate were challenged. A petition was sent to Parliament stating that his claims to lands near London and in Yorkshire could not be verified[8]. He informed the House that he would not defend his return, so his election was declared void, and a new one ordered[9]. Despite this, he stood again, and was victorious, although a third of Tiverton's electorate declined to take part in the second contest.

---

[1] 1935, 319.
[2] ib.
[3] cited in O'Gorman 1989, 233.
[4] DRO R4/1C68.
[5] DRO R4/1/Z/PO15.
[6] Craig 1977, 308.
[7] TivLib folio 3/461.
[8] JHC 1833, 17.
[9] ib., 380.

The prelude to Parliamentary reform had been the fundamental changes in the relation of church and state. The monopoly of the Church of England in the nation's politics was broken. The repeal of the Test and Corporation Acts in 1828 had enabled many Dissenters as of right to enter public office. Discrimination had once been practised even on the most basic level: W.P. Authers cites the case of a Tiverton woman with no shoes who was given a pair on condition that she used them to go to Church not to Chapel[1]. Such was the confidence given by the law that Tiverton's Independent and Congregational churches, united under the remarkable Rev. William Harvey Heudebourck, decided to replace the Steps Meeting House with a new chapel. The last service was held in the old building in April 1831 and just a week later the foundation stone of the new structure was laid, while

> 'the worldly and vain were looking on and making a noise and confusion outside the barricades which inclosed the site of the intended Building but those who loved the holy and simple religion of the Fishermen cared not for their contempt'[2].

As for Catholics, it is always difficult to determine the number living locally. Bishops' questionnaires show that at no time were there more than a dozen willing to declare their faith. The Emancipation Act of 1829, however, changed things completely; it had allowed the most prominent Catholic in the area, Charles Chichester of Calverleigh Court, to stand in the 1832 Parliamentary election. The family's chaplain, Father Jean-Marc Montier, made his will in 1833, leaving instructions to build a chapel and appoint a priest to serve the 'poor Catholics' in the Tiverton area[3]. Land was bought from John Heathcoat alongside the road leading out of the town towards Calverleigh and Rackenford, and the first stone of Saint John's Roman Catholic Church was laid in November 1836.

Although the law had come to the aid of different religious communities, intolerance, or at least inflexibility, was still for many years common enough in Tiverton. One case came to light in April 1833, shortly after Blundell's School had admitted nine-year old Philip Ezekiel, the son of a Jewish draper of Fore Street[4]. Letters from his father, Benjamin, to the Master, the Rev. Alldersey Dicken, and the Feoffees[5], claim that Rev. Boulton, the Usher, dismissed Philip after just eight days. The boy was told not to return unless he agreed to repeat the Catechism. Ezekiel pointed out that Dr Dicken had previously told him that there would be no difficulty admitting the boy on religious grounds. The matter was obviously put right as young Ezekiel remained at

---

[1] Authers 1974, 35.   [2] ib.
[3] cited in Snell 1892, 286-7.
[4] who was either the same man or a relative of the Ezekiel who engraved the map of Tiverton in Dunsford's Historical Memoirs.
[5] DRO 1148 add 4M/22/3 and 1148M add/36/463.

the school until 1837, and two of his brothers were later admitted[1]. The Feoffees were faced with a greater crisis in the following year, when George Coles, the arch-critic of the Corporation, turned his venom on them. It all seems to have started when Coles tried to promote his son, Augustus, as a candidate for a closed Exhibition. The boy approached the Rev. Rayer, one of the Rectors of Tiverton whose right it was to choose the scholar, but was informed that the place had already been awarded to Francis Dunsford. Writing to his father, Augustus added that it had been granted 'at a private examination... and at a good luncheon to boot at the lordly mansion of the Rev. Mr Rayer'. Coles complained to Rayer, then to Balliol College, and even threatened to write to the Charity Commissioners. Balliol, however, rejected Dunsford as he fell short of the required standard. The Coles family's expectations were raised, only to be dashed when they were informed that the Exhibition would be left open for another two years, then offered again to Dunsford[2].

A problem that affected Tiverton, and a good many other towns, was the number of 'distressed travellers' begging for money. The Tiverton Mendicity Society was established in June 1833 to care for these people and to 'detect and punish vagrant impostors'. Their method was to provide the beggar with a ticket, not cash, which could be exchanged for one pound of bread, four ounces of cheese or bacon, a pint of beer, and lodging for a night at the Society's rooms. In the morning, he or she was escorted out of the town and ordered not to come back for a year, on pain of being sent before the magistrates. During the Society's first year 731 individuals applied for this relief, of which 664 were successful[3]. The Poor Law Amendment Act was introduced in 1834 to save money. It was based on the harsh notion that poverty among the able-bodied was a moral failing and would no longer be relieved as before. Parishes were grouped into Unions, each of which had to maintain a Workhouse, a place that was to be synonymous with misery for the next 100 years. Tiverton became the centre of one such Union, and began to receive paupers from no fewer than 26 other parishes, including Bampton, Cullompton, Halberton, Silverton and Thorverton. With this extra burden, it was clear that a new larger Workhouse was needed. The first step was for the Board of Guardians to buy the site[4]. The architects chosen were George Gilbert Scott and William Moffatt, and local masons George and John Beck, builder Samuel Gath, along with Thomas Ward and John Gath were appointed to construct the building which was eventually opened in 1837[5]. Under the law, the able-bodied would receive relief only if they were inmates of the Workhouse. The old or sick, however, would still be entitled to payments at home. The parish had been allowed for centuries

---

[1] *Blundell's Register.*
[2] DRO 1148M add/36/469a.
[3] TivLib folio 4/619.
[4] Harding 1845, iii, 55.
[5] DRO R4/1/Z43.

to take children receiving poor relief and place them *ad hoc* as apprentices. This was a source of very cheap labour. A regulated system, however, had been introduced in March 1833 which allocated children according to the value of the farms. Farmers were to take one child for every £100 of the annual value of their land; those valued between £50 and £100 also had to take one but would receive 2s in the £ from smaller tenements until the £100 was made up. Houses valued at £14 and over were also obliged to take one apprentice[1].

Although mainly aimed at the north of England, the Factory Act of 1833 had outlawed the employment of children less than nine years old. It went further; those between nine and thirteen were restricted to nine hours work a day, and all factory children were to be given two hours' daily schooling. The effect this had on John Heathcoat's Factory cannot be accurately determined, but in addition to the examples already given (see p.208), the minutes of an 1828 Vestry meeting included an order to produce 'a list of all paupers having children above six years of age... in order that enquiries may be made as to their earnings at the factory'[2]. It is even possible that this enterprise was exempt from the legislation, because factories designated as silk mills did not have to comply.

Heathcoat, at this time, was building on part of the Factory site. As well as replacing the foundry[3], he was putting up a house on Boysham for Ambrose Brewin, his business partner and the suitor of his daughter, Caroline. Nowadays hidden away on the Factory site, Exeleigh House was designed as an elegant stuccoed villa, and was accessible by a bridge crossing the Exe until this was swept away in 1960. John Heathcoat was also working on a land-draining machine, which he patented in 1832 and 1834. This invention, often referred to as the 'bog machine' in his accounts, 'although 20 tons in weight has been placed on a bog where it is believed nothing heavier than a hare or a rabbit ever ventured before'[4]. It had been tried near Bolton and was soon to be transported to Ireland. Sadly, however, it never crossed the sea. It sank in a peat bog near Dumfries where, one assumes, its remains still lie.

In the election of January 1835 Heathcoat was safely returned as one of Tiverton's M.P.s, capturing well over 90% of the vote. Kennedy, on the other hand, finished just 50 votes ahead of the Tory Chichester[5] and, 'from considerations affecting his health, profession and other circumstances'[6], resigned shortly afterwards. In truth, he had been trying to sell the seat for a while, but failed because he kept raising the price. It was eventually bought for £2,000 by the Foreign Secretary, Henry Temple, Viscount Palmerston. He was not opposed at an election, memorable only because 'his dress seems to have been by far the loudest thing about it - white hat, white trousers and blue

[1] DRO R4/1/Z/PV4.   [2] DRO R4/1/Z/PV8.
[3] DRO 4302B/B21.   [4] *EFP* 11.9.1834.
[5] Craig 1977, 308.   [6] cited in Bourne 1982, 541.

frock-coat with gilt buttons'[1]. Palmerston was to serve Tiverton for the next 30 years, most of them with Heathcoat. He quickly became associated with the Tiverton Races, although, certainly in the early days, he considered them tiresome. He was expected to act as steward for their duration, and commented that it was a duty to be performed towards his constituents, especially soon after an election[2].

Meanwhile, the Commissions appointed in 1831 to enquire into the management of the nation's boroughs were coming to their conclusion. They found that

> 'Corporation funds are frequently expended in feasting and in paying the salaries of unimportant officers... These abuses often originate in negligence... in the opportunity afforded of obliging members of their own body, or the friends and relations of such members'.

Tiverton had been investigated in October 1833, and the Commissioners were questioned closely throughout the proceedings by George Coles and William Chapple, the strongest critics of the Corporation[3]. Few were surprised at the eventual verdict:

> 'in no place we have visited do the pernicious effects, arising from the connexion between a corporation having the right to return Members of Parliament and an influential nobleman as patron of the borough, appear to be more clearly displayed than in the borough of Tiverton. The management of the public affairs by the corporation has neither deserved nor obtained from them the confidence of the inhabitants'[4].

Despite opposition in the Lords, the Municipal Reform Act reached the statute book in 1835, and changed the governance of boroughs and their corporations throughout the country. The terms of the Act included the replacement of closed corporations by elected borough councils. All male ratepayers over the age of 21 years who had been resident for three years would have the vote. The first Tiverton list of voters contained no fewer than 764 names, underlining the wider representation that the Act had brought about[5]. Tiverton's councillors would stand in three newly created wards, and would serve for three years. These councillors were to choose a group of aldermen who would hold office for six years. There would be a paid Town Clerk and Treasurer, and the council would be required to form a police force. The 'old regime' made sure that little of benefit remained for their successors. They assigned Mayor's Tenement at Bolham to John Wood to pay off debts of £300[6], the furniture of the Mayoralty Room

---

[1] Bourne 1982, 542.
[2] *Palmerston*, 301.
[3] *EFP* 24.10.1833.
[4] *Parliamentary Papers 1835*, vol XXIII.
[5] DRO R4/1/C145.
[6] DRO R4/1/C94.

was sold, and the remainder of their wine stocks was doled out among themselves[1]. The incoming councillors received little favour from the Crown either. The King at first refused to grant the borough the right to hold Quarter Sessions because of its relatively small population and the low number of prisoners tried each year. However, after reconsidering, and making a proviso that a new gaol be built, the right was granted[2]. The Commissioners of Woods and Forests refused to renew the lease on Elmore, and in February 1836 they ordered its sale by auction[3]. The grip of the oligarchy had finally been broken without violence. What we now consider a traditional liberty, the right of ratepayers to choose their representatives, had at last been established by law[4].

---

[1] Snell 1892, 106.   [2] DRO QS294B/6.

[3] the eleven lots, totalling 16 acres, were sold for £1,400, but the Treasury pointed out that the Tiverton Municipal Charities would not be allowed to keep all of it (TivLib folio 1/22).

[4] the establishment of the borough council, however, seems to have signalled the decline of the Parish Vestry, hitherto the most representative body in the town.

15 The Ratepayers' Borough

William IV died on June 20th 1837, and was succeeded by his niece, the 18-year old, Victoria. The Victorian Age was to be a time of constitutional monarchy, Parliamentary government, peace, progress, and unprecedented industrial and commercial expansion which transformed the face of Britain and created an Empire that became the envy of the world. The young Queen's Coronation was celebrated to excess in Tiverton. At the Factory, John Heathcoat treated his employees to a hot dinner of mutton and beef, followed by plain and fruit puddings[1]. Two years later, many of the Factory workers found themselves making the bridal veil worn by the Queen on her marriage to Prince Albert of Saxe-Coburg which took place on February 10th 1840.

Victoria's accession was followed by a general election, which in Tiverton resulted in an impassioned campaign. Heightened emotions were mainly due to Benjamin Bowden Dickinson's decision to stand. The old Corporator aroused many pent-up feelings. One printed sheet asked of him:

> *'Did you not employ Mr Patch to go to London to oppose the Municipal*
> *Reform Bill and you mortgaged the Corporation property at Bolham to pay*
> *him, did you ever attend to any public duties except for the purpose of doing*
> *mischief... have you not, whilst residing at Knightshayes, been as little known*
> *and as useless to the town of Tiverton, as if you had lived at Madeira'*[2].

Another handbill posed the cryptic question 'When did Dickinson ever protect the poor and distressed? Remember Mary Warren!'[3]. Even the worldly-wise Palmerston was surprised by some of the tactics used, and embarrassed that his own supporters, whenever Dickinson attempted to hold a rally, unloaded barrels of cider in the fields nearby to lure away his audience[4]. To the relief of many Liberals, when the votes were counted, the sitting members were returned. Heathcoat had polled 323, Palmerston 246, but Dickinson was only 66 behind with 180[5].

In the Census of 1841, Tiverton's population exceeded 10,000 for the first time. Nationally, the death rate was revealed to be falling, and there was a large movement of people from the countryside to the towns, especially London and the manufacturing centres of the Midlands and the North. Tiverton was both a market and a factory town. Between 1811 and 1821 its population had increased by 2,000, coinciding with the arrival of Heathcoat and the establishment of the Lace Factory. In the Census of 1831,

---

[1] DRO 4302B/B33/5.
[2] TivLib folio 3/503.
[3] TivLib folio 3/548.
[4] Bourne 1982, 571.
[5] Craig 1977, 308.

9,766 persons had been recorded - the previous dramatic rise was levelling off - and in 1851 a 19th century peak of 11,000 was reached. The population had indeed risen, but the town of Tiverton had not spread correspondingly. Some houses had been built on new sites on the outskirts yet the housing stock in the town remained the same as it had been for centuries. The resulting overcrowding, and the heavier burden placed on the sewage system and water supply, would inevitably challenge the Borough Council when it became evident.

The rough track leading from Withleigh Vicarage down to Groubear Bridge which, before the turnpike road from Tiverton to Nomansland was built in 1837, was one of the area's 'main rads'.

Meanwhile, improvements to the roads were pursued. Although authorised eight years earlier, the new road from Penny Park to Nomansland was begun in 1837, the costs being borne almost entirely by subscription[1]. The starting point for the road was

---

[1] the largest donation was the the Rev. George Sharland Cruwys' £1,000, in addition to which he gave as much of his land as was needed (DRO 1092A/P53).

by the newly-built Roman Catholic Church, from where it ran up the hill soon to be given the name Long Drag[1], and on towards Nomansland. It is, of course, still in use as the present B3137. Crossing the small stream between Wayland and Quirkhill proved to be a major problem, solved only by a 35-foot high bridge, whose existence is barely discernible to the modern traveller. Tollhouses were built at the bottom of Long Drag, and where Tombstone Lane crosses the new road just above Wayland, and at Withleigh at the point where the former main route dropped down to Groubear Bridge[2], the boundary of the parish. This road was the final part of a network of turnpikes for Tiverton, making the town accessible from all directions along well-made surfaces. The fact that the routes are still in use is proof enough of their good planning and construction.

In 1836, for the first time in its history the tolls taken on the Canal had topped £1,000[3]. This was still far, far short of the £10,000 a year projected 20 years earlier. The staple trade was the transport of lime, from which the producers were making good profits. John Chave delivered almost 7,000 hogsheads to the Tiverton wharves in a single year, and his profit was almost 30%[4]. The Basin at Tiverton was the focus of an important industry; at one time there were 20 limekilns in use, making it one of the largest such enterprises in the country[5]. The remains of some of the kilns can still be seen there, while others are preserved in name only at nearby Lime Kiln Road. When the waterway was at last opened to Taunton in 1838, a greater variety of goods began to reach Tiverton. The expansion also brought to Canal Wharf Number One the Taunton firm of Goodland, Quant and Company, 'coal, stone coal, coke and salt merchants'[6]. Meanwhile, a threat to both the canal and the turnpike roads was already emerging in the shape of the Bristol and Exeter Railway Company.

The routes mentioned are to be seen on a unique set of maps produced in 1842. They resulted from the Tithe Commutation Act of 1837, which standardised tithe payments[7] into a rent-charge based on the price of grain. To enforce the legislation, agreement on this rent-charge was needed between the landowners and the occupiers. For Tiverton, this was forthcoming in 1841, amounting to a rent increase of some 3%[8]. The mammoth task of mapping the parish could now begin. For tithe purposes

---

[1] named Long Drag not because of the ascent, but because during the long descent the drags, or dragshoes, used to slow down the wheels of carriages and wagons, had to be applied for a considerable distance.
[2] DRO R4/1/Z34.   [3] Hadfield 1955, 199.
[4] DRO 58/9/Box 73/3.
[5] for a full treatment of the subject see Leach 2000.
[6] from bill heading (Saint Peter's MSS Envelope B).
[7] some parishes paid in kind, others in money, still others in a mixture of both.
[8] *EFP* 30.4.1841.

Tiverton was divided into its four ancient portions of Clare, Tidcombe, Pitt and Priors, and a fifth portion of All Fours had been created, mainly out of the parkland which had once belonged to the Castle. In February 1841 a contract had been signed with a Cornish firm to produce maps of the portions at a scale of three chains to the inch, together with a book of reference[1]. For some unknown reason, the contract was negated, and a new one drawn up with William Richards, a local land surveyor. The detail of the maps and apportionments, which together give the owner and occupier's names for every plot of land, together with its name and size, are invaluable to anyone studying genealogy, place-names, land tenure, topography, or the history of settlement. One additional condition attached to the second contract was to produce a map at a scale of one chain to the inch of that part of the town within a half-mile radius of Coggan's Well, much of which was exempt from paying tithes. Although this very useful circular map does not have an accompanying book of reference, it does show the town itself in considerable detail.

One authority has suggested[2] that changes in education could well be considered the essential feature of the Age of Reform. For later employment and enjoyment of life, growing numbers of children needed to be taught to read, write and count – a basic elementary education. Any notion that this should be universal, compulsory, free and secular, imposed by the state, was, however, utterly alien to early Victorian society. Whereas some countries, such as France and a few of the German states, had introduced public education systems in the early part of the 19th century, responsibility in Britain rested in the hands of the churches, chapels and private charity, where it always had been. Furthermore, rivalry between religious denominations would frustrate national reform for decades. Tiverton, in some respects, had better educational endowments than most towns. The Chilcott School had taught an elementary education (and more) to boys who could afford it since 1611. The Bluecoat Schools, founded in the 18th century, were flourishing financially. Indeed, following a complaint of their surplus of funds[3], the Trustees bought new premises for £1,000 in Castle Street[4], which were opened at the end of 1841[5]. Many 'Dame schools' had also grown up during the 18th century, run by tutors in their own homes or, more cheaply, in the pupils' homes. These are rarely documented, although one such school, teaching art, is known from a single advertising card found at Tiverton Castle. This referred to a Mr Benezech who, in 1796, offered to teach drawing, landscapes and figures, to scholars attended twice a week at their houses. He also ran a private academy at his apartments for an hour on Tuesdays and Fridays for six young ladies at a guinea per quarter and a

[1] Harding 1845, i, 264-5.
[2] Woodward 1938, 455 *et seq.*
[3] *JHC 1837,* 669.
[4] *Bluecoat School Minute Book.*
[5] *ib.*

further guinea registration, and the same for young gentlemen on Mondays and Thursdays[1]. By the middle of the 19th century some 20 or more of these Dame schools existed in Tiverton.

Sunday Schools had been established in the town since 1786 and were, it seems, particularly successful. W.P. Authers estimated[2] that in the 1840s about one third of children in the parish regularly attended some form of instruction on Sunday. The original intention that they were to be non-denominational was still held to be important by many. The grocer, Hugh Risdon, a fervent Nonconformist, put a notice in his shop window on Angel Hill which read

> *'If these Schools are for the instruction of the Children of all Classes without respect to sect or party and if the Children of Dissenters will be allowed the advantages of instruction there and to go at the same time with their parents to their respective Chapels on the Lord's Day - if these Schools are liberal and unsectarian in their spirit - may they flourish, but if not, may they perish. God Save the Queen'[3].*

Children attending Sunday Schools were rewarded with occasional treats. One such occasion was the Congregational Church's summer outing in 1839. The children walked to Robert Were's farm at Farleigh, where 'they formed an immense double circle on the lawn in front of the house'. Following a short address and prayer, they shared a large vessel containing half a hogshead of coffee and copious amounts of cake.

> *'After tea, at the sound of a horn, the Scholars scattered themselves over the field for amusement and exercise, and so continued until the shade and coolness of the evening warned the party to return'.*

They filed back to Saint Peter Street, where they entered the chapel and, once another address had been heard and 'some sweet verses' had been sung, they ended the day[4].

Most important were those schools supported by subscribers to the National Society, formed in 1811 'for promoting the education of the poor in the principles of the national church', and the British and Foreign School Society of 1814 which enforced bible reading but excluded denominational teaching. Both types had large classes taught under monitorial supervision by older children. In Tiverton, their school buildings are conspicuous even today. The National School[5] on the west side of Saint Andrew Street had opened in 1818 for 350 children, but demand was so great that by 1840 other premises were sought. A new location was chosen on the opposite side of

---

[1] Mahood 1953, 133.   [2] Authers 1974, 37.
[3] *ib.*, 36.   [4] *ib.*, 38-9.
[5] National Schools were organised by the Church of England, whereas the British and Foreign Schools were nonconformist.

the street, bounded on the north by Saint George's Churchyard. The school was designed by Hayward of Exeter with two schoolrooms for boys and girls separated by the master's and mistress's accommodation, and opened at Whitsun 1841[1]. With its plain, functional Saint Andrew Street façade still intact, this houses part of the Tiverton Museum of Mid Devon Life. At the entrance to the Lace Factory, John Heathcoat laid the foundation stone for a much grander, Elizabethan-style British and Foreign School in June 1841, promising to spend £2,000 on it[2]. Some who attended this school were very young indeed. Ann Norman began at the tender age of one year and nine months, whereas William Davey of Wellbrook, and William Whitfield were six months younger[3]. Obviously, this school acted as a nursery, freeing mothers to work in the Factory. By the 1850s the National and British and Foreign School Societies were receiving quite considerable government grants[4]. The Societies had also established training colleges, whose certificated pupil-teachers had begun to take over from monitors. Nevertheless, a Government Commission's proposal to set up locally elected school boards was deferred, and the deadening system of payment by results was imposed on Victorian education. By the late 1850s an estimated 95% of children nationally were receiving some education, and in Tiverton the percentage was probably even higher[5]. Of course, at this time it was not compulsory or free. Even the 2d a week to attend the Heathcoat School was, in at least one instance, too much. John Lentel of Elmore could not return for his second week of schooling as he was 'occasioned by poverty'[6]. Few children attended school regularly and most left before the age of eleven.

Education for older children was restricted to those who could afford the time and money it took to secure the classical education that alone qualified for admission to the universities. Apart from private academies, most old grammar schools had fallen into decay as their endowments and salaries were overtaken by rising prices. Some, however, were flourishing. Tiverton's Free Grammar School (Blundell's) was famous for the scale of its buildings, the number of pupils, the quality of teaching, and the size of its academic and landed endowments. From the beginning, Masters had raised their income by taking boarders. The Rev. Henry Sanders was appointed in 1834 to a school of about 100 boys, most of whom were boarders. He could accommodate at least 40 in his own house, charging each one 50 guineas for washing and tuition. His pupils came from far and near, among them Frederick Temple, the future Archbishop of Canterbury, and Richard Dodderidge Blackmore, author of *Lorna Doone*, whose first pages describe the school of the novel's hero, Jan Ridd. Little had changed in the organisation of Blundell's School. The 25 Trustees administered the lands in South

---

[1] Harding 1845, iv, 101.
[2] Harris 1985, 14.
[3] DRO 2745C/EFA1.
[4] subject to match-funding and inspection.
[5] Authers 1974, 37.
[6] DRO 3029C/EFA1.

Devon[1], collected rents, made repairs to buildings and paid the Master the statutory £50 a year and the Usher £20. Rents were raised, but salaries were fixed. Consequently, each year there was a surplus sometimes as much as £300. Like the Bluecoat Charity, the Trustees of Blundell's looked to the Court of Chancery for advice on how best to employ their rising funds. Among the reformed electorate of Tiverton, however, criticism was forthcoming. George Coles, the scourge of the Old Corporation, wrote in 1836 to Sir Thomas Dyke Acland, one of the Trustees. He roundly denounced the recent building of dining rooms for the Masters as 'one of the most unnecessary and profligate specimens of expenditure of the funds of a charitable institution I have ever met with'[2]. This was only the beginning of what would become a long, acrimonious and expensive dispute. The new Borough demanded a greater say in the running of its greatest benefaction, and a return to what they saw as the explicit intentions of its founder.

The episode is best accessed through Harding's full, yet concise, contemporary account in his *History of Tiverton*. His interest in the school is relatively easy to understand; not only had he been a pupil at Blundell's for six years from 1801, but he also had a son there in 1837. Nevertheless, his links to education in Tiverton were not restricted only to the one school, as in 1841 he became secretary of the body responsible for the new National School in Saint Andrew Street[3]. Other than these snippets of information, very little is otherwise known about Lieutenant-Colonel William Harding who, in April 1845, published the first part of a *History of Tiverton*. This two-volume work is divided into five parts, a format similar to that used by Dunsford in 1790. Harding, however, clearly had access to many more documents, notably the papers of the Greenway Charity. He made extensive if not imaginative use of the extra material, but the best of his work are those chapters that update Dunsford, especially the lengthy and authoritative treatment of the proceedings in the Blundell's case.

According to Harding[4], the first complaints against the School were aired at a meeting of Tiverton's Reform Association early in 1837. Following this, a petition was sent to the House of Lords listing the 'abuses in the management' of the School. These

---

[1] the Tiverton properties had nearly all been sold by 1825.
[2] (DRO 1148M add/36/476).
[3] TivMus 2000.266.39.
[4] (Harding 1845, iii, 141). Harding cites as his authority for this reference a little-known publication, issued in 1836-7, by George Boyce. This work was never completed; there exists a Part I of 88 pages, Part II of 40 pages, and Part III, containing 68 pages. Boyce's intention was to rewrite and update Dunsford's Historical Memoirs, but ill health halted the work after 1837, and led to his death early in 1841. I have managed to locate only two copies of the work, one in the Bodleian Library, and one in private hands. I was fortunate to be given access to this latter copy, but was sadly disappointed by its content; it added nothing to Dunsford's work regarding Tiverton before 1790, and Boyce's work on the period after that date was clearly available, and used by, Harding.

included the charges for instruction, the introduction of boarders who were accused of bullying and, worse, depriving local boys of scholarships, and of the Trustees themselves who were mostly not resident in or near Tiverton. In December 1838, a public meeting resolved to communicate these concerns, and others, to the Earl of Devon, the Chairman of the Trust. Among the critics were John Heathcoat M.P., the Mayor, the three rectors, two doctors, George Coles and other prominent citizens. They respectfully reminded the Trustees of Peter Blundell's intentions: to provide a free classical education primarily for Tiverton children, rich or poor, up to 150 in number; only when there were fewer could 'foreigners' be admitted as boarders, and even then only with the consent of the town's principal tax-payers. Their final point was that, in view of present needs unforeseen by the founder, a wider curriculum with free instruction in mathematics and the living languages should be introduced without delay. A petition sent to Chancery in 1839 by the Trustees shows that they, in fact, agreed with much of this. However, they failed to convey their good intentions in time, and the Committee, feeling slighted, prepared for a battle in the courts. In February 1840 the Vice Chancellor of the Court of Chancery dismissed what he considered 'a foul libel on the Masters and Feoffees', but reserved costs and allowed the town to proceed by information. Knowing what was likely to ensue, he urged both parties to consider the expense to Blundell's Charity of further proceedings.

His advice went unheeded. A venomous pamphlet war had already begun[1]. One of many such papers, signed (in Latin) 'an Old Boy of Blundell's School'[2], refers to the petitioners as 'a set of political fungi, more than half of them never heard of in Tiverton twenty years ago'. It then launches into a tirade against the more prominent signatories, declaring that Heathcoat's motto should have been 'let the cobbler stick to his last', and, equally, Mr Talley 'should stick to his plough'. Of the petitioners, he declares

> 'many of them being of the lowest class of mechanics, and therefore far below that class which Blundell intended to benefit, when he said none should be entitled below a Grammar Scholar'.

However unwillingly, town, gown, and Trustees were locked in bitter dispute. Blundell's was not the first, and would certainly not be the last, school to suffer from envy, prejudice, class-consciousness, reactionaries, or would-be reformers, or from the Court of Chancery. Commissions of enquiry sat at the Three Tuns in Tiverton, and in London, from September 4th to October 12th 1844. They heard 91 depositions on behalf of the town, 56 for the Trustees and 52 for the Masters, in response to 30 questions put to witnesses.

---

[1] some are in the War Memorial collection, and many are included among the 336 items relating to the case kept at Blundell's School.
[2] TivLib folio 1/33.

The Vice Chancellor finally published his judgement in October 1846. Ironically, this was a year too late to be included in Harding's analysis of the case. Few were satisfied when so much had been expected. His decision to base his opinion on the dubious precedent of the Manchester Grammar School case was inept, and even then Blundell's had to wait a further six years for its new scheme of management. Meanwhile, it was decreed that a Classical education was to be maintained free of charge, but subjects such as mathematics, writing and French could be paid for; only free scholars would be eligible for Exhibitions or Scholarships. Then came the débâcle. 'Neither the Master nor the Usher ought to receive any payments from, or in respect of, any of the boarders, or ought to take any boarder'. Of those signing the petition only 11 townsmen had argued for this. The salaries of the Master and Usher were to become a charge on the foundation; the Feoffees were to pay them £400 and £200 a year respectively, but in bad years they went short. The last of the boarders left in June 1847. The Rev. Sanders was presented with a magnificent silver kettle[1] and inkstand, and went off to become Rector of Sowton. His successor, the Rev. John Bickley Hughes, took on 40 pupils in 1848, most of them day-boys. Boarders continued to be admitted as 'foreigners', lodging in the town[2].

It had all been a waste of opportunity and money. What had begun as proposals from both sides to reinvigorate and reform Blundell's had ended in frustration and bitterness between the Trust and the borough's leading citizens. All this at a time when the railway was coming near, and the aspiring middle-classes were looking for places to educate their sons as gentlemen. Many petitioners had expected such an influx of families, but they did not come, and John Heathcoat's plans to develop and build 'superior dwellings... on a field called the Circus'[3] had to be abandoned for some 30 years. Only the lawyers gained: in all some £5,900 was lost to Blundell's foundation when the costs of the Chancery case were awarded against the Trust.

The possibility of social unrest in pursuit of political aims was always of great concern, and there were fears that such a threat was growing. The 1832 Reform Act and much of the subsequent legislation had brought little immediate response. To radicals in search of universal suffrage the Act had been just a beginning, and one of them, William Lovett, in 1838 produced the People's Charter. Its

---

[1] donated to the school in 1986 by a direct descendant.
[2] at places like Mr Brown's Boarding School at Wilderness House, which advertised for young gentlemen attending Blundell's in addition to offering 'the advantage of commercial instruction' (cited in Mahood 1952, 75-6).
[3] *ib.*, 74-7.

supporters, soon to be known as Chartists, advocated annual parliaments, votes for all men, secret ballots, the abolition of property qualifications for M.P.s, payments of M.P.s, and electoral districts with populations of equal size[1]. When Parliament ignored these demands there were widespread disturbances. One particular crime associated with social unrest was arson. Perhaps there were fears of this in Tiverton, as one of the Borough account books speaks of persons 'apprehended for incendiarism' in 1840[2]. The situation probably explains the two carbines and bayonets kept at the entrance lodge of John Heathcoat's Factory[3]. No further trouble arose, however, and even the Parliamentary election in June 1841 passed off peacefully in the town. The Chartists did not field a candidate, but a Westexe butcher, William Rowcliffe, championed their cause. His constant heckling earned him the grudging respect of both Heathcoat and Palmerston who, after the withdrawal of the Conservative candidate, were returned unopposed.

A daring crime that took place in January 1842 jolted the Borough into action. Nine men escaped from the Gaol, and one of them committed a violent assault while on the run[4]. All nine were eventually recaptured and subsequently transported[5]. It was too easy to escape; all that was needed, it was claimed, was a 'spike nail'. The grant of a Court of Quarter Sessions in 1836 had been made on condition that the Borough built a new Gaol, but nothing had been done. The break-out prompted an immediate response. A site in Saint Andrew Street, beside Hobby Horse Lane, was conveyed to the Borough Council[6]. The purchase money was supposed to come from the sale to John Heathcoat of the Corporation's properties at Bolham and Chevithorne[7]. The foundation stone of the new Prison was laid in March 1844, and the local builders Joseph Perkins, and John and Charles Beck began the work[8] before it was realised that there was not enough money to pay for it. John Heathcoat offered a loan for the whole sum, £3,500, but it was decided to borrow £1,000 from George Voysey of Saint Andrew Street at 3½% rate of interest, and the remainder from Heathcoat who had insisted on 4%[9]. The architect of the new Gaol was Gideon Acland Boyce, the son of a Tiverton bookseller. Boyce had been educated at Blundell's, and in 1830 was the collector of the Land Tax for the town. He was a prolific architect, and much of his work has survived. The Gaol, at least in part, of course is still standing and retains its

---

[1] all the points of the Charter have since been absorbed into British constitutional practice, with the exception of annual elections.
[2] DRO R4/1/T41.
[3] DRO 4302B/A8.
[4] *EFP* 25.8.1842.
[5] DRO R4/1/T41.
[6] DRO R4/1/C94 and DRO 49/9/6/127.
[7] he acquired Mayor's Tenement at Bolham for £1,530, and Berry's Tenement for £600 (DRO R4/1/C94).
[8] DRO R4/1/C94.
[9] DRO R4/1/C308.

splendid classical façade, although the building is now divided into flats as part of the aptly named Bridewell Court. He was also responsible for the British and Foreign School at the Factory, which now houses the Factory Shop, and Saint John's Roman Catholic Church at the bottom of Long Drag in Gothic style.

The Municipal Corporation Act of 1835 had recommended the establishment of a police force in Tiverton. Nine years later, the Borough Council still maintained that it was 'neither desirable nor expedient to establish a regular paid police force'. Their decision was reversed in December 1844, but only by the Chairman's casting vote[1]. A motion to fund the police out of the Liberty Rate was opposed by the Parish Vestry, who thought this would be unfair, because those living in the rural areas would receive less protection for their money than would those within the town, and asked for a subscription instead[2]. Nevertheless, the Council passed the original motion, and a force of one superintendent and three constables[3] was soon settled into a building adjoining the Town Hall. Strict regulations were imposed; each constable was to visit all parts of his beat three times an hour, and any officer found talking to female servants or other females in the street, or smoking on duty, would be reported[4]. The benefits were immediate. The *Exeter Flying Post* soon announced that at night Tiverton was 'much more reputable... a certain class of females not being allowed on the streets after 11pm'[5].

Church building went on apace in the 1840s. It was proposed to build a chapel at Chevithorne, and the London architect Benjamin Ferrey[6], a former student of the great Pugin, was chosen. The building which was dedicated to Saint Thomas, was consecrated in June 1843[7]. It had been funded by subscription, with one of the largest contributors being the Rev. William Rayer, Rector of Tidcombe. He also gave its church plate[8], determined the seating-plan[9], and, in 1850, was to make substantial provisions for the curate, organist, clerk, sexton, as well as for the maintenance of the building[10]. An Independent Chapel was built in Elmore in 1843, with a burial ground added. This building had come about through the persistence of the Rev. Heudebourck in the face of much opposition. On the west side of Saint Andrew Street, the plot of land where the old National School had stood was bought by the Bible Christians, a group which had broken away from the Methodists. They established their Providence Chapel on the site, though at first the congregation was meagre, just one preacher on

---

[1] DRO R4/1/C4.   [2] DRO R4/1/C315.
[3] *EFP* 26.12.1844.   [4] DRO R4/1/C317.
[5] 15.4.1845.
[6] he is best known in the Tiverton area for the design of Huntsham Court in 1869.
[7] DRO Chanter 62.   [8] Chanter 1919, 107-8.
[9] DRO 2986A/PW1.   [10] DRO 2986A/PF1.

trial and seven members[1]. Saint George's Church was closed from 1841 while extensive repairs were carried out, which included a new roof, the complete renewal of the seating and the installation of a new organ[2]. The costs were largely met from Mary Peard's bequest. The most ambitious plan, however, was to build a chapel for the hamlet of Withleigh. William Carpenter of Higher Withleigh donated the land, his son gave £25 as well as the stone from his quarries[3], and the building costs were met by subscription[4]. The site chosen was in a field called Chapel Close where the medieval Saint Katherine's Chapel had once stood. Nevertheless, according to two itinerant preachers, Messrs Dealtry and Burgess, all this church-building was in vain as the End of the World was due on October 10th 1845. They offered salvation for half a crown to anyone willing to undergo total immersion in the Lowman. Burgess was still soliciting candidates in the town in November, having deemed postponement of the End until 1847[5].

Yet more building was going on in Westexe, where John Heathcoat made good his intentions to provide suitable housing for his workers. In 1845 he bought part of Frosts Meadow, on the edge of which was to be 'the intended new Melbourne Street'[6], Tiverton's first example of town planning. Meanwhile, he began the process of buying up large amounts of property. He purchased the Subscription Rooms in Fore Street, the venture having proved something of a failure[7], and houses in the Pit, the area beside the river to the south of Exe Bridge[8], as well as ground near Waldron's Almshouses[9]. His landed interests were not restricted to the town, for in 1845 he added Norwood Plantation[10], Deepaller and Lower Pitt[11], Lythecourt[12], and would follow these with the purchase of Wayland and Coxmoor[13].

Tiverton's fledgling police force was called into action in May 1847. News had arrived of food riots at Exeter and Cullompton, and trouble seemed imminent. The fears were well founded, as a crowd 500 strong gathered at Lowman Green and began, after dark, to smash the windows of all the town's bakeries. They then marched to Gornhay where the farmer, William Chapple, was known to have a huge store of grain. After shots were fired from the farmhouse, 'some gentlemen' persuaded the crowd to calm down and allow Chapple a chance to speak. He came out and promised to deliver a thousand bushels of corn into the Market on the following Tuesday[14]. This seems to

---

[1] DRO 2514D/1.
[2] Harding 1845, iv, 56.
[3] DRO 2987 addA/Z.
[4] DRO 2987 addA/PW6.
[5] *EFP* 27.11.1845.
[6] (KEO Box 2). The street was named after Lord Melbourne, the Prime Minister.
[7] Harding 1845, i, 239.
[8] DRO 213M/T55.
[9] KEO Box 2.
[10] DRO 2547M/T185.
[11] KEO Chest 49.
[12] DRO 49/9/6/253b.
[13] KEO Chest 49.
[14] *EFP* 20.5.1847.

have satisfied the crowd, and they dispersed peacefully. On the following day, however, 200 railwaymen, working nearby, marched into the town[1]. Presumably, their action was in support of the earlier activity, but nothing came of the incident. In the 'hungry forties', despite the repeal of the Corn Laws in 1846, the price and supply of corn could still provoke violent protests.

Nationally, the Chartist movement experienced a revival. The slump in trade during 1847 saw them once more a headline threat. They secured sympathy and support in Tiverton; many people sent contributions to the Chartist Land Company, a group intent on setting up commune-like settlements throughout the country[2]. In the 1847 General Election, they put forward one of their national leaders, George Julian Harney, to stand in Tiverton against the Foreign Minister, Palmerston. Harney, a journalist[3], was a very intense, dedicated man. His sober appearance was in stark contrast to that of Palmerston, an Irish Regency beau bedecked in bright blue coat and white pants. The contest drew reporters from the national dailies and for a brief period made Tiverton the focus of British, even European, attention. The speeches of both men were bold and emotional, with Harney declaring to the Tiverton crowds that it was farcical to speak 'of our Indian Empire, and our colonial possessions, when you have not one foot of soil in your own country to call your own'. In the opinion of the working-class radical press and the Tiverton populace, Palmerston was handed a 'thorough thrashing on foreign policy'[4]. At one time, a show of hands proclaimed Harney and Heathcoat as the people's choice. However, the crowd was, of course, largely unqualified to vote. Harney's reaction was to withdraw in protest against the electoral system, leaving Heathcoat and Palmerston again unopposed[5].

The railway finally reached Tiverton in 1848. The 4¾-mile stretch from Tiverton Junction into the town was opened on June 12th amid scenes of great celebration. The list of amusements announced that

> 'two legs of mutton will be suspended on top of poles in Fore Street, to be climbed for and removed; jumping in sacks; driving wheelbarrows blindfold; a pig will be let loose from the door of the Guildhall and become the property of who can catch it and retain it by holding the tail only; a hopping match; treacled cakes to be jumped for'[6].

It had been a long timing coming. Early in 1836, the directors of the Bristol and Exeter Railway had called a meeting to inform the Tiverton Turnpike Trustees of their

---

[1] Snell 1892, 306-8.   [2] Hadfield 1970, 22.
[3] he had met both Marx and Engels on many occasions, and persuaded them to write for the *Northern Star*, a newspaper of which he was the editor.
[4] Schoyen 1958, 152.   [5] Ridley 1972, 443.
[6] TivLib folio 2/200.

wish, as part of the route to Exeter, to lay a branch line to Tiverton[1]. An Act of Parliament to build the line was secured in the same year, and the planning and surveying began. Despite the good news, many people were disappointed that it was to be a branch line and the town would not be on the main line. Their disappointment, however, was nothing compared to that of the Canal and Turnpike operators. The threat to both was obvious. As the railway would be following virtually the same route into Tiverton, it seemed that nothing could stop it from taking the coal and lime trade from the Canal. The Turnpike Trustees saw the arrival of the railway as a catastrophe, claiming that they were already losing at least £1,500 a year from the Cullompton and White Ball tollgates[2]. The sixteen or so stagecoaches that ran into the town would soon cease[3]. The Trustees could do little, apart from cut down on their expenses. They decided that from 1849 the Treasurer, Clerk, and Surveyor would take a 25% reduction in their salary[4]. The situation was not without irony. In 1848, the turnpike roads and the Canal had made a profit – by carrying building materials for the railway.

A spate of arson attacks took place in the vicinity during 1849. Newspapers like the *Exeter Flying Post* tended to portray the incidents as wanton vandalism rather than anything more organised. In successive weeks from November, Beauchamp Farm (Washfield), Churchill Farm (Loxbeare), and the property of Dry Hill (Stoodleigh) were all set on fire. No matter what the newspapers thought, the actions of the local landowners reveal that they, at least, believed the incidents were motivated by poverty and high rents. Soon after the Stoodleigh fire, the Rev. John Pitman, who had land nearby, reduced his rents by 10% and gave £1 to each of the labourers working for his tenants. None of his farms was attacked. The landowners' fears increased during the winter, as severe weather put many labourers out of work[5]. The Rev. Robert Carew of Bickleigh followed Pitman's example by returning 5% of his tenants' tithe payments, and his kinsman Thomas of Collipriest gave back 10% of the half-yearly rents. Following conflagrations at Leigh and Loxbeare Bartons, it was the turn of Tiverton itself in March 1850. Fourteen houses adjoining the Prince Blucher in Westexe were burnt. Why arsonists had chosen a residential area in the town is not known. Yet these worrying incidents stopped as abruptly as they had begun. Within the space of six months, there had been six serious fires, all without demand or explanation.

W*hite's Directory* of 1850 has nothing but praise for Tiverton. As well as containing a general history and description of most of the prominent buildings, along with a most useful list of professional men[5] and tradesmen, it claims that Tiverton 'is considered one of the healthiest and principal

---

[1] *EFP.*
[2] DRO R4/1/Z21.
[3] Kanefsky 1977, 67.
[4] *EFP* 9.3.1848.
[5] so many that a Relief Fund in Tiverton provided bread for over 500 people.

towns of Devon'[1]. However, the unseemly reality of the conditions in which most Tivertonians lived was officially recognised just a year later. June 1851 saw the publication of a report by Thomas Webster Rammell, a Commissioner of the Board of Health, on the 'sewerage, drainage, and supply of water and the sanitary condition of the inhabitants of the borough of Tiverton'. The report had been requested by some of its leading citizens following a cholera outbreak in 1847. From the evidence presented, Tiverton was undeniably a town with many serious faults. As Rammell noted

> *The general aspect of the town, meaning the principal streets in the old part of it, is cheerful and prepossessing; so much so, indeed, that the stranger could barely expect to find the masses of filth and corruption which a closer inspection of the back quarters, where the poorer portion of the population dwells, would bring to his view.'*

Surprisingly perhaps, the Gaol and Workhouse were singled out for rare praise:

> *'The comfort and cleanliness of both are in striking contrast to the miserable dwellings of the working people of the town generally.'*

The extent of housing for the poor can be seen in the figures provided in the report; 70% of dwellings in the town had a rateable value of less than £5, whereas in the rural area this category contained just 23% of the housing stock. The water supply still depended heavily on the Town Leat. For many people it was the only available water for laundry, washing, and even drinking, but it was found to be taking house slops, and run-off from cesspits, pigsties, and stables[2]. In Westexe, the Factory Leat served the same purpose as the Town Leat, but effluent from the Factory often added to its pollution. As for the sewers, many had become broken or severely damaged, and were often found to have an insufficient gradient thus leading to a rapid build-up of deposits. Even where they existed, only about one tenth of the houses were connected. In many parts of the town - the upper parts of Bampton Street and Barrington Street, Water Lane, Town's End, Silver Street, Bartow's Causeway, part of Gold Street, and Westexe[3] – sewers simply did not exist.

Most revealing are Rammell's observations made on a four-day tour of the town. The careful descriptions of vile conditions make dreadful reading. In the upper part of Bampton Street, for example, was

---

[1] p.308.

[2] one witness, William Hole, stated that the Leat flowed for 85 yards in his garden, and every year he cleansed his section of some 16 cart-loads of black and green deposit.

[3] it was pointed out that although Westexe contributed one third of the rates, it too was devoid of sewers.

Joyce's and other premises. - Five dwellings; one privy; against which is a nest of piggeries, with dung-heaps. Joyce's wife died of cholera last year. Same description applicable to premises adjoining on the upper side, excepting that these have a slaughter-house in addition. All the sulliage runs into the street. Next premises much of the same character, but still more close and confined. Another slaughter-house, against which is the privy. The dwellings upon the three last sets of premises, are in the most dilapidated condition, the roofs thatched, the windows hardly admit any light. A more abominable collection of filth was never allowed to accumulate.

Everywhere, Rammell encountered dung-heaps, slaughterhouses, open cesspits, and human waste running in open gutters. He also visited the town's three vagrant lodging houses, in one of which he was told that at fair-times as many as three or four vagrants would sleep in each bed.

The recommendations of the report were radical and wide-ranging. Rammell suggested piping the water from the Town Leat into all houses and supplying the labouring class with bathhouses and washhouses. New sewers would be required, and their outfall was to be carried clear of the town. The cesspits and open pools that caused so much offence would be removed, and all houses provided with privies. He proposed the registration and regulation of slaughterhouses and lodging-houses, as well as the laying-out of public walks and pleasure grounds.

Nevertheless, many inhabitants viewed 'with disgust the Rammell report and consider the same a slander on our town'[1]. A petition headed by John Heathcoat and 11 councillors, containing 800 signatures, was sent to the Board of Health objecting to the findings[2]. The estimated cost on the rate, 2d a week[3], was thought to be prohibitive, and without Heathcoat's support Rammell's report remained literally a pipe dream. However, the Borough Council made some creditable attempts to improve a bad situation. In the very same week as the report was issued they sanctioned work at Lowman Bridge. The bridge itself was to be rebuilt, all the nearby weirs and embankments removed, and the river bed lowered[4]. This would speed up the flow of water, so the discharge from the sewers would escape faster. This last problem would be further eased by channelling their outflow into a covered elm drain, which would empty only into deep water[5]. It was also decided to build a sewer in the rapidly growing northern Westexe, into which all occupiers of land were compelled to carry their drains[6]. Such work, however commendable, could never be more than a piecemeal temporary solution.

---

[1] DRO R4/1/Z77.   [2] TivLib folio 8/1132.
[3] 1d a week to pay for improving the water supply, and 1d to pay for drainage.
[4] DRO R4/1/C4.   [5] DRO R4/1/C5.
[6] *EFP* 27.11.1851.

Rammell's was not the image that Tivertonians fancied for their town. The one promoted a few years later by the *Stranger's Guide* was much more agreeable. Published in 1855, the booklet was unashamedly targeted at tourists who, with the arrival of the railway, could now be expected. The unsuspecting visitor was told of Tiverton's 'providential exemption from epidemical disease', and the Town Leat, which 'still continues a blessing to the town, conducive alike to the health and convenience of all within its influence'. Great emphasis was placed on the availability of fishing on the Exe, and the fact that near Howden 'the side of this hill offers many pleasant building sites'. Nowhere does the *Guide* attempt to lead the visitor into the alleys and courts investigated by Rammell, but its author, a reporter on the *Dumfries Chronicle*, could hardly be blamed for that.

John Heathcoat and Company came into being in 1852. The business was now a partnership between John Heathcoat and his son-in-law Ambrose Brewin, joined by John's nephew, Thomas Hallam, and his grandson John Heathcoat Amory[1]. Clearly, it was still very much a family business. During the year, another of John's nephews, Thomas Heathcoat, journeyed to Paris, Lyons, Marseilles, Messina and Genoa[2]. The visits to Italy probably paved the way for the later expansion into silk production. The Factory at Tiverton, however, remained by far the most important production centre - important for the town as well as for the Company. At this time over 1,200 were employed there, comprising 279 male adults, 683 women and girls, and 259 youths and boys[3].

John Heathcoat and Ambrose Brewin were instrumental in setting up Tiverton's first dispensary. The town's ratepayers had called a meeting in May 1852 to consider the matter, mainly at the insistence of a Dr Clutterbuck, who had recently arrived from Australia. He obtained a large donation from Heathcoat and Brewin[4], which made the project possible. Later meetings were held to determine just who should receive treatment. As with Anna-Maria Turner's gift in 1828 (see p.216), those already in receipt of parish relief were exempted, as were those entitled to medical assistance from benefit societies or clubs[5], together with servants earning £5 a week or more[6]. Premises were soon obtained, and the Dispensary opened in Kiddell's Court, on the south side of Fore Street[7].

The same two benefactors also gave generously toward the extensive repairs and alterations needed at Saint Peter's Church. The Rev. John Bickley Hughes, Master of Blundell's, and a founder member of the Exeter Diocesan Architectural Society, had

---

[1] (DRO 2685 add/F27). John Heathcoat was to provide £80,000 of the firm's capital of £120,000.
[2] DRO 4302B/F7.
[3] the figures are for 1846.
[4] *EFP* 10.6.1852.
[5] TivLib folio 4/625.
[6] DRO R4/1/Z77.
[7] DRO 3761R/Tiverton.

already listed the building's shortcomings. In his opinion, the heavy gallery over the chancel drowned the voice of the priest, another in the north aisle spread a dim light, and a third blocked the tower arch and window. The font was lost among the high pews in the nave, and equally lofty pews in the chancel concealed the neglected altar. The east window was blocked by woodwork, and the preacher spoke from the pulpit not to the congregation, but into the candelabrum[1]. Nevertheless, Hughes' list of faults dealt only with the fittings inside the church.

TIVERTON CHURCH, 1853.

TIVERTON CHURCH, 1857.

Saint Peter's Church from the north-east:
before restoration (top), after restoration (bottom).

---

[1] 1857, 37-8.

The fabric of the building itself called for more substantial work. The walls were out of perpendicular, the parapets and battlements were in danger of falling down, and some of the buttresses had been undermined by rainwater. There was desperate need for space in the churchyard, so it was decided to demolish the Church House and other buildings there[1]. Although work did not begin until 1853, preparations were made years before. The Churchwardens' Accounts in 1849 record a payment of £1 10s for work that included cleaning the chandelier before its removal to Holcombe Rogus Court[2], recently purchased by the Rector of Tidcombe, William Rayer[3]. The sounding board of the pulpit and part of the medieval rood-screen[4] later joined the chandelier. All of the work was paid for largely by voluntary contributions. Out of the initial £3,000 subscribed, Heathcoat gave £500, Brewin £250, Frederick Owen Patch £205, and the Earl of Harrowby £179 10s[5]. To make up the expected shortfall, the Vestry allowed a further £1,250 to be raised from the rates[6]. Before work could proceed, permission was obtained for Saint George's Church to conduct marriages and burial services[7]. The architect appointed to direct the work was Edward Ashworth of Exeter[8].

The Victorian restoration continued for three years. All of the galleries were removed, along with much woodwork, and the 17th Century pulpit was replaced by an inferior example, poorly carved in Caen stone[9]. In the end, virtually the whole of Saint Peter's was rebuilt. Apart from the tower, the Greenway Chapel, part of the south aisle, and the piers and arches of the chancel, most of the present building dates from this period. As with similar long-term projects, the final costs were considerably more than the initial estimate. By 1855, there was a deficit of about £2,000, but Tiverton soon saw an opportunity to make up the shortfall. The Bath and West Agricultural Society had decided to hold that year's show in the town, so an exhibition of works of art was planned to coincide with the event. The hope was that this would raise sufficient funds

---

[1] DRO R4/1/Z/PV4.   [2] D&C 6027/5.

[3] Baring Gould 1920, 104.

[4] the candelabrum and sounding-board were returned.

[5] TivLib folio 4/660.   [6] DRO R4/1/Z/PV4.

[7] DRO Faculty Petitions/Saint Georges 1.

[8] this must have been a prosperous period for the local building industry, for new schools had been built in Bampton Street (1847), and at Elmore (1848), both paid for by Ambrose Brewin, and a school near the church at Withleigh was opened in 1849. Apart from Saint Peter's, an Independent Chapel was erected at Bolham, and an extensive 'restoration' was planned at Cove. It was later decided to construct the Chapel on a new site, albeit only feet away from where the earlier structure stood. The new Cove Chapel was opened in November 1856, little over a year after Thomas Daniel had laid the foundation stone. As the church was on a new site, it should have been relicensed for marriages, but the fact was overlooked for some years. Matters were put right by the passing of the Marriages Confirmation (Cove Chapel) Act in 1873, which legalised all of the marriages performed there since the rebuilding.

[9] Welsford 1973, 6.

to pay for the restoration work and to build a hospital for the town[1]. The Tiverton and West of England Exhibition of Works of Art and Industry, as it was named, would be staged in a temporary building constructed over the Market Avenue from Fore Street[2]. In order to attract more visitors, the Turnpike Trustees agreed to waive the tolls at the North Devon Gate for the three days of the Bath and West Show, which was held at the Loughborough Fields[3]. Both events went ahead as planned, but whereas the Agricultural Show drew great crowds, receipts from the Exhibition did not cover even half of the Saint Peter's shortfall, let alone enough for a hospital[4]. A renewed appeal for subscriptions, however, brought in all but £400 of the building costs, which had risen to £6,000[5]. At the end of June 1856, the parish church was finally re-opened amid much celebration[6].

While work inside the Church had been going on, the problem of the burial ground was tackled, once the Church House and other buildings had been demolished. Of the yard itself,

> 'the accumulation of soil mainly composed of the results of human decay rose to the height of several feet above the original level of the ground', and when making fresh interments it is hardly possible to avoid disturbing graves of recent formation, resulting in scenes of a painful and demoralizing character'[7].

Tiverton's solution was to be the same as that taken elsewhere at this time, and one which Rammell had recommended. An Act of Parliament was obtained in 1855 to discontinue burial in Saint Peter's and Saint George's Churches except in existing vaults, and to open a cemetery on the outskirts of the town. A nine-acre field beside the old Bampton Road was bought for the purpose, and an agreement made with the local builder, Joseph Perkins, to drain the ground, build boundary walls, and construct a lodge with entrance gates. Two chapels were added, one for Anglicans, the other for Dissenters, designed by Gideon Acland Boyce[8]. The Cemetery was ready in little time, and the first interment, that of Charles Harris, a six-year old boy from the Workhouse, took place on June 4th 1855[9]. Trouble soon arose, however. A complaint was made to the Burial Board that there was not a single nonconformist member among them[10]. Feelings intensified when a Parish Vestry petitioned for the closure of all the Dissenters'

---

[1] DRO R4/1/Z77.
[2] DRO 3171M/T46.
[3] DRO R4/1/Z4.
[4] *EFP* 26.7.1855.
[5] Snell 1892, 413-6.
[6] but not everyone joined in the festive events; some did not believe that donkey-racing was compatible with the occasion (*EFP* 3.7.1856).
[7] DRO R4/1/Z77.
[8] DRO R4/1/Z57.
[9] DRO R4/1/Z56.
[10] DRO R4/1/Z61.

burial grounds; those of the Independents at Elmore and Saint Peter Street, the Baptists in Newport Street, and the Wesleyans in Saint Peter Street[1]. The intention was to have all burials at the Cemetery. The greatest controversy, however, concerned the boundary between the Anglican and Dissenters' sections. Bishop Philpotts of Exeter, a man not famed for his tolerance of Dissent, made it known that if the wall separating the two groups were not raised from two to four feet or more, he would withdraw the licence for burials. The Burial Board reluctantly stated their determination not to comply, and the matter had to be taken before the Court of Queen's Bench[2]. The dispute was eventually settled in June 1858, with judgment on all points in favour of the Burial Board[3]. Nevertheless, the Board chose to compromise; the boundary was not to be a wall, but a path marked by stones, and in October, Bishop Philpotts at last performed the consecration ceremony[4].

Fear of Catholicism was just one factor that led to the building of a third town church, this time in Westexe[5]. This heavily populated part of Tiverton was served by a single religious building, the Roman Catholic Church at the bottom of Long Drag Hill. John Heathcoat gave land for the new church, but first the area needed to be cleared of 'a great number of unsightly cottages' in order that two new streets could be built for better access. These were to be Church Street and Saint Paul Street, and, of course, Saint Paul's Square was also created. Ambrose Brewin had agreed to meet most of the building costs, and in April 1854 the foundation stone was laid of what was to be a most handsome church, designed to hold 1,000 worshippers. As Saint Peter's was undergoing its rebuilding at the time, a license was granted to hold services in the shell of a building in Melbourne Street until the new church was finished[6]. Meanwhile, at the opposite end of the town, in Elmore, an Anglican chapel was being built[7]. The Baptist Church was also being enlarged, and its congregation used the Public Rooms in Fore Street as a temporary place of worship[8]. All this building was directed to the spiritual welfare of the various denominations in mid-Victorian Tiverton. The new church in Westexe, dedicated to Saint Paul, was opened in January 1856. Special permission was sought to open the building before its official consecration, which was delayed because Bishop Philpotts had bronchitis. Three months later he had recovered, and the service went ahead, with his chaplain, the Rev. Robert Carew, preaching the sermon[9]. Sadly, Ambrose Brewin did not live to see the event. He had died in August 1855, aged only 47, and was buried in the Heathcoat family vault in Saint Peter's Churchyard.

---

[1] DRO 2514D adds1-5/857.
[2] *EFP* 27.11.1856.
[3] DRO R4/1/Z53.
[4] DRO Chanter 63.
[5] Welsford 1973, 64.
[6] DRO Faculty Petitions/Saint Pauls 1.
[7] DRO Faculty Petitions/Tiverton 3.
[8] Snell 1892, 165.
[9] *EFP* 2.5.1856.

The Age of Reform was characterised by generous voluntary subscription to good causes and worthy enterprise. Tiverton provides many examples. A school was desired at Chevithorne, and in little time £500 had been collected, with the Rev. Rayer alone contributing £200. When it opened in 1857, it proved such a success, attracting more children than anticipated, that it was soon necessary to employ an extra teacher[1]. In Fore Street a soup kitchen was established in 1855 in part of the Athenaeum, formerly the Public Rooms, to feed those who could find no work or who were poorly paid[2]. At a penny a quart, no less than 14,000 quarts were sold during the winter of 1857[3]. The introduction of the Penny Post in 1840 had led to the need for pillar-boxes. The Postmaster-General sent two to Tiverton in April 1857, and the Paving Commissioners decided that one would be placed at the north-east end of the recently-built Saint Paul Street in Westexe, and the other at the corner of Bampton Street and Newport Street[4]. Private enterprise also brought about change. The foundation stone of Dunsford's Bank in Fore Street was laid in June 1857, on the site now occupied by the NatWest Bank. The rooms under the Town Hall, which the Bank had rented from the Borough for the previous 80 years, could now be surrendered, and were soon being used by William Partridge, a solicitor[5].

Victorian educational reforms led to a sharp rise in the level of literacy. This, in turn, made the public hungry for information. To go some way to satisfying this appetite locally, Tiverton's first newspaper was founded. The first issue of the *Tiverton Gazette and East Devon Herald* appeared on April 27th 1858, costing one penny, and, despite a brief spell under the guise of the *Mid Devon Gazette*, the *Tiverton Gazette* has been with us ever since. Its founder was Robert Were, a young man of just 22 years of age, who produced the newspaper in Saint Paul Street. It began as a four-page issue, containing not only information related to Tiverton and the area but also national and international news. The venture seems to have been an immediate success as it was enlarged to six pages in 1861. Its young editor, Robert Were, died in 1863, after which the ownership of the *Gazette* passed to George Rippon.

The newspaper's launch came two months too late to report the resignation of the Government led by Tiverton's M.P., Palmerston. His defeat in the House was a result of his failure to respond to France's accusation that Britain was harbouring refugees who were planning to murder Napoleon III. Tiverton was alone in sending a memorial of support for Palmerston's position[6]. He retained his seat for the borough in 1859, after some lively verbal sparring with the Radical Rowcliffe at the hustings[7]. On this occasion, though, Palmerston's fellow-member was George Denman, not John Heathcoat.

---

[1] DRO 2986A/PE1.
[2] DRO R4/1/Z77.
[3] *EFP* 24.3.1858.
[4] DRO R4/1/C350.
[5] DRO R4/1/C96.
[6] *EFP* 25.3.1858.
[7] see Lorne 1892, 188-9.

Heathcoat had decided it was time to retire from public life due to failing health[1]. Not surprisingly, the workers at the Factory made a collection, and in May 1859 presented him with an inscribed silver inkstand, gold pencil case and pen[2]. Having no son to succeed him, his grandson, John Heathcoat Amory, already a much-respected young man, took charge of the firm. Heathcoat's health deteriorated, and on January 18th 1861 he died at Bolham House, aged 77. Tiverton lost the man who single-handedly had brought work to the town at a time when its traditional textile trade was at its lowest ebb. He had always given generously to a wide range of projects, and served the town as a Member of Parliament for 27 years. His skills as an innovator were succinctly described by Isambard Kingdom Brunel who, when referring to his lace machine, said

> *'it appears to me one of the most complete mechanical combinations, in which*
> *the author displays uncommon powers of invention'* [3].

The whole town mourned Heathcoat; every shop closed on the day of his funeral. So many people wanted to attend the service that Saint Peter's could not accommodate them all and hundreds were made to stand in the churchyard. Differences were put aside for the day. Political rivals stood alongside each other, and Dissenting ministers were invited to take part in the service alongside the Anglican clergy. He was laid to rest in the plain table-vault to the north of Saint Peter's, where his wife had been buried some 30 years earlier. After the funeral, the people of Tiverton met to decide on how to commemorate him. They concluded that a bronze statue set on a granite pedestal would be the most appropriate memorial[4], but the plan progressed no further. One can only assume that his family did not want such a conspicuous representation of someone, whose name, above all, would always be associated with the town.

---

[1] TivLib folio 3/586.
[3] cited in the *EFP* 30.1.1861.

[2] *Western Times* 21.5.1859.
[4] DRO R4/1/Z79.

248

16 Civic Pride and Progress

Tiverton's new Town Hall, designed by Henry Lloyd and completed in 1864.

By the early 1860s, Tiverton's Town Hall was considered too small. The old building could not accommodate the dignified Council Chamber expected of a Victorian Borough Council and its growing number of public servants, and so a competition was organised to design a new one. Of the 62 submissions, the drawings of Henry Lloyd of Bristol were chosen. The old structure was demolished, the materials sold, and loans taken to cover the £6,500 needed for the replacement. The tender of Williams and Parish for the construction work was accepted, and work was well under by the end of 1862. It was, however, not simply a case of reusing the old site, as the old Town Hall was an island surrounded by streets. To accommodate the new design the top end of Saint Andrew Street had to be moved to the east, requiring a portion of Saint George's Churchyard. Permission was obtained from the Bishop of Exeter to move the boundary wall back towards the church, and to resite five vaults and tablets to a more 'convenient place'[1]. The polygonal end of the new structure overcame the problem of neatly turning the corner from Angel Hill to Saint Andrew Street. The building is a

---

[1] DRO Faculty Petitions/ Saint Georges 2.

particularly showy and eclectic design, in a style once described as Franco-Venetian, with a tall French château roof. This epitome of civic pride was completed in the spring of 1864, one of the last operations being to lay a granite crossing between it and Saint George's[1]. It was expected that Palmerston, the Prime Minister, would open the new building on May 19th, but he excused himself, saying he was 'less strong', and 'affairs in Europe are critical'. His absence was resented, and his place alongside the Borough's other M.P., George Denman, was taken by Earl Fortescue. The crowd, after listening to addresses from the two celebrities, called for their local favourite, the radical Rowcliffe. He came forward, and induced a loud three cheers for Gladstone, the darling of the Liberals[2].

Moral improvement through education and the Church was the way to progress, or so it was generally believed. The isolated hamlet of Lurley, although within the parish of Tiverton, lay about two miles from the town, making access to schooling and religious education difficult for the local children. Sir Thomas Dyke Acland, who owned much of the land there, provided a building in Lurley to be used 'as a school room for poor children of Tiverton, Loxbeare and Calverleigh or for performance of divine worship or as a bible class'[3]. His concerns were shared by those clerics who attended the Rural Deanery Chapter meeting at the end of 1863. One of the subjects before them was 'how to counteract the increase of immorality in our parishes and whether there are any assignable causes for the increase'. After much deliberation, they laid a lot of the blame on the ease with which marriages could be dissolved or even avoided. They had heard of 'fathers allowing their sons £200 to keep mistresses because that was more economical', and of overcrowding in labourers' cottages where 'there could not exist much delicacy'[4]. Indeed, immorality was the reason for opposing any revival of the Tiverton Races in 1864[5]; drunkenness, gambling and disorderly behaviour were cited as the main objections[6]. Nevertheless, the revivalists heavily outnumbered the objectors at a public meeting in May, and the Races were re-instated for a period[7]. Intoxication, however, led the Tiverton police force to tighten their regulations. One of their number, P.C. Quick, on more than one occasion had been reported for being drunk and disorderly. Eventually, his behaviour led to a final warning[8], and a general order that no officer, even when off duty, was to enter a public house or skittle alley[9]. Concern about decency and crime in Tiverton turned to horror on the discovery of a child murder in 1865. A newborn infant was found with its throat cut in the mill leat in Westexe. News of the incident spread far, as the Government

---

[1] DRO R4/1/C68.   [2] *EFP* 25.5.1864.
[3] DRO 2987 addA/PW2.   [4] DRO 2864/E3.
[5] they had lapsed for six years.   [6] DRO R4/1/Z79.
[7] (*EFP* 4.5.1864). They continued intermittently for a further 20 years.
[8] DRO R4/1/C59.   [9] DRO R4/1/C60.

offered a reward of £50 for information leading to the prosecution of the perpetrator[1]. The money was never claimed. Perhaps some poor desperate woman was unable to feed yet another child, and the result was the heinous crime – or so it was believed.

Poverty always existed, and so did corruption. A fraud was revealed at the Workhouse in 1865, when it was discovered that one of the Relieving Officers, a Mr Doble, had been diverting funds into his own pocket. One of his scams was to pay relief to paupers after their death[2]. He was summarily dismissed, and another colleague resigned before his errors, too, were fully revealed. Many of Tiverton's poorer people were angry over this swindle, especially as it had been perpetrated by those in authority. The resentment was exacerbated by labour disputes in the town. During 1865, two groups went on strike for increased wages. The joiners had already refused an extra 2s a week when a group not usually associated with militancy, Tiverton's washerwomen, joined them[3]. They demanded an extra 3d a day and one less hour for those at the tub. All seems to have been solved amicably as there are no reports of disturbances.

In the 1865 General Election Palmerston was returned with John Walrond, the Conservative squire of Bradfield. He ousted the Liberal Denman by just three votes. For the first time in the Borough, the Liberal hold was broken. Among Walrond's first actions was one of apparent generosity: a subscription of £80 was raised to buy 'sundry articles' to give to the heads of poor families in the town. Was this some compensation for the defeat of their man, the more radical Denman? The *Exeter Flying Post* pointed out that the gifts were accepted, despite the election handbills of the Radicals, which had proclaimed 'Men of Tiverton, do you want charity or your rights?' One of the recipients allegedly gave the retort 'Rights be blowed, the free distribution of food amongst us does not interfere with our rights'. Soon after the election Lord Palmerston died. Tiverton marked the day of his funeral by the tolling of church bells, and a special edition of the *Gazette* was produced, recording his career with a supplement, sombre in appearance, with black column divisions reflecting London practice. A public meeting was called to consider a suitable memorial to the late Prime Minister. No decision is recorded, but a reference was made over 12 months later to the 'pedestal inscription for the bust of Lord Palmerston'[4]. For at least one Tivertonian, there was good reason to keep his memory alive. Palmerston had favoured John Cann, a photographer, with a sitting shortly before his death. This was to be the very last image of the man, and Cann was soon selling copies of the photographs[5]. The statesman was

---

[1] *EFP* 14.6.1865.
[2] *EFP* 31.5.1865.
[3] Porter 1984, 64 and 72.
[4] DRO R4/1/T3.
[5] *EFP* 8.11.1865.

commemorated when the Three Tuns was renamed the Lord Palmerston in 1870[1]. In the by-election caused by Palmerston's death, George Denman joined Walrond in the Commons after defeating the Tory Sir John Hay.

Frances Walrond, mother of the M.P., died at Knightshayes in November 1866, leaving a fortune of just under £14,000[2]. She was the widow of Benjamin Bowden Dickinson who had taken the name Walrond on the death of her father in 1845. Frances' son, John, now sold most of the family lands in Tiverton, including a share of the valuable Clare House which was bought by Elizabeth Hole who already owned the rest of it[3]. More important, John Heathcoat Amory, who had been married three years earlier[4], took the opportunity to purchase the much-prized Knightshayes. Walrond agreed to sell at a price of £45,000, which included the 600 acres of land known as the Knightshayes Estate, comprised principally of Zeal, Marsh, Allers, Marley and Coydon[5]. Despite both parties' desire to finalise the deal, legal technicalities, mainly concerning the right to title, took two years to resolve[6]. Heathcoat Amory made many other purchases after his grandfather's death, and his propensity for property transactions no doubt led to his appointment as chairman of the Tiverton Land and Building Company, formed to purchase land for building[7].

The workers at the Lace Factory submitted a bold request for a wage rise in 1866. They were probably encouraged by the partial revival in Britain's textile trade, which followed the end of the American Civil War. The conflict had severely disrupted transatlantic commerce, especially the shipping of cotton to Britain so vital to the northern factories. The Tiverton workers asked for 1s a week extra, but were happy with the 8d offered[8]. The town's masons, carpenters, and the men employed at Thomas Ford's brewery were also successful in obtaining pay rises during the year[9]. Tiverton's apparent prosperity was not reflected everywhere in Devon. There was sporadic rioting throughout the county in the following year because of the high cost of provisions.

The money earned by children was often needed to supplement the family income. This, of course, affected attendance at school, especially at busy times in the

---

[1] this once impressive building on the north corner of Fore Street and Bampton Street continued as an hotel until it made way for retail development in 1961. Today his name remains in Palmerston Park, a housing estate in Westexe.

[2] DRO 1926B/W/W25.   [3] DRO 1926B/W/E20/18/2.

[4] in April 1863 he married Henrietta Mary, the daughter of William Unwin of the Colonial Office, and his wife Jane, one of the wealthy Grants of Glenmoriston. (DRO 2987 addA/PZ1).

[5] DRO 1926B/D/E6/8.   [6] DRO 1926B/W/E20/17/3.

[7] (DRO 1926B/W/E20/17/5). The Company did not have a long life, as it went into liquidation in 1885. The only development which it appears to have completed and sold before its demise was on the site known as Crowden near Wilcombe.

[8] Porter 1984, 70.   [9] *ib.*, 64 and 72.

agricultural year when children were much in demand. Summer holidays were given at a time when many would have been absent during the harvest anyway. The first mention of another practice appears in the Chevithorne School logbook in 1868. The Master recorded on October 5th 'rather thin school, owing to many children, especially those of the poorest people, being kept away to collect oak-mast for pigs', and later adds 'the mast being in great abundance, this nuisance threatens for some time'. According to this source, the acorn harvest did not end until November 2nd. The farmers were blamed for the absences, as some of them gave the children as much as 1s 4d a bushel. It was decided later that dividing the school holidays between harvest and mast-gathering[1] would ease the problem. Discipline in schools was tight at this time. Given the number of pupils it probably had to be. Incidents were often chronicled in the school log books, those of Chevithorne being unusually detailed. Punishments ranged from admonition to firm action: 'had occasion to speak sharply to a few children on their ragged and dirty appearance', and 'detaining children after school until they had learnt their previous evening's homework', as well as 'Henry Loosemore, severely caned in front of the whole school for stealing penholders and pens from the master's desk', and Thomas Parr who was punished for 'writing obscene language upon his slate'[2]. When children were beyond discipline in school or at home, there were reform schools. Two special schools had been set up in Devon; the Devon and Exeter Reformatory Farm School for Boys, situated in Brampford Wood, just outside Exeter, and the Reformatory and Refuge for Girls, which was in the city. Tiverton could send its miscreants to these establishments at a cost, which, in the case of one Rhoda Gardner in 1868, was recorded in the Borough's account book[3].

Tiverton's fairs were always a great attraction for the local children, and often took priority over attending school. They were of great antiquity, having existed for well over 600 years, but changes were introduced in 1869. Their dates were altered, severing their link to the Church calendar. The one held on the second Tuesday after Trinity Sunday was moved to the first Thursday in June, and the Michaelmas Fair was to be staged on the first Thursday in October[4]. They retained many of their medieval features, however, and it was not rare to see performing bears in the streets. At the 1869 Michaelmas Fair one such animal caused an uproar. The bear and its Italian owner, Giovanni Rossi, were both accommodated at Mrs Rookes' lodging-house in Westexe, the bear sleeping in a stable. In the morning, it was discovered that the beast had killed two of her rabbits, as well as damaging a wall. Rossi was willing to pay only for the rabbits, and hurriedly left

---

[1] DRO 752C/EFL1.
[2] *ib.*
[3] DRO R4/1/T57.
[4] DRO R4/1/C6.

town. He was brought back, however, and made to face the Borough Court, where he was fined 20s[1]. Hawkers attended the fairs in large numbers, but their presence was sharply criticised by Tiverton's Mayor in 1870. He said that, in his opinion, they had become a 'great curse to the poorer classes' and often led them into buying goods of inferior quality 'at a high rate upon a system of credit'[2].

By then, the second Reform Act, passed in 1867, had widened the franchise to embrace all male householders. Many considered this a risky move, believing that a Trojan Horse had been created. Disraeli, who sponsored the Bill, however, maintained that the working classes were in essence Conservative in their outlook. The Act, which nationally added nearly one million to the electorate, swelled the number of Tiverton voters from about 500 to 1,155. They would have to wait to exercise their right, as the 1868 General Election was not contested in the borough. The sitting Tory M.P., John Walrond, preferred the North Devon constituency, and no one from his party replaced him. Consequently, both Liberal candidates, the other sitting member, George Denman, and John Heathcoat Amory, were returned unopposed.

In the same year as his grandson followed in his political footsteps, John Heathcoat was remembered in another way. His name was given to one of the wards in the partially completed Tiverton Infirmary and Dispensary in Bampton Street[3]. It was fitting that he should be associated with the institution; after all, it was mainly through his exertions, and those of Ambrose Brewin, that the first Dispensary in Kiddell's Court had been founded. Indeed, Brewin had given two spacious houses in Bampton Street to be used as the Infirmary, but it was thought more practical to build anew on the site. The building received its first in-patient in February 1868, and continued to treat Tiverton's sick to 2004, only recently being superseded by a new Hospital.

Heathcoat Amory embarked on having Knightshayes built in a style fit for an M.P. One of his first moves was to gain some privacy for the property; the public road passing close to the house was stopped up, and a new road made from Longhayne Meadow near Firebeacon through 'Allers Vale' to Moorhayes Cross[4]. The site chosen for the new mansion was a little further north than Dickinson's house, but on the same alignment. On April 17th, 1869, the owner's four-year old son, Ian Murray Heathcoat Heathcoat Amory, laid the foundation stone. The occasion was one of great celebration. Tents had been placed near the site, and were filled with food for all those invited. The building work was to be undertaken by Fletcher of Salisbury to designs by the renowned architect William Burges[5]. The house was built in the Gothic style on a

---

[1] *EFP* 6.10.1869.   [2] DRO R4/1/C68.
[3] TivLib folio 4/629.   [4] DRO R4/1/Z4.
[5] by this time, he had already worked on the cathedrals at Lille, Brisbane, and Cork.

nearly symmetrical plan, with projecting gabled wings flanking the main block, and a low service wing attached on the right. The creepers, still a prominent feature of the façade, were part of the original plan, intended to soften the harsh contrast between the two main types of material used – the reddish Hensleigh stone and the Ham Hill dressings. Burges also designed the stables, the walled garden, and the entrance lodge. While working on Knightshayes, he was commissioned to design a parsonage at Chevithorne[1]. This building was begun in May 1870, with the cost being borne by Heathcoat Amory.

Knightshayes Court – a mansion built for John Heathcoat Amory M.P. The foundation stone was laid in 1869, and the architect originally employed was William Burges.

Knightshayes Court and Chevithorne Parsonage were both first inhabited in the summer of 1871[2]. A week at the end of January 1872 was given over to house-warming festivities at Knightshayes. On the Tuesday a shoot took place over the grounds of Chettiscombe Manor, and in the evening 200 guests, drawn from the county, danced in the new ballroom. Charades took up most of Wednesday, although the previous

[1] DRO 3406Z/Z2.   [2] DRO Chevithorne MF6.

255

night's ball had lasted well into the early hours. The week ended with another ball, this time for 250 dignitaries of the town and local farms. All of these activities must, however, have taken place in little more than the shell of the house, as work was by no means complete. Soon after the festivities, we do not know exactly when, or for what reason, John Heathcoat Amory and William Burges parted company[1]. Burges was replaced by John Dibble Crace, a very able designer, and much less flamboyant. The present Knightshayes bears witness to Burges' departure. At the west end of the building he had planned a massive tower over the staircase, but only the base was built. Had this been completed it would have been the most conspicuous feature of the building's skyline, flanked by the crenellated chimneys already built. Similarly, not all Burges' detailed interior designs were used, but his sumptuous Great Hall is a reminder of what could have been achieved if he had stayed to complete the work.

In one of his public duties, however, John Heathcoat Amory did not escape criticism. As he had been appointed a Tax Commissioner, the Tory *Exeter Flying Post* loudly proclaimed his absence from a meeting called at Tiverton in November 1871 to debate income tax. The subject aroused strong feelings among professionals and tradesmen. At the gathering, many men stated that often their 'honest returns' had been ignored, and heavier burdens had been imposed upon them. Their argument seems to have been valid, as the tax paid in Tiverton had risen in one year from £1,333 to £2,069. The justifiable complaints were apparently acted upon, as the assessment dropped back to £1,346 in the following year[2].

The Elementary Education Act of 1870 brought widespread reform nationally. Local school boards with the power to levy rates were set up, and schools were to be built in all districts that lacked Church schools. As Tiverton was already adequately provided with elementary schools, no new building resulted from this legislation. On the other hand, the Endowed Schools Act, passed a year earlier, was eventually to lead to great changes locally. It was based on the findings of a Royal Commission charged with investigating educational endowments, and proposed extensive reforms in the provision of secondary education. Commissioners would draw up suitable schemes based on a grading system: First Grade schools would prepare pupils for the universities; Second Grade for a career in commerce, and Third Grade establishments would provide an education somewhat better than elementary schools. Time was given for interested parties to make their views known and, in the case of schools with endowments exceeding £1,000 a year, to submit their own Draft Schemes. A group was formed in Tiverton during 1870, which included John Heathcoat Amory, now a Blundell's Trustee, Dr Mackenzie, who had given evidence in the Rammell enquiry, and many Old Blundellians, foremost among them the engine driving the group,

---

[1] possibly Burges' work appeared too fantastical and expensive.
[2] DRO 1169A/LT92.

256

William Partridge, a solicitor. They believed Tiverton could support five secondary schools. This, they proposed, could be achieved by the removal of Blundell's to a new location, even at this early date suggesting Horsdon[1]. The old buildings could then be used as a Second Grade boys boarding school; a new site was to be found for a similar school for girls, and Third Grade schools for both sexes would occupy the Chilcott and Bluecoat premises. The Commissioners left the final decision on the future of Blundell's to the Trustees, many of whom wanted the school to remain where it was. Without such a move, however, the Committee's plans were unworkable. It was decided that Tiverton was not to have any Second Grade schools. The Commissioners' scheme was to form two good fee-paying establishments from the Bluecoat and Chilcott schools. These would became the Tiverton Middle Schools – one for girls, housed in the former Bluecoat School, the other for boys, on a new site a little further up Castle Street. They also approved a new Scheme for Blundell's that took effect from 1876. As well as laying down standards for an entrance examination and re-ordering the curriculum, two drastic changes were instigated: head money was introduced - the new Headmaster, A.L. Francis, was to receive a smaller salary than before, but it would be supplemented by tuition and boarding fees as it had been before 1846. The school was to be administered by 18 Governors - nine chosen locally, one by the Masters, seven co-opted, and the other was to be the Lord Lieutenant or his representative.

Meanwhile, a by-election took place in November 1872, brought about by George Denman's appointment as a Judge of the Common Pleas. The contest was between John Walrond, supported by the recently-formed Conservative Working Men's Association, and the Liberal William Massey. During their canvassing both candidates made much of Tiverton's lack of crime. By September the white flag over the Gaol, signifying the dearth of prisoners, had been flying for 111 days and was to stay up until December[2]. The hustings themselves, however, were a lack-lustre affair. Gone were the days of Palmerston, Harney, and Rowcliffe. The only event of note was on polling day itself, when the 77-year old John Hawkings collapsed and died while placing his vote[3]. The result of the poll, a victory for Massey by just 30 votes[4], did lead to some excitement; the Conservatives' reaction to this narrow defeat was immediate. Harsh words were aimed at 'Massey's Vigilance Committee' regarding the positions of the voting booths. This had been the first election in the town under the terms of the Ballot Act, which made voting by secret ballot compulsory. One of the booths had stood near the entrance to the Factory gates, and the Conservatives implied that the Liberal

---

[1] on the subject of the move, and the events leading up to it, see Jenkins 1982.
[2] *EFP* 4.9.1872.   [3] DRO 2960A/PR32.
[4] Craig 1977, 309.

Heathcoat Amory had monitored the voting of his workers. The comment was made at a Tory meeting that 'if the factory were taken away the Liberals would find themselves in a pretty dilemma'[1]. The confidence of the Tiverton Tories was regained at the end of 1873. Despite Liberals taking the four Council seats in the Westexe and Castle wards, the remaining two Lowman places were both filled by Conservatives[2]. Their mettle was again tested in the following year at a General Election. The voters, of course, included no women, although some even then were determined to alter this position. Tiverton Borough Council had received a letter early in 1873 from Lydia Becker of the National Society for Women's Suffrage along with a handbill exhorting the removal of the 'electoral disabilities of women'[3]. In the election of 1874 Disraeli's Conservatives won the national contest, but Tiverton returned Liberals, Massey and Heathcoat Amory. Again Walrond lost narrowly, this time by just 24 votes[4]. John Heathcoat Amory's support was rewarded by a knighthood on the insistence of the outgoing Prime Minister, Gladstone.

By this time, Tiverton was largely being bypassed by the railway system. Although the branch line from Tiverton Junction had arrived in 1848, no further routes had been established. Progress elsewhere, however, threatened Tiverton with a loss of trade. Its status as a centre between north and south Devon had been greatly affected by the opening of the Taw Vale Railway from Exeter to Barnstaple in 1854. Worse was the Devon and Somerset Railway's line from Taunton to Barnstaple, which began operating in 1873. Much of Tiverton's trade had traditionally been drawn from places along this route, from the towns of Wiveliscombe, Dulverton, Bampton, and South Molton, as well as the many small villages in between. Those links were in danger of being severed. There had been plans for two railways in the early 1860s; one to run south down the Exe Valley from Tiverton to join the Bristol and Exeter's main route[5], and another to connect Tiverton to any Taunton-Barnstaple line[6], but both had been abandoned. Now they became imperative, and hasty revival followed. Renewed investment in the Tiverton and North Devon Railway was called for. Both M.P.s enthusiastically backed the project; Heathcoat Amory invested £3,000, and Massey

---

[1] *EFP* 13.11.1872.
[2] *EFP* 5.11.1873.
[3] DRO R4/1/C67.
[4] Craig 1977, 309.
[5] for much of this route, the railway would run parallel to the turnpike road. Nevertheless, early in 1864 the Turnpike Trustees decided not to oppose the Railway Company's plan. In fact, the Trustees were in no position to fight, as they owed more than £42,000 to their investors. The Bristol and Exeter Railway, having seemingly defeated the Turnpike Trustees, turned to the Grand Western Canal. They purchased the waterway in 1864 for £30,000, and three years later closed the section of canal between Taunton and Lowdwells.
[6] for which a new company, the Tiverton and North Devon Railway Company, was formed.

£2,000[1]. The Company obtained a new Act of Parliament in July 1875, authorising it to lay a track from Morebath to Tiverton, a distance of 8½ miles. The line would run down the Exe Valley as far as Bolham, where it would strike away from the river and head for Brick House, Pinnex Moor, finally across Blundell's Road to terminate at Tiverton Station[2]. The southern Exe Valley route was to leave the main line at Stoke Canon, run northwards to enter Tiverton in Westexe, and end at a point near Broad Lane[3]. From there, a short length of track was needed to cross the River Exe and connect with the Station[4]. Yet both routes were to take a long time to complete.

In 1873, a fire destroyed most of the properties on the lower eastern side of Bampton Street. As on so many previous occasions, disaster was perceived as an opportunity for improvement. The decision was taken to widen this part of the street. It was estimated that the Borough Council would need just over £2,000 to buy the premises involved[5], which included the Shoulder of Mutton and the Ship public houses, a cobbler's shop occupied by William Henry Stoyel, the town's Post Office, and Goodland's butcher's shop[6]. In addition to this amount, the costs of the alterations to the street itself would bring the total to about £3,500. An application for the whole amount was made to the Public Works Loan Commissioners[7], a body established in the previous decade to facilitate urban renewal. The old Paving Commissioners handed over their duties to the Borough Council at the end of 1875, urging them to name the town's streets and number the houses[8]. This subject had been raised in a letter from a commercial traveller to the *Tiverton Gazette* over ten years earlier. On his first visit to the town, he had been armed with a list of potential customers in the form 'Mr A in such a street, Mr B another street'. He had foreseen no problem, but when he began to look for street signs he found none! He ended his letter:

> *'If your authorities are so hard up they can't afford to do it, let them stick lists in the commercial houses to raise wind for a bit of paint to name streets at each corner, and I warrant funds will come (in a year or two) from members of my fraternity'.*

---

[1] *EFP* 24.2.1875.   [2] DRO DP318.

[3] in 1876 the Bristol and Exeter was sold to the Great Western Railway Company.

[4] permission was obtained for a footpath to run alongside the track from Westexe to Saint Andrew Street, and the Bishop of Exeter consented to alterations to the glebe land near Pitt Rectory in Saint Andrew Street, where once there was a farmhouse, complete with tithe barn and cowsheds (DRO Chanter 206).

[5] DRO R4/1/C6.

[6] (DRO R4/1/C94). Yet, two years after the fire the intricacies of property ownership in the street had not been completely unravelled. The main problem centred on one individual, John Hungerford Snook. As a Lieutenant in the army he was stationed at Malta then the Cape of Good Hope, so was difficult to contact.

[7] DRO R4/1/C69.   [8] *EFP* 29.12.1875.

His advice had not been taken, and responsibility for the matter now rested with the Council. The Paving Commissioners, in their final year, did get some work done; the path through Hit or Miss Court, joining the Works with Castle Street, was paved, and a length of pavement from Saint Peter Street to Angel Hill Terrace was laid[1], using an experimental surface of vitrified brick.

The Council had been under threat of legal action from the Devon County Asylum since 1866. This institution had an arrangement to take the town's lunatics, but a charge of 3s 6d per patient was levied on boroughs like Tiverton that did not contribute to the County Rate[2]. The Council refused to pay, arguing that the Guardians of the Poor should bear the cost[3]. The Asylum threatened to begin legal proceedings, and to eject Tiverton's patients. In 1874, they did indeed discharge eight of the town's female patients, who were transferred to Fisherton House near Salisbury[4]. The issue of mental illness had been tragically highlighted during the previous year. Captain Walter Palk Carew, who lived at the Castle with his young wife, on one occasion was found wandering around the churchyard with a drawn sword in his hand, and on another he attempted to drown himself in the Exe. His father had him placed in an asylum near Bristol, where, sadly, using a knife concealed in his clothing, he cut his own throat and died[5].

The problem of sanitation again challenged the town in June 1875. The mortality rate had risen over the previous few years, and was the subject of a meeting of the Borough's Sanitary Committee. Severe winters accounted for many of the deaths, but a large number resulted from fever. Impure water sources and badly constructed sewers were blamed. An outbreak of scarlatina during the year emphasised the need for urgent action, and the fact that half the casualties lived beside the River Lowman[6] highlighted the area of greatest concern. The Committee decided to commission another report[7]. The author was an engineer, A.W. Estridge, who presented his findings in 1877. They revealed the depressing conditions still prevailing, despite Rammell's recommendations a quarter of a century before. Twyford Place housed 17 families but had only three privies; Londonderry Cottages had two for 10 families; Broad Lane's 21 families shared eight. In the town as a whole there were 1,643 families with access to 491 pumps; 243 families with no water supply at all; 865 privies and a mere 229 W.C.s[8]. The Borough Council resolved to improve the situation, and work began on two schemes, both recommended by Rammell. The problem of

---

[1] DRO R4/1/C349.
[2] DRO R4/1/Z46.
[3] DRO R4/1/Z47.
[4] TivMus 88/1077/1/9.
[5] *EFP* 18.6.1873.
[6] DRO 3171M/Z7.
[7] *EFP* 2.6.1875.
[8] DRO R4/1/C67.

disposing of sewage polluting the Lowman took time. The first proposal was to carry the waste away by means of an intercepting sewer and spread it over Collipriest Marshes. It was hoped this action would severely reduce the cases of fever that occurred in the Elmore and Lowman areas, but, ironically, the disturbance of the riverbed was blamed for a sharp rise in sore throats[1]. The Council later amended their decision, choosing instead to purchase fields belonging to Great and Little Holwell and build a sewage farm there[2]. A solution was achieved more swiftly for the other scheme. Part of the Gaol premises in Saint Andrew Street had fallen out of use, so it was decided to use the space to build Tiverton's first public baths[3]. They were an immediate success; 4,387 people used the facilities within the first 17 weeks[4].

Good health and habits, especially sports and active recreation, were promoted usually by voluntary clubs and societies. Tiverton could boast Bicycle and Athletic Clubs by 1880, both of which held their annual meetings at the Cricket Field in Elmore[5]. Total abstinence from alcohol became a popular cause. The Church of England Temperance Society supported the Tiverton Coffee House Company, which opened its Fore Street premises in 1879. To finance the organisation 700 shares were sold at £1 each, and the first chairman was the Rev. George Hadow, Rector of Tidcombe, who had been instrumental in getting the enterprise started[6]. Another worthy venture was being undertaken at Eloise Heathcoat's Bolham home. There she was training orphan girls as domestic servants as well as maintaining other 'young ladies in reduced circumstances'[7]. Her sister, Caroline Brewin, who died in 1877, gave her own two schools in Elmore and Bampton Street to the Tiverton School Board, and the houses that her husband had bought near Saint Paul's Church were left to Queen Anne's Bounty[8]. Another grand old lady of Tiverton, Elizabeth Hole, also died in 1877. Her chief property was Clare House which, complete with its 'pine house' (for growing pineapples) and 'vinery'[9], was put up for sale. The purchaser was the Rev. Henry Venn, Rector of Clare. Although an Anglican, he could not have helped being impressed by the new Baptist Chapel which had just been completed on the opposite side of Newport Street. History was made when the Borough Council attended its

---

[1] *EFP* 2.7.1884.

[2] construction of the sewage works did not begin until 1886, however, and was carried out by William Edmondson of London at a cost of £3,656 (DRO R4/1/C71).

[3] DRO R4/1/C70.

[4] of whom, it was clearly thought important, '645 were ladies' (DRO R4/1/C17).

[5] *EFP* 15.9.1880.　　　　　　　　　　　　　[6] *EFP* 26.2.1879.

[7] (Snell 1892, 389). Eloise died a spinster in 1880.

[8] (DRO R4/1/C95). Queen Anne's Bounty was a fund established to augment the income of incumbents in impoverished benefices.

[9] DRO 49/9/26/8.

dedication, for it was the first time that Tiverton's governing body had taken part in a service in a Nonconformist building[1].

Historical sources tend to portray the extremes of society; the rich, landed, families, the extreme poor, and criminals. Similarly, unusual events make the headlines, not everyday happenings. It is therefore a joy when documents survive that were produced by 'middling people' concerned with day-to-day living. Into this category fall two diaries written from 1875 to 1890 by William Norris, the tenant farmer of Loxbeare Barton[2]. Although he did not live in the parish of Tiverton, he had land there and what social life he enjoyed occasionally took him to the town. One such occasion was when 'me and Annie' went to the Devon County Show at Tiverton in May 1876, a day finished off with a visit to the Theatre in the evening. More frequent were his trips to the nearby farm of Fulford, where 'me and Mr Carpenter played Frank Ferris and Mr Poole at whist'. Indeed, evenings out usually took place in the winter months – work took priority during the long summer days. Both volumes are full of details of the current farming practices: 'ploughed the six acres of turnip ground at Lurley', 'sowed the Lurley wheat arrish to oats', and 'tilled potatoes in Wringford Field, manured with four pounds of guano per yard'. Yet nowhere is there the slightest indication of the national decline that had begun to affect agriculture. Clues must be sought elsewhere. A letter written in 1877 concerning two cottages at Rock, near Cove, does appear to hint at the slump[3]. The tenant states that one of the buildings is in ruins and the other scarcely habitable, and that he is unable to help keep his workers there without an abatement in rent. Britain's arable and livestock farmers were finding it harder to compete with foreign producers, who were helped by improved storage and refrigeration as well as the greater ease of transport. The price of English wheat stood at 56s 9d a quarter in 1877, but cheap imports from North America saw to it that for the rest of the century the price would not get within 10s of that figure. The effects would be profound.

Blundell's Old Boys' annual dinner in July 1878 resounded with talk of the prospect of the school's removal. By then, most of the Governors were in favour of a move, especially the Earl of Devon and Frederick Temple, Bishop of Exeter, along with the Headmaster, A.L. Francis. They believed that a new boarding school on a larger site with better accommodation and spacious playing fields would bring an increase in scholars, whereas to remain in the cramped, unhealthy site beside the Lowman would lead to an inevitable decline in Blundell's fortunes. A public meeting held a month after the dinner came to the opposite conclusion; removal would deprive local boys of the advantage of Peter Blundell's will and Tiverton of trade. With the town and gown apparently again at loggerheads, it was thought wise for the Governors to cease holding

---

[1] Harris 1985, 16.
[2] DRO 500M/F1-2.
[3] DRO 1926B/SH/E1/2.

their meetings in the Town Hall[1]. Fearing, like many, that removal would mean demolition of the old school, the solicitor and town councillor, R.F. Loosemore, persuaded the Society for the Preservation of Ancient Buildings (SPAB), formed only in the previous year, to take up their cause. One of the group, William Morris the renowned decorative artist, was especially active. It must be remembered that, at this time, there was no legal protection for historic buildings, and so SPAB's endeavours consisted mainly of its Committee members pleading by letter to appropriate Governors of the School[2]. The intervention of the Charity Commission was called for by the town, but to no avail. The Governors' intentions were upheld[3]. The purchase of the site at Horsdon went ahead[4], and the Earl of Devon laid the foundation stone of the new School in June 1880. The work was carried out in red Halberton stone, with Doulting stone mullions and quoins, to designs by Hayward of Exeter. The new Blundell's School was opened on May 9th 1882.

New buildings for Blundell's School at Horsdon, drawn by Hayward and Son of Exeter, architects.

But what to do with Old Blundells? Even before it fell empty, a few Town Councillors proposed that it should become the town's lunatic asylum. When put to a

---

[1] DRO R4/1/C70
[2] for a full appreciation of the proceedings from SPAB's point of view, see Richmond 1989.
[3] *EFP* 12.2.1879.   [4] DRO 49/9/3/99.

Council meeting this suggestion, thankfully, was outvoted by 19 to two[1]. The first use made of it was for an exhibition under the patronage of the North Devon and Tiverton Decorative Arts Society. As well as works of art, a pipe allegedly smoked by Sir Walter Raleigh was on show, as was a new type of telephone transmitter[2]. When the exhibition closed, the building was bought by the brewer, Thomas Ford, on condition that the façade remain virtually unaltered, a proviso which allowed much of the interior to be gutted and transformed into six residences.

John North Singleton, who had been the Factory Schoolmaster from 1842 to 1878, died in 1883, leaving his considerable library to Tiverton's Baptist congregation, of which his father had been pastor. He laid down strict rules concerning the books. They were to be the property of the pastor and Sunday School officers, and were to be made available to any member of the congregation who joined the library at a cost of 1d a week[3]. The library was cherished by Baptists for well over a century, until its disposal in the 1990s. In the 1880s, two relatively new religious groups became established in Tiverton. The Plymouth Brethren had been formed in the 1830s, and for many years held a tent mission in a field at Shillands. They set up a permanent base in 1884 in what was known as the Iron Room Chapel off Saint Andrew Street, on part of the site now occupied by the Tiverton Museum. It was little more than a shed, and had been almost totally forgotten until extensions to the site in 1974 revealed a pit containing a flight of four steps[4]. The other group was the Salvation Army, founded by a Methodist minister, William Booth, in 1865. They began ministering in the East End of London, from where they quickly spread out, establishing mission stations in most towns to feed and house the poor. Their first efforts in Tiverton, however, were not particularly well appreciated. Complaints were received from the residents of Angel Hill[5] in May 1885 of the noise and obstruction caused by 'certain persons known as the Salvation Army'. Tempers flared at the end of the year when the Army's doorkeepers barred three young men from entering their meeting. It barely needs saying that these incidents did not deter the members or their message.

The Tiverton and North Devon Railway's track from Dulverton to the station at Tiverton was finally opened in July 1884. Shops closed for a half-day holiday and there was much celebration in Tiverton as well as along the route. In contrast, the opening of the Great Western Railway's line from Stoke Canon to Westexe, in May 1885, was barely noticed. There was comparatively little display in either Tiverton or Exeter,

---

[1] (*EFP* 11.2.1882). The matter was finally resolved in 1886 when the Borough Council agreed to send the town's patients to the newly-built asylum at Exeter (DRO R4/1/C7).
[2] *EFP* 31.5.1882.   [3] DRO 3958D add/17.
[4] Authers 1975, 130.
[5] the fact that they held their first meetings here probably accounts for the area being known by some Tivertonians as 'the Citadel'.

although the inhabitants of Thorverton were more joyful[1]. As Snell points out[2], everything possible had now been done for Tiverton as far as railway connection was concerned, but it had taken too long.

With the passing of the third Reform Act in 1884, which enfranchised agricultural labourers, the electorate was trebled and England was very near to being a democracy for men. Before this new batch of voters had the opportunity to enter the polling booths more disturbing legislation was passed. The Redistribution of Seats Act (1885) redrew parliamentary constituencies with the intention of making them all roughly equally representative (about 50,000 persons in each). Boroughs with a population of less than 15,000 inhabitants lost their franchise. Tiverton, long entitled to choose two members, now became part of the Tiverton Division[3] of 9,349 electors, with just one M.P. to serve its interests. Elections would never again have quite the same monopoly of local interest and political passion. The people of the town would no longer necessarily be voting for their man; he could now be 'a foreigner'. Indeed, two newcomers contested the 1885 General Election, when the Tory William Hood Walrond defeated Sydney Stern, a Liberal, by more than a thousand votes[4].

Tiverton had lost one of its Westminster representatives after 270 years, and it was soon to lose an arrangement that had existed for at least 700 years – the ancient ecclesiastical portions of the parish. Clare, Pitt, Prior's, Tidcombe were to go, together with the later addition of All Fours. The Rev. Dr. Frederick Temple in 1884, Bishop of Exeter, succeeded in getting the Benefices (Tiverton) Consolidation Amendment Act through Parliament. This enabled him to redraft boundaries, with permission from the patrons. The rural churches of Withleigh, Cove, and Chevithorne were elevated to parish status, each being given an area of land for their support, and Saint Paul's (Westexe) parish was enlarged. The remaining land was divided between Saint Peter's and a new parish, Saint George's. Seeing that the former had the greater population it was to offer the most valuable living. As for the clergy, it was to be a case of whoever survived the longest would get the biggest prize. The Rev. Henry Venn of Clare eased the situation by resigning early in 1885, and shortly afterwards the Rev. Michael Thorne, Curate of Prior's, died, as did the Rev. William Knight of the temporary unit of Pitt-Clare. This left just one survivor, the Rev. George Hadow, who had been the portioner of Tidcombe. He now became Rector of Saint Peter's, and the Rev. Walter Edmonds was appointed as the first Vicar of Saint George's. While this re-organisation was taking place, considerable work had been done on Saint Peter's Church. Henry

---

[1] *EFP* 6.5.1885.   [2] 1892, 292.

[3] comprising 'the petty sessional division of Cullompton, the borough of Tiverton, and the petty sessional division of Wonford outside the parliamentary borough of Exeter' - from Morebath south as far as Dawlish (Snell 1892, 376).

[4] Craig 1977, 260.

Septimus Gill paid for a new clock in 1883, which was fixed on the east face of the tower, and still today rings out its unique chimes[1]. At the same time, the opportunity was taken to rehang the six smallest bells and carry out other repairs in the belfry[2].

The fiftieth anniversary of Queen Victoria's accession was celebrated in expected style in June 1887. For many months before, Tivertonians had been pondering over what type of lasting memorial would be appropriate. In February, the town's Debating Society invited suggestions, among which were the construction of a river embankment and the provision of a free library[3]. There would be a long wait for these. The idea which was finally chosen, however, was the brainchild not of a Tiverton resident but of a citizen of London. John Coles, who had been born in Washfield, offered the Borough Council a sum of £1,000 to buy land for a 'people's park'[4]. His gift was readily accepted, and the 3½ acre Govett's Field opposite the entrance to Villa Franca was chosen[5]. Another adjacent plot of equal size was purchased from the owners of the Castle for a further £1,000. The Golden Jubilee festivities began on Monday June 22nd 1887, starting with a concert by the Musical Society at the Drill Hall in Newport Street. At dawn on the following day, Saint Peter's Society of Change-Ringers began their Jubilee 'touch', a succession of peals specially composed for the occasion. At 10 o'clock in the evening massive bonfires were lit on Exeter Hill, Seven Crosses, and Van Post. Wednesday was to be the main day of the celebrations. The church bells rang out at seven in the morning and a band paraded around the town. Later, a large procession assembled at the Town Hall and walked to Saint Peter's Church, where a Thanksgiving Service was held. Afterwards, lunch was served in the Market Place for 1,000 men and women above the age of 50 years, followed in the afternoon by at least 2,000 children walking to the new park where tea was provided[6]. The evening saw a torchlight procession through the streets, and the official proceedings concluded with a firework display. Many people continued to celebrate in their own way well into the night in the town's public houses, which had all been granted a special two-hour extension[7]. Although People's Park had been used during the festivities, it was not officially opened until June 23rd 1888, a day of incessant heavy rain. Not surprisingly, the crowds were smaller yet enthusiastic. The recreation area had been embellished

---

[1] although the dial, measuring seven and a half feet across, cost only £20, the total costs amounted to £182, including carriage to Tiverton Railway Station. Grasons, the clockmaker in Fore Street, installed the mechanism. The hours are struck on the 29cwt bell and the changes chime on the others.
[2] Saint Peter's MSS. [3] *EFP* 16.2.1887.
[4] DRO R4/1/C71. [5] DRO 3271B/T15.
[6] *EFP* 25.6.1887. [7] DRO 440P/R1.

with a bandstand, the gift of the late Alderman Lane, and near the northern entrance there was a fine drinking fountain presented by the Rev. George Hadow[1].

The north-eastern entrance to People's Park and the keeper's lodge.

Such large gatherings of people sometimes resulted in drunkenness and minor thefts, but generally, there was little crime in these years. The white flag over the Gaol, acclaimed in the Election of 1872, was often to be seen. Tiverton had achieved a commendable level of moral awareness, social discipline, and living standards. The town's police force dealt mostly with minor offences. The Tiverton Court registers include such cases as that of John Howe of Gold Street, a young man fined 8s for having two recently-killed wild birds. Two lads of 12 and 13 were ordered to pay 5s each and do seven days' hard labour for throwing stones in Westexe[2]. But one terrible event that happened just a month after the Jubilee celebrations stained the reputation of the town. The body of 37-year old Archibald Reed was found in the Exe, near the Rag. His throat had been cut from ear to ear. He was an employee of the Tiverton Fishery Association and, before that, had been assistant keeper of Mr Unwin of Hayne House. While in both jobs he had attempted to catch a gang of poachers operating in the area, and it was likely that he had encountered the same gang on the night he was murdered. The finger of blame pointed to one Thomas Western, a Bickleigh thatcher and notorious poacher, whom Reed had earlier implicated in a court case. He was immediately arrested, but soon released. A reward of £100 offered by the Borough's

---

[1] *EFP* 23.6.1888.   [2] DRO 440P/R2.

Watch Committee was soon raised to £125, and a letter was sent to Queen Victoria imploring her to offer a free pardon to anyone giving information leading to the murderer's conviction[1]. Yet despite extensive and long-lasting investigations the perpetrator was never found.

[1] DRO R4/1/C71.

17 The Turn of the Century

The Local Government Act of 1888 created county councils, whose duties were mainly those formerly carried out by the county J.P.s, with the important exception of justice. They became responsible for, among other things, lunatics, bridges, roads, poor relief, and police. Councillors were elected by all ratepayers and were to serve for three years. At this early stage Devon County Council had no chamber of its own, so the first meeting was held in one of the courtrooms at Exeter's Rougemont Castle. Tiverton's first two representatives were prominent citizens distinguished by their status and generosity, Sir John Heathcoat Amory and Thomas Ford junior[1]. The Act also established rural district councils, one comprising those parishes around Tiverton and to the east of the town, including Cullompton. Tiverton retained its Borough Council, however, with all its powers intact.

At this time Sir John Heathcoat Amory paid for major alterations at Chevithorne Church, where, he had commented, the harmonium was 'very wheezy' and ought to be replaced by an organ, and the smoky stove should be changed for a new heating apparatus[2]. Vestries were built and a transept added to form the Amory Chapel for the exclusive use of the family[3]. His benevolence was not restricted to the Anglican Church, for he offered the Plymouth Brethren a home at the Heathcoat Hall in Wellbrook Street for a small rent[4]. The Ford family had also become very important in Tiverton. Thomas Ford senior had started a brewery in 1852, and five years later moved his offices to Fore Street, now the site of Tesco. The brewery was relocated in 1859 to a spot beside the River Lowman, where Phoenix House now stands. By the 1880s, it had become the largest brewery in the Southwest. Perhaps following the example of John Heathcoat, Thomas Ford was aware of the prestige and respect to be gained from rewarding his employees. In 1890, he made over ten cottages in Chapel Street for the use of retired brewery workers[5].

John Francis Ellerton was Mayor in 1889, the first Conservative to hold the post for a great number of years. It seems that the origins of a future institution began during his term of office, when the Borough Council was offered a collection of 792 geological specimens from a Miss Elizabeth Croker[6]. Charles Marshall Hole, in his letter of acceptance as Town Clerk, intimated that it had been a long-held wish of a number of townspeople to establish a museum. The items were housed in the clock tower of the

---

[1] DRO Z9/Box 94/2.
[2] DRO 286A/PW1.
[3] DRO Faculty Petitions/Chevithorne 1.
[4] Authers 1975, 130.
[5] *EFP* 1.2.1890.
[6] they had belonged to her father Dr John Gifford Croker, an authority on geology.

Town Hall[1], where they were soon joined by a portrait of Martin Dunsford given by one of his descendants, and a collection of Devonshire mosses[2]. Despite the enticement of being able to exact a full penny rate under the Museums and Gymnasiums Act (1891), the Council were unwilling to provide either a public museum or library[3]. The *Exeter Flying Post* reported that the Tiverton Debating Society, had begun a subscription list for a library, only to find that a few months later the response was slow. Nevertheless, the town was host to the members of the Devonshire Association in 1891[4]. This happened not through the exertions of the Borough Council but by the efforts of the newly appointed secretary of the Association's local branch, Alfred Thomas Gregory, the editor of the *Tiverton Gazette*[5].

Despite a reluctance to provide cultural facilities, the Borough Council were making progress on what obviously were more pressing matters. Water consumption was rising in the town all the time, both for domestic and, increasingly, for industrial uses. A plentiful supply was urgently needed. In 1888 permission was sought from the Rev. William Rayer to search for an underground source at Bingwell, but he refused. The Council did, however, obtain the right to prospect on the adjacent property of Warnicombe. Boreholes were sunk and water found. At a depth of 20 feet, the shaft was yielding 11,000 gallons a day, but, although this was considered sufficient to make up the town's needs[6], it was decided to drill further into the hillside. By May 1892 68,000 gallons were coming from this source every day[7], but the hot summer caused so great a demand that Alderman Tom Haydon offered water from his springs at Allers near Chettiscombe, which added a further 50,000 gallons a day[8]. This was by no means a long-lasting solution, however; that would have to wait until the problem of storage had been overcome. In September 1890, eight years after its first domestic use in Britain, Parliament passed the Tiverton Electric Lighting Order[9]. Within a couple of years Thomas Ford's brewery was lit with electricity from works he had built on the Lowman[10], but the Borough Council were dithering over how and when to implement the Act.

---

[1] DRO R4/1/C7.   [2] DRO R4/1/C72.

[3] and the Town Clerk prophetically remarked 'nor do I think there is much probability of them doing so' (DRO R4/1/C73).

[4] this was actually the Association's second visit to the town; their first was in 1865, just three years after the group's formation.

[5] Gregory, a native of Bath, had taken over the *Gazette* in 1877 at the young age of 25 years, and was one of the leading Methodists in the town.

[6] plans were made to join these works with the town main (DRO R4/1/C20).

[7] *EFP* 7.5.1892.   [8] *EFP* 9.7.1892.

[9] *EFP* 20.9.1890.

[10] (*EFP* 17.6.1893.) Two years later, Ford joined forces with the Knights of Bridgwater and Starkeys of North Petherton and Taunton to form Starkey, Knight and Ford.

In fact, they made a decision that seemed to fly in the face of progess; in 1895, while most people realised that electricity was going to be the power source of the future, the Council bought the Tiverton Gas Works from Heathcoat and Company for £20,000[1]. In this same year, the Council finished numbering Tiverton's houses, a task proposed 33 years earlier. The Council had bought blue plaques with white enamel numbers, and supplied one to each of the town's 1,600 properties[2]. The Borough Council, no doubt influenced by Blundell's provision in 1889 of a sanatorium for boys with infectious diseases[3], decided that the town should have a similar establishment. A site on the Halberton Road was investigated in 1895[4], but, again, time took its toll and the Isolation Hospital at Post Hill did not materialise until June 1901.

Sporting occasions in and around Tiverton were popularised by the railway's ability to bring day-trippers to the area. Events like the annual meeting of the Tiverton Athletic Club often attracted competitors from far afield. In 1893, there were athletes present from the Edgbaston Harriers, London Athletic Club, and teams from Cradley Heath and Cardiff[5]. The meetings were so popular that, a few years later, a request for 200 tickets from Bristol had to be politely refused as 'such a number cannot be given to any one person'[6]. Not every class of rail passenger was welcome. In October 1890, an illegal prize-fight took place on land at Plushayes, about two and a half miles east of Cove. The boxers were Morgan Crowther of Cardiff, a future contender for the World Featherweight Championship, and Bill Johnson of Leeds. Much like the raves of the 1990s, the venue had been kept secret by all that took part, yet they came by rail. The reason, it was reported, for staging the fight in such a remote spot was that there was little chance of discovery by the police[7].

Tiverton School Board acquired the premises of the Athenaeum[8] in Fore Street in 1885. The rooms were to house the Science and Art Schools, which almost immediately attracted as many as 500 pupils. Much of the success was due to the enthusiasm and ability of Emil Scales Perkins, the Headmaster of the School of Art. In 1891, when elementary education became free in the Borough, the Government made funds available for technical instruction. Perkins was quick to realise the opportunities such money could provide, and devised a scheme accordingly. Government funding, he argued, could be used to widen the curriculum to include manual and commercial subjects, and to provide an assistant art master and a science master, and make technical education available at the Middle Schools. His plans were supported and adopted by all Tiverton's schools, and he was appointed Director of the scheme. A large building,

[1] DRO R4/1/C73.
[2] DRO R4/1/C22.
[3] DRO R4/1/C20.
[4] DRO R4/1/C8.
[5] *EFP* 9.9.1893.
[6] DRO R4/1/X1.
[7] *EFP* 11.10.1890.
[8] formerly the Subscription Rooms.

at Tiverton's Technical and Science School, to include a chemical laboratory, science, manual and shorthand class rooms[1], was planned on a site in the south-west corner of Wilderness Field[2]. The range of subjects taught was impressive:

> art - *design and ornament, perspective, sciography[3], architecture, clay modelling, light and shade work, decorative monochrome, figure drawing;*
>
> technology - *brickwork and masonry, carpentry and joinery, chemistry of brickmaking;*
>
> manual work - *wood carving, carpentry and joinery*
>
> commercial subjects - *shorthand, typewriting;*
>
> science - *geometry, machine construction, building construction, chemistry theoretical and practical, electricity, mathematics, mechanics, physiography and geology[4].*

Prebendary Percy Scott's appointment as Rector of Saint Peter's in 1895 prompted a break with long tradition following discussions as to where he should live. Tidcombe House was considered to lie too far from the church, so a house closer to Saint Peter's was needed. The first suggestion was Clare House, but its position near the Market and the Drill Hall, both constantly in use for meetings, dances, and other functions, made it unsuitable[5]. Scott proposed the construction of a new house, and his wish was granted. The site chosen was part of a field called Castle Orchard, bordering People's Park. Meanwhile, Tidcombe House, with its 'vinery containing 10 vines and large nutteries'[6], was sold for £4,600 to Mrs F. Harmar, the daughter of a former rector, William Rayer[7].

Meanwhile, Sir John Heathcoat Amory was bringing many new practices to the family business, and to the hunt. In February 1895, the Company was advertising for women homeworkers to add chenille spots to the Factory-made lace[8]. The journey to work at the Factory for women and girls was to be much quicker, for in 1898 the Company placed a bulk order to purchase bicycles[9]. In the previous year, the Factory and the nearby school were first lit by electricity[10] and the former was soon connected by private telegraph to Knightshayes, Hensleigh, Worth House, and the Estate Office in Leat Street[11]. Family and business were now just an arm's length away! Sir John, together with his son-in-law William Unwin and Prebendary Scott had taken over the Tiverton Coffee House Company in 1894[12], but his support of temperance did not hamper the Knightshayes Estate cider production. Centred on Lythecourt, its output

---

[1] DRO 3115C/EAA4.
[2] given by Sir John Heathcoat Amory.
[3] shadow drawing.
[4] DRO 3115C/EAA12.
[5] DRO Faculty Petitions/Tiverton 11.
[6] DRO 1044B/M/95n.
[7] *EFP* 20.1.896.
[8] *EFP* 9.2.1895.
[9] *Western Times* 7.4.1898.
[10] DRO 2745C/EFL3.
[11] KEO Box15.
[12] *Western Times* 23.2.1894.

had reached almost industrial proportions. During 1897 an application was made to the Borough Court for a license in order to sell the drink 'at the cider cellars' to be 'consumed off the premises'[1]. The Devon and Somerset Staghounds decided to establish a pack of hounds at Tiverton in 1896. It came as no surprise when it was announced that they would be kennelled at Knightshayes, and would be known as Sir John Amory's Staghounds. He himself was to be the master, his son Ian the horn, and the de las Casas brothers of Worth House, Washfield, were chosen as whippers-in[2]. Sir John was not one to take matters of bloodstock and improvement of the hounds lightly, as can be seen a few years later when a staghound was imported from France to augment the pack[3]. The reason for the second pack was the increase in deer numbers, which could not be controlled by the main pack at Exford. The area hunted was divided between the two; Sir John's hounds being allocated the land south of the Barnstaple-Taunton railway line, measuring about 30 miles by 20[4], and those at Exford hunted to the north.

Queen Victoria's Diamond Jubilee was, of course, celebrated with gusto in 1897; the festivities included the time-honoured tea with sports and fireworks. As a permanent memorial, the Council agreed to provide a new ward at the Infirmary[5], which was added two years later. People's Park, the scheme that had marked the Queen's Golden Jubilee, underwent changes also. The Council had taken over its maintenance in 1896, and decided to make an entrance from Bartow's Causeway. The Commissioners of Queen Anne's Bounty donated the strip of land needed from the plot of Saint Peter's Rectory. New parks were also planned at Elmore and Westexe. The engineers and ironfounders, Stenners, owned the Elmore ground[6], whereas that at Westexe was part of the ancient glebeland of Pitt. Heathcoat and Company gave £600 of the £1,500 purchase price of the Westexe land[7], and the remainder eventually came from bazaars, fêtes, and subscription[8]. Again, Queen Anne's Bounty generously gave part of their land in Saint Paul's Square for an entrance to the Recreation Ground[9], which was formally opened in June 1900.

Hardinge Stanley Giffard on his elevation to the peerage in 1898 chose the title Viscount Tiverton of Tiverton. An eminent lawyer, Lord Chancellor, and former M.P.

---

[1] DRO 440/PR4.
[2] one of whom, Manuel, in 1899 was to marry Dorothy Helen, the second daughter of Sir John Heathcoat Amory.
[3] DRO R4/1/C75.
[4] *VCHSom vol II*, 580.
[5] *EFP* 29.5.1897.
[6] DRO R4/1/C74.
[7] DRO R4/1/T4.
[8] a short-term loan of £900 was secured from Brighouse Corporation (DRO R4/1/T4).
[9] DRO R4/1/C27.

for Launceston, his choice stemmed from the fact that one of his ancestors was Roger Giffard, the 17th century owner of Tiverton Castle. In gratitude for the honour that he had bestowed upon the town, the Borough Council conferred the Freedom of Tiverton on him at the end of the year. Indeed, at this time the Council justifiably took pride in many of their projects and the general appearance of the town. Lately, the provision of gas lamps in Westexe had proved successful, prompting some townspeople to comment that they no longer had to 'grope about the courts in the dark'[1]. The onus to provide facilities was shifting on to the local authority, whether Borough or County Council. They were often restricted as to what they could achieve, of course, for they were accountable to the ratepayers. On the other hand, individual benefactors, whom Tiverton never seemed to lack, were free to provide whatever they wished or deemed necessary. The eastern portion of the town towards Blundell's School had been greatly enhanced by two such individuals, G.E. Cockram and William Partridge. They had bought and built 40 'good-class houses' at Horsdon where, before 1892, 'one had been'[2].

Construction work suffered a setback during 1898 when most of Tiverton's masons and bricklayers went on strike. One immediate effect was that Graters refused to sign the contract to build the wall at the Bartow's Causeway entrance to the People's Park[3], and the considerable work going on at Horsdon was severely curtailed. The strikers were adamant, and the *Western Times* reported that at the end of April over a dozen had left Tiverton to find work in South Devon, South Wales, and even Chatham. Indeed, 1898 was to be a year fraught with problems for the town and its Council. It had begun with a serious fire at Hartnolls, Bolham, which resulted in 18 of the building's 21 rooms bring destroyed. This incident exposed the shortcomings of Tiverton's fire service. On its outbreak, just two of the five alarms around the town were sounded, and, even then, it took the engine an hour to reach Bolham. Once there, the hose was found to be defective and of little use. Searching questions were asked at the next Council meeting, and prompt action was forthcoming. As well as ordering £600 to be borrowed to provide another engine[4], the Council decided to unite the town and country brigades. Until this time they had operated separately, a situation that on many occasions had resulted in reluctance to cover the other's patch.

The Council then addressed the problem of disposal of Tiverton's domestic rubbish. Current practice was to dump it on Tom Haydon's land at Prescott, but complaints were often made about the smell and the rats. By this time, many larger towns and cities were using incinerators, but they were very expensive to buy. One alternative was to take the rubbish by rail to Bickleigh, from where it could be taken to a nearby dump.

---

[1] *Western Times* 14.1.1898.
[2] Gregory, 1932, 24.
[3] DRO R4/1/C27.
[4] DRO R4/1/C10.

The cost of this method was estimated at £1 5s a week compared with £1 4s to take it to Prescott[1]. The Borough Council ignored both of these methods, and took the easiest course – they renewed the agreement with Haydon for a further five years[2].

Yet another emergency faced them at the end of 1898. A dispute had arisen over access to the river walk at Collipriest. Many of the townspeople used this pleasant promenade, believing they had a right to do so, but Charles Carew, the occupier of Collipriest, disagreed. A Council Committee investigated the matter[3], and legal opinion was sought[4]. By the following June, the position of all parties seemed clear. Carew was willing to allow access to the walk only as a benevolent gesture, whereas the Borough Council claimed ancient right of use. On Saturday, September 19th 1899 some Borough Councillors led a very large crowd of 4,000 Tivertonians to Collipriest to perambulate and claim the walk which extended, so it was alleged, from the bottom of Saint Andrew Street all the way to Bickleigh. This demonstration passed without incident. On the following day, the gates to the walk were locked, but on the approach of a group of the Council's employees, they were swiftly opened[5], thus ending the confrontation, albeit temporarily[6].

Following the outbreak of war against the two Boer republics of Transvaal and Orange River Colony in South Africa in October 1899, thousands of British troops poured into those regions, including a small number from Tiverton. The town was kept informed of events and, along with the whole country, celebrated the raising of the siege of the British forces at Ladysmith in late February 1900. Detonators were let off at the railway station, the streets were festooned with streamers, and in the evening a torchlight procession was held[7]. At the Heathcoat Schools the pupils lined up in the playground, the Union Jack was hoisted, and cheers rang out for the Queen, the Ladysmith garrison, and, loudest of all, for General Redvers Buller, the Crediton man who had raised the siege[8]. Further celebrations were held in May when Mafeking was relieved. Tiverton tradesmen decorated their shop windows with portraits of Baden-Powell, the stout defender of the settlement. In the following month, Tiverton's compassionate citizens raised over £50 for Mafeking's women and children who had suffered during the siege. There were many local casualties in the War, some caused by disease. One was Private Garnett of the Coldstream Guards, the lodge keeper at

---

[1] DRO R4/1/C21.
[2] DRO R4/1/C97.
[3] DRO R4/1/C75.
4 DRO R4/1/C9.
[5] *Western Times* 19.9.1899.
[6] tempers rose again in 1906 when the Council announced its intention to erect a sign indicating the walk, and Carew declared he would resist such a move.
[7] *Western Times* 6.3.1900.
[8] DRO 2745C/EFL1.

Knightshayes, who died of enteric fever in April 1900[1]. The spectre of war hovered over proceedings when Frederick Temple, now Archbishop of Canterbury, was honoured with the Freedom of the Borough in October. The day began in a sombre mood with a service at Blundell's Chapel, where he dedicated a memorial window to those pupils who had lost their lives in South Africa[2]. Later, he visited the old school where, on walking around the buildings, he brushed aside some laurel bushes to show the gathered crowd the initials on the wall that he had carved when a pupil. The day continued with a reception in the Town Hall, where he was feted as a Tivertonian, no doubt by virtue of its having been his place of education.

On January 22nd 1901 the death of Queen Victoria brought to a close the longest reign of any English monarch. She had been responsible for reinvesting the crown with popularity and dignity, and her activities during the Boer War – visiting hospitals, inspecting troops, and attending medal ceremonies – ushered in the modern notion of royalty. Full mourning was observed, black shutters were put up at many shops in Tiverton. A special meeting of the Borough Council was convened, which voted to send an address of condolence to the Royal Family[3]. Three months later ideas were being put forward for a permanent memorial by which the town could remember all she had done. Should the town build a gymnasium, Victorian almshouses, a monument on Angel Hill, a Free Library, or a clock tower at Lowman Green? The last was chosen, and it was further hoped that the names of the men of the Borough who had served in South Africa should be inscribed upon the tower[4].

News of Tiverton casualties did not cease. Lieutenant H.G. Spring, son of the Rev. Spring of Deepway, was killed, as was Major S.B. Moore of Tiverton Castle. At the end of May 1901 Sir John Heathcoat Amory's estate agent, H.J. Coulson of Lythecourt, and his wife heard news that their son, Gustavus, a Lieutenant in the King's Own Scotch Borderers, had been killed in action. Shortly afterwards they were informed that he was to receive a posthumous Victoria Cross. He had given his life in an attempt to save his corporal, and prevent artillery falling into the hands of the Boers. A brass tablet in Saint Peter's Church preserves the memory of the 22-year old. Intense patriotism could tolerate no cowards it seemed. Newspapers often named and shamed deserters. Two had appeared in the Tiverton Police Court in April, having run away from a court-martial. They were ordered to wait for an escort to return them to the army authorities. Newspapers also exposed the disgrace of the refugee camps into which Boer families were forced. Public sympathy forced the Government to introduce a scheme for educating Boer women and children, for which teachers were required. Despite the

[1] *Western Times* 11.5.1900.
[2] *Western Times* 5.10.1900.
[3] *Western Times* 25.1.1901.
[4] *Western Times* 30.4.1901.

spartan accommodation and shortage of rations in the camps, many volunteers made the journey. Among them were Kate and Lottie French, whose father was headmaster of Tiverton Boys Middle School, as well as a Miss Butterworth of Tiverton[1].

Victory was finally celebrated in June 1902. Shops closed, thanksgiving services took place, and sports were held at the Athletic Field. Edward VII's Coronation should also have taken place at the end of the same month but was postponed at short notice because of the King's illness. Tiverton, however, like many towns, had already finalised preparations to mark the occasion. A large tea had been arranged, and postponement meant the perishable goods had to be eaten on that day. Of the three bonfires built, at Van Post, Exeter Hill and Hill Top, only the last was lit. The rearranged festivities on August 9th were undertaken somewhat half-heartedly and on a much reduced scale, as most of the money had already been spent. Between the two Coronation dates, Tiverton had turned out to cheer General Buller, who had come to distribute prizes at Blundell's Speech Day.

If southern Africa had become the grave of many, it proved to be the making of others. According to the *Western Times*, Edwin Dunning, who had just moved into Stoodleigh House, had made a fortune in the region. Another success was Hugh Marshall Hole, the son of Tiverton's Town Clerk. He worked for the British South Africa Company, and in July 1901 had been sent on a special assignment as far north as Aden to see whether 'a permanent supply of natives suitable for mining work could be obtained'. This was an important first step in the introduction of Arab workers to eastern Africa. Such was the respect that he commanded that, less than a year later, he was made responsible for the funeral arrangements of no less a person than Cecil Rhodes[2].

The War had given impetus to the desire for the social improvements that characterise the reign of Edward VII. A local branch of the Young Men's Christian Association was founded in Tiverton in 1901. The newspapers remarked how odd it was that the formation of a local group had taken so long, seeing as the founder of the organisation, the Dulverton-born Sir George Williams, had been a pupil at the Chilcott School. Several of the returning soldiers approached the Borough Council requesting land for allotments. A suggestion to use part of the Greenway land near Broad Lane, in Westexe, was refused as the Charity was unwilling to divide the eight acre property. The Council were making some moves on the subject of an electricity supply, beginning in 1900 when they appointed their first electrical engineer[3]. While the Council hesitated, Sir John Heathcoat Amory, not for the first time, showed the

---

[1] *DSN* 6.2.1902. [2] TivLib folio 5/73.
[3] *Western Times* 13.2.1900.

way. In the following year, he stated his intention to place turbines at Bolham Weir to supply electric lighting to Knightshayes[1]. This prompted the Council to publicise their plan to provide power for the town from a plant near Washfield Mill[2]. Before the year was out, however, the scheme was abandoned, leaving an engineer's bill of £290. The Council then chose to ask Tiverton's 1,800 ratepayers whether they actually wanted electric lighting once the conditions were right. Surprisingly, only 341 replied, of whom 305 said 'No'. The Council, undeterred, decided to install lighting in 1903 as a municipal venture. Tenders were invited to set up the scheme, and, despite strong competition from a German firm, Suter and Company of London were appointed[3]. During the discussions, a few of the more vociferous councillors had questioned Heathcoat's sale of the Gas Works in 1895. They felt that the Company had sold the Works to the Council at a very good price (for them) knowing that when electricity was introduced, gas would largely be rendered obsolete. Ian Heathcoat Amory strongly refuted these allegations in the Council Chamber. The provision of a library for Tiverton was another issue that had been debated for a long time. Two offers of money for it were forthcoming in 1903; one of £2,000 from the philanthropist John Passmore Edwards was declined in favour of the other, £2,500 from Andrew Carnegie. The Scottish-born steel industrialist had made a fortune in America and, now in his retirement, was establishing libraries and educational institutions throughout the English-speaking world. Whereas he covered the costs of building and equipping each library, he insisted that the local authorities provide the site and maintain the institution. Tiverton Borough Council could not decide whether to accept his offer or not, but sent a letter informing him that the matter was under consideration[4]. By this time, not surprisingly, the Council had earned a reputation for hesitancy and indecision, rather than innovation and enterprise.

Meanwhile, in 1901 a scholarly curate, the Rev. Edwin Spencer Chalk made two interesting discoveries in Saint Peter's Church. First, he found the *Benefactions Book* in the vestry, the existence of which had for long been ignored. This volume, compiled on vellum between 1656 and the end of the 1700s, is a record of many of the original gifts to the people of Tiverton, and probably formed the basis for Dunsford's summary of the town's charities. Another important find were some carvings, described as 'four gilded boys in willow'[5]. These were believed to have been made by the great Grinling Gibbons (1648-1721), whose work adorns Saint Paul's Cathedral. The Rev. Chalk, during his curacy, and, later, while rector of Kentisbeare, wrote many articles, and books, on a wide range of subjects, including folklore, politics, and history. His greatest

---

[1] DRO R4/1/C34. [2] DRO R4/1/C77.
[3] *DSN* 15.10.1903. [4] DRO R4/1/C77.
[5] *Western Times* 19.11.1901.

work was the *History of Saint Peter's Church* which, although now almost a hundred years old, remains the best authority on the subject. Further interest in the town's past was generated in 1902 by the discovery of a large collection of documents at Sandon Hall in Staffordshire, home of the Earl of Harrowby. Among the papers was a vast amount of correspondence between various citizens of Tiverton and members of the Ryder family, their patrons and, for a long time, their Members of Parliament. The Earl informed the Borough Council of the find in September, and generously offered the collection to Tiverton, on payment of the expenses incurred in sorting and listing them. The Council accepted the papers, bound in 26 large volumes, along with a box of letters that had been subsequently discovered[1]. Soon after their arrival at the Town Hall late in 1903, the author and historian, Frederick J. Snell, asked the Council for permission to see them[2]. He was a native of Tiverton, had attended Blundell's School, and went on with a scholarship to Balliol College. At the young age of 30, in 1892, he published his *Chronicles of Twyford*, the key source for the history of 19th century Tiverton, to which he added a continuation to the year 1896. Not surprisingly, Snell's request to look at the Harrowby Papers was granted, but it was made clear that 'as many of them appear to be of a private nature' any proposed publication would be subject to the approval of the Mayor and Town Clerk[3]. Nothing resulted in print from his investigations, and the papers seem to have been ignored for almost a generation.

By the end of 1903, preparations were under way for the 300th anniversary of the founding of Blundell's School due the following year. Arthur Fisher, a Tiverton solicitor and Old Blundellian, intended to publish an edition of the School Register, which would include an historical introduction and a bibliography of the literature, illustrations, and manuscripts relating to the school. The finished volume fell somewhat short of the original proposal, but is still indispensable. The Borough Council enthusiastically took part in the preparations for the anniversary. They named the new streets near the School; hence Lodge Road, Old Road, The Avenue, Blundell's Avenue and Horsdon Lane came into being[4]. They donated £50 towards the Tercentenary festivities[5], and agreed to combine the event with the presentation of the Freedom of the Borough to John Coles, in recognition of his gifts to Tiverton. Both events were celebrated over two days. On June 29th a procession filed out of Old Blundells, headed by the Tiverton Town Band and the School Cadet Corps. On leaving the old school, they were faced with streets colourfully bedecked with decorations, and

---

[1] DRO R4/1/C10.   [2] *ib.*

[3] DRO R4/1/C78.

[4] (*DSN* 14.1.1904). The opportunity was also taken to give names to Belmont Road, and in Westexe, Princes, King and Queen Streets.

[5] DRO R4/1/C35.

a massive temporary arch spanned Gold Street. It seemed as if all Tiverton lined the streets, and above them banners were tied to the upper storeys of the shops. The long procession, including 300 boys, walked to Saint Peter's Church, where a Thanksgiving Service was held. Afterwards, a lunch took place at the School, to which invitations had been sent to the county's mayors and M.P.s, as well as the Masters and Fellows of Balliol and Sidney Sussex Colleges. The day continued with the unveiling of a portrait of Archbishop Temple, presented by John Coles, followed by tea for all the Blundell's boys. In the evening many private dinner parties were held, while at the School there was that most Edwardian of entertainments, a *conversazione*[1]. The following day was largely given over to the presentation of the Freedom to John Coles. At this time he was a London J.P., the Governor of the Hudson's Bay Colony, Chairman of the Clerical, Medical and General Life Assurance Company, and, locally, a Governor of Blundell's School. He had given generously to both town and School. His money had provided People's Park in 1887, a physics laboratory at Blundell's in 1898[2], and in the year of his Freedom he gave £350 for a new laundry at the Infirmary in the town. After a service in the School Chapel, the presentation was held in the Town Hall. As night drew on the Town Band played in the grounds of Blundell's, brightly illuminated, just like the town's parks.

In 1902 under the Balfour Act, local school boards were abolished, and their duties passed to Local Education Authorities. These new bodies were to be funded from local rates, and were given powers (and money) to establish and maintain new secondary and technical schools, as well as to develop existing elementary systems. The Middle Schools in Tiverton - the two former Bluecoat Schools in Castle Street and Chilcott's – were to be administered by a single body. One problem was how to maintain the existing charitable benefits available to pupils once they had finished elementary education. The solution was to offer a number of competitive free places to children aged 11 or 12 to continue their education, which, in practise, accounted for about one quarter of the secondary school places. Amalgamation was not completed until 1906, when the provisions of Chilcott's School were absorbed. At this date, the school was closed and the long-serving Master, Mr Cowell, retired with a modest pension. Clearly, the remaining Castle Street schools did not have the requisite facilities, especially

---

[1] a meeting or assembly for conversation, especially on the subjects of art, literature or science.
[2] Coles's son, George, later assumed the surname Pinckard on succeeding to his uncle's property. He was also a benefactor to Blundell's, giving £1,000 in 1886 to be used for the foundation of scholarships (*EFP* 11.8.1886).

playing fields and laboratories, demanded by 20th century education. A new site would be necessary[1].

The Act of 1902 also sparked off something resembling a rebellion in Tiverton and several other towns. Many Nonconformists objected strongly to their rates being used to support Anglican schools. A large number of people refused to pay the education portion of their poor rate, among them an influential group of the town's tradesmen, including H. Henson, the Bridge Street outfitter, and H.C. Wakefield, the draper. They also refused to have any fines paid on their behalf and distress orders were therefore made on their goods[2]. Their cause was strengthened in 1906 when the Mayor of Tiverton himself, Henry Mudford, was brought before the Magistrates Court, for refusing to pay. Although he was not jailed, across the country many of his fellow-believers were. This issue was no doubt partly to blame for the demise of the Tory government in the General Election of 1906.

M otorised road traffic was beginning to make a noticeable impact soon after this. Although cars had been legally allowed to use the highways only since 1896, a decade later they were replacing other modes of transport. Once the proposed Tiverton to Witheridge railway scheme[3] had been abandoned, the G.W.R. were urged to establish a motor car service between the two centres. This, too, did not materialise. In 1905 the Motor Act was necessary to curb dangerous practices, and it was not long before offenders were being brought to court. The first Tiverton case

---

[1] meanwhile, in 1904 the Technical School had developed a special department for the training and instruction of pupil teachers. When the Secondary Schools came into being, they took over this work, and the department developed into the Teachers' Centre. In 1904, the Devon Education Committee decided that children under three years of age should not be admitted to schools. This signalled the end of the 'babies' class' at the Factory School, which had been little more than a crèche enabling mothers (and older siblings) to be free to work.

[2] tenders were invited for the goods of these persons, but, most of their property found its way back to them (*DSN* 29.9.1904)

[3] some Tivertonians had advocated a light railway from the town to Witheridge in 1896, largely in response to a proposed railway route from Crediton to Witheridge. Such a route would endanger Tiverton's considerable trade with the area north of Cheriton Fitzpaine (DRO R4/1/C74). Indeed, Witheridge and its surrounding parishes was a prize worth fighting for; the Maunders' butter factory there had begun to take away milk supplies from Tiverton, sometimes resulting in local shortages. A public meeting early in 1897 heard that the Borough Council would be willing to put up a quarter of the costs of a line to Witheridge, and it was firmly believed that the Light Railway Commissioners and the Great Western Railway (which had taken over the Tiverton and North Devon Railway five years earlier) would both contribute similar amounts, leaving the remaining quarter to be raised locally (*EFP* 20.2.1897). The route was surveyed and published, but the scheme went no further.

concerned Herbert Eglinston, chauffeur to a Chesterfield man, who was accused of 'driving in a manner dangerous to the public' in Westexe, without using either 'horn or gong'[1]. Later in the year John Nott, engine driver of Witheridge, appeared, charged with driving a locomotive on a road less than 16 foot wide and more than 100 foot long without anyone in front to warn approaching vehicles[2]. Another driver, Tom Jones of Crosslands, Halberton, was fined 10s for driving a locomotive at a speed more than four miles per hour[3]. Heavy steam traction engines like the ones driven by these men quickly destroyed carefully-laid road surfaces. The greatest amount of damage was caused around Cove, especially after Tiverton Council took a lease of Cove Cliff Quarry in 1906[4] and began extracting large amounts of the stone which was to be used for most local building work. Tiverton's streets also took a battering from the increase in traffic, and harder-wearing surfaces were always being sought. At one time, it was suggested that creosoted pine blocks often used in other towns, should be used to pave Gold Street[5].

During 1906 Heathcoat and Company announced a new pension scheme for its workforce, based on employee contributions. This was an important innovation, coming three years before the introduction of the state Old Age Pension. But this was not a totally novel idea at the Factory; the Heathcoat scheme replaced an informal arrangement by which many employees had received a lump sum on leaving the firm's employment[6]. Finances there were clearly in a healthy state. In the previous year Sir John had bought the Chevithorne Barton Estate for £21,000[7], and the remaining eighth share in Buckhayes from the trustees of John Newte's Educational Foundation. In 1907, the Company acquired a site in Cowick Street, Exeter, where it was expected that between two and three hundred hands would be employed in lace-mending rooms and offices. Indeed, 1907 was to be a joyful year for the family and Company alike. On June 24th Sir John's youngest daughter, Mary Christal, married Lesley Butler, the son of the Irish peer Lord Dunboyne, at Saint Peter's Church[8]. Festivities marked the wedding and did not subside, for on the following day it was announced that all workers were to receive a bonus, 5% of their previous year's wages[9]. A formal acknowledgement of the town's gratitude to Sir John came in October, when he received the Freedom of the

---

[1] *DSN* 8.6.1905. [2] DRO 489P/R1.
[3] DRO 440P/R8.
[4] William North Row granted the lease on very favourable terms; the Council were to pay an annual rent of £30, in addition to 4d per cubic yard of material extracted (DRO R4/1/C95).
[5] DRO R4/1/C23. [6] *DSN* 15.2.1906.
[7] covering just under 1,000 acres, this property comprised Chevithorne Barton, Colcombe, Shepherd's Barn, Craze Lowman in Tiverton and North Kidwell in Uplowman. (KEO Chest 49).
[8] DRO 2960A/PR22. [9] *DSN* 25.7.1907.

Borough[1]. Not since the days of the Courtenays had Tiverton been home to so prestigious a family. The Heathcoat Amorys brought 'high society' to the area. Their summer garden fêtes at Knightshayes became legendary, and included such fads as 'living chess', in which human pieces were directed around a giant chessboard laid out on the lawns[2]. For those who preferred equestrian events, there were many opportunities to follow Sir John Amory's Staghounds, and the family steadfastly supported the Tiverton Polo team, whose star players were the four de las Casas brothers of Washfield.

The White King and Queen from a living chess game, played at Knightshayes Court on August 2nd 1906.

John Coles and Thomas Ford continued to bestow gifts on Tiverton. In 1906, a house next to the Infirmary was to become the John Coles' Nursing Institution, with the donor offering £500 toward the cost of the necessary alterations. An inscription

---

[1] the family's year was brought to a delightful conclusion when Sir John's son, Captain Harry, received the Cross of the Order of Isabella La Catolica. This unusual award was conferred on him by the King of Spain, as Harry, who was secretary to the Duke of Portland, had been in charge of the arrangements during the King's stay in England with the Duke (*DSN* 24.10.1907).
[2] in 1906 the local newspapers gave a full account of the proceedings, complete with a list of the moves (*DSN* 9.8.1906).

high up on the side of the building still testifies to this gift, but is rarely noticed by passers-by. At the end of the year he also gave £100 to convert the redundant Chilcott School, where he and his son were both educated, into a gymnasium[1]. As for Thomas Ford, in 1907 he decided to provide a clock tower on Lowman Green, an idea first mooted to commemorate the death of Queen Victoria. He purchased a piece of ground, at the centre of which stood a cabstand, and gave it to the Borough Council[2]. The tower, designed by J. Donkin, was built of Bath stone and, somewhat unusually, has three faces, each with double lancet windows and illuminated clock faces. The formal ceremony of handing over the keys of the tower to the Council took place on Saturday, May 16th, 1908. The event was held at five in the evening, a time set by Thomas Ford so that 'the working classes could be present'.

The curious Stockdale pyramid in the Cemetery, designed by, and housing the remains of William Colebrooke Stockdale, and those of some of his family.

A few months before the opening of the clock tower, what is possibly Tiverton's most curious, and least known, construction was built. It is not to be found in one of the streets, but in the Cemetery. This is the pyramid designed by William Colebrooke Stockdale to house his own remains, and those of his family. Stockdale and many of his

---

[1] *DSN* 8.11.1906. [2] *DSN* 14.2.1907.

ancestors had been prominent in the East India Company, and had previously lived at Tiverton where he married the daughter of a Mayor of the town, John Wills[1].

But then came natural disaster. A powerful earthquake in southern Italy on December 20th 1908 spelled ruin for Heathcoat's interests there. The company had two sites in the region, one at Gazzi, a suburb of the city of Messina on the island of Sicily, the other at Villa San Giovanni, which lay across the Straits of Messina on the Italian mainland. Both enterprises were destroyed, and one fifth of the workforce of about 400 lost their lives. At first, it was thought that William Skinner, the manager, and some of his family had perished. Fortunately, they were found alive, whereas a young Tiverton man lodging with them, Frank Wood, of Exe Vale Terrace[2], was killed.

A month later, Miss Elizabeth Hallam died. She was a niece of John Heathcoat[3], and like other members of the family, she, too, had been very generous to Tiverton. She gave £1,000 to the Infirmary in 1894, and soon after her death her great-nephew gave £500 to endow a 'child's cot' there. During her lifetime she had donated large sums to the town's dissenting congregations: £1,000 to the Baptists, and £500 each to the Congregationalists, Wesleyans, and Bible Christians. Nonconformists were now not only very respectable but also well supported. Indeed, Church and Chapel were probably stronger and more influential than ever. When the Heathcoat Hall in Wellbrook Street was wanted as a gymnasium for the Factory, the Plymouth Brethren were in need of another meeting place[4]. Sir John Heathcoat Amory gave them a site in King Street, where their Gospel Hall was built and opened in July 1909. The Methodist movement, since its inception, had experienced many a schism: the New Connexion broke away in 1797, the Primitive Methodists in 1811, Bible Christians in 1815, and the United Methodist Free Churches in 1857. In 1907, all except the Primitive Methodists joined to form the United Methodist Church[5]. Pressure was put on Tiverton's inns and hotels for accommodation in April 1908, when the annual meeting of the Devon Congregational Union was held in the town. Meanwhile, the Baptists welcomed an evangelical mission in November, led by Herbert Booth, the son of the founder of the Salvation Army. His visit ended with a bioscopic lecture entitled 'The Entrancing Story of the Early Christians', the poster for which reassuringly proclaimed that the scenes would be 'intensely realistic but in no sense revolting'[6]. Changes were also taking place in the town's Anglican churches. At Saint Paul's, in

---

[1] *DSN* 5.3.1908.   [2] *DSN* 7.1.1909.

[3] she was the daughter of the second marriage of Thomas Hallam, whose first wife had been John Heathcoat's sister.

[4] since their move in 1892 from the Iron Room Chapel on the Museum site.

[5] the Primitive Methodists, the Wesleyan Methodist Church, and the United Methodist Church affiliated in 1932 to form the Methodist Church.

[6] DRO 3958D add2/63.

1909, it was agreed that 'all stonework throughout the church should be freed from the unsightly yellow-wash'[1], the font was moved, the chancel floor raised, and the vestries enlarged[2]. Meanwhile, at Saint Peter's, the font was taken out[3], and replaced by a new one in memory of the Rev. Alan Arthur Clarke Jervoise.

The most extensive construction work, however, was secular. The Devon County Council was building the Tiverton Middle Schools on part of the land known as The Wilderness, given by Sir John Heathcoat Amory. The site covered more than three acres, so there was space for the buildings, a playing field, and even allotments. A competition had been organised to design the school, and of the 235 entries received, a Mr Ashford of Birmingham was chosen as winner. Sir Thomas Acland laid the foundation stone in November 1909 and the buildings were ready for use in December of the following year. At last there was a selective school, supported by ancient legacies, and absorbing recent institutions such as the School of Art. Similarly, in Westexe, the LEA's new Heathcoat School, designed to accommodate over 300 pupils, was soon under construction in King Street. Opened in 1913, the school, with its large playground and nearby park, was an enormous improvement for the people of Westexe.

Tiverton Middle School which opened in 1910, later becoming the Grammar School, and now Castle School.

Early in May 1910 Edward VII fell seriously ill with bronchitis, and did not recover. His reign had been notable for the raft of social reforms introduced by the Liberal

[1] DRO Tiverton Saint Pauls PV1. [2] DRO Faculty Petitions Saint Pauls 3.
[3] the old font was rehoused in the mission church at Elmore (DRO Faculty Petitions/Tiverton 15).

government, most of which were designed to reduce poverty. Free school meals were made available to poor children in 1906, and a school medical service was established in the following year. The Small Holdings and Allotments Act of 1907 encouraged Councils to provide land for labourers so they could become more self-sufficient. Tiverton Borough Council, in the following year, purchased a field alongside the Cemetery for this purpose, prompting the people of Westexe to demand a similar facility on their side of the river. An Old Age Pensions Act was passed in 1908, improving the lot of the elderly; and labour exchanges were formed with the intention of easing unemployment.

Soon after the King's death Thomas Ford informed the Borough Council that he wanted to give the town a statue of Edward the Peacemaker. They gladly accepted his offer, but where would it go? The whole matter soon descended into farce. Ford suggested three possible locations – outside Saint George's Church, near Saint Peter's, or even by Coggan's Well – but later hardened his stance, and threatened to withdraw his offer altogether unless the statue was prominently placed[1]. He eventually relented, but his second choice of Lowman Green was not amenable to the Council who suggested a site in the middle of the road outside Old Blundell's. The position eventually agreed is where the statue now stands, on a bay beside the newly repaired Lowman Bridge, and in full view of Gold Street – a bay paid for by Ford himself. Who should unveil the statue? Mr Ford had no wish to perform the ceremony himself and, failing a member of the Royal Family, the Lord Lieutenant of Devon was to be asked[2]. The unveiling by the Countess of Portsmouth eventually took place on Empire Day, May 24th 1912, watched by a great multitude. As well as attending this event, the schoolchildren of the Borough each received a newly-minted threepenny-bit as a gift from Ian, Sir John Heathcoat Amory's son[3].

Private benevolence continued to improve Tiverton's educational facilities. As the new Middle School had subsumed the functions of the Technical and Science Schools, the old buildings stood empty, but not for long. Miss Lazenby of Eastfield paid for a domestic science centre to be established in the redundant chemical laboratory and, fittingly, was invited to open it in December 1911[4]. At Blundell's they were planning a new science block with lecture, and demonstration rooms, to which John Coles contributed £500. A.L. Francis, the Headmaster, received an unexpected cheque in May 1912 for £1,000 from George Oliver May of New York, an Old Boy who had become senior partner of the American branch of Price Waterhouse and Company.

---

[1] DRO R4/1/C28.
[2] DRO R4/1/C29.
[3] DRO 3029C/EAL2.
[4] *DSN* 28.12.1911.

May expressed the wish that the money should be used to found a scholarship[1]. In the following month, £2,000 came from Colonel William Dicken, a descendant of the former Master, Alldersey Dicken. Francis received yet another gift in June, but not of money. It was a letter, Tiverton's first airmail post, dropped from an airplane piloted by a Monsieur Salmet. His flight over the town was witnessed by large crowds which gathered at Post Hill, the railway bridge near Blundell's, and in a field just below Knightshayes where the plane landed.

Unlike gifts from individuals, those from Government had to be paid for. In 1909 the budget proposals made by the Liberal Government to finance their generous social reforms and increased defence spending, faced strong opposition. The Chancellor, David Lloyd George, was proposing a surtax on higher incomes, 20% death duties, and hefty increases in the tax on alcohol. The People's Budget, as it became known, was, not surprisingly, rejected by the House of Lords, and this led the Government to resign. Nevertheless, the Liberals were returned in the 1910 General Election, but with a smaller majority[2]. The swing to the Tories in the Tiverton Division resulted in Walrond's increased share of the vote over the Liberal candidate, Ian Heathcoat Amory. The Government was challenged in the next few years by bitter labour disputes in traditional industries. In 1910 Winston Churchill, the Home Secretary, sent London police officers and, later, troops to avert riots by coal miners in South Wales who were demanding a minimum wage. A national coal strike was called for in 1912, and the anticipated longevity of the stoppage forced the Tiverton Borough Council into action. To conserve the supplies of coal the Lighting Committee advocated that public lamps should be extinguished one hour earlier each night, and at the beginning of April it was decided to leave half the town's lamps unlit[3]. Before more stringent measures were necessary the miners returned to work with the promise of a minimum wage.

Women, too, became militant in pursuit of the right to vote. In March 1912, a Tiverton branch of the National Union of Women's Suffrage Societies was formed, and, it seems, was bent on action. A parcel full of ink was found in one of the town's post-boxes in the following year which, as well as ruining many of the letters, was accompanied by a slip of paper reading 'No safety to life or property until women get the vote'[4]. One month after this incident, Emily Davison threw herself in front of the King's horse at the Derby, and her death gave rise to a suffragette pilgrimage from

---

[1] *DSN* 16.5.1912.

[2] under the threat of introducing as many as 600 peers, the Liberals forced through the Parliament Bill in August 1911 by which legislation that had passed the Commons in three consecutive sessions could no longer be vetoed in the Lords. Support for this Bill had also come from Irish Nationalists who saw its success as likely to ensure the passing of the (third) Home Rule Bill.

[3] DRO R4/1/C32.   [4] *DSN* 15.5.1913.

Land's End to London. The group arrived in Tiverton in the middle of July and held a peaceful open-air meeting in the town.

The Liberals' social reforms were noticeable, especially the introduction of old age pensions. At the Tiverton Workhouse in 1910 payments had been made to 40 indoor and 273 outdoor paupers, but three years later the numbers had dropped to 21 and 24[1]. Furthermore, following the opening in 1913 of a home for them at 'The Elms' in the hamlet of Shillingford, Tiverton's pauper children were no longer forced to live in the Workhouse. Sickness, unemployment, and maternity benefits were also brought in during the year and would benefit many. The seriously ill or the heavily pregnant could now be sustained without having to work. The employees at the Lace Factory were presented with yet another innovation in February 1913, as the outlines of a profit-sharing scheme was laid before them. Not surprisingly, the plan was eagerly accepted.

Housing conditions, too, were tackled at this time. Although there had been a lot of building in Westexe and Elmore too many people lived in the crowded, squalid courts, where the detestable sanitary conditions exposed 60 years earlier still prevailed. Improvements were at last underway, however. The Borough Council embarked on what would become its greatest achievement of all, the building of council housing, or artisans' dwellings as they were often known. By the end of 1912 the first site, on part of Bennett's Close, at the higher end of Chapel Street, had been bought for just under £1,200[2]. As with the Town Hall and the Middle Schools a competition was opened for architects. The eventual winner was Mr S. Thompson-Clothier of Street in Somerset. His drawings were to be translated into 114 houses, of three types:

    class A, comprising 3 bedrooms, parlour and kitchen, costing £180 each,

    class B, the same but without a parlour, at £135,

    class C, with just 2 bedrooms and living room, at £107 each[3].

By the end of the year, the Council had contracted Grater and Sons to build the first batch of 18 dwellings[4]. The houses, of course, needed a name. At Council meetings they had already been jokingly called 'Gregory Buildings', after Councillor Alfred T. Gregory, who had first suggested building them. The provisional title of 'Corporation Gardens' was adopted, but finally changed to Council Gardens[5].

Just when Tiverton seemed to be on the verge of great improvements, it lost two of its most charitable citizens. In September 1913, at the advanced age of 94, Thomas Ford died. The *Devon and Somerset News* remarked 'if a man has realised value by his

---

[1] *DSN* 28.8.1913.   [2] *DSN* 26.12.1912.
[3] *DSN* 17.4.1913.   [4] DRO R4/1/C97.
[5] in connection with this building scheme, the Council began widening both Chapel Street and Watery Lane (DRO R4/1/C26).

industry in his native town he has some share and responsibility in it'. Despite his numerous earlier gifts, his estate still amounted to over £80,000[1], of which he left £1,000 to the Infirmary. Less than a year later, on May 26th 1914, came the sad news of the death of Sir John Heathcoat Amory. Perhaps the *Western Morning News* best summed up his life:

> *'Much of the wealth that he derived from the lace trade he devoted largely to purposes of public utility and private benevolence, and while he enjoyed the highest reputation as an employer, he was also well known as a good landlord and he made himself popular by the energy and enthusiasm which he threw into the provision of sport'* [2].

---

[1] *DSN* 20.11.1913.   [2] 28.5.1914.

18 The Great War and Depression

While everyone's eyes were fixed on Ireland, where a civil war seemed imminent[1], the heir to the Austrian Empire was killed by an assassin's bullet in Sarajevo on June 28th 1914. This murder by a young Serbian nationalist led unexpectedly, but inexorably, to the most terrible war in European history. The event immediately invoked the pattern of alliances: at the end of July Austria declared war on Serbia, Russia mobilised, Germany responded and France followed suit in a patriotic fervour. When German armies invaded Belgium to attack France, Britain declared war on August 4th, 1914. Within a month, Tiverton began to see the immediate effects. Units of army and naval reservists were assembled at various depots. Recruitment meetings were held, often in the open-air, and a constant stream of men volunteered to join up. The Borough Council were jolted into action and, even at this early date, it was announced that the 'utmost economy possible' would be necessary, and steps were taken to trace 'all aliens in the area'[2]. Tiverton's unmarried policemen had joined the reservists, so the Chief Constable ordered vacancies to be filled and a large force of Special Constables to be sworn in. Plans were made to defend the neighbourhood; Boy Scouts were to help guard local bridges, whereas the waterworks were placed under the protection of the Civic Guard and Blundell's School Officer Training Corps. Mayor Alfred Gregory was informed that Tiverton was to become a military sub-depot, and up to 270 men could be expected. He arranged accommodation for them at the new Drill Hall in Westexe, the Heathcoat Hall, the Electric Theatre[3], and at the old Liberal Club on Angel Hill[4]. In January 1915, after Zeppelin raids on the Norfolk coast initiated nation-wide precautions, Tiverton Council ordered that no outside lights were to be lit after 7 p.m., and people would be warned of an impending raid by a hooter at the Gas Works[5].

This was not to be the short war everyone expected. Criticism of the War Office, especially over the shortage of munitions, led to the formation of a Coalition Government in May 1915[6], and the suspension of parliamentary elections. Locally, the

---

[1] the aspirations of the supporters of the Home Rule movement had been opposed by an eruption of Unionist sentiment which saw the formation of the Ulster Volunteer Force. To counter the UVF, the Nationalists, in November 1913, launched their own military grouping, the Irish Volunteers. Both sides gathered arms, and war was expected.

[2] DRO R4/1/C12.

[3] itself a drill hall until 1912.

[4] DRO R4/1/C45.

[5] DRO R4/1/C12.

[6] Asquith's Liberal government was forced to include Conservatives and a single Labour member.

mayor, Alfred Gregory, was expected to hold office for the duration of the conflict[1]. One of his first decisions was to announce that the Borough Charter Tercentenary, due in August, would be marked only by church services. With 500 Old Boys already in uniform, Blundell's School abandoned the annual speech day, and memorial certificates were given instead of prizes. Local children became actively involved in the war effort; making sandbags, knitting socks, and making jam for the troops[2]. Girls from the Heathcoat School collected 2s 6d each week towards the rent and coal for a Belgian refugee family who had been allocated one of the newly completed Council Gardens houses[3].

Heathcoat's Factory was pressed into action to help the war effort. By November 1914, it was producing kilts for Scottish troops and, later in 1915, net for gas masks[4], while the foundry made components for artillery shells. The Heathcoat Amory family were exemplary in the war effort. In October 1915, Knightshayes was given over for use as a Voluntary Aid Detachment Hospital for wounded soldiers, with Lady Amory acting as assistant commandant[5]. To welcome the first arrivals Starkey, Knight and Ford's Brewery sent a cask of ale. The patients there soon numbered 60, and for them, and the troops billeted in the town, a 'soldiers' and sailors' rest' was opened in Fore Street, as was the Mayoralty Room[6].

William Henry Stoyel of Bampton Street boasted of having 15 grandchildren on active service. He was not alone; since 1914 over a million volunteers had joined Kitchener's Army. Because of the enormous casualty figures, however, in May 1916 Britain had to resort to military conscription[7]. Tribunals were set up with power to grant exemptions to essential workers, and to hear objections from conscripts or their employers. For those who disagreed with the tribunal's decision, a Devon Appeal Tribunal was instituted, with Sir Ian Heathcoat Amory in the chair. Inevitably, there was a great shortage of manpower in the countryside, which, it should not be forgotten, was also stripped of many of its horses[8]. Lowering the school-leaving age to 12 years eased the situation. The Heathcoat Factory was able to employ girls to operate the lace machines, and boys were released to work on the land, where the workforce was further increased in 1917 by the appearance of prisoners-of-war. Local farmers were allocated

---

[1] *Obituary* 1942, 30-1.   [2] DRO 2745C/EFL2.

[3] the first group of Belgians had arrived in the previous November and by March 1915 there were over 100 in the district.

[4] (*DSN* 13.5.1915). Gas was first used by the Germans at Ypres in April 1915, and production began at Heathcoat's within a month.

[5] *DSN* 11.11.1915.   [6] DRO R4/1/C13.

[7] this was the first time conscription was resorted to by Britain, and all males aged between 18 and 41 were called up.

[8] the Tiverton district, even in 1914, had provided 125 horses for cavalry duty and a further 80 for pulling artillery (*DSN* 27.8.1914).

a handful of German and Austrian captives[1]. Huge losses of shipping in the U-boat campaigns cut imports drastically, so great emphasis was placed on producing food at home. Every piece of land was to be used; an acre of the Tiverton Cemetery was ploughed up and planted with potatoes[2]. By 1917 it was necessary, for the first time, for the Government to impose food rationing.

For four years an endless stream of news of men killed, wounded, or 'missing, presumed dead' afflicted Tiverton, as elsewhere. Inevitably, nearly all the victims were young, tragically deprived of promising futures. Just one example was Harold Rudall of Chapel Street, killed in action in 1916, who, before the War, had been in great demand for his footballing skills. In June 1916 three Tiverton men were feared lost on *HMS Indefatigable*, and news came from distant Iraq that the Mayor's only son had died at Mosul[3]. The human toll of war was unprecedented and unceasing. A roll of honour of former pupils of Heathcoat's Boys' School, serving or already dead, contained over 500 names by January 1917. Two months later, a similar roll for the Borough held over 1,000 names, and by August no fewer than 852 Old Blundellians had already taken part in the War, of whom 105 had been killed.

The headstone in Tiverton Cemetery marking the grave of Private Thomas Sage V.C.

In December 1917, the ultimate military honour, the Victoria Cross, was awarded to a Tivertonian, Private Thomas Sage. He had been working at the Starkey, Knight,

[1] *Western Times* 22.2.1918.   [2] DRO R4/1/Z52.
[3] *Obituary* 1942, 30-1.

and Ford Brewery before he volunteered for service, and was told he would not be allowed to serve overseas until he had surgery on his leg. He could have had an immediate discharge, but refused, so eager was he to join up. He won the V.C. for his actions in a shell hole when one of his company had been killed in the act of throwing a grenade. Sage instantly recognised the certain outcome of an explosion, so he threw himself on top of the grenade. He saved his comrades but suffered severe wounds to his thigh[1]. The Borough Council voted unreservedly to give the hero an official welcome home, and to make him a gift of War Bonds and Treasury Notes[2]. They kept their word; and in March 1918 the Tiverton hero was met at the railway station and, after a civic reception, left for his Westexe home accompanied by a crowd of several thousand. His future was assured when he became caretaker of the Drill Hall.

The German offensive of 1918 failed to break the Allies; Russia was embroiled in civil war, and made peace, the Americans eventually appeared in battle, and the War ended almost as surprisingly as it had begun. The news of the November 11th Armistice reached Tiverton that day. The *Western Times* recorded that 'the factory employees left their work, and others joined later'. Sir Ian Heathcoat Amory announced the good news to the children of the Heathcoat School as 'the greatest victory ever known in history'[3]. Servicemen gradually returned home – men like Corporal Jutsum of Patcott Farm, who had been a prisoner-of-war for nearly two and a half years, and Private Walter Hoare, a captive for 15 months. Many of them had horrific tales to tell, but most kept their experiences to themselves. One sad victim was Lieutenant Harold Hatt who returned in February 1919, but went missing almost immediately. His cap was found on the banks of the Exe near Brampford Speke, and soon after his body was discovered near Bickleigh.

Several of those who had fought in the War contracted tuberculosis, and in Tiverton, as elsewhere, a sanatorium was much needed. Sir Ian lent a site near Bolham, overlooking the Exe Valley, where a simple wooden structure made of two army huts was put up in July 1920[4]. Although the building was originally for ex-servicemen, pressure was soon put on the Borough Council to make it available for the rest of the townspeople. The disease was indeed taking a toll in the town; in November, the Viney family of King Edward's View suffered their fourth fatality in three years from this 'white death'[5].

Peace was not officially celebrated in Tiverton until July 19th 1919, on a day that also brought the first rain for three months. The weather did not deter the procession of 500 soldiers, the tea in People's Park, or the evening's bonfire on Exeter Hill.

---

[1] *Western Times* 28.12.1917.
[2] for which over £30 had been subscribed (DRO R4/1/C45).
[3] (DRO 3029C/EAL3). He had only three months earlier lost his brother, Ludovic, who died in France from his wounds.
[4] DRO R4/1/C25.   [5] *ib.*

Anyway, there was a second chance to rejoice, as a Peace Pageant had been planned for August 15th. This time, the sun shone and crowds of people made their way down to Collipriest where they were treated to a procession of tableaux showing scenes from the town's history. The event had been organised almost single-handedly by Alfred Gregory[1]. The pageant was to be one of his last public duties, for he declined to serve a ninth term as Mayor because of failing health. The town and the country rewarded his long stint in office during the wartime years. The Borough Council presented him with the Freedom of the Borough, and in the following year, he received an O.B.E. from the King.

The carnage of the War was to be recorded on memorials the length and breadth of the country. At Saint Peter's Church, a Memorial Chapel was located in the east end of the north aisle, separated from the main body of the church by a screen. Three oak-framed brass tablets recording the 56 men of Saint Paul's parish, Westexe, were unveiled in October 1920[2], and in the following month, the large stone Celtic cross at Blundell's School was revealed, together with the tablets recording the names of the 195 Old Boys who had died[3]. During 1919, the Borough Council purchased the Angel Hotel, with a view to turning it into a permanent War Memorial. The idea was to provide a Library as well as a large hall for public use, and there were to be memorial tablets on the outside of the building in addition to a roll of honour in the entrance hall[4]. Initially, the plan involved little alteration to the Hotel and, on Armistice Day 1920, the Library, the first phase of this War Memorial building, was formally opened by Mrs Emily Lazenby of Eastfield[5]. John Coles had given £500, but he did not live long enough to see the opening ceremony. He died in 1919, leaving an estate valued at almost half a million pounds.

The expanding American economy and disruption caused by German reparations led to a decline in traditional British industries that was to characterise the inter-war period. The result was widespread unemployment which, by the summer of 1921, affected more than a fifth of the nation's workforce. At Tiverton, the situation became so serious that the Guardians of the Poor suggested that relief should be paid not by them but by the Borough Council, who should also provide work for the men[6]. Schemes were indeed devised; several men were employed on road improvements, and

---

[1] *Obituary*, 1942, 30-1.
[2] DRO Faculty Petitions/ Tiverton Saint Pauls 8.
[3] *Western Times* 5.11.1920.   [4] DRO R4/1/C45.
[5] she declared it free to all, adding that readers would be allowed access from 6-9pm on each weekday, and 2-5pm on Tuesday, Thursday and Saturdays.
[6] *Western Times* 21.10.1921.

the Council sent a group of 26 to clear woodland on the Acland estate at Killerton[1]. Wages were reduced at the Tiverton Gas Company, and in the early months of 1922 many local farmers attempted to lower labourers' wages from 38s to 34s a week. Most seriously for Tiverton, a lack of orders in September led to a three-week closure of the Lace Factory.

A General Election was called in November 1922, the first in which women were to have the vote. What peacetime never achieved, the War had. During the conflict, women and girls had worked on the railways, in service industries, making armaments, in factories, in mines, and on the land, so there was no longer any reasonable excuse to exclude them from helping to determine the nation's future. Nevertheless, under the 1918 Act only those over the age of 30 were eligible to vote, unlike men who could vote at 21; full electoral equality had to wait another decade. The 27,000 electors of the Tiverton Division were faced with a three-way choice: Weston Sparkes of Dawlish stood for the Conservatives, the Liberals were represented by Francis Dyke Acland, and there was a Labour candidate, Frederick Brown. The Tiverton poll resulted in the Tories narrowly defeating the Liberals, with Labour coming a distant third[2]. Weston Sparkes died early in 1923, causing a bye-election, notable as being the first of two family contests between Francis Dyke Acland and his cousin Colonel Acland-Troyte who stood as a Conservative. On this occasion the Liberals were victorious by a majority of 400[3], only to see this drastically reduced to just three votes in the General Election of December 1923, one of the narrowest margins in British political history. This election ushered in the first-ever Labour government, supported by Liberals. Labour's subsequent treaty negotiations with the newly established USSR, however, caused many Liberals to abandon their parliamentary bedfellows. Consequently, yet another General Election in October 1924 saw the Tories under Stanley Baldwin score an overwhelming victory. In the Tiverton Division Acland-Troyte won comfortably.

The War had brought about many social changes, not least to the gentry. High wages, taxes, and death duties bore down on many with large landed estates, and one remedy was to reduce numbers of servants. A few chose to open their stately homes to the public to generate an income, others decided simply to demolish them, but the easiest way was to sell off all or part of what they owned. Large sums of money were involved, and many an ancient family became divorced from its heritage. In 1922, the North Row's Cove Estate went on the market, with the main residence of Cove House being sold to Frank Shearman of Stoodleigh Court for over £10,000[4]. A similar sum

---

[1] DRO R4/1/C45.
[3] *ib.*

[2] Craig 1969, 331.
[4] DRO 547B/P2207.

296

was paid for Castle Barton, Tiverton, when the Carew Estate with property in Tiverton, Bickleigh and Halberton, was sold for over £30,000[1].

Council house building was resumed with renewed vigour and pride after the War. In Tiverton, the 50 houses at Council Gardens, begun in 1913, had to be finished before a start could be made on more than 100 at Westexe[2]. The rural areas were also provided with labourers' cottages: ten at Bolham, six at Chettiscombe, four each at Chevithorne, Longhayne, Cove and Withleigh, and two at Seven Crosses[3]. The Borough Council purchased further building sites in 1924. Land at Loughborough was offered by Captain John ('Jack') Amory[4], and many small plots were bought on the north side of the Chettiscombe Road, opposite People's Park[5]. The Borough Council sold these sites to private builders to construct houses for sale rather than rent, a method encouraged by Neville Chamberlain's 1923 Housing Act, which subsidised such building.

Whereas new houses were provided with up-to-date facilities, the majority of those in Tiverton still had shared access to water. The Streets Committee undertook a survey of mains running water available to the various sections of the town in 1926. The old courts still exposed the greatest need. The 13 houses of Rudd's Buildings had access to just two taps, Church Square's eight houses shared one, Chapple's Buildings had a single tap for eight houses, and, worst of all, the 13 houses of Taylor's Court had use of just the single tap[6]. The Borough Council again set out to find suitable schemes to improve the town's water supply. In the meantime, a great deal of importance was placed on the municipal baths next to the Bridewell in Saint Andrew Street[7]. For many, they were the only place where they could take a bath. Other concerns that impinged on public health were the town's slaughterhouses and the disposal of its refuse. The Borough Council had voted to establish a public slaughterhouse on a site at Horsdon, near where, it was hoped, the market would relocate. This abattoir would replace the handful of existing enterprises sited in the town that, for early 20th century taste, had become unacceptable. One slaughterhouse in Barrington Street had 'a paved and drained yard, two-stall shippen, manure pit and furnace'[8]. The public was no longer prepared to put up with such activities in the middle of town. As for the disposal of

---

[1] *Western Times* 29.9.1922. [2] DRO R4/1/C13.
[3] DRO R4/1/C48. [4] DRO R4/1/C47.
[5] which eventually became the Park Road estate (DRO R4/1/C95).
[6] DRO R4/1/C26.
[7] at this time, the baths were in need of repair. Offers were made, however, to build new swimming baths at Loughborough – a gift of £1,000 from J.R. Turner, a former resident of Tiverton, and the land from Sir Ian Heathcoat Amory (DRO R4/1/C95). In spite of Tiverton Swimming Club preferring alterations at the old baths, the new ones were begun at the end of 1923. The Loughborough Baths were provided with 57 'dressing boxes' and seating for over 100 persons, and took their water from the Leat which flowed into the Factory (DRO R4/1/C14).
[8] DRO R4/1/C95.

household refuse, the search for a long-term site was eased when the Carpenter brothers leased a piece of their land at Coldharbour to the Council[1].

In 1923, the only obstacle to Tiverton's electric lighting scheme had been the siting of the generating works. The location chosen, in Blundell's Road beside the Gasworks, had aroused considerable opposition from the residents of the neighbouring Lodge Estate. As soon as they realised the advantages of a nearby electricity supply, however, they dropped their objections[2] and building work proceeded rapidly. The Electricity Works had an initially modest customer-base of 31 in 1924, but by January 1925, it could boast 107 consumers. Electricity opened a new world; the modern, clean, but dangerous, power supply could be used to run a growing number of household appliances. The consumer goods revolution had begun. Shops were needed to sell the goods, and a new trade of electrician was much in demand to maintain not only the appliances but also the supply itself. Just a couple of years later Stenner and Gunn were offering 'complete electric lighting installation', as were E.V. Twose of Halberton and H. Pincott of Gold Street, described as electrical engineers. Broadcasting, by the BBC fed a rapidly rising demand from 1922. Locally, sales of wireless sets soared after the chimes of Big Ben were broadcast through loudspeakers at Lowman Green on New Year's Eve 1925. Even the Workhouse was to have a set, as long as it came 'without any charge on the rates'[3]. Stenner and Gunn gave one, so inmates especially enjoyed the 1926 Christmas broadcast from Canterbury Cathedral. Radio would have an enormous effect on family life; whereas newspapers brought yesterday's events, radio brought immediate news. People could now hear a wider range of music than ever they had; accent became important; and the voice of experts and entertainers was now available in the home.

The return to the gold standard in 1925 led to a rising pound, a decline in the annual value of British exports and a general fall in wages. The ending of Government subsidies to mines and competition from cheap German coal forced colliery owners to consider pay reductions. The miners rejected any such proposals and went on strike on May 1st 1926. They appealed to the Trades Union

---

[1] (DRO R4/1/C95). All was well until April 1926 when it was reported that the tip was on fire. This was a relatively common occurrence on such sites, and at first did not cause much alarm. However, two engines pumping water on to the flames did not put out the fire, so the Council employed six men for eight days digging back the tip. Still it was not extinguished, and it was decided to cover the tip with earth (DRO R4/1/C26), and as much as five months later the Public Health Committee voiced its alarm that the site was still smouldering (DRO R4/1/C52).
[2] *Western Times* 19.10.1923.   [3] *DSN* 1.1.1925.

Congress for support. The result was the first General Strike[1]. Tiverton Borough Council introduced emergency measures over the use of coal at the Gas and Electricity Works, and plans were made to ration it in the town. Civil unrest was expected, for 90 special constables were enrolled[2]. The Strike was a tragedy that mercifully ended after nine days, but miners continued their protest for months to come. Although railway services were disrupted for over a week, Tiverton itself was little affected by the stoppage. The press took pains to point out that the only 'union men' on the Borough Council, three bricklayers and a carpenter, had taken part in the strike[3], whereas the workers of Starkey, Knight and Ford were each given a 10s bonus 'for remaining loyal'.

Tiverton turned to more sociable events. A delightful wedding took place in March 1927 between a local woman and a Londoner, whose name was to become synonymous with enjoyment. William 'Billy' Butlin, listed on the register as 'amusement caterer'[4] married Dorothy Cheriton, a 25-year old from William Street. The summer months were the time for trips to the seaside or further afield, and a handful of businesses applied to the Borough Council for omnibus licences. Locally, the Witheridge Transport Company was prominent, but Mark Howe and Sons of Newport Street, and Eastmond and Sons of Gold Street also obtained licences[5]. Rail, however, was the preferred method of transport of the 300 Tivertonians who travelled to Rhyl in North Wales in 1927 in order to watch the solar eclipse. The many hundreds that gathered on the hills around Tiverton, however, were denied a glimpse of the phenomenon by almost total cloud cover[6]. Their disappointment was to be alleviated by the October Carnival, proclaimed by the newspapers as 'the best ever!' One regular feature not to be missed was the 'World's Fair', which in this year was held on the Athletic Field[7]. It comprised a circus, side-shows, and firework display, which attracted no less than 6,000 paying customers. The financial outlay was relatively low as most of the performers were local, among them 'Binkie the Educated Horse' and 'Bruno the Bear and his Terpsichorean Act with his Trainer'[8].

Tiverton's main streets, as now, saw constant change. During resurfacing in Gold Street and parts of Fore Street in 1928 many people petitioned the Mayor asking whether it was intended to return the streets to their previous state where 'plentiful

---

[1] indeed, men of all industries were being attracted to the unions at this time, with the enigmatic leader of the Transport and General Workers Union, Ben Tillett, speaking at a meeting at Tiverton in March 1926 (*DSN* 18.3.1926).

[2] *DSN* 13.5.1926.   [3] *DSN* 6.5.1926.

[4] DRO 2960A/PR25.   [5] DRO R4/1/C42.

[6] *DSN* 30.6.1927.

[7] having outgrown its previous location in the Market.

[8] *DSN* 30.10.1927.

water flowed down both sides'; he assured them that this would be so[1]. By this date, Fore Street was not only home to seven national banks[2] but also a handful of chain stores. Indeed, two of them were expanding; W.H. Smith and Sons had purchased 40 and 42 Fore Street[3], while Timothy Whites bought the former New Inn property at 43 Fore Street. Gold Street was soon to be adorned with new shop fronts for Clapp's Café and Eastmond's[4]. A major construction project was underway on Angel Hill, where the second phase of the War Memorial building was taking form. The work included straightening the curved frontage of the old Angel Hotel. A shortfall in the costs was partly made up by encouraging people to subscribe 6d per brick (although they cost just 1½d each). The foundation stones of the present War Memorial building were laid in May 1928 by three of Tiverton's most charitable ladies, Mrs Emily Lazenby, Miss Marjorie Gregory and Lady Amory, and it was ready for its grand opening in the following April. The ceremony was performed by Lord Mildmay, the Lord Lieutenant of Devon, with, most appropriately, the British Legion forming a guard of honour[5]. The War Memorial Trust also owned the level stretch of ground beside the Exe to the rear of the building, which was put to good use when tennis courts were laid out by a newly-formed company, Tiverton Hard Courts Limited[6].

The large workforce at Heathcoat's was courted during the 1929 General Election campaign. Meetings were held at the Factory as well as at the Heathcoat Hall. The sitting member for the Division, Acland-Troyte, warned that the firm was successful mainly because of the policy of protecting British products by taxing foreign imports, whereas under the Socialists the Factory would be nationalised and jobs put in jeopardy[7]. The threat of unemployment made in the speeches was particularly poignant, as soon it would rise dramatically. In the previous year Tiverton Borough Council had been asked whether work could be found for men and boys from industrially depressed areas. It quickly answered to the effect that the local Employment Exchange was unable to find sufficient work for its own[8]. When the results of the General Election were announced at the Town Hall, it was little surprise that Acland-Troyte had retained his seat[9]. Nationally, however, a Labour minority government was formed under Ramsay McDonald[10].

---

[1] *DSN* 30.9.1928.
[2] the London Westminster and Parr's; the National Provincial and Union Bank of England; Fox, Fowler and Company; Lloyds Bank; the London Joint City and Midland Bank; Barclays Bank and the Devon and Exeter Savings Bank.
[3] they already occupied number 42.   [4] *DSN* 21.3.1929.
[5] *DSN* 4.4.1929.   [6] *DSN* 26.1.1928.
[7] *DSN* 23.5.1929.   [8] DRO R4/1/C52.
[9] Craig 1969, 331.
[10] although the Labour candidate for the Tiverton division, Wreford-Glanvill, came third in the poll, the rise in interest in the party encouraged the establishment of a Labour Club in Tiverton.

The problem of Tiverton's water supply again needed to be faced. The growth of the town, especially in the Elmore and Westexe districts, was making demands that existing sources could not meet. A report commissioned by the Borough Council in 1927 concluded that a reduction in usage was not possible, that the 'present supply is impure and inadequate', and that no minor scheme was economically viable. The Council were urged to consider pumping water from the Exe at a cost of £30,000, but were understandably cautious about such a large undertaking. They agreed to adopt the scheme only as a last resort, and decided to investigate the possibility of obtaining supplementary supplies from elsewhere[1]. A year later, many of the councillors' hopes were raised by a firm of water diviners, who had discovered considerable supplies along the upper reaches of the Town Leat. It was decided to recommend developing these sources leading down to Allers, which had an estimated daily yield of 300,000 gallons[2]. Curiously, even this discovery did not prompt immediate action.

Perversely, an abundance of water was to pose a threat in December 1929. The River Lowman burst its banks, covering Lowman Green to a depth of $3^{1}/_{2}$ feet, and flooding the Gas and Electricity Works. It also carried away a large number of empty barrels from the Starkey, Knight, and Ford Brewery, many of which were last seen floating out to sea at Topsham[3]. On April 5th what were described as the worst tropical storms for 50 years brought just under $1^{1}/_{2}$ inches of water. There was a landslide at Rock Cottages near Cove, and Hamlin's Mills in Saint Andrew Street were seriously affected. Just as so often before, Lowman Green was again rendered impassable. Such events were sadly never rare in Tiverton, and invariably the same two areas were affected – Lowman Green and lower Saint Andrew Street. This was mainly because the River Lowman was still hindered in its course by weirs, narrow stretches, and an accumulation of silt and rubbish. The Borough Council resolved to clean out the river, and to widen it at Collipriest, Saint Andrew Street Bridge, Old Blundell's and the Athletic Field[4]. Unfortunately, these measures would not be enough.

During emergencies, Tiverton's Police Force was much in demand. For years, Devon County Council had been trying to persuade the Borough to incorporate the force into the County Constabulary, but Tiverton jealously guarded its control[5]. Even the Government had tried tactics verging on blackmail to bring about a merger. Tiverton had applied for a reduction from 10 to 8 officers in 1920, as it was a 'peaceful, happy and law-abiding place'. The Home Office replied that no fewer than 10 would be permitted, 'but if Tiverton amalgamated, eight would be sufficient'. At this time, the

---

[1] one alternative source that was suggested were the streams at Sidborough, near Templeton (*DSN* 6.10.1927).
[2] *DSN* 11.10.1928.   [3] *DSN* 12.12.1929.
[4] DRO R4/1/C55.   [5] *DSN* 19.6.1919.

Borough's 11 men constituted the smallest independent municipal force in the whole country[1]. There was vigorous competition for vacancies, evident on the retirement of one of the constables when over 200 applications were received for the post. Despite its lack of numbers, the force availed itself of the most up-to-date technology available. 'Police telephone plants' were introduced during 1930 at the Palmerston Corner and in Westexe. These were telephones by which the public could communicate directly with the police station, and were fitted with a red light that glowed when a call was being sent. Another innovation during the year was the decision to appoint a traffic warden for the Borough[2]. This proved so successful that the post was continued in preference to recruiting an extra constable.

Tragedy struck on Witheridge Moor in Christmas week 1930. While hunting, Sir Ian Heathcoat Amory's horse took a tumble, and rolled over its rider, causing multiple injuries[3]. Despite surgery and constant treatment, he died on Sunday, January 4th, 1931, in his 66th year. The funeral service, held at Saint Peter's, bore testament to his popularity, as more than 3,000 people attended, of whom half had to stand outside the church. A quiet interment at Chevithorne followed. Benevolent to the very end, Sir Ian bequeathed £5,000 to the Factory Employees Pension Fund. His gift was especially generous, as at this time business was slack. Indeed, in January, the Factory was on half time, but this did not deter the workforce from making a collection to erect a memorial to him outside the counting house.

Captain John, Sir Ian's eldest son, succeeded to the title and inheritance. One of his first pronouncements was that no profits could be shared out in 1931, because of the drop in orders to the Factory. This was one of the consequences of the worldwide slump in trade following the Wall Street Crash of 1929. Yet he did not curtail his benevolence to Tiverton. Local newspapers had carried reports that the Infirmary had outgrown its premises in Bampton Street, and needed a new building[4]. The Hospital Committee decided in August 1931, however, that the time was not right to go ahead with a new site (and would, it seems, not be so for another 75 years). Sir John's solution was to donate sufficient land as was needed to extend the William Street site northwards[5]. As well as providing for the sick, he was also instrumental in founding one of Tiverton's most enduring sports clubs. He purchased Bradford Farm, just off the Halberton road, in 1931 with the intention of letting part of it as a golf course. It is not too difficult to see where the source of his enthusiasm for this sport originated. His wife was the

---

[1] being fewer than Carmarthen with 12, Congleton 13 and Clitheroe 15 (*DSN* 27.2.1930).
[2] DRO R4/1/C55.   [3] *DSN* 25.12.1930.
[4] 'on a high position outside the town', at a considerable cost of £30,000 (*DSN* 21.2.1929).
[5] plans were soon drawn up for a £20,000 extension - almost as much as that estimated for a new building.

redoubtable Joyce Wethered, who had already won the British Women's Open Championship in 1922, and was to repeat the feat after her marriage in 1924, 1925 and 1929. She is still widely regarded as the greatest British woman golfer of all time. There had been a golf course of sorts in Tiverton for many years at the Athletic Field, but other demands on the land meant that the game could be played there only on very rare occasions. One hundred and seventy people had already indicated their enthusiastic support for a new course. Over half of the £4,500 needed as capital to start the club had already been promised, and to spur on other investors Thomas Ford, despite the prevailing financial climate, guaranteed a 5% return on all money advanced[1]. The course was opened at the end of May 1932, with the first match being played between James Braid, five times English champion, and E.H.W. Kenyon the reigning Irish Open champion[2].

Tiverton's unemployed numbered 100 in November 1930, but rose to 174 by January 1931, and was to stand at 258 by the end of the year[3]. Whereas, schoolteachers, the Armed Services, and civil servants were forced by the Government to take a 10% cut in their salaries, Tiverton Borough Council narrowly rejected a motion to reduce the wages of its employees. Large numbers of people took to the roads, actively looking for work on tramp. Having nowhere to stay, they often sought shelter in the nearest workhouse. Overcrowding became so serious at Tiverton that, during one weekend in March, 36 of the inmates had to stay in bed because there was no other space for them. A temporary solution was to use the Workhouse Chapel as a tramps' ward, although this gave rise to strong objections[4], and relief was felt in all quarters in November when 35 Chapel Street was converted from a lodging-house into a 'hostel for wayfarers'. Nationally, unemployment figures had reached 23% in the summer of 1931. Desperate proposals to cut unemployment payments and other social services split the Cabinet and led to the temporary resignation of the Labour Prime Minister, Ramsay McDonald. No single party wanted to take responsibility and so a coalition, the National Government, was formed under him. Nevertheless, the numbers out of work continued to rise. In August 1932 at Tiverton they reached 321. This local peak reflected that of the Southwest where 16.4% were out of work, but was far below the figures in Scotland and Wales, where the figure was more than 38%[5]. This was not the full story, however, as in some areas heavily dependent on traditional industries, such as coal, cotton and shipbuilding, unemployment was often 90%. What was particularly worrying locally was the large number of farm workers being put out of work and applying for relief. One who felt great sympathy with these men was Harold Shapland who, on being appointed Mayor, announced that the Council would forego their usual

---

[1] *DSN* 23.4.1931.
[2] *DSN* 26.5.1932.
[3] *DSN* 12.11.1931.
[4] *DSN* 2.4.1931.
[5] Flanagan, 1991, 118.

municipal banquet, and the money would be spent 'on those less fortunate'. Whenever work was offered, it was eagerly grasped. A group of 30 or so men from the Tiverton area took the opportunity to travel to Jersey to help lift the early potato crop[1], while others were put to work 'curing dangerous corners' on the roads around the town[2].

In April 1933, it was announced that, once the enlargement was complete, the Infirmary would be renamed the Tiverton and District Hospital. A concerted effort was begun to raise the remaining money, although not all such worthy efforts were successful. Kenneth Bareham, the organist at Saint Peter's, had brought in considerable funds in the previous two years by showing his home-made local-interest films. His third such venture, however, was a financial disaster, leaving him with considerable bills and forcing him to sell his equipment[3]. The shortfall for the Hospital was, hopefully, to be met by an Olde English Fayre planned for June. Despite the economic climate, the organisers did not hold back. There was a Folk Dance Festival with 200 dancers; the new bowling green in The Avenue was opened in time to stage events, and 174 entries were received for the Tiverton Tennis Tournament held behind the Town Hall. The main venue was Knightshayes Court, which hosted a gymkhana, dog racing, and a children's carnival. The highlight of all this was a display put on by the British Hospitals' Air Pageant[4]. Famous pilots, such as Charles Scott[5], performed stunts, and people were taken on short flights around the area. The £3,000 receipts from the Fayre were supplemented by a very successful Carnival, all of which provided a much-needed boost for the new Hospital's funds.

Gregory Eastmond, the well-known draper of Gold Street, was an innovator of the time. Following a visit to London with John Hamlin, the miller of Saint Andrew Street, the two men decided that Tiverton ought to have a purpose-built modern cinema like those they had seen in the capital. On a site just off Fore Street, they built the Tivoli, which opened in December 1932 with the film *Jack's The Boy*. Its use has not changed during the years, and it is now the only cinema in the town. As with the Tivoli, Eastmond was responsible for another notable building of the period[6]. In 1934, he obtained permission to build a house on Deyman's Hill[7] whose design was unusual for

---

[1] *DSN* 25.2.1932.   [2] *DSN* 27.10.1932.

[3] *DSN* 2.2.1933.

[4] local fascination with aerial exploits had been heightened earlier in the year as one of the RAF pilots who broke the long-distance non-stop flying record Flight-Lieutenant G.E. Nicholetts, was the son of a former Tiverton bank manager (*DSN* 15.6.1933).

[5] Scott had flown from England to Australia.

[6] the other cinema, the Electric Theatre in Newport Street, was given a new 'art deco' façade about this time.

[7] DRO R4/1/C56.

Britain, let alone Tiverton. The building is a striking example of the Bauhaus style, which had originated in contemporary Germany[1].

Gregory Eastmond's house at Deyman's Hill.

Bauhaus was not, unfortunately, the only thing emanating from Germany at this time. The Depression was leading many people towards extremist political views, including Fascism. A right wing, anti-Communist movement had brought Mussolini to prominence in Italy in the 1920s, and later Hitler's Nazi Party in Germany. Sir Oswald Moseley had formed the British Union of Fascists in 1932, and in the following year an Exeter member of the group was selling copies of their paper *The Blackshirt* in Tiverton[2]. Indeed, in March 1935, a packed Heathcoat Hall would listen attentively to a talk uncompromisingly entitled 'Blackshirt Policy', given by their Director of

[1] for an authoritative article on this building see Wickham 1992.
[2] *DSN* 28.10.1933.

Propaganda, William Joyce, later to become known as Lord Haw Haw[1]. Various attempts were being made to improve relations between Germany and Britain, and even in Tiverton a student from the University College at Exeter, Karl Heinz Schwebel, lectured on the subject to the Tiverton Rotary Club in February 1934[2]. More prophetic, though, was the title chosen for the debate of the first meeting a month earlier of the very respectable local Discussion Society – 'Can War be justified?' This group was to meet at members' homes, and had Derick Heathcoat Amory, Sir John's younger brother, as its chairman, with the librarian, Stanley Mahood as its vice-chairman[3].

Many endured hardship during the winter of 1934. The large numbers of Tiverton's unemployed and poor led to the Provident Coal Society's distributing more than 600 tickets for free supplies. The Relieving Officers gave those in extreme distress coupons that could be exchanged for groceries[4]. Fortunately, the economic situation did begin to improve, and unemployment was slowly reduced nationally, but remained constant in the depressed areas. The Borough Council could, with increasing confidence, look ahead, and join in the building boom of the 30s. Encouraged by the Housing Act of 1933, which had promoted the replacement of substandard housing by modern rented accommodation, the Council drew up its first list of properties to be demolished as part of a slum clearance plan. It consisted of 21 houses; two in New Inn Court and Trickey's Court, five each in Water Lane, William Street and Phoenix Lane, and single properties in Pinkstone's Court and Salter's Buildings. From the outset, the William Street properties posed a problem. Their owner, Rose Ashton, claimed that the premises were virtually the only form of income she had, and that she was willing, if necessary, to put them into a habitable state[5]. A second list soon followed, comprising 20 'back-to-backs', all in Westexe, which would be converted into 10 houses[6]. Yet no demolition would take place for another 30 years.

At long last a fundamental problem could be addressed. Plans for the town's water supply were revived in 1934[7]. The Council were on the point of seeking Parliamentary powers to proceed with a scheme to extract water from the Exe at Bolham when objections were raised by a small number of councillors, led by D.M. Thomas, and backed by the Tiverton Ratepayers' Association. A public meeting was called, and was attended by over 1,200 people. Of those present, only 70 were in favour of the Exe scheme. Back to the drawing board went the Council and appointed yet another expert

---

[1] *TG* 19.3.1935.   [2] *DSN* 22.2.1934.
[3] TivLib M1.
[4] it was discovered in many cases that the poor were getting cash from the shopkeepers either as change or as payment for their coupons (*Western Times* 29.3.1935).
[5] *DSN* 8.11.1934.   [6] DRO R4/1/C16.
[7] the decisions of 1928 (see p.*) had apparently been largely forgotten.

to produce yet another report. R.G. Hansford Worth, a water engineer of Plymouth, in October gave details of the estimated yields of the various sources:

Norwood	70,000 gallons
Allers	64,000 gallons
stream at Allers	120,000 gallons
Knackershole	150,000 gallons
Warnicombe	16,000 gallons

In his opinion, a supply derived from the Town Leat supplemented by the stream rising between Knackershole and Coombe, near Cove, would be sufficient to meet the town's demands. He estimated the cost of such a scheme would be £18,500, including two large reservoirs of 300,000 and 56,000 gallons[1]. The Council readily adopted the plans. Land was purchased at Knackershole and at Allers, both for very reasonable sums, and by September 1935 the Council had arranged the borrowing of £20,500 for the works[2].

Money was also required for other Council projects. Over £1,000 was raised to equip Rock Close in Saint Andrew Street as an Infant and Maternity Clinic, and two houses at the top of Saint Andrew Street were converted into the Council's Gas and Electric Department showrooms and offices[3]. A further £1,225 was needed to buy the field called Old Park, next to the recreation ground in Westexe, so that it could be turned into extra public walks and pleasure grounds[4]. In 1935, the Hospital Committee decided to continue with the planned major alterations and additions, which included the provision of maternity wards and the installation of central heating throughout the building. Nevertheless, the funding was by no means assured. The deficit at the beginning of the year was almost £10,000, despite a gift of £1,000 from Arthur Chamberlain, President of the Committee. Fund-raising activities were plentiful and the Carnival, as always, boosted the funds. The full amount needed, and more besides, came at the end of the year by way of an unexpected legacy from a former Tivertonian, Isabella Hallett of Knightshayes, Hendon, who left about £20,000 to the Hospital[5].

Tiverton celebrated King George's Silver Jubilee in May 1935 with a mass tea in the Market and a commemorative mug for every child. There was a giant bonfire on Exeter Hill and many of those in receipt of Public Assistance were given a bonus. The King did not see out his Jubilee year, dying of bronchitis in January 1936. The outpouring of public grief, so widely covered by the press and radio, was partly due to the suddenness of his passing and, it has been said[6], that the nation was not only mourning its King, but also its past. In Tiverton over 1,000 people marched in procession to Saint Peter's for a memorial service. Edward, the Prince of Wales, was proclaimed King in

---

[1] DRO R4/1/C16. [2] DRO R4/1/C95.

[3] DRO R4/1/T54.

[4] (DRO R4/1/C95). When finished in 1938 the grounds would have a paddling pool and an area of water for sailing model boats.

[5] *DSN* 13.12.1935. [6] Mowat 1955, 563

Tiverton on a particularly rainy day, in spite of which many men crowded around the Town Hall with their hats off.

Just a month after the Jubilee celebrations, Tiverton mourned one of its most prolific writers and historians. Frederick John Snell, died on May 25th 1935, in his 73rd year. He had been educated at Blundell's, from where he obtained a scholarship to Balliol College. His writings encompassed a range of subjects, and his books include *The Autobiography of a Poacher* and *A Book of Exmoor*, but, most importantly for Tiverton, the *Chronicles of Twyford* and *Palmerston's Borough*. A passion for his native town and county permeates all his work, and his attainments had been acknowledged in 1932 when he was granted a pension in the Civil List[1]. His last years were spent in the old tollhouse known as North Devon Cottage, at the bottom of Long Drag. Less than a year later, Tiverton lost another of its scholarly historians. The Rev. Edwin Spencer Chalk, once curate of Saint Peter's Church, died in August 1936 and was buried at Kentisbeare where he had been Rector[2]. He had written many articles and books, and contributed his edited notes on the Harrowby Manuscripts to the *Notes and Queries*. *The History of Saint Peter's Church* published in 1905, remains his greatest work, and is still indispensable to modern students.

---

[1] *DSN* 14.7.1932.   [2] *Obituary* 1936, 25-7.

19 World War II and its Aftermath

On December 5th 1936, Tiverton's fearful old enemy returned when fire destroyed the Lace Factory. Despite the efforts of the town's fire brigade, reinforced by crews from Exeter, Taunton, South Molton, Crediton, and Cullompton[1], the blaze in the five-storey main building was so ferocious that whole floors collapsed under the weight of heavy machinery. Firemen could do nothing to save much of the building, but they did prevent the inferno from spreading. A smouldering shell was all that was left of the factory John Heathcoat had bought when he came to Tiverton 120 years earlier. The damage amounted to over £100,000[2]. While many people despaired for the future of the business, almost immediately a new building was being planned. Fortunately, the silk-piece goods section was largely unaffected, and elsewhere much of the damaged machinery was salvaged. Production was maintained whilst replacement winding-frames were brought from the north of England. Within months what had threatened catastrophe had been overcome by the response of management and workforce; indeed, the future seemed assured. Little over twelve months after the fire, in January 1938, Lady Joyce Amory laid the foundation stone for the new Factory building. It was in use by July.

1937 was a year of celebration nationally and locally. In May, Tiverton, along with the rest of the country, acclaimed the Coronation of King George VI, who had come to the throne only because of the abdication of his brother, Edward. Tiverton Foxhounds and Staghounds' annual spring point-to-point meeting at Pileywell Farm was a resounding success, attracting over 2,000 spectators. Festivities continued with July's memorable Agricultural Show. On this occasion, many favourable comments were made about the progress of Young Farmers' Clubs, especially pleasing for H.F. Shapland of Prescott, then secretary of the Devon Federation[3]. The floats in the Autumn Carnival saw the humorous side of some very serious issues. One poked fun at Hitler and Mussolini and another depicted the situation of the town's water supply[4].

Meanwhile, the process of building a public abattoir had begun at Horsdon. The Borough Council had invited tenders for its construction, and had purchased the surviving slaughterhouses in the town. Frank Cook's premises at Canal Hill, Percy

---

[1] DRO R4/1/C65.   [2] *ib.*

[3] the Young Farmers' Club founded at Withleigh in 1929 was the first in Devon.

[4] progress was, however, being made, for the site for the Allers reservoir was bought in the following year (DRO R4/1/T54).

Chave's in Broad Lane and Ernest Burt's at Horsdon, were all closed down[1]. In March 1938, however, the Council's future building plans were challenged. Controversy surrounded the proposed new senior school for the town. The suggestion to have classes with both sexes was heavily criticised, especially by the Heathcoat's Old Girls Association, but a far greater reaction greeted the announcement of the suggested location for the school. Wellbrook Field had been suggested, but this was also considered desirable for housing. At a Council meeting in July the school won the day by a single vote, with part of Cottey House Farm and a field at Cherry Gardens[2] being allocated for residential development. Housing, for once, took second place.

Row of old cottages at Little Silver – although considered by many to be slums not fit for habitation, they survived well into the 20th century.

The term 'slum clearance' was first applied to Tiverton's courts in 1933. They could no longer be seen in isolation; the very word 'slum' equated them with the worst housing to be found in places like London's East End, Manchester, or Glasgow. According to one Tiverton councillor the dwellings at Little Silver housed people 'who don't live there, they simply have horrible shelter'[3]. The results of a house occupancy

---

[1] DRO R4/1/C99.
[2] adjoining the Cowleymoor Railway Bridge
[3] *Western Times* 18.11.1938.

inspection carried out in April 1936 exposed the extent of overcrowding and the dire need for extra housing in the town:

266	houses were occupied by	1 person
6		1½ (a child counted as ½)
599		2
189		2½
407		3
87		3½
208		4
61		4½
97		5
30		5½
45		6
15		6½
13		7
2		7½
7		8
3		8½
2		9
1		9½
1		11½.

By this time the surrounding villages, such as Washfield, Uplowman and Bickleigh, were already described as 'old people's settlements' because their youngsters had moved into Tiverton[1]. The Borough Council were determined to ease the housing shortage, and at the end of 1936 had announced that new estates were to be built at Shillands and Watery Lane[2]. Some councillors in April 1938 even demanded that housing be given priority over the much-needed water scheme. Councillor Sir John Heathcoat Amory stated in more considered terms, however, that the greater part of the rates should be devoted to both the water and housing schemes but economy should be practised on smaller projects.

Anxieties over foreign affairs, as we all know, dominated the late 1930s. Nationalist parties had come to power in Germany and Italy, under the leadership of Hitler and Mussolini respectively. The greater threat was from Germany, which was believed to be rearming at a great speed. As early as 1936, Devon County Council wrote to the Tiverton Borough Council imploring them to form an air-raid committee[3]. What must have seemed a comical adventure for Tiverton's schoolchildren, but a terrifying development for their parents, took place in October 1938, when the youngsters were

---

[1] *Western Times* 15.10.1937.   [2] DRO R4/1/C57.

[3] they further suggested the Committee ought to be divided into three sections, dealing with anti-gas, transport and decontamination (DRO R4/1/C16).

fitted with gas masks[1]. This followed directions from a Government, which, despite Chamberlain's appeasement of Hitler in the previous month, was taking no chances. Tiverton's Baptist Church announced at the beginning of 1939 that 'it will doubtless be a year of political unrest, unless the totalitarian states are moved by the spirit of God'[2]. Tiverton was allocated 158 Air Raid Wardens, who practised throughout the spring often alongside the regular police, the special constables and even Boy Scouts. Mass evacuation from cities and towns most at risk was planned, and the Rural District Council was informed in April that as many as 5,400 children could be sent to their area[3].

Regardless of the threat of war, Tiverton Borough Council defiantly announced an ambitious five-year programme in April 1939. The projects, estimated to cost over £190,000, included the public slaughter-house, a new market, refuse destructor, new council depot, the erection of 262 houses (mostly in Westexe South), the extension of the electricity mains to Lurley, and a new senior school which alone would cost over £40,000[4]. Two months later they celebrated the fulfilment of what was, up to that date, their most ambitious scheme. The new pumping station and filter at Allers was opened. With a reservoir capable of holding half a million gallons of water, Tiverton's water supply seemed for once assured.

Hitler pursued his demands for territorial expansion, acquiring Czechoslovakia and threatening Poland. The notorious Russo-German pact in August made war virtually inevitable, and Germany's invasion of Poland forced Britain and France to declare war on September 3rd. That very day an air-raid warning was heard, a false alarm but not unexpected. Mass evacuation of children had already begun. Air Raid Wardens patrolled the towns and cities, and total blackout was introduced. There were to be no street-lamps; heavy black curtains covered every window; vehicle headlights were shielded, and any visible light generally resulted in a court appearance. The importance of morale was constantly emphasised by government propaganda and, not least, by Heathcoat's Factory. They announced that the families of those employees who had enlisted would have their rent and rates paid for them[5], and in 1940 Sir John Heathcoat Amory endowed a Heathcoat Trust Fund with the considerable sum of £100,000[6]. At the outset Tiverton's Hospital was emptied to make way for possible air-raid victims,

---

[1] (DRO 752C/EFL5). The fear of air raids was clear to all who watched the newsreels of the Spanish Civil War or even H.G. Wells' *The Shape of Things To Come*.
[2] DRO 2514 D add3/233.
[3] by June it was announced that up to 200,000 evacuees were to be sent to Devon and Cornwall. Halberton, at least, had foreseen such plans in January, for they conducted an accommodation census just in case of mass evacuation (*Western Times* 27.1.1939).
[4] DRO R4/1/C16.   [5] *Western Times* 3.11.1939.
[6] *DSN* 15.8.1940.

and makeshift mortuaries were designated[1]. The public, however, was often shielded from potentially depressing information, especially the scale of expected casualties. At one stage, the Tiverton Burial Board were requested to provide 200 grave spaces for members of the Forces and to be ready to accommodate a further 2,000 military casualties 'arising in consequence of war operations in the vicinity', as well as spaces for 1,000 civilians[2]. Such information must have been a heavy burden on those few who were aware of these plans.

On the other hand, it was an exciting time for Tiverton's children who, as early as the first week of the conflict were joined by more than 140 evacuees. They were all ordered 'to leave white paint and sand bags alone', and 'to carry their gas masks to and from school, to take cover quickly should the siren give warning'[3]. Initially, the provision of shelters was utterly inadequate, as shown by the Heathcoat Boys School records[4]. In the event of an air-raid the children in Standard I were to proceed to a shelter near 'the church' (presumably, Saint Paul's), whereas Standards II and III were to remain in the school. Of this last group, the boys living in Westexe could go home, but the rest were to walk to Seven Crosses if the weather was fine, otherwise they were to scatter throughout the school. As for the Girls and the Infants Schools by the Factory, they would get some shelter in trenches dug on the Ham.

Troops were stationed in the town almost from the beginning; the first were men of the Durham Light Infantry along with the 5th Battalion of the Somerset Light Infantry. The Chilcott School was commandeered for use as a store[5], and troops were given accommodation at the old Liberal Club premises in Bampton Street[6]. The Park Parachute Company took over part of the Lace Factory[7], and camouflage nets were later produced at Exeleigh House[8]. Tivertonians willingly participated in the many schemes drawn up to help the war effort. Thirty acres of the golf course were given over to cultivation as part of the Dig for Victory campaign[9], and, later, a field in Broad Lane[10] and the level part of the Old Park were tilled. People were asked to contribute scrap iron and other metals which were to be melted down and reused. The Borough Council set an example by getting rid of the remnants of the First World War still scattered over the town. As well as the tank on Lowman Green, there was a cannon in the People's Park and two howitzers at Blundell's School. All were sold for scrap to the local dealer,

---

[1] at Mark Howe's motor showroom in Bampton Street, Chave's old slaughterhouse in Broad Lane, a room in the Methodist church in Saint Peter Street, one of the Cemetery chapels, the Fives Court at Blundell's, and the Club House at the Golf Course (*DSN* 13.6.1940).
[2] DRO R4/1/Z50.   [3] DRO 3029C/EAL3.
[4] *ib.*   [5] DRO 4401C/ESM1.
[6] *Western Times* 24.11.1939.   [7] *TG* 5.9.1989.
[8] beginning in the autumn term of 1941 a teacher from the Heathcoat School with 20 girls spent three afternoons a week there helping in the process (DRO 2745C/EFL4).
[9] cited in *Western Times* 7.6.1946.
[10] part of the site earmarked for the proposed new Senior School.

E.B. Janes. Food rationing was introduced in the first week of January 1940, and by March, after a bitterly cold winter, Tiverton was experiencing a severe shortage of coal. Nevertheless, there was little complaint. Indeed, the dangers of dissent and careless talk were remembered; there was always the chance that the enemy was listening. Suspicions were aroused by the presence of two Austrians and a German who lived near Tiverton's waterworks, giving rise to fears that they might contaminate the water supply with arsenic[1].

In the first months of the War, despite dreadful expectations, the skies did not see the assault that was expected. Apart from bombing raids in September 1939, Britain had not come under serious attack. On the other hand, German U-boats had inflicted considerable damage on Allied shipping in the Atlantic and North Sea. The sinking of the *Admiral Graf Spee* in the Battle of the River Plate in December was a cause for national pride. One of the crew of *HMS Exeter*, which took part in this action, was a Tiverton man Leslie Frost. On his return in the following April, the Borough Council made a presentation to him[2]. But the situation on land changed dramatically during the spring of 1940; German troops overran Norway and Denmark in April; Belgium and the Netherlands succumbed shortly after and France was invaded in May. The so-called 'phoney war', a period of relative stagnation was well and truly ended. On the eve of the Battle of France, Chamberlain gave way to Winston Churchill and a coalition War Cabinet. Churchill promised 'blood, sweat, toil and tears' in pursuit of victory. Within three weeks, the Allied forces were driven back to the Channel coast and, by a miracle of logistics, were evacuated, mostly from Dunkirk. The Germans then launched intensive air raids on the Channel ports and the whole of southern England in July 1940 – the Battle of Britain had begun, and the prospect of invasion was all too real.

Local Defence Volunteer forces had been formed in May 1940, soon becoming better known as the Home Guard. Although nowadays they are often mocked, their role was of immense value. A force of over 700 men came forward in the local area and was organised into seven platoons and a task force. Tiverton itself was too small to be targeted from the air, but was not immune to stray hits. On the night of July 31st six bombs hit Belmont Road, destroying the front of a house in Ivy Terrace and causing lesser damage elsewhere in the street. Another bomb was jettisoned in the Exe Valley near Bolham, and, possibly during the same raid, others were dropped in the fields near North Sidborough Farm[3]. These incidents, and the fear of further bombs prompted an urgent response. Fire watching, made compulsory under Government orders, was bolstered by the appointment of a local Fire Guard staff officer. More reassuring to the people of Tiverton, however, was the Council's decision to build substantial air-raid

---

[1] *DSN* 6.6.1940.   [2] DRO R4/1/C16.
[3] where the craters are still visible.

shelters. They were located at Lowman Green, the Bampton Street entrance to the Market, in Saint Paul's Square, in Phoenix Lane, in the yard of the White Ball, and in Chapel Street[1]; each was capable of accommodating about 250 people. The cellars under the Town Hall were to be available during daytime raids.

Extensive bomb damage caused to a house in Ivy Terrace, Belmont Road, on the night of July 31st 1940.

Mass bombing raids of southern England increased evacuation now that fearful anticipation had become reality. By the end of 1940, Tiverton had received over 1,100 children, mainly from the London area, and in the night raids of 1941 the Borough Council was informed that a further 500 would be coming from Bristol[2], and 1,000 from Plymouth. Crowds often welcomed larger groups on their arrival at the Station, where they were registered. People lined the streets as children were escorted to the Market for a medical inspection. From there they were either dispersed around the town or loaded on to buses bound for the surrounding parishes. By February 1942, it was calculated that Tiverton had taken over 2,600 evacuees[3]. In May and June 1942,

---

[1] DRO R4/1/C16.   [2] DRO R4/1/add C1.
[3] (*DSN* 6.6.1940). Not all stayed for long, however. A couple of Bristol children made their parents travel to Tiverton and take them home, after a local shopkeeper had told them the town was always being bombed (*DSN* 27.2.1941).

air raids on Exeter brought nearly 350 people up the valley to safety, and following damage to the city's slaughterhouse 1,400 animals were sent to the Horsdon abattoir[1]. The sheer numbers of evacuees often put a severe strain on Tiverton's resources. Occasionally there was not enough time to organise a family to take the children and so emergency accommodation was used. The Elmore Mission Room, the Gospel Hall, and the Congregational Church schoolroom often performed this function. Communal feeding stations were also set up, first at the Masonic Lodge in Castle Street, later supplemented by one at the Heathcoat Hall[2]. A much-needed hospital for children was established just outside the town at Ashley Court. Schools, especially, were put under great pressure. The Heathcoat Schools alone admitted an extra 355 children during this time[3], and the peaceful village school at Chevithorne received over 140[4]. One further hardship brought by the children, especially during the winter months, was the washing and drying of all their extra clothing. Help arrived in March 1942 in the form of a mobile laundry for the use of all those households with evacuees. Life must have been so different for these youngsters who, as one clergyman remarked, 'bring their gifts of quick life to us'[5]. Overall, Tiverton coped well with the influx.

Day-to-day living was complicated by rationing[6]. Basic allowances varied as the Ministry of Food decreed. On average, a typical weekly allowance for one person was:

bacon or ham	4oz
meat	1s 2d worth
butter	2oz
cheese	2oz
margarine and cooking fat	4oz
milk	2 or 3 pints
sugar	8oz
whole egg	one
(powdered egg was available from the summer of 1942)	
tea	2oz
sweets for each child	3oz

As can be imagined, a cook's greatest asset was often resourcefulness. Nevertheless, everyone became resigned to this hardship, firmly convinced that the sacrifice was necessary, as indeed it was.

---

[1] DRO R4/1 addC/1.   [2] ib.
[3] DRO 2745C/EFA18.   [4] DRO 752C/EFA1.
[5] (DRO 2514 D add3/236). These gifts, according to some, included scarlet fever and scabies (DRO R4/1/add C5).
[6] beginning in January 1940, with bacon, ham, sugar, and butter, the restrictions were to include meat three months later, then tea, margarine, cooking fat, and cheese in July. In the following year jam, marmalade, treacle and syrup were put on ration in March, eggs were controlled from June, and milk from November. Much to the annoyance of children, sweets were added to the list in July 1942. Additionally, clothing was rationed from June 1941 and soap from January 1942.

The National Savings Scheme, begun during the 1914-18 War, was used to great effect at this time. Several families actually became richer during the War: often both parents were working, wages rose, and, because of rationing and the unavailability of many goods, the opportunity to spend was limited. Many people saved their money and willingly gave large amounts to the various national campaigns for the war effort. Tiverton excelled in these schemes. For War Weapons Week in February 1941, the Borough and Rural District Councils set a target of £100,000, but collected a staggering £351,533[1]. During the summer each firm, shop, and school in the town set out to raise money to provide specific military equipment. Bampton Street School was to contribute enough for two Tommy guns, Elmore School 40 small bombs, Hamlin's Corn Mills two soldiers' uniforms, Thorne Brothers an anti-tank rifle, the Council's Gas and Electricity Departments 3,000 rounds of ammunition, Stenners one parachute, and so the list went on[2]. An astounding landmark was achieved in December when it was announced that War Savings in the Borough and Rural District Councils had passed the £1,000,000 mark. In the following year, after raising over £320,000 for Warship Week, their efforts were recognised by the Lords Commissioners of the Admiralty who presented plaques to both Councils; the Rural District Council adopted *Motor Torpedo Boat 60* and the Borough Council the corvette, *HMS Bluebell*[3].

The few deaths in Tiverton which can be directly blamed on the conflict did not result from enemy action but from traffic accidents involving military vehicles. At the end of 1940, an army lorry mounted the pavement at the top of Angel Hill and clipped two prams. The baby in one was thrown out, but miraculously was uninjured. The other pram, containing the only child of a couple who lived in Rackenford Road, was dragged along the street and the infant killed[4]. Two similar incidents occurred in April 1941, both involving army lorries, resulting in the deaths of a 52-year old local woman and a five-year old evacuee from Bristol.

In the last week of December 1941, Alfred Thomas Gregory died[5]. As Mayor, he had steered Tiverton through the Great War, just as John Lewis was doing through the current conflict. Gregory had been a Governor of Blundell's School, the editor of the *Tiverton Gazette* and an author of some note. His best-known publication is *Recollections of a Country Editor*, a detailed account of life and events in Tiverton from the 1870s to the 1930s. He also wrote a biography of Robert Raikes, the founder of the Sunday School movement. Gregory himself had been active as a teacher and preacher

---

[1] *DSN* 27.2.1941.   [2] *DSN* 24.7.1941.
[3] built in 1940, the *Bluebell* had been engaged in hunting U-boats in the North Atlantic.
[4] *DSN* 23.1.1941.   [5] *Obituary* 1942, 30-1.

in the Wesleyan Methodist Connexion until 1926, and in his will he left £500 to pay the superintendent minister of the Tiverton circuit[1]. Another death earlier in the year had brought an unexpectedly large bequest to Saint Peter's Church. James Luther Greenway, the owner of a great iron works at Ludlow in Shropshire, left in all more than half a million pounds. He claimed descent from Tiverton's John Greneway, and, because of this, bequeathed £1,500 to the Rector and Churchwardens of Saint Peter's for the maintenance of the Greenway Chapel, as well as £4,000 to the Greenway Charity[2].

In the dark days of 1942 the Government had the vision to plan for peace. The Beveridge Report, published in December 1942, promised full employment and 'freedom from want by securing to each [person] a minimum income sufficient for subsistence'. The future Welfare State would care for the citizen from the cradle to the grave. Just over a year later, the Butler Education Act (1944) was to provide secondary education for all, with no school fees to be charged in any local authority establishment. To implement this the stages of education were redefined. 'Primary' meant children from two years to 11 or 12, and would be compulsory from five years of age. Secondary Education was to be compulsory to 15 years, and included youngsters from 11 or 12 to 18 or 19. Beyond was Further Education to cover the vast range of activities for older pupils, including university, technical and art instruction, and studies for adults. To fulfil the objective of the Act which stated that secondary education was to be delivered according to 'age, ability, and aptitude', it was necessary to provide three types of school with separate curricula – Grammar, Technical and Modern. Hence the principle of selection by '11-plus' tests was extended.

Like the Government, the Borough Council tried to conduct 'business as usual', although heavily burdened with war-related duties. In November 1942, it was finally agreed that the town's Police Force should be merged into the County Constabulary. The conditions were to be mutually beneficial; Tiverton would become the headquarters of the County's 'C' division[3], and the officers' future would be assured, with Chief Constable Beynon appointed Superintendent of the Division. All the arrangements were implemented in the following January. One of the Borough Council's more pleasurable decisions was also made in this month. They agreed to confer the Freedom of the Borough on one of Tiverton's most distinguished residents, Miss Katherine Maud Lazenby of Eastfield. She was to be the first, and only woman to receive the honour. The list of her achievements, especially in the sphere of education, is impressive. She had been Justice of the Peace for the county, Governor of Tiverton Middle Schools and the Science, Art and Technical School for 33 years, a member from

---

[1] *DSN* 1.4.1942. [2] TivLib Cuttings Book 3.
[3] after a temporary period as a separate 'T' Division.

1898 (and chairman from 1924) of the Tiverton School Board, from 1903 a member of the Tiverton Borough Education Committee, of which she was chairman 1925-35, as well as chairman of its Medical Sub-Committee[1].

A fter Pearl Harbour (December 7th 1941) the whole world was at war. At first, the Allies were everywhere in retreat against the Axis powers, but slowly the tide turned - in North Africa, at Stalingrad, and in 1943 with the invasion of Sicily and the Italian mainland. Plans for a Second Front, a massive assault on northern France, were at last becoming realisable, and Tiverton began to feel the effects of a growing American presence. To begin with, the U.S. Navy established a small store at Collipriest[2], with many of the men housed at Howden. For ease of communication (and, probably, to keep the troops out of the town as much as possible), a temporary bridge was put up across the Exe between the two camps[3]. Collipriest became the headquarters of the U.S. 4th Infantry Division; the Divisional Signals and Cavalry Reconnaissance troops were encamped there[4], and were visited, we are led to believe, by General Patton and General Eisenhower, the Supreme Commander. One of the men staying in Tiverton, working for an Intelligence Unit, was J.D. Salenger, who became the world-famous author of *Catcher in the Rye*. Later in 1943 a unit, numbering over 150 men, from the U.S. 80th Chemical Smoke Generating Company was stationed at Halberton[5].

The presence of American troops sparked a wide range of emotions, actions, and reactions. The town was alive with their strange accents and 'high living'. Dances were popular[6], and the Tivoli and Electric Theatre cinemas were much in demand. Indeed, the avid American appetite for 'movies' and abundant female company persuaded the Borough Council early in 1944 to agree to open the town's cinemas on Sundays[7]. Tragically, traffic accidents involving military vehicles continued. In late 1943, Ellen Perry, a 54-year old woman of Rix Cottages, was knocked down and killed by an American lorry driven by a black Texan named Paris Spriggs. He was subsequently court-martialled for manslaughter. Shortly before the Normandy landings most

---

[1] DRO R4/1 add/C1.
[2] their largest naval store in Britain had been established not far away on the Exeter city golf course (Wasley 1994, 124).
[3] DRO R4/1 add/C5.   [4] Wasley 1994, 145.
[5] their role of laying down smoke-screens was to have great importance when the invasion of France began in June 1944.
[6] Tiverton, during the War, was treated to the music of such bands as those of the Royal Artillery, the Royal Ordnance Corps, the Czech Air Force and the RAF Silver Wings Band (Wasley 1994, 93) as well as many American acts. Saint Paul's Church and Blundell's School both served as venues for concerts by the London Symphony Orchestra.
[7] but admission was to be confined to men and women from the services accompanied by one friend only (DRO R4/1 add/C10).

Americans had left Tiverton, but enough remained to be noticed. The Council's Public Health Committee remarked that in the Athletic Field they had thrown oil into a ditch, which subsequently flowed into the River Lowman, and in September 1944 the Highways Committee reported that their trucks had caused damage in the Market[1]. In the same month, the American forces presented a plaque to the Borough of Tiverton in recognition of the kindness shown to them during their stay.

Yet another accident resulted in death in November 1944. An American jeep hit and killed an Italian prisoner-of-war on the Uffculme road, and injured a local woman and her daughter. Although the American authorities assisted an enquiry into the death, the jeep in question was never identified[2]. There was apparently not too much concern raised about the death of the Italian. In the previous year, a prisoner-of-war camp had been established just outside Tiverton, on the Old Race Course[3], where the first inmates were Italians. At first, security seems to have been lax. The *Western Times* reported in October 1944 that the POWs, who were allowed 'to exercise within defined limits' in the town, had been abusing this privilege and were distributing 'crude pamphlets bearing Fascist slogans'[4].

Allied troops landed on the Normandy beaches on June 6th 1944, D-Day, and the Germans were slowly driven back. Paris was liberated in August, and by October the invasion of Germany itself was imminent. It seemed, too optimistically as it proved, that the end was in sight, and there was a general scaling-down of military controls in Britain. This led in November 1944 to the Military Authorities transferring 1-2 The Larches, the Elms in Station Road and Elm Cottage on the Rackenford Road to the Ministry of Heath to house evacuees[5]. The Germans, however, launched the Ardennes Offensive in December, but its failure did mean that victory was finally in sight[6]. The end of the war in Europe - VE Day - was celebrated on May 8th 1945. The lights had come on a month or two earlier, and plans were hastily made to hold events all over

---

[1] DRO R4/1 add/C6.   [2] *Western Times* 17.11.1944.

[3] the site now occupied by the High School and East Devon College.

[4] (*Western Times* 24.11.1944). We do not know the category of man detained in the camp, but the newspaper suggested that they had been taken from other camps 'because of their subversive tendencies'.

[5] the Evacuation Committee said they did not really need them, however, and suggested they should revert to private use (DRO R4/1 add/C6).

[6] but not before tragedy befell *HMS Bluebell*, Tiverton's adopted ship. The Borough Council was informed in February 1945 that she had been torpedoed in the Barents Sea, near Murmansk; sinking in 30 seconds with 90 of the crew, and leaving only 12 survivors (Tiverton Town Clerk's Office).

Tiverton. Schools closed at 4 p.m. on the day before the festivities, and stayed shut for two days[1]. Everyone, it seems, turned out to sing, dance, and feast the day away. Pianos were brought outside to accompany the singing, and parties were held in almost every street and court. Three months later, after Hiroshima and Nagasaki, the Japanese capitulated. The war was over at last.

Throughout the conflict there had been reports of troops missing or taken prisoner, and sometimes there were happy conclusions. Chief Petty Officer Pellow of Angel Hill was on board the destroyer *HMS Jackal* when it was sunk in the Mediterranean, but everyone's worst fears were allayed when news came that he was safe in a hospital in Alexandria[2]. Similarly, after the fall of Singapore in January 1942 nothing was heard of R.H.V. Reed of Tiverton until reports 22 months later stated that he was alive and well, but held by the Japanese. The others, like these two men, who had survived the War, gradually returned home, but 78 Service personnel of Tiverton had made the ultimate sacrifice.

A General Election was called for July 1945, after Churchill's Coalition Government was brought to an end and all parties fought independently. Lieutenant-Colonel Derick Heathcoat Amory, who had been wounded at Arnhem in 1944, took on the Conservative mantle[3], and was joined in the contest by the Liberal C.H. Blackburn, another Lieutenant-Colonel, and the Labour candidate, G.C. Thompson, a man engaged in the London textile industry. As part of the Victory celebrations, the workers at Heathcoat's Factory had been promised two weeks annual holiday instead of the usual one, but the Labour and Liberal candidates considered this a ploy by Heathcoat Amory to win votes, so the workers had to be satisfied with a single week. Nevertheless, he won the election with a majority of more than 8,000 votes over the Labour candidate[4].

Nationally, the Labour Party swept to its first General Election victory with an overwhelming mandate to implement wide-ranging reforms. The Bank of England, coal, electricity, railways, roads, canals, docks and harbours were to be nationalised. The basic industries had been under Government direction during the War, so nationalisation had already taken place in practice if not in theory. Existing social services were dramatically extended in a National Insurance Scheme to provide benefits for unemployment, sickness, industrial injury, and old age. Emergency grants for pregnancy, maternity, widowhood, and burial were made available. Perhaps most

[1] DRO 3029C/EAL3.   [2] *DSN* 20.5.1942.
[3] after receiving a knighthood in the New Year's Honours List, Lieutenant-Colonel Gilbert Acland-Troyte did not stand for the Tiverton Division he had held since 1924.
[4] Craig 1969, 331.

acclaimed was Aneurin Bevan's National Health Service Act (1946), which promised medical care for everyone, regardless of their ability to pay[1]. As we have seen, the Education Act of 1944 had provided secondary education for all, but in Tiverton the existing schools required reorganisation before this could be implemented. Planning took a long time; the changes would not be practicable until the beginning of 1947. The Middle Schools in Barrington Street became the Tiverton Grammar School, taking those pupils who passed the 11-plus test, whereas the Heathcoat Boys' School in Westexe became the Heathcoat Secondary Modern School for Boys and Girls, taking in children from 11 years of age. The establishment of the Secondary Modern and Grammar Schools in Tiverton led to a large influx of pupils from the surrounding areas which had no such schools of their own. Children began to travel daily from the villages of Silverton, Thorverton, Halberton and Sampford Peverell[2].

John Lewis had been Mayor of Tiverton throughout the War and in 1945 he was re-elected for the seventh successive term, equalling Gregory's First World War record. Like him, he was also given the Freedom of the Borough for his unstinting work. After the rigours of the wartime years, he could now participate in duties that were far more pleasant. He welcomed the Lord Mayor and Mayoress of Plymouth, who visited Tiverton to thank the people who in 1941 had taken in 153 girls and staff from the Devonport High School[3]. Unknown to almost everyone, during the conflict the ancient charters and documents of the Borough of Poole had been stored in the strong-room of Tiverton's Town Hall. These were now returned to Dorset[4]. History was made in the local elections in the autumn of 1945, when the first woman was elected on to the Council. Two had stood, Mrs Alice Maud Gardiner in Castle Ward, who was defeated, and Mrs Winnie Rooks who won a seat for the Westexe ward. Two years later, Charles Bulgin Williams became the town's first Labour councillor, winning one of the Westexe places. Many a council meeting of this time seems to have been enlivened by the offerings of a radical Welshman, Councillor Dai Thomas, one of whose suggestions was to requisition Knightshayes and Collipriest for the use of homeless families[5].

Thomas' inflammatory proposal highlights the importance given to the town's housing problems. Even before the D-Day landings, Sir John Heathcoat Amory had urged the Council to begin building again, suggesting that possibly regulations should be relaxed once peace came. Early in 1945, the Westexe South site was purchased, and negotiations were under way to buy land at Cottey House Farm. Houses were being built on both sites in the following year. The contract to build 42 homes on the former had been won not by a large firm but by a consortium of four local companies – John

---

[1] although it did not come into effect until 1948. By 1950 95% of the population were enrolled with NHS doctors.
[2] DRO 3029C/EAL4.
[3] *Western Times* 16.3.1945.
[4] DRO R4/1 add C6.
[5] *Western Times* 14.12.1945.

Grater and Sons, Bamsey, Marshall and Company, F.R. Randoll, and F.J. Emmett[1]. Tiverton's first batch of prefabricated buildings, of a type known as Airoh houses[2], were unloaded at the Cottey House Farm site in September 1946. R.G. Carthew asked for permission in October to place two caravans in an orchard beside Park Hill. He had served in the Army for six years, and claimed this was the only type of accommodation he could get in the town. Although the Council acceded to his request, they were worried they may have set a dangerous precedent. The site, of course, did develop, and is now known as the Underhill Park.

Pre-fabricated temporary housing at Cotteylands was begun in September 1946.

Despite austerity, post-war Tiverton delighted in the renaissance of social activities. For the celebrations held in 1946 to commemorate the Victory anniversary there was an all-day cricket match, children's fancy dress parade, free cinema shows for the young, a boxing tournament, and the Tiverton Harriers' first athletic meeting for many years. Many ex-servicemen were keen to promote sport in Tiverton. One was Ken Holland. In 1948, as secretary of the Harriers, he approached the Council for permission to wear the Borough Seal design on members' vests and trunks[3]. Already a well-known rugby and water polo player, Ken had set up a record time of three hours

---

[1] DRO R4/1 add C6.
[2] made from aluminium salvaged from aircraft pieces, they were manufactured at the British Aircraft Corporation's works at Weston-super-Mare.
[3] DRO R4/1 add C7.

for canoeing from Exeter to Tiverton earlier in the year. He was given a great honour when chosen to carry the Olympic torch for part of its journey through Devon on its way to Torbay, where the Games' yachting events took place. New life also dawned on the town's social scene. The Operatic and Dramatic Society was reborn, and townspeople voted overwhelmingly in favour of Sunday opening for the cinemas[1]. They flocked to the summer's Swimming Gala, which included special events for the POWs still at the Bolham Road camp[2], and the much-loved autumn Carnival was revived. The Tiverton Agricultural Show was restarted after a seven-year break, even if rationing led to some restrictions - the dairy classes could not be held, and the control of feedstuffs meant that cattle and sheep entries were down. For the first time, bread rationing was introduced in July 1946, leading to the Tiverton Golf Club's decision to resow part of the course with corn. It has perhaps been generally forgotten that at this time Britain was in receipt of food aid from the Commonwealth, especially the West Indies and Australia[3], and tinned food occasionally arrived as gifts from the Canadian and American Red Cross.

Heathcoat's expanded into Cornwall in 1946. Initially, they used part of the old Council offices in Redruth, but later moved to Carn Brea, an unoccupied WAAF station near Portreath, where, it was hoped, more than 200 people would eventually be employed[4] making surgical stockings and knitted elastic fabrics. Meanwhile, at Tiverton a new weaving shed was being planned, and was in operation by the end of 1950, stocked with Swiss and American looms. The immediate post-War years saw the Company increase its exports, and on a few occasions local labour could not meet the demand. Derick Heathcoat Amory was involved in the United Europe Movement[5], and was no doubt influential in the firm's decision in November 1947 to give work to refugees. The company advertised for local people willing to provide board and lodgings for seven Polish-Ukrainian girls. Tiverton also became the home of a much larger group of refugees a little later, victims of the Cold War that for the next 40 years would divide Europe with an Iron Curtain between Western democracy and the Communist East. After the last of the German POWs left the Bolham Road Camp in December 1948[6], the site was used as an agricultural hostel run by the Devon Agricultural Executive Committee. The men accommodated there included a group of 74 Yugoslavs who had escaped from the Communist take-over in their homeland. They were immediately made welcome, and became a much-respected and integral

---

[1] although this had been conditionally granted to the troops during the War.
[2] *Western Times* 1.8.1947.   [3] DRO R4/1 add/C6.
[4] *Western Times* 28.8.1946.   [5] DRO 4302B/F36.
[6] although four stayed in Tiverton as they had married local women.

part of the town's population. In January 1949, they held an Orthodox Christmas celebration in Saint Peter's Church[1]. A wedding service conducted by a priest of the Orthodox Church took place there in the following May between one of their number to a Ukrainian girl working at the Factory.

Not all visitors to Tiverton were so well appreciated, however. A certain Gameel Seoud was suspended in April 1949 for two weeks from the Grammar School after hitting the woodwork master on the back of the head with a jack plane[2]. Some of the local children appear to have been no better behaved. In the previous month, as a change from the usual activities 300 Sunday School pupils went to the War Memorial Hall to watch a two-hour religious film. This did not turn out to be the enlightening experience envisaged by the clergy. The raising of Lazarus was met with howls of laughter, and the *Western Times* reported that the Vicar of Saint George's had referred to the children as 'little savages'[3]. School exchanges and visits to the Continent began again in this period. The Grammar School sent a party of 21 girls and six staff to Switzerland in April 1949, and received a West German girl and three Austrians in the Summer term. All of these visits seem to have passed without a hitch, until a group of scouts from Blundell's School travelled to West Germany in August. The 23 boys marched through the streets of Munich, once the centre of Nazi rallies, proudly sporting their school colours, red, black and white, and badges emblazoned with the letters NS, for National Service. Unfortunately, the same colours had been those of the Hitler Youth Movement when NS stood for the Nazionalisches Sozialismus Partei, the official title of the Nazi Party. The incident was reported in the press, where, it was said, not surprisingly their appearance caused German heads to turn. International relations were not severed, however, as we find ten young German girls working at the Heathcoat Factory a few months later.

Foreign links emphasised the export drive and the expansive optimism of the time. This is no better illustrated than the distribution of the Tiverton Chamber of Trade's publicity leaflet in 1948 when they boasted that 10,000 brochures had reached 32 countries 'and even penetrated the Iron Curtain'[4]. But on the home front, this same group was proposing drastic changes to the centre of Tiverton. They wanted a new market near the railway station; an idea first mooted twenty years before, and thought the original site would better serve the town as a car park. Such large-scale developments were made possible under the powers of compulsory purchase given to local authorities by the Town and Country Planning Act of 1947. This complex legislation, which established many of the planning procedures still in use today, sought to map out the future scene by means of development plans. With local

---

[1] with a lay reader reading most of the service, but the rector opened the proceedings and pronounced the blessing (*Western Times* 14.1.1949).
[2] DRO 4401C/ESM2.   [3] *Western Times* 18.3.1949.
[4] *Western Times* 17.3.1950.

councillors wielding such powers, outbursts of men like Councillor Dai Thomas seemed almost threatening. He agreed with the removal of the Market to the Horsdon area, but suggested the vacant space be sold to businesses and the proceeds used to provide an all-year swimming pool, a public hall to seat 1,250 people and a gymnasium. Any support for his golden vision was lost when he announced his suggested site for the pool and gymnasium: he envisaged pulling down Greenway's Almshouses to make room for them[1].

Building in the town was taking place at as rapid a rate as regulations permitted. The Heathcoat subsidiary, E.V. Twose Ltd, was putting up a new factory at the Lowman Works, and, nearer the centre of the town, the Old Brewery adjoining the District Hospital was being converted for use as an ante-natal clinic. Yet the greatest expansion was Council housing. As well as conventional houses, the Cowleymoor estate was provided with state-of-the-art Hawkesley aluminium bungalows and Cornish Unit homes[2]. A significant milestone was reached in July 1951, when the 500th Council house, 100 The Walronds, was opened. Possibly, to coincide with this event, the whole estate underwent a beautification, with flowers, shrubs, and trees being planted. As the southern gateway to Tiverton this estate has always been of particular visual importance.

Once travellers from the direction of Exeter had passed The Walronds, however, they entered the narrow bottleneck that was Westexe South. A one-way system had been introduced; town-bound vehicles entered by way of Broad Lane and Brewin Road, and traffic going to Exeter passed from Bridge Street to Westexe Halt. In addition, it was proposed that the houses of Pinkstone's Court be demolished to make room for a car park. These alterations were seen as only temporary, as the Council knew they would have to take drastic action sometime in the future. One idea put forward would solve not just the Westexe traffic problem but also the poor state of the Canal, at this time no more than a stretch of stagnant water. The proposal was radical: to purchase the 'town' part of the Canal, fill it, then surface it so that it could form part of a south-eastern bypass for the town. This thoroughfare would lead from the Halberton Road, across Tumbling Fields, to the Walronds[3]. The growth of the Cowleymoor estate was also creating serious traffic problems, especially in Chapel Street which was, and still is, extremely narrow. To remedy this, it was suggested (even then) that a new road be built to connect the estate with Blundell's Road. Was it wise to build in Westexe South and, to a lesser extent, at Cowleymoor as both areas had always been prone to flooding? Heavy rains at the end of October 1949 exposed the threat. The Athletic Field, Sawmills and Gas Works were flooded; a foot of water covered the Exe Valley railway line, and the bottom of Saint Andrew Street was under

---

[1] DRO R4/1 add C1.   [2] pre-fabricated concrete houses.
[3] *Western Times* 30.3.1951.

five foot of water. This deluge temporarily delayed work on the Blundell's Road car park, which eventually opened just weeks before further flooding occurred. Building work at Cowleymoor was halted for a while in January 1950 because of yet more floods, and again a month later. Something clearly had to be done. It was thought that widening the stream from Higher Moor Farm into the Lowman[1], as well as clearing the bed of the Lowman itself would solve the problem.

Although austerity continued, the Festival of Britain in 1951 was a celebration of the country's achievements and aspirations. The main exhibition in London took place in the area between Westminster and Waterloo Bridges, once devastated by air-raids. Just when it appeared that those dark days of the War could be forgotten, George VI died suddenly on February 6th 1952. A man never destined to be King had applied all his effort to a demanding task. He fostered a great sense of solidarity with his people, epitomised by his refusal to leave Buckingham Palace even during the height of the Blitz. At a time of such optimism, his loss seemed so much greater.

---

[1] DRO R4/1/ addC7.

20 Expansion and Local Planning

O n February 6th 1952, Tiverton's beadle, Charles Baker, exclaimed 'God Save the Queen!' to a large crowd assembled outside the Town Hall. The Mayor, Hedley Carpenter, then proclaimed the accession of Elizabeth, the 25-year old daughter of the late King. Although George VI's loss had deeply saddened the nation, the weather dealt the cruellest blow to Devon and Somerset in this year. Continuous and torrential rain on August 15th led to disastrous flooding in the northern parts of both counties. Worst affected of all was the Lynmouth area, where swollen rivers sent huge boulders cascading down the narrow valleys. Such was the scale of devastation that much of the town was destroyed and the final death toll reached 34. At Tiverton, no lives were lost, but there was considerable flood damage. The Lace Factory was inundated, as were many houses in Westexe South and the Borough's largest estate, the Walronds, which had undergone extensive landscaping only in the previous year. While the nation's attention was rightly drawn to Lynmouth it was pointed out at a Devon County Council meeting that many of Tiverton's poorest inhabitants had also been affected and should not be forgotten[1].

Once the immediate effects of this disaster were behind them, Tivertonians began to consider the prospect of a 'new Elizabethan Age' in 1953. Festivities for the Coronation were planned in detail. The Borough Council levied a 1d rate to pay for the celebrations, and 2,700 souvenir mugs were purchased for the town's children. The Council also decided to name the perimeter road of the growing Cowleymoor estate 'Queensway' in honour of the succession. The Fire Brigade cleaned the Lowman Green clock tower, and a huge bonfire 25-foot high was built at Seven Crosses. When Coronation Day, June 2nd, came, Tiverton was a blaze of red, white and blue. Almost every entrance, street, and court was festooned with bunting and decorations; banners were hung across the roads, and triumphal arches spanned paths and streets. Though the Coronation ceremony in Westminster Abbey was the first major event to be broadcast on television, at this time few owned a set. Anyway, most people preferred to celebrate together in the open air. The town's official events focused on a mammoth parade, which wound its way through the streets. All of the official organisations and bodies were represented, including the British Legion, the Royal Air Force Association., the Red Cross, Twyford Lodge of the RAOB, the Sea Cadets, Police, Town Band, as well as over 1,000 schoolchildren. The crowds that lined the route cheered them all,

---

[1] some help for the area came from unexpected sources. The 'sympathetic Jamaican people' sent gifts of sugar to many places ravaged by the floods, including Tiverton (*DSN* 10.9.1952). It must be remembered that sweets and sugar were subject to rationing until the following year

and afterwards most people returned to their own streets and courts where they held parties that continued well into the night.

The new reign, it was hoped, would usher in a time of optimism after the bitterness of the previous decade. The youthful Queen, herself a mother with children, was seen to embody this hope for a brighter future in which young people would play a vital role. This was certainly happening in Tiverton, where the voters had elected the Borough's youngest councillor, Brian Homer. In July 1953, he shared the stage at the Tiverton Labour Party's first ever gala at the Athletic Field, where the guest speaker was Harold Wilson, later Prime Minister. These were exciting times for Tiverton's schoolchildren. When the new term began in September, 120 five to seven-year olds from the growing estate at Cowleymoor moved into their new school, and in the following year Saint John's Roman Catholic School was opened on its Melbourne Street site[1]. At last, the Borough Council began to clear some of its substandard housing. In October 1954 12 cottages at Little Silver were demolished[2], although, ironically, these were not part of the planned programme - the 40 or more houses contained on the first two lists compiled for the slum clearance plan in 1933 were still standing. For most of those fortunate enough to escape the condemned buildings, home was to be made in a new house on one of the Council estates. The sites at Cotteylands and Cowleymoor were growing fast, as was Wilcombe, where no fewer than 540 Council houses were planned. Despite the rapid rate of building, it was estimated that at least seven years were needed to clear the waiting list for these houses.

According to the local press, one problem of the new estates was that many of the inhabitants failed 'to attach themselves to any organised religion'. To remedy this situation, at least for the children of Wilcombe and Cowleymoor, the Tiverton Council of Christian Congregations set up in 1954 an experimental bus service to convey them to various Sunday Schools[3]. A more permanent solution would be for this part of Tiverton to have a church of its own, and plans for such a building were announced as early as May 1954. The new church was to be part of a proposed reorganisation of the Tiverton parishes by which Chevithorne would be detached from Saint Peter's[4], Elmore Mission Church and the Nonconformist Chapel in the Cemetery would both be knocked down, and their sites, along with that of Saint Peter's Church House in Castle

---

[1] *DSN* 13.10.1954.
[2] (DRO R4/1 add C2). Three similarly awful cottages had been knocked down six years earlier
[3] *Shapland Scrapbooks*.
[4] so that it could be held in plurality with Cove.

Street, would be sold. Radical as these suggestions were, they were nothing compared with the almost incredible proposal to demolish Saint George's[1]. The threat of removing this unique building generated outrage locally and attracted considerable attention from further afield. The Georgian Group, a national society, supported the preservation of the church, as did Lewis Horrox of the University College of the Southwest at Exeter, whose protest appeared in the *Sunday Times*[2]. Most notable of the critics was the poet John Betjeman who wrote an article, 'City and Suburban', which appeared in the *Spectator*[3]. Before it was published, however, the Bishop of Exeter emphatically stated that he did not intend to authorise the demolition. Was this a resounding victory for public pressure, or had the plan to destroy Saint George's never really existed?[4]

Labour disputes on opposite sides of the world affected Tiverton trade during 1955. John Heathcoat and Company had constructed a new factory on a nine-acre site on the outskirts of Melbourne[5], which was to be stocked by goods sent by sea. When the ship reached Australia, however, a dock strike prevented its unloading, and it was forced to return to Britain. A widespread rail strike in June 1955 temporarily increased road traffic through Tiverton. Many local lorries were commandeered to convey meat from Tiverton Junction to the London markets, and Heathcoat's Factory was forced to cancel all Saturday working because materials could not be delivered.

Some of the town's growing traffic problems were about to be eased. The daily congestion of vehicles in Westexe South was resolved by removing all the buildings on the west side to make a 30 foot-wide road with ten-foot pavements. In all, 57 properties had to be purchased; this was achieved by April 1957[6]. A similar remedy proposed for William Street in 1956 would involve the demolition of the cottages on the south side of the street. The problems of traffic flow in this part of the town were inextricably linked with the central market area. We should remember that the only access to the Market was from Bampton Street, which had to serve both the stock and pannier markets. Even at this time, cattle were being driven through the streets. What should be done with the Market area, was a question asked then, and still not quite answered now. The town's Chamber of Trade suggested a central car park should be provided there[7], and another idea was to build a new entrance from Newport Street, which would at least enable traffic to circulate.

---

[1] *DSN* 2.3.1955.   [2] TivLib folio 7/60.

[3] TivLib folio 7/56f.

[4] the interest generated by this incident was put to good use, as a timely appeal was launched to repair and restore the carvings on the outside of Saint Peter's Church (*DSN* 27.4.1955).

[5] in 1959 this enterprise was merged with Elastic Webbing Property Ltd of Collingwood, Victoria, and many of the key operatives returned home.

[6] *DSN* 10.4.1957.   [7] *DSN* 8.2.1956.

In June 1956 Derick Heathcoat Amory formally handed Mr and Mrs Les Osment the keys of 1 New Buildings, Westexe South, the 1,000[th] house built by Tiverton Borough Council. This was a significant achievement of local authority initiative, and came just five years after the completion of the 500th house. The investment put into housing and the speed of construction were paying dividends. In the same year, 40 flats and seven houses were completed within ten months on the Westfield site, just off Howden Road. Tiverton workers also benefited from this site, as the contract stipulated that no less than 75% of the men employed were to be local.

Mr and Mrs Les Osment receiving the keys from Derick Heathcoat Amory to Tiverton Borough Council's 1,000th house.

Britain's economy prospered in the 1950s under a succession of Conservative governments. More people began to own cars, televisions and refrigerators, and the volume of exports rose. Stenners were particularly successful at this time, their sawmilling equipment being in great demand across the world. In the spring of 1957, they even received an order from the USSR[1], which, despite the Cold War, still needed access to expertise from the West. Many Commonwealth countries also showed interest in Stenners' products, and often sent representatives to the factory. A few years before, delegations from Kumasi and Accra in the Gold Coast (now Ghana), as well as Victor

---

[1] (*DSN* 22.5.1957). It was interesting in that William Authers believed the saw was going first to a research institute, where it would undergo a thorough examination.

Bryan, Trinidad's Minister of Agriculture and Lands, all toured the production area[1]. Growth in overseas orders made expansion possible. Stenners, together with E.V. Twose (Manufacturing) Ltd, and Twose-Farmex Ltd, all subsidiaries of Heathcoat's, bought 1½ acres of the old Gasworks site on the Blundell's Road to enlarge their workspace. The parent company, enjoying similar success, began a £250,000 development at their Leat Street site[2].

The Managing Director of Stenners at this time was William ('Bill') Authers, a man enthusiastically involved in most aspects of Tiverton life. As well as holding a senior position with the firm, he was also a prominent Congregationalist, a Governor of Blundell's, a local historian of style, and a Borough Councillor. He contacted the Council of the township of Tiverton in Rhode Island, USA, with a view to forming links between the two communities, and they responded with the gift of a silver salver in September 1957[3]. So began a close connection between the two Tivertons that continues to this day. Bill Authers also took a keen interest in the collection of miscellaneous objects kept by the Borough Council in what it chose to call its museum, in reality a poky little room directly under the clock tower of the Town Hall. None of the objects had ever been sought; people had simply given them to the Council for safe-keeping. There were cases of stuffed birds, local mosses, geological specimens, fossils, paintings, documents and books. Bill Authers compiled a catalogue of these items, and by October 1957 a Committee had been established with the intention of forming a 'proper Museum'[4].

Some questioned the Borough Council's commitment to this enterprise. After all, just four years earlier they had decided to return the Harrowby Papers to Sandon Hall. Councillor Stanley Punchard had voiced his strong objections to getting rid of what was (and is) the most important single collection of 18th century documents relating to Tiverton. The Honorary Secretary of the Devonshire Association, Mrs Thomas, said the organisation would greatly regret Tiverton's losing the collection. Nevertheless, they were overruled, but not without winning some concessions. Before the papers were formally returned an adequate listing and index would be made, copies of which were to be kept locally[5].

In October 1957, William Gore Allen published *John Heathcoat and his Heritage*. It is both a biography of the founder of Tiverton's Lace Factory as well as a history of the

---

[1] *DSN* 2.7.1952.
[2] including the construction of two new buildings and additions to the existing finishing and rubber-covering plants, as well as installing further knitting machines and looms (*DSN* 11.12.1957).
[3] DRO R4/1 add C2.   [4] DRO R4/1 add C/10.
[5] Denys Jacobs, a tutor of the University College of the Southwest, offered his services to perform this work, which was, however, not completed until 1970.

later enterprise. Although the section dealing with Heathcoat himself is considered by many to be more eulogistic than factual, the remainder of the work is of considerable value. The same author, six months later, released *The Reluctant Politician: Derick Heathcoat Amory*, one of John Heathcoat's most distinguished descendants. The title of the book echoes the description by a contemporary who said that Derick was 'one of those strange beings with apparently no real political ambition' but 'profoundly respected because of certain qualities of character'[1]. Tiverton's M.P. had been Minister of Agriculture since 1954, and in January 1958, ambitious or not, he was appointed Chancellor of the Exchequer by Harold Macmillan.

One of his first duties was the official opening of Tiverton Grammar School's new £50,000 extensions. Significant as these additions were, they were dwarfed by the new £148,000 Secondary Modern School (now the Tiverton High School) begun in the summer and opened in January 1960. Built on the Bolham Road site where the POW camp had once stood, it had originally been planned for Wellbrook Field, but this had become the site for a new Heathcoat School that was also opened in 1960. Furthermore, in 1958 newspapers had asked the question 'New Technical College for Tiverton by 1961?' The answer was in the affirmative, and the East Devon Technical College on the Bolham Road, was soon under construction. With this last institution, the Education Act of 1944 would be fully implemented. Despite the great strides made in the provision of education in the town, the way in which schools were run was open to criticism. It has been sometimes said that pre-war attitudes prevailed among the managers who controlled the schools, and often there was little input from the teaching staff. This sometimes led to a situation where the managers challenged innovative teaching techniques.

Personal, municipal and corporate successes were celebrated during 1959. In January the two Heathcoat Amory brothers, Sir John and Derick, were awarded the Freedom of the Borough, and both were called upon during the year to open more facilities in the town. Bill Authers' dream of a museum finally came to fruition with the formation of a Museum Society, whose first President (and constant benefactor) was Derick Heathcoat Amory. In June 1960 he opened its first modest premises[2], just two rooms in Councillor Victor Broomfield's house on Angel Terrace. The public's interest was pleasantly encouraging; in the first fortnight over 2,000 people came to look around. Sir John, for his part, laid the foundation stone of a new foundry at the Lowman Works in July. Indeed, the Heathcoat Company's position in world markets

---

[1] cited in *DSN* 12.2.1958.
[2] the event, however, happened just a few days after the death of Allen Stanley Mahood, who had been librarian of the town for over 40 years, and would have been justifiably proud of Tiverton's latest asset.

was such that for this year on the cover of its magazine it could place an international figure, the film star Jayne Mansfield - wearing the firm's elastic-net tights, of course! Among other Tivertonians who enjoyed success during 1959 was Harold Shapland who had been elected President of the English Bowling Association for the year, and Mary de la Mahotière (née Carpenter), a native of the town, who brought out her new book, *The Newspaper Children*.

Plans laid years before were, in many cases, only now being realised. Progress with slum clearance was at last gathering momentum; a further 19 houses in Chapel Street had been declared unfit for habitation, and, in Westexe, Steer's Court and Candy's Court were demolished, as were parts of Westexe South. The scheme to widen William Street, and provide a 60-place car park went ahead[1]. In October 1959 the Market extensions, which included a new sale ring, dairy cattle shed and stock pens, were formally opened. Although this pleased local farmers, the increase in the rabbit population had been worrying them for some time. In 1956 the Devon Farmers' Union had declared the county a 'clearance area', and had enlisted the aid of the man-made myxomatosis disease. Locally, some measure of success had been achieved by early 1960. The Tiverton and District Rabbit Clearance Society, formed in the previous year, was supported by 92 local farmers or landowners who, between them, owned over 10,000 acres. They had already killed over a thousand rabbits, mainly by trapping or shooting, but a considerable number had been gassed. Nationally, it has been estimated[2] that myxomatosis and other methods killed as many as 99% of Britain's rabbits at this time, and only now are the numbers rising again. On a lighter note, it appears that a much stranger animal, completely unknown to farmers and town-dwellers alike, was on the loose in Tiverton. Early one July morning in 1960 people near Lowman Green woke up to find green footprints leading from near the Clock Tower across to the statue of Edward VII. The prints climbed a short way up the plinth, then turned back, and retraced their steps. Journalists of the *Devon and Somerset News* dared to suggest that an Abominable Snowman who walked through green snow was to blame!

Tiverton was flooded four times during October 1960, and on the last occasion Little Silver was cut off from the rest of the town. Although Lowman Green was under water, some people saw the humorous side of the situation: a sign appeared outside the Prince Regent Hotel inviting customers to 'Come inside, and get wet!' Business, of course, suffered. The Sawmills on Blundell's Road managed just one

---

[1] this led to the razing of the cottages opposite the main entrance to the Hospital, a couple of houses each in Bampton and Barrington Streets, as well as the huddled housing of Richards' and Gillard's' Buildings between those two streets.
[2] Rackham 1986, 48.

full day's work in the month. Much, much worse was to come, however. Heavy and incessant rain fell on December 4th, resulting in the River Exe between Dulverton and Tiverton rising 12 feet in an hour. A torrent swept down the valley covering some places with as much as eight feet of water. Fortunately, Tiverton did not suffer to that extent, but many parts of Westexe were under two feet, with over 500 homes affected. Emergency shelter was made available, and canteens set up in the schools. Members of the Durham Light Infantry with the use of DUKWs[1] and army lorries distributed meals to victims in their own homes[2]. Blundell's School rapidly assembled a flood squad of 50 pupils who worked alongside some Red Cross workers who had been drafted in. Disasters such as this exposed the lack of local emergency services, so it is not surprising how much the people of Tiverton appreciated the assistance of the School's Cadet Force. Hard work and determination soon cleared away the worst of the water and mud, but the stench remained for months.

Westexe South during the flood of December 1960.

When the emergency work had been completed and there was time to study the effects of this deluge it was revealed that water had entered more than 3,000 homes in

---

[1] amphibious vehicles, so-called after their military code designation.
[2] DRO 2745 add2C/EFL7.

the Exe Valley, with Tiverton, Exeter, and Exmouth being worst affected[1]. Yet, unbelievably, little was done. The opportunity for preventative work while water levels were low in the summer of 1961 was not taken, even if in October, the River Board began to remove hundreds of tons of shingle and debris from the downstream area of the old Exe Bridge. By the end of the year a Flood Prevention Scheme had been devised, but like many other plans it would take years to be implemented however conspicuous the need.

Derick Heathcoat Amory was elevated to the peerage as Viscount Amory of Tiverton in 1960. In the following bye-election of November, the young Robin Maxwell-Hyslop held Tiverton for the Conservatives, with a majority of more than 3,000 votes. In July 1961, before taking up an appointment as High Commissioner in Canada, Viscount Amory opened the new packing and despatch warehouse[2] at the Heathcoat Factory. He used the opportunity to promote his vision of the Common Market, saying that 'if Britain could enter on satisfactory terms, the advantages were clear'. The country applied to join in October, but negotiations would end in January 1963 with de Gaulle's emphatic *'Non'*.

While floods never damaged Fore Street, fires and the hand of man (or machine) did. A blaze in April 1960 gutted the Co-op Stores and Timothy Whites at the top of Gold Street. Damage to both properties amounted to over £40,000. The decision was taken to knock down only a part of Timothy Whites' store, but the Co-op's premises were demolished completely and the site was taken over in 1962 by Eastmond's to build an extension to their Gold Street premises. This key area at the junction of Fore Street, Gold Street, and Bampton Street would soon become the architectural hotch-potch it remains today. Rossiter's the pharmacists were building a modernistic new four-storey building on the corner of Bampton Street and Gold Street, where Thorne Brothers ironmongery had stood. The greatest desecration, however, was to take place across the road at the Palmerston Hotel. This prominent, grandiose period building, a landmark in the town with a national reputation for its past hospitality, was to be demolished and replaced by further retail development. It is almost impossible to find compliments about the resulting buildings of this area; one celebrated authority on Devon's architecture describes it as a hideous jumble of angular frontages[3]. This was not a time for sentiment let alone respect for history. The new Westexe South opened in October 1961, with a long row of modern shops on the western side of the street. On an even more ambitious scale, details were released of the projected creation of a new town centre for Tiverton based on the Phoenix Lane and Hammett's Lane area. The development was to include a shopping precinct, a large car park, and a bus station. A town centre still remains elusive.

---

[1] Shorter *et al* 1969, 49.
[2] the long building stretching along Leat Street.
[3] Cherry & Pevsner 1989, 814.

The imposing Thorne Brothers shop on the corner of Bampton Street and Gold Street, which was replaced in 1962 by a modern four-storey building housing Rossiter's, the chemists.

Developments of the early 1960s were by no means restricted to the retail sector. The Borough Council continued to build houses for rent. Higher Cotteylands was already occupied, and discussions in 1962 centred on whether to buy the fields between that estate and the rest of Westexe. Doubts had been cast on their suitability for housing, as the land was so wet. Nevertheless, construction went ahead. By this time, most homes, whether new or old, had many up-to-date consumer goods, including a television set, but because Tiverton was surrounded by hills reception was poor. This was largely remedied in 1961 by erecting a master aerial on top of Exeter Hill, which was part of a new television relay system. The Tiverton Dealers' Retail Company was formed to deliver this service to households for a £5 installation fee and 2/6d a week thereafter. Meanwhile, great strides were being made with the provision of educational facilities. The East Devon Technical College was opened on Bolham Road in November 1962, just a year later than planned. The large estate at Wilcombe was provided with a school for 240 local children a year later. This brought the number of new schools built in Tiverton during the previous decade to three – Cowleymoor, the County Secondary School, and now Wilcombe. Blundell's School was planning a major building project, which was to include a new school hall, dining hall and kitchens, a new music school, as well as an extension to the chapel and six extra classrooms.

Tiverton's major employers, in keeping with the prevailing trend, also carried out large building projects. The £50,000 Medland, Sanders and Twose complex was constructed on the former Gasworks site, and nearby the Tiverton Sawmills had been purchased by E.V. Twose (Manufacturing) Ltd. On the northern edge of the town, a six-acre site across the Exe from Heathcoat's Factory became the location for the Globe Elastic Thread Company[1]. This was a particularly busy time for Heathcoat's; they were proposing to move into the former Bristow's Factory in Mill Street, Crediton, and in December 1962 they contracted the House of Dior to act as fashion advisers for some of their clothing ranges. Furthermore, the Company was providing the expertise for a firm in New Zealand called Helanca Yarns. There were changes, too, at Tiverton's second-largest employer, the brewery of Starkey, Knight and Ford, which in 1961 began bottling and distributing the products of the Danish company, Tuborg. The management had already entered into an agreement to exchange certain products with Whitbreads, and so it came as little surprise in October 1962 when it was announced that they were proposing a £3.8 million take-over of the Tiverton business. The deal was made, and within two years, a new brewery and bottling plant at Howden was planned. To some it was sad to see the end of local control of a traditional industry, but Whitbreads brought with them a new chapter in working conditions and a national wage scale. Heathcoat's would no longer dictate earnings in the town.

Progress on all fronts was temporarily checked in the first week of 1963 by deep snow, which covered fields and town alike. Further falls caused widespread disruption, and RAF helicopters were needed to deliver essential supplies to the more remote farms like those near Seven Crosses. The River Exe was frozen either side of Exe Bridge, and the ice did not break until the second week of February. The combination of blocked roads and continued chilly temperatures resulted in a severe coal shortage that lasted through to March. One unfortunate victim of the weather was Tiverton's former Borough Surveyor, William Duncan Arthur. While shovelling snow away from his home at Castle Bar on Exeter Hill, he collapsed and died.

The Beeching Report on Britain's railways was published in this year. It was an attempt to rationalise a system whose losses were no longer supportable. Branch lines

---

[1] a business formed by an agreement between John Heathcoat and Company and the Globe Manufacturing Company of Fall River, Massachusetts, U.S.A.

were doomed, as was steam. Many of the report's recommendations had been issued in the previous year, so Tiverton knew it was going to lose the Exe Valley route, but believed that the service to Tiverton Junction would be safe. In October 1963 Westexe Halt saw its last passenger[1]. It was further announced that the Taunton-Barnstaple line would close and, somewhat unexpectedly, so too would the passenger service from Tiverton to Tiverton Junction. The town, it seems, had been lulled into a false sense of security. It had missed the opportunity to mount a strong opposition and now it was too late. The decision to cut all rail access seemed incomprehensible to many, especially as Tiverton was expanding. In addition to new estates at Pinnex Moor and to the north of Loughborough it was announced during 1963 that Tiverton was one of 11 towns in the county scheduled for further large-scale development[2].

Everything seemed to be in a state of change; not all of it could claim to be progressive even if it was planned. There seemed to be little respect for the past and, in the case of young people, little respect for authority. Bernard Shorland, Headmaster of Uffculme Secondary School and President of the Devon County Teachers' Association, summarised the era as 'the time of teddy boys, telly watchers, pop singer squealers and gym-slip mothers'[3]. Such views were not new; journalists had feasted on them for almost a decade. But young people had many redeeming qualities which, it was hoped, would be developed by the Youth Centre that opened on Bolham Road in August 1964. This was not only a first for the town but for the whole county. Appropriately, the Borough Council in this year chose as its Mayor, the 35-year-old Brian Homer. He epitomised a generation that had grown up through the War years: in 1946 he had won the All-England Sea Cadet Corps breast-stroke championship, became a councillor at the age of 25, and played hooker in the victorious Devon team which won the County Rugby Final in 1957.

Tiverton's long tradition of care for the elderly and infirm was enhanced by the opening in September 1964 of the community centre at Amory House in Saint Peter Street. The 300 members of the Tiverton Aged People's Association benefited enormously from this facility, which is still in use today. Purpose-built housing for older residents became a feature of the town; the bungalows in King Street, Westexe, had been inhabited for almost five years, and one proposal for a development in Chapel Street was as old people's flats. The need for such housing had been growing for some time, due to many reasons. Improved health meant people were living longer and, on a more local note, a high percentage of those living in the buildings designated for

---

[1] Clinker 1978, 143.

[2] this was the beginning of the idea of population 'overspill' from the major cities, and Tiverton, it was proposed, could take 4,000 people immediately.

[3] *DSN* 29.5.1963.

demolition were elderly. Similarly, several of those still working on the land were of the older generation, and it was becoming more economical for them to live in council housing in the town and travel to work. For those who became ill, Belmont Hospital had been offering specialist care for the elderly for well over a decade[1]. Tiverton had another cherished medical facility. Tidcombe Hall was the second home opened by the Marie Curie Foundation, which, for the next 45 years, would offer palliative care for cancer sufferers.

The Borough made the most of the 350th anniversary of receiving its Charter of Incorporation. In October 1965, a week-long programme of events was organised to mark the occasion, including a colourful pageant of 80 tableaux depicting the town's history. One of the more auspicious ceremonies took place in People's Park, where Mayor Victor Broomfield invited Princess Marina to plant the 'Charter Oak', a sapling from Windsor Park. The intention was to plant 350 trees around the town, one for each year since 1615[2]. For many people the highlight of Charter Week was the arrival in Tiverton of the locomotive that had become known as the 'Tivvy Bumper'. The last passenger service from the town to Tiverton Junction had run on October 5th 1964[3], prompting F.G. Britton to suggest that one of the engines ought to be preserved. Sir John Heathcoat Amory purchased the 'Bumper', built 30 years earlier, and presented it for display[4]. Amid great celebration it was delivered to the Goods Station with Viscount Amory at the controls, and duly handed over to the Museum Society. By this time, the Museum had moved[5] to the former National School in Saint Andrew Street, but could not contain its latest exhibit without special accommodation. Until this was built, the engine was given an outdoor temporary[6] home on a plinth in Blundell's Road.

The Tivvy Bumper was not to be the only new feature on Blundell's Road. In 1965, Vivian Scott of Pinnex Moor House announced plans to build a motel near the Elmore Football Club's ground[7], while, nearby, the Church of England finally commissioned the new church promised years before to serve the Wilcombe and Cowleymoor areas[8]. One dream, however, was not to materialise. Sophia Loren was asked to attend Blundell's School summer fête by one of the masters after a group of boys had been

---

[1] despite a complete refurbishment of the building, it still had the stigma of having been the Workhouse, and was referred to as such by many older people.
[2] the scheme enjoyed such success, however, that it continued until 1995, by which time over a thousand trees had been planted.
[3] the line was retained for freight only for another couple of years.
[4] Hateley 1977, H44.
[5] from its humble beginnings on Angel Terrace, by way of the Chilcott School.
[6] temporary, however, was to mean 14 years.
[7] it opened in August 1967.
[8] the building, dedicated to Saint Andrew, followed the designs of the architect, Anthony Rome, and was eventually consecrated on September 29th 1971.

beaten for breaking bounds to see her in a film at the Electric Theatre. Only at the very last minute came the disappointing message that she could not be spared from filming 'Arabesque'. If the Headmaster had been somewhat embarrassed by the national media coverage given to this incident, the School came into the news more positively in May 1967 when the Queen Mother opened the new buildings on the north side of the road. Later in the month, the Roman Catholic Chapel of Saint James in Old Road was dedicated, to serve the needs of the Catholics of the nearby large estates. The rapid growth in the eastern part of Tiverton had led to some confusion over street names: there was Willow Close, Willow Crescent and Willow Avenue, as well as Wilcombe Avenue, Close and Grove. The answer was to change them by honouring some of those who, as we have seen, contributed to Tiverton's history. The names of Gregory, Temple, Mackenzie, Harrowby, and Sage now grace the street map. Wilcombe Avenue was changed to Hermes Avenue to mark Tiverton's adoption in 1966 of the Royal Navy's newest aircraft carrier, *HMS Hermes*.

Failure to implement its flood prevention scheme[1] after clear warnings made events in Tiverton in December 1965 a national scandal. A downpour left 150 properties under as much as four feet of water, with Westexe yet again worst affected. This disaster prompted demands for immediate action. The projected scheme had three main constituents: to rebuild Exe Bridge[2], whose four piers, it was said by some, seriously hampered the passage of floodwater; to clear a substantial amount of material from the riverbed; and to build high concrete walling downstream from the bridge. Where was the traffic to go while the bridge was being rebuilt? The solution was to revive a plan first mooted in 1956 to build another road across the Exe[3]. At that date, the idea was for a road to run from the foot of Long Drag across the Exe near Head Weir to join the Bampton road between Velvains and Rix Cottages, but now the route was to be constructed further downstream. A new stretch of road would run from Shillands, over the Leat and the Exe, past the growing Kennedy Way industrial estate to join the Bampton Road near the Youth Centre. Not only would this cut down the volume of traffic wanting to go through the town, but also allow the old Exe Bridge to be completely rebuilt. Work was carried out comparatively rapidly; the road was begun

---

[1] little had been done apart from removing some shingle from below Exe Bridge.
[2] early in 1958 the Exe Bridge Trustees gave Devon County Council £2,500 to take responsibility for the structure, which was repointed and grouted by its new owners.
[3] to reduce the volume of traffic passing through the town.

in March 1966 and opened in the following spring. Demolition of Exe Bridge began in July 1967[1], and was soon followed by the removal of more than 150,000 tons of earth and stone from the river channel and banks before the building of the retaining wall. The new concrete single-pier bridge was opened to traffic in November 1968, but the whole scheme was not finished until the spring of 1970.

During 1968, Sir John Heathcoat Amory succeeded in saving a bit of 'old Tiverton'. The Borough Council wanted to remove the lamp standard that had stood on Angel Hill for 90 years, but his offer to have it repaired made them relent, and the well-known landmark remained. The rush to develop often left no time for the considered investigation of what was being swept away. Although it was too late for most of Fore Street, further mindless destruction would be strongly challenged by the Tiverton Civic Society, established early in 1968. This group received some response almost immediately after its foundation. Tesco declared they would retain the fine Georgian façade of 37 Fore Street[2]. It was propped up while the shop below was being altered, but the upper storeys became dangerously unstable, and in the end a brand new frontage was necessary. What we have today is just an illusion. There was a sympathetic restoration, however, of the old Corn Market in Bampton Street (numbers 18-22) by the Market and Almshouse Trust. On a much larger scale, a new shopping centre was being planned for the Market and Bampton Street areas. It seems as if the focus of the elusive town centre had moved; the former choice, Phoenix Lane, was to become the centre for transport services.

From the early 1960s the Tiverton area had been threatened by overspill - the term given to the plan to move large numbers of people from the inner city areas of London and the West Midlands to more sparsely-populated localities. Figures for the proposed influx had fluctuated widely; at one time 4,000 new arrivals were forecast, at another a new town of 40,000 people had been proposed for the Culm Valley or even nearer, at Sampford Peverell[3]. The location of a new settlement was clearly influenced by the proximity of the proposed M5 motorway and, to a lesser extent, the planned North Devon Link Road. At the outset, Devon County Council were strongly in favour of the scheme, but as opposition mounted their stance softened and they began to consider holding a referendum on the issue. Meanwhile, Tiverton Borough Council had begun negotiating directly with the Greater London Council over a limited intake, but a split developed between the Planning and Development Committee who were opposed to

---

[1] it was soon obvious that the structure, generally thought to have been built anew in 1818, had in fact been built around an earlier bridge. Some of the timbers found in situ were thought to be of 16th century date if not even earlier, and examples of these can now be seen outside the Museum.
[2] the former home of Sir John Duntze, and later the offices of Starkey, Knight and Ford.
[3] DRO R4/1 add C3.

the scheme, and the Tiverton Trades Council who believed it would bring new industries and employment. Following the Borough Council's vote against the issue in September 1968, the word 'overspill' was fortunately forgotten.

The Countryside Act, passed in 1968, allowed for the establishment of Country Parks where people could enjoy their leisure hours. A few local enthusiasts, most notably Bill Authers and Colonel Dennis Harwood, realised a golden opportunity of reviving the disused Canal. There had been no shortage of suggestions over the years as to what to do with the waterway - fill it in and use it either for agriculture, or to build on, or, as we have seen, surface it and use it as part of a southern relief road for Tiverton. In 1966 Bill Authers had persuaded the Borough Council to look into the costs of clearing the Canal, and in 1967 enthusiasts voiced a hope of restoring the 11-mile section from Tiverton to Lowdwells. The Act bolstered their efforts, and support for the plan to make it a Country Park was so strong that in October 1969 over 800 people met at the Basin. After encouragement from the Chairman of the Preservation Committee, and Tiverton's M.P., Robin Maxwell-Hyslop, they set out to walk from the Basin to Greenham. Everyone realised that if the Canal was to have a future as a leisure area much work would need to be done.

Tiverton's growing population led to necessary additions to the town's schools. In 1967 extensions were needed at Wilcombe, athough the school had only been built for four years. Elmore School's cramped, old premises had long been recognised as inadequate for 20th century teaching, and in 1968 a new building was under construction alongside the existing school at Cowleymoor. The new school, however, kept the name of Elmore Junior School. Far more drastic plans for local education seemed to be on the horizon. In January 1969, Devon County Education Committee approved plans to establish comprehensive schooling in North Devon. Would Tiverton be next? A comprehensive system would necessarily bring to an end the 11-plus selection for the Grammar School, as well as the Middle School system, then current in Tiverton. Sides were taken immediately. Councillor John Lake vociferously defended the *status quo*, whereas John Lello, the Head of the Grammar School, saw the Bolham Road site as ideal for a switch to comprehensive education. While the great debate went on, it was the behaviour of some of Tiverton's youngsters that grabbed the local headlines. John Lello's older pupils were asking him to provide a smoking room in the Grammar School's Sixth Form Centre, but he emphatically refused. Under-age drinking in the town was also giving cause for concern. Tiverton's licensees, in their defence, complained that, with the fashion for long hair, it was difficult enough to determine the sexes let alone establish their ages. More serious, however, was the fact that several youngsters were tempted by drugs. At a lunch-time service in Saint George's Church a local Baptist minister pointed out that 'young people were hanging about in shop doorways and on street corners, idly kicking their heels, looking for something in life - this is the ideal situation for the drug pusher'. The police were seizing small quantities of cannabis locally, and it was admitted that it was being picked up in London and brought down to Tiverton and distributed at 'two local places of entertainment'[1].

Nothing seemed immune to change or challenge at this time. In 1969 the textile interests of John Heathcoat and Company, the main employer in Tiverton for over 150 years, were taken over by the multi-national Coats Paton group. Assurances were made about the future of the Company as it was pointed out that 30% of the shares would remain with the existing holders, many of whom were employees. Nevertheless, subsequent events did little to instil confidence. Nationally, the textile industry was depressed, so it was no surprise when short-time working was introduced at the Factory. In March 1971, 103 workers were forced to register as unemployed. Fortunately, this remained in operation for one month only, but more bad news came in April 1972. The decision to cut 30 jobs through a re-organisation of the Tiverton narrow fabrics division was followed two weeks later by the announcement of 140 redundancies at the firm's Helanca division. The question was asked whether this was the action of 'an industrial physician wielding a skilful scalpel to cure an ailing concern or a hatchet-man axing ruthlessly?'[2]. When the company's annual statement was issued in August, no one was surprised to hear that the group was trading at a loss.

This must have made depressing news for the ailing Sir John Heathcoat Amory. He died peacefully three months later, aged 78. Born at Hensleigh, he had served with the 4th Devons in the First World War, and in the Second was a Major in the Home Guard. Tiverton had benefited in many ways from his kindness. In 1949, he had given Alexandra Lodge as a care home; shortly before his death he offered the old baths site to the Tiverton Red Cross and, jointly with his brother, donated £100,000 toward the new swimming pool on the Bolham Road. For many years, he had made it known that he wanted to leave Knightshayes to the National Trust. His wishes were followed, and in 1974, 100 years after his grandfather had been knighted, the house and gardens were opened to the public.

Britain's entry into the European Economic Community at the beginning of 1973 aroused mixed emotions. Whereas local industrialists appeared relatively happy with the prospect, farmers were far more reserved. On one hand, they were promised more money for their products, but on the other, they became subject to all sorts of additional rules and regulations. In Tiverton, Europeanism of a social kind took the form of a 'twinning' with the French community of Chinon, and, by the end of the year, plans were under way to find a similar German partner. Both associations have endured.

---

[1] *DSN* 8.9.1970.
[2] nationally, Coats Paton had already reduced their textile labour force by 5,000 (*DSN* 18.4.1972).

Although unemployment was growing and trade, in general, was in recession, some businesses in Tiverton bucked the trend. The Saint Andrew Street mills were to re-open, a £1 million extension at Whitbread's site in Westexe promised to create 30 to 40 jobs; and it was announced that the likely relocation of Ford and Lock Supermarket's headquarters to Tiverton would result in 100 more. The Grand Western Canal was finally designated a Country Park in 1973, and it was hoped to have horse-drawn boats working along part of the route within a year or two. Alderman Authers, who had received an M.B.E. in July 1971, staged an exhibition at the Museum on the subject of the Canal that was visited by more than 5,000 people[1]. Celebrations continued with the visit by the Queen Mother on July 1st. At the invitation of the Rev. Charles Nye she attended the Thanksgiving Service to mark the 900th anniversary of Saint Peter's Church[2]. Three weeks later, Tiverton gave a rousing welcome to the crew of *HMS Hermes* who paraded through the town to celebrate the ship's being given the Freedom of the Borough.

These festivities took place against a background of worsening national economic conditions. Since the Second World War Britain's economy had suffered from a series of alternate booms and slumps partly caused by manufacturing decline, the loss of markets, the failure to modernise management, and strike action. The problems for government were occasionally severe, even critical. Although these episodes were often short-lived, nonetheless they could be extreme in nature, and this was one such period. By the end of 1973 there was a severe oil shortage because of conflict in the Middle East, which, compounded with a strike by miners, had led to an urgent need to conserve fuel stocks. Edward Heath's Tory Government was at one time forced to introduce a three-day working week. The immediate effect of this in Tiverton was 300 extra people signing on at the Unemployment Exchange, and within a month, Globe Elastic laid off 20 workers. In January 1974, John Heathcoat and Company predicted they could maintain 80% production, but the sudden cancellation of export orders for nylon bobbinet in May seriously hampered the business. The situation was made much worse at the end of the year when 120 workers in the elastic-covering division had their hours reduced. Nationally, the political situation had become highly volatile. The Conservative Government resigned and Harold Wilson formed a minority Labour Government in March 1974. Later in the year, another General Election saw Labour returned with a majority, albeit meagre. Tempers were often raised on the hustings. It was even suggested in the local press that an ex-officers' and gentleman's junta be formed to 'fight the trade unionists, layabouts and thugs who are ruling the country'.

---

[1] interest was further heightened by the publication in November of *The Grand Western Canal* by Helen Harris, who had been brought up in Tiverton.

[2] although it is almost certain that Tiverton's church was founded much earlier than 1073, historical accuracy was not of the greatest importance on this occasion.

On both occasions, however, the Conservative, Robin Maxwell-Hyslop, held on quite comfortably to the Tiverton Division.

In such circumstances, communities up and down the country were falling into line with the Local Government Act of 1972. Reform was necessary, but few foresaw its consequences. Existing local authorities, with their limited resources, could simply not afford or administer all the public and personal social services thrust on them. The Act's measures were drastic and far-reaching. On April 1st 1974 the 1,424 local government areas of England and Wales were reduced to 456. Tiverton Borough Council was one of the casualties, being swallowed up by a new District Authority, based on Tiverton and Crediton. Rackenford and Witheridge wanted to join with Tiverton, but in opposition to their wishes, and rejecting any historical or cultural affinity, central Government decided the two parishes were to become part of the Barnstaple grouping. Nevertheless, the Tiverton-Crediton area was encouraged to take in Teignmouth, a part of Saint Thomas Rural District, as well as Dawlish Urban District. Tiverton refused. What was to be the name of the new authority? The suggested titles were East Devon and Mid Devon District Council, Nine Rivers, Mid-East Devon District Council, Saint Boniface, Exe-Creedy District Council, Redvers (proposed by Bill Authers), Mid Devon District Council, and East and Mid Devon Area Council. Initially, the Joint Steering Committee chose the last-named, but we know what the eventual choice would be. Tiverton attempted to make the transition with the least amount of fuss. At the beginning of 1974, it was decided that the new parish council - in essence, what the Borough Council was to become - would still be known as a Town Council, and its Chairman would be termed Mayor. A subsequent meeting agreed to perpetuate the annual Mayor-choosing ceremony. The final meeting of the Borough Council was called at the end of March[1], and the changeover went ahead with little trouble. Fittingly, Eric Shapland, whose father and grandfather had also held the office, was the last Mayor of the Borough under the conditions of the Charter of 1615.

---

[1] DRO R4/1 add/C4.

21 The Hub of Mid Devon

The new Mid Devon District Council was to have no honeymoon period. From the start, its duty to implement Government policies as well as its own met with strong criticism. In April 1974, just three months after the formation of the Council, Tiverton's Chamber of Trade led a countywide rates revolt by advocating the temporary withholding of payments[1]. When it was revealed that Councillors had claimed £30,000 in expenses during the first year[2], there were loud calls from the public for scrutiny of their submissions. Housing issues are always guaranteed to arouse strong opinions, no more so than in 1974. Despite a long and commendable record of providing rented accommodation there was still a serious shortage, which became much worse. House-owners in Tiverton became angry when the Council announced their intention to buy up properties in privately owned areas in order to rent them out[3]. Government policy offering Council tenants the chance of purchasing their properties removed many houses from the stock, and placed them out of the reach of those people for whom they were originally built. Prevailing economic instability caused the Government to halt Mid Devon District Council's plans to build 137 houses for rent. The same reason was given for the postponement of the construction of a multi-storey car park and a proposed £200,000 development of Amory Park[4].

Tiverton's Mayor in 1975, the Liberal Frank Suter, predicted that the area's unemployment figures would cause the greatest concern in the time ahead[5]. He was right. The first set of statistics in the following year showed unemployment in the Tiverton and Cullompton area at 6.4% of the workforce, significantly higher than the national average of 5.1%. Throughout the year, the figures rose[6], and by the summer of 1977 one in ten local people were out of work. To reduce the rising national numbers, the Government set up the Manpower Services Commission to establish sponsored schemes that provided work of a sort, mainly for youngsters and the long-term unemployed. Locally, the first posts created were for one young man to help repair and redecorate Tiverton Castle and another to train as a salesman at Soundy and Son

---

[1] an action committee was formed at a meeting attended by members of Devon's 35 Chambers, with Tiverton's Vivian Scott as Chairman.

[2] *DSN* 8.6.1976.   [3] *DSN* 5.2.1974

[4] furthermore, the South West Water Authority said they could no longer support any further major industrial or residential development in Tiverton until the town's sewerage disposal system had been improved (*DSN* 18.10.1977).

[5] *DSN* 13.5.1975

[6] including a handful of workers at Weldcontrol's Howden factory and some 30 white-collar jobs at Heathcoats.

in Gold Street[1]. Such jobs were to multiply as the months went on.

Yet there would be cause to celebrate in 1977. Harold Shapland received an M.B.E. in the New Years Honours list, and Ron Davey fulfilled a lifetime's ambition as the stalwart conductor of the Tiverton Youth Orchestra when it was announced that they were to play at the Royal Albert Hall. For the Queen's Silver Jubilee commemoration, every child in Tiverton was to receive a mug. While the Town Council failed to commit themselves fully to any such gift, especially as over 6,000 would be needed, the indefatigable Mary Turner, Mayor for the year, typically ignored such frustrations and launched her Silver Appeal to cover the costs[2]. Beginning with Palmerston Park in February, various streets and areas in and around the parish announced plans to hold parties. When the first week of June finally arrived, Tiverton was decked in red, white, and blue, and everyone seemed to join in the festivities. The weather did not always help, however; at the opening of the Elizabethan Fayre the crowds were showered with hailstones.

Many of the children who took part in the Jubilee celebrations were affected by the fundamental changes to Tiverton's schools that were implemented in September 1977. The Grammar School was to be lost to a comprehensive system. Its pupils, and those from the Heathcoat Secondary School, aged between 13 and 19, were to move to Bolham Road. The Grammar School site would be split into the Caroline Brewin First and William Shapland Middle Schools. Elsewhere, the growing population in the Wilcombe and Tidcombe areas had made necessary the building of the Sunningmead Infants School in 1975 and in 1979 a new first school was under construction in Tidcombe Lane.

The opening of the Job Centre at Coggan's Well House in January 1978[3] brought the unemployment crisis right into the centre of Tiverton. Anyone could now see just how many people were visiting the office to 'sign on', and the few cards on display reflected how scarce jobs had become. The number of young people out of work across the country prompted Callaghan's government to introduce the Youth Opportunities Programme. The idea was to prevent school-leavers going straight on to the dole by offering some sort of work, often very poorly paid and, almost invariably, temporary. The effects were further to disillusion school-leavers and to give a false, if politically desirable, impression of the unemployment figures[4]. For the adult unemployed, the Manpower Services Commission had created more schemes. Although often termed

---

[1] *DSN* 1.3.1977.   [2] *DSN* 28.12.1976

[3] about the 400th such building since the modernisation of Britain's employment service about four years earlier.

[4] at the end of the 1979/80 school year, the Programme engaged 59 of Tiverton's school-leavers (*DSN* 26.8.1980).

'Mickey Mouse jobs', they were all meant to include a serious training element. Heathcoat's by 1983, were employing 60 people under such Government schemes in return for subsidies.

Kaba Locks, a little-known Swiss multinational company, began production in January 1979 on the Howden industrial estate. There, too, another firm, Spenco, celebrated its first million pounds' worth of orders in July. Such rare successes were to be found only in secondary industries; the longer-established firms experienced continuing decline. A dearth of orders in the early summer led to a 13% cut in the workforce at the Exeleigh Foundry[1]. A few months later, Lowman Engineering was hit particularly hard by a national engineering dispute, forcing them to announce 20 redundancies. All through 1980 unemployment figures continued to rise in the Tiverton area, reaching a total of 1,000 in December. At Stenners, where a three-day week had already been imposed, 1981 began with 72 of the workers losing one further day a week[2].

Lord Amory of Tiverton died peacefully in his sleep at Chevithorne Barton on 20th January 1981. Thus ended a long and distinguished life dedicated to town, county, and nation. He had served as Chancellor of the Exchequer in 1958, and later as Governor-General of Canada, as well as being Chancellor of the University of Exeter. He was the only holder of a title that consequently lapsed. For many people in Tiverton, his death was overshadowed by the threat of redundancy. In April, Heathcoat's reduced the workforce by 45 to 610, and a further 38 workers began part-time working. The new Globe Elastic factory went on a three-day week in June, and in Fore Street the Co-op Stores announced it was to close, making eight workers redundant. More important, three months later Whitbread decided to close their Fore Street brewery site, with the loss of 75 jobs. Tiverton's largest building firm, C.P. Unwin, was wound up in March 1982, throwing 130 men out of work. The Falklands War, during the spring of 1982, diverted media attention away from the fact that Britain's unemployed now numbered over three million. Of this figure, the Tiverton area could count almost 1,500, one in eight of the workforce.

In 1981 local industrialists, Trades Union representatives, and County Councillors had pleaded to the Mid Devon District Council to take the initiative and to discuss in-depth the local unemployment situation. What could they do? They were in an invidious position; if they did nothing, they were accused of not caring or hiding their heads in the sand, and when they did take the initiative, they were invariably criticised for squandering the ratepayers' money. Besides, Government policies often hampered

---

[1] only months after a £600,000 extension had been finished there.
[2] it was pointless looking outside the town for work; in February, Fox Brothers announced that they were to close their operations at Uffculme and Cullompton with the loss of 53 jobs, and at Silverton, Reed and Smith's Paper Mill were to shed a further 16 jobs.

their plans. In 1980, the widening of Westexe North was put on hold, and the ban on council house building, originally just a temporary measure, looked likely to remain for a long time[1]. The last decision at least averted a confrontation, as the Council had been planning to build between 40 and 60 houses in the space between Leofric Road and the Cemetery[2]. Another dispute had arisen in 1979 when the Council initially refused to make houses available for Vietnamese refugees. Undeterred however, Eric Shapland, the District Council Chairman, made impassioned humanitarian pleas that eventually won over his colleagues who, in September, allocated four homes in Tiverton[3].

Despite hard times, Tiverton's twinning with the German town of Hofheim had been inaugurated in the summer of 1980 and a German party was suitably fêted at the Town Hall. The building itself, however, became the focus of dissent, when it was decided to equip one of its cellars as a radiation-proof war-room. This provoked an angry reaction from local CND supporters who demonstrated against the decision. Divisions also appeared over the proposed plans to develop the centre of Tiverton. In 1981 the Chamber of Trade, ever protective of its interest, approached the District Council's Planning Committee with a hope of imposing a ban on the establishment of further building societies, estate agents and other non-retail businesses in the heart of the town, but their request was rejected. More contentious were the proposals announced as early as 1982 to pedestrianise Fore Street, establish a new library in Beck Square, and develop the land at the rear of the Town Hall into grand new Council offices necessitated by a growing bureaucracy.

As ever, things were changing in Tiverton, among them some traditions that were centuries old. The cattle market had been condemned two years before, and when it closed the local magistrates in 1982 decided there was no reason for all-day drinking in the town on market days and so it should cease. The Perambulation of the Town Leat was the unlikely occasion for another innovation, when sexual equality was championed by the participation of two withy-girls from Blundell's[4]. In October, the last marriage ceremony took place at Cove Church, and the building was declared redundant[5], ending a centuries-old chapter of ecclesiastical history. But one development was more than welcome and would prove a successful local initiative. During 1984, John Heathcoat and Company negotiated the return of the Factory; they bought back the 75% stake that had been held for the previous 15 years by the Coats

---

[1] by this time, 400 Council tenants had applied to buy their homes.
[2] against the strong wishes of residents on the Pinnex Moor estate (*DSN* 15.4.1980)..
[3] *DSN* 25.9.1979.
[4] in September 1975 Blundell's School admitted its first girl pupil, 16 year-old Arabella Ashworth. Early in the following year the school was to consider taking day girls from the age of 13 (*DSN* 3.2.1976).
[5] DRO 1400 add3/PR3.

Paton group[1]. This immediately halted the gradual reduction of the factory's workforce, which, under this management, had fallen from over 1,000 to about 530 workers. In the year following the buy-back numbers actually began to rise. The change at Heathcoat's coincided with a new look in Westexe North where the row of flats and shops on the west side of the street was officially opened in April 1985. Another project to come to fruition in this year was the £800,000 Melrose Unit at the Belmont Hospital. It was designed to accommodate 20 'elderly confused persons', and took its first resident in October. Plans – never in short supply – were announced at various times through the year of the intention to build a new theatre in the town, a 'retirement complex' around Pinnex Moor House, and to convert the house itself into a residential home. The opportunity was available to celebrate all these events with Tiverton-produced libations, as the first batch of 1,700 bottles of wine became available from the Highfield Vineyard[2].

Tiverton was at last becoming more accessible. Construction of the first stage of the North Devon Link Road, the 6½-mile section from Junction 27 of the M5 to the Bolham Road, had begun in March 1982. A year later, one of the approach roads, past the Hartnoll Hotel, was improved, and such swift progress was made with the Link Road itself that the first stage was opened in March 1984. Work could begin in the following year to construct a road from Blundell's Road to connect with it near Higher and Lower Moor. Proposals for industrial growth in this area met with negligible opposition, even plans for a large residential estate near Higher Moor were acceptable, although the District Council would have to defy Government cuts to build it[3]. On the other hand, as soon as the construction of an out-of-town shopping centre in that vicinity was proposed there was a strong outcry from Tiverton's shopkeepers, who feared that such an establishment would lead to the abandonment of the town centre[4]. Another new road was planned to run from Westexe to join the Eastern Distributor Road near the Tiverton Hotel. The route was roughly that of the old railway line. The land flanking this relief road, now the Great Western Way, was seen as ripe for development. The old Whitbread Brewery site beside the Lowman attracted the greatest interest, and the greatest controversy. One of the first schemes, offered in 1983, was to build a supermarket there, along with about 35 Georgian-style houses and an equal number of sheltered houses for the elderly. Safeway were first to show interest in the site, but by 1986 KwikSave had become the prime candidate. Whoever would eventually build there, Tiverton shopkeepers once again heard the death-knell of town

---

[1] *TG* 26.6.1984.
[2] unkindly named Château Long Drag (*TG* 26.6.1984). This was not, of course, the first vineyard in Tiverton; Yearlstone had been operating for the previous seven years.
[3] and to begin the 100-house development at Lower Farleigh.
[4] *TG* 5.6.1984.

centre trading. The remaining land, lying between the proposed supermarket site and Saint Andrew Street would also became a planners' battlefield. The Council were advised to buy it for car-parking, but the flamboyant entrepreneur, Dan McCauley, who owned Globol Chemicals at Bampton, had his eye on it as well. His concept was to turn it into a shopping complex and theatre, complete with underground parking.

Others shared McCauley's vision of a theatre for Tiverton. A location close to the East Devon College had already been proposed, but in 1986 the cheapest alternative was taken - to refurbish the New Hall, despite its lack of parking. Indeed, land near the College had become as attractive for developers as that at the bottom of Phoenix Lane. The College itself had already allocated £1 million for additions to its premises, and the land on the opposite side of Bolham Road was the desired location for a very ambitious scheme. The seven acre site was earmarked for a leisure complex with an 11-court regional indoor tennis centre, indoor bowls rink, squash and badminton courts, snooker tables, gymnasium, sauna, solarium, and a 52-room hotel with conference and health facilities, fast-food and sports shops[1]. This, like many other grand projects of the time, never progressed further.

Equally ambitious, but ultimately achievable, were the proposals for a development at Blundell's School. An Old Boy, the Canadian tycoon, Christopher Ondaatje, had given over £1 million to construct a multi-purpose hall, to include a theatre/lecture room, three art studios, and a number of rooms suitable for exhibitions and meetings. Meanwhile, the School's governing body, together with Lowman Manufacturing and Knightshayes Estate applied in 1987 to construct more than 150 houses on land between the School and Tidcombe Lane. This aroused fierce local opposition, which gained valuable support from the Nature Conservancy Council when it was discovered that the area was home to Devon's only sizeable bed of the humble lesser pond sedge. In 1988, Tidcombe Fen was declared an SSSI (Site of Special Scientific Interest), scuppering any building plans. Nearby, the Marie Curie Foundation warned that they could not afford the cost of the necessary refurbishment of their hospice at Tidcombe Hall, so it would have to close. Queen Elizabeth the Queen Mother, among others, expressed deep regret at this proposal. People rallied to the cause and the sum needed, a little less than £½ million, was found, and all were led to believe that the hospice's future was secure.

The General Election in the summer of 1987 returned Margaret Thatcher's Tory

---

[1] the District Council soon found themselves in trouble over this scheme, as they foolishly agreed to lend the developers £1,000 towards the costs of submitting their planning application (*TG* 5.8.1986).

regime for its third term. The Prime Minister, who had won her way in the Falklands and against miners, now turned to education. Not only did the Education Reform Act introduce the National Curriculum, it also challenged the right of local education authorities to administer education in their own areas. Chaos was widely predicted by teachers; Tiverton was vulnerable, as falling pupil numbers already threatened the existence of the William Shapland and Caroline Brewin schools as well as Bolham First School. A greater upheaval was to follow. At the end of 1990, the Ministry of Education announced the plan to reorganise Tiverton's schools. As expected, Middle Schools taking 9 to 13-year old children were abandoned. In future, all those above 11 years of age would transfer to Tiverton High School, and from there all sixth-form students would progress to the East Devon College. The College was preparing for the extra numbers; a new technology building under construction would incorporate a lecture theatre, six computer teaching rooms, a microelectronics laboratory, information-processing workshops, and a design studio. The changes would leave state-funded primary education in the town at Tidcombe Lane, Wilcombe, Two Moors (formerly Elmore and Cowleymoor), Castle School (formerly the Caroline Brewin and William Shapland Schools), Heathcoat Primary, and Saint John's Catholic School, and the only rural school within the old borough remained that at Bolham[1].

One of the Thatcher Government's most unpopular innovations was the Community Charge, which abandoned the principle of a property-based local rate for an undisguised poll tax. In November 1989 it was made known that the amount payable by every adult in Mid Devon would be about £210. Officers of the District Council expected it would be difficult to administer, and a large group of Tory M.P.s, including Tiverton's Robin Maxwell-Hyslop, were angry at the way the new system was being imposed. A fine balance would be needed between cutting local public services and raising the amount of tax. The Council's situation was made worse by the £350,000 worth of uninsured damage to their property resulting from freak January storms - costs that had to be borne by the taxpayers. Their telephone switchboard was jammed as the poll tax bills went out[2]. Several persons chose not to pay, but many more were unable. Liability orders were issued to non-payers, whose names and addresses appeared in the newspapers, and by the end of 1990 bailiffs were ready to move in. At a single session in February 1991, Tiverton magistrates issued almost 850 liability orders[3]. Mid Devon District Council along with many others protested to the Government demanding the abolition of the tax. Popular pressure won the day, and the 1991 Budget saw the restoration of a charge rated on a scale of property value.

The new Council Tax could not reverse the trend of cuts in local services. Care for

---

[1] Saint Aubyn's, a private preparatory school, at this time flourished as never before.
[2] an event that coincided with the second largest earthquake ever recorded in Britain.
[3] *TG* 5.2.1991.

the elderly was especially under threat. Alexandra Lodge in Old Road was closed in the autumn of 1991, leaving Charlton Lodge in Broad Lane as the only Council-run care home in the town. Early in the following year concern was also raised about Belmont Hospital, which had been functioning as a geriatric unit for many years. In a large-scale reorganisation of local health provision, it was proposed by the N.H.S. to replace the facilities there with a much smaller unit, to build a new hospital for Tiverton on the Belmont site, and locate a cottage-style hospital at Cullompton[1].

Employment prospects reflected national trends. The LeGrove and Globe Elastic factories had closed on Kennedy Way, putting a combined workforce of 80 on the dole. The Nitrovit mill in Saint Andrew Street was shut down, and in 1989, following a health scare concerning listeria in chicken, Lloyd Maunder laid off more than a third of its poultry workers[2]. Stenners announced a string of redundancies, which, by April 1991, had halved the company's workforce. At Whitbreads it was hoped that reorganisation would avoid the loss of 94 workers, but this was not to be the case; and at Tiverton Poultry Packers 20 jobs went early in 1992. Nevertheless, there were rare successes. Heathcoat's Yarns and Fibres division took the last remaining site on the Lower Moor Business Park, where they hoped to expand their workforce, and in September 1992 Hepco Slide System's new £3.5 million office and manufacturing complex was opened on the same Business Park. The unemployment figures, however, revealed the overall situation very clearly; at the end of 1992, almost one in seven local people were out of work.

Despite the prevailing gloom some welcome developments were realised – and a lot more were at least planned. Castle Street's unique appearance was tastefully enhanced, with antique street-lamps and cobbled banks flanking the Leat. Much more ambitious was talk of a £12 million scheme to develop the Market area. Shopping malls, arcades, and other enhancements were proposed[3]. The traffic problems that would result once this work began put pressure on the District Council to proceed rapidly with the construction of the Great Western Way and the multi-storey car park at the bottom of Phoenix Lane. A previous decision, however, seemed to put paid to the Market vision; the District Council had already granted the Janes Trust permission to build workshops to the east of the Pannier Market on part of the land earmarked by the developers. The administrators of the Trust maintained their right to build there. Meanwhile, work went ahead on the new car park in Phoenix Lane. The design was striking, a multi-

---

[1] *TG* 28.4.1992.

[2] in 1992, following a serious fire at the plant, a further 85 jobs were shed, but these were quickly restored.

[3] *TG* 14.7.1987.

storey structure in brick with the appearance of a whimsical château. When it was completed in October 1992, work on the Great Western Way had yet to begin. A champion for this cause was found in Angela Browning, who became Tiverton Division's first woman M.P. in 1992[1]. Her constant pressure on the Government was successful and the go-ahead on the new road was sanctioned in December.

Development amply repaid the fortunes of Tiverton Town Football Club in the nineties[2]. They announced a major building plan in May 1992 costing £60,000, which included a new grandstand[3]. Success for the team, managed by Martyn Rogers, came in the following season. They reached the final of the FA Challenge Vase, but lost 1-0 to Bridlington at Wembley. On a regional level, they were runners-up in the Great Mills League Premier Division, and in Devon they won the Saint Luke's Cup and the Les Phillips Cup[4]. After a couple of seasons consolidating their position as a team of regional importance Tiverton Town again embarked on a sustained run of success. In the climax of the 1997/8 season they again reached Wembley in the final of the FA Carlsberg Vase. This time they defeated the gritty Tow Law Town side from Durham to the delight of hundreds of their fans who had travelled to London by the coach-load. The following Tuesday's *Gazette* proclaimed 'Ours At Last'. Few believed they could repeat this success, but come the spring of the following year, Tiverton had once more booked their place in the final. The *Gazette* revelled in the occasion. Full coverage was given, and a special souvenir supplement was printed in advance of the occasion on May 16th. Tiverton overcame their opponents, Bedlington Terriers, by a single goal, and brought the Cup back to Tiverton again[5].

National sporting recognition had also came to the Tiverton BMX Club in the summer of 1992, when they were chosen to host a round of the national championships. Their track at Cowleymoor was hastily upgraded to stage the event, which attracted a large number of enthusiasts. The club had been formed in 1981, and had produced a number of champions. Nevertheless, despite successes on the BMX track, in the various youth football teams, and elsewhere, it is perhaps symptomatic of our times that the anti-social behaviour of a small number of Tiverton's young people invariably monopolised the headlines. This was the case in February 1994 when 20

---

[1] she replaced Robin Maxwell-Hyslop who retired from the seat, following his knighthood in the 1992 New Year's Honours List.

[2] for a full treatment of the history of the club, see Miller 1995.

[3] at this time Elmore Football Club received a tempting offer of £2 million for their Horsdon Park ground (*TG* 17.8.1993). The interested party was the supermarket giant Tesco, whose ambitions to build a large store in that area of Tiverton are only now coming to fruition.

[4] Tiverton Town's success in the F.A. Vase continued in the 1993/4 season, when they reached the quarter-final, only to be beaten by the Norfolk side, Diss Town.

[5] the *Gazette* celebrated with yet another souvenir supplement.

hypodermic syringes were found in litter bins in the Market Car Park. Worse, it was alleged that children as young as 12 were buying pure cocaine that was easily available locally[1]. Under-age drinking and vandalism were also said to be commonplace. Some thought it was time to 'get the kids off the street'[2]. This was literally the option taken, as a drop-in centre for the town's youth was opened in the following year in one of the former cattle sheds of the Market. This facility seemed to attract those youngsters for whom the Youth Centre near the Swimming Pool was too organised and regulated.

The pedestrianisation of Fore Street and Phoenix Lane eventually went ahead in the early months of 1994. In many towns, this had been seen as the answer to local traffic problems and failing business, but opinions in Tiverton were mixed[3]. Several local traders saw the move as a threat to their livelihood, believing that people would not want to walk to their shops. Time alone would tell. Of immediate concern was an improvement in the physical appearance of the area. The sweeping view from the new multi-storey car park up Phoenix Lane to Fore Street would be broken by small trees[4], and a small haven of peace was created by a garden dedicated to the Burma Star veterans. The centrepiece of this area, however, was to be a fountain. A spectacular burst of five powerful jets of water sprouting to an impressive pinnacle was envisaged, but something resembling a blocked drain was all that would be achieved. At Tiverton's first Spring Festival, in May 1995, Phoenix Lane was the venue for one of the most innovative performances, the percussionists, Weapons of Sound. More sedate surroundings accommodated other attractions, such as the Western Sinfonia and the Bournemouth Sinfonietta. Whereas the Spring Festival has continued to involve several local organisations and individuals, the diversity of performers in the earlier years has, sadly, not always been maintained. The Mid Devon Show is another event, begun at this time, which has enjoyed continued success. Although inaugurated in July 1994, it was in essence a revival of the old Tiverton Agricultural Show, last held in 1971. The event is staged on a site at Hartnoll Farm beside the Halberton road, and the first meeting attracted 15,000 people[5]. The organising committee sought to serve the whole of the Mid Devon area, as well as providing a shop window for local traders and producers. In this they have succeeded.

---

[1] *TG* 28.6.1994.   [2] *TG* 15.2.1994.

[3] results from opinion polls differed widely. A *Gazette* survey showed a 2:1 ratio against pedestrianisation (*TG* 21.6.1994), yet a poll conducted by the town's traders showed 94 for, 58 against, and 64 'don't knows' (*TG* 5.7.1994).

[4] the last of the Charter trees were planted here, thirty years and more than a thousand saplings after the first ceremony to mark the 350th anniversary of the Borough Charter of Incorporation.

[5] held annually ever since, the Show continues to attract large attendances.

The National Lottery began in 1994, creating instant millionaires and making lots of money available for good causes. Hundreds of small organisations benefited from National Heritage Lottery grants, and there was no shortage of suggestions on how to spend larger sums – perhaps Tiverton could be provided with an ice-skating rink, a model farm, or a heritage centre. The Museum was one of the earliest applicants, submitting plans in 1996 for re-displaying the galleries and building a new entrance facing Beck Square. The eventual result has carefully maintained the external appearance of the old National School, at the same time enhancing the aspect from the car park. The future of some other buildings caused controversy and, in one particular case, a great deal of anger. 'Back-door privatisation' was the term used to describe the move in 1996 to sell Tiverton's Post Office in Bampton Street to an unnamed firm, placing at risk the jobs of 10 workers[1]. Plans to relocate the service to Market Walk angered many locals, but despite the intervention of Angela Browning M.P., and a 10,000-name petition, the move went ahead early in 1997. With the benefit of hindsight, it must be asked what all the fuss was about, as the new Post Office functions well, as does the sorting office, which remains on the old site. The redundant Heathcoat Middle and Sunningmead schools were favoured as sites for housing development, but, fortunately, not by local residents. They wanted to retain both buildings, and use them as community centres. In both instances determination resulted in success. In May 1996, the proposed Old Heathcoat School Community Centre received an anonymous donation of £60,000 towards the purchase price of £250,000 and, in spite of inevitable delays, the keys to the property were handed over to the fundraisers in September 1997. Progress with Sunningmead was a little slower. Despite opening in 1999, serious problems with the heating system delayed its being fully functional until the following year. Meanwhile, two former schools were put up for sale as surplus to Council requirements, Chilcott's and the original Elmore School in Chapel Street.

Tiverton still needed and expected a new hospital, new District Council Headquarters, and a new Library. Eventually, a combination of factors has led to their practical realisation over the past five years. Proposed changes in health care provision introduced some urgency into making a start on the hospital. When the Local Health Authority announced its intention to close Belmont Hospital it was thought a new building would be ready in time to transfer the patients. However, closure was fixed for 1998, far too soon for a new building whose site had not even been established at that time. The Melrose Unit was spared, and all the other patients were transferred to the existing District Hospital. Meanwhile, many Tivertonians were surprised at the interest shown in the derelict Globe Elastic site on Kennedy Way. Not only was this being

---

[1] *TG* 20.2.1996.

viewed as the possible location for the new hospital, but it was also favoured for Mid Devon's Council headquarters. This, we must remember, was a location which had previously been contaminated by some of the noxious chemicals used at the factory[1], and many people were (and some still are) not convinced that the site is clean. Nevertheless, it was chosen for Tiverton's new 73-bed Hospital, and here work began in 2001 on the cartwheel-design building[2]. Elsewhere there was regret and even anger when the Marie Curie home at Tidcombe was put on the market in Autumn 1999. The Foundation in March 1998 had scotched rumours of its intentions[3], but within six months came the announcement that the hospice was indeed going to close. A day-care centre, housed in part of the Police Station on Canal Hill, would compensate in part for the facilities lost at Tidcombe.

Historically, of course, the Millennium should have been celebrated in 2001, but no one could wait that long! Various events were scheduled for the end of 1999, and as the date approached, boffins predicted computer failure due to the Millennium Bug – planes would fall out of the sky, and missiles would be unintentionally launched. Nothing of the sort happened, but many a fortune was made averting the expected apocalypse. Tiverton's civic response to the Millennium was, to say the least, hardly traditional. All there is to remember of the occasion can be seen at the entrance to the Burma Star garden in Phoenix Lane; a holly tree was planted next to an engraved Cornish granite slab, taken from the Town Hall steps, under which a time capsule was buried.

Closures always hit hardest when the institutions are long established. Such was the case with Tiverton magistrates' court which, along with that at South Molton, stood down on the orders of the Lord Chancellor. Brian Homer, Chairman of the Devon Magistrates' Courts Committee for over 24 years, could see no economic sense in the decision[4]. Yet, despite an appeal in June 2000, the judgement was not changed. Consequently, the costs of justice to individuals, if not the Lord Chancellor's Department, have risen accordingly. News of another probable closure came in July 2000, as the 170-year old Twose Company had called in the administrators. The firm was taken over in the autumn by Alamo Group (Europe) Limited, who stated that manufacturing would cease at Tiverton, and 36 of the 41 workforce were likely to be made redundant.

The location of Mid Devon District Council's headquarters was at last settled during 2000. Kennedy Way had been given up to the Hospital, a site behind the Town Hall would be too expensive and its design had met with strong opposition from National Heritage, so the new building was to be located at the bottom of Phoenix Lane, beside the River Lowman. No two buildings could look as different as the Town

---

[1] *TG* 13.10.1992.
[2] in the meantime, there were further cuts in maternity services at the District Hospital and hysterectomy surgery also ceased.
[3] *TG* 10.3.1998.
[4] *TG* 8.2.2000.

Hall and Phoenix House; each was built to accommodate the ever-increasing numbers involved in local government, and, it seems, both may still be necessary to do this effectively. Two birds would be killed with one stone, as the new building would incorporate the long-awaited Tiverton Library, first planned for Beck Square in 1974.

Agriculture has always been prey to headline-hitting health scares. During the 1990s the major threat was perceived to be BSE, the so-called 'mad cow disease', and its links to Creuzfeld-Jakob's disease. Many people were dissuaded from eating beef or any product derived from cattle. Hundreds of already-beleaguered farmers were placed under an intolerable strain; Devon County Council hardly helped their plight when instructions went out to take beef off school menus. Few believed it was possible for the situation to get worse. It did, however, when the outbreak of foot and mouth disease in 2001 had its devastating effect. In February, the first case was noticed in Humberside, and unchecked movement of stock saw it spread across the country within a few days. By the second week of March, cases had been reported at Morchard Bishop and Crediton. Precautions were taken: the public was told to stay away from farmland; farmers virtually barricaded themselves on their property; and events such as the Devon County Show and Mid Devon Show were cancelled. An outbreak occurred at Calverleigh in April, resulting in the slaughter of all the stock. In June, there was a surge in local cases, affecting five farms around Clayhanger and Huntsham. A month later, the number of cases dropped, and although the stench of the pyres was still in the air, restrictions began to be eased. Mid Devon was declared free of the disease in August but, as some had feared, continuing tests led to its discovery in a flock of sheep at Chevithorne, and 300 animals were slaughtered. Fortunately, this proved to be the last incidence of foot and mouth locally, and the whole county was officially declared free of the disease at the end of November. The effects of the outbreak are still being felt. For many farmers, already impoverished by years of falling returns, this was the final straw. Several with a long family tradition in agriculture left the land, while others sought alternative forms of income. For a few, diversification has become the answer, whether by establishing an environmental or natural attraction for tourists, or through converting farm buildings into accommodation. It is perverse that, at a time when the public's interest in the countryside is at its greatest, the numbers sustained by traditional farming are at their lowest ever.

Although foot and mouth restrictions hampered travel in the countryside throughout 2001, major building work started in the town. In August, the first turf was cut on the Exe Valley Leisure Centre site. The old swimming pool was demolished and the new Centre rose with admirable speed. Opened in March 2003, it has attracted a number of people to its swimming pools, fitness centre, sports hall, and outside courts and pitches. Another landmark building, Phoenix House, combining the new District Council headquarters and Library, was under construction throughout 2003. This one, clean-cut building is designed to accommodate all the Council's offices, replacing no fewer than seven separate sites scattered throughout the town[1]. Its opening at the beginning of 2004 hit the headlines for the wrong reason; when it was discovered that the architects had failed to provide the £5 million building with a letterbox.

Phoenix House, the Mid Devon District Council's headquarters and Tiverton Library, built on the site of Starkey, Knight and Ford's Brewery.

If anything can be said to characterise development in Tiverton in recent times, it is the ping-pong of planning. Invariably, the same game is played; applications are submitted, strong opposition is mounted, plans are revised, quite often a different group opposes the revision, and back and forward they pass until they are either dropped or they progress in a much diluted form. We have become accustomed to this in the prime example of the Tiverton Market Enhancement Scheme. Much must have been spent already on the various versions of this. Planning applications are often opposed on health grounds nowadays, such as those concerning two particularly

---

[1] the sale of some of the Council's redundant buildings - Great House, the registrar's office in Saint Peter Street, and the former housing office in Bampton Street – is expected to bring in an estimated £500,000 (*TG* 20.5.2003).

controversial and topical proposals received by the District Council during 2002. Bampton Down, the high ground to the east of Cove, was suggested as a site for a wind farm, where turbines would stand over 300 foot high. Whereas this application was resolved peacefully, the other matter ended in a serious act of vandalism. A 50-foot mobile telephone mast was erected at Elmore Football Club's ground, but opposition on health grounds, mounted locally, persuaded the Council to consider its removal. The matter seemed to have reached a stalemate, when some 'persons unknown' took the law into their own hands and toppled the mast. It has since been re-erected. Developments on the outskirts of Tiverton often attract the most vociferous criticism. In 2001, East Devon College announced their far-sighted plans for expansion, which would include a new refectory, social area, and hard-court sports arena. The scheme, in two or three phases, would cost more than £6 million, which, for an establishment catering for 800 full-time and 3,500 part-time students, was considered a worthwhile investment in the future. The means by which this project is to be funded, however, has met with considerable opposition. The College's desire to sell land on Kennedy Way, perhaps to a supermarket chain, and turn one of the sports fields into a housing development, is being challenged. East Devon College maintains that its very future depends on being able to expand its facilities, and is waiting for the issue to be resolved.

The District Council, often the arbiters of such developments, were facing serious questions about their own housing stock during 2003. The dilemma was whether to retain ownership of council housing or, as many other authorities have already done, transfer them all to a housing association[1]. Tenants' views were tested, and in November councillors voted in favour of the transfer. The shortage of affordable housing for local people, especially the younger ones, was highlighted by the costs incurred by the Council for bed-and-breakfast accommodation for the district's homeless. The amount spent in 1999-2000 was £15,000, but had risen sharply within three years to £250,000. There has been no shortage of suggestions to ease this situation, including the use of Belmont Hospital, or the District Hospital (now it is empty), or to build anew on the old allotments at Palmerston Park. Again, we must wait.

Land suitable for residential development is difficult to find. This is hardly surprising, as all the prime sites were taken up by earlier generations. Modern developers are left with the increasingly marginal land in the flood plains of the Exe and Lowman, on the steep hillsides to the south and west of the town, and on poorly drained land to the north[2]. Such sites include the large estate at Moorhayes, eventually to comprise over 1,000 homes, the proposed 32-acre business park at Gornhay, and the Oakfield site at Brickhouse Hill.

---

[1] *TG* 11.11.2003.
[2] just how many recent developments involve the name 'moor'?

The speed of physical expansion surprises many; one set of statistics reveals the reason. In the 1801 Census 6,505 people lived in Tiverton's 1,221 dwellings, an average of more than five persons per dwelling, but now just over 17,000 people inhabit 8,300 dwellings, just over two people per house. The population has grown by two and a half times, whereas the number of dwellings has risen sevenfold, and still cannot meet demand. The growth of the town does, however, seem to have come up against one barrier – the North Devon Link Road. Fears have been raised, especially in the villages of Bolham, Chettiscombe and Chevithorne, that once this road has been crossed developments will engulf their communities.

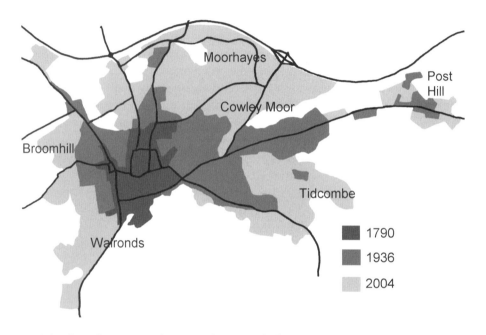

The physical expansion of Tiverton from Dunsford's time to the present, most of which has taken place since 1900.

In September 2003, three former members of Mid Devon District Council were granted the Freedom of the Borough of Tiverton. They were former Air Vice-Marshal Donald Attlee, who had been Vice-Chairman, Chairman and leader of the Council[1], Jack Harris, a retired police officer, and district councillor for 26 years, and Eric Shapland, who had been Chairman and member of the Council from 1973-95, as well as Mayor in 1973, and member of the former Borough Council from 1967. The septennial Perambulation of the Town Leat gave Tiverton another opportunity to

---

[1] representing Culmstock and Uffculme.

celebrate its past in the same month. Well over 600 walkers followed the Bailiff of the Hundred from Coggan's Well to the source of the Leat on Norwood Common, celebrating the gift made some 750 years earlier. The presentations of the Freedom of the Borough and the Perambulation show that Tiverton still has a sense of occasion, even if it fails in many ways to promote its heritage.

But what of present-day Tiverton? Although its link to the rail network lies some four miles to the east at Tiverton Parkway, access by road has improved enormously in recent years. There are high-speed connections along the North Devon Link Road to Barnstaple and the coast as well as to the M5. This is of great benefit to those who live locally, but, inevitably potential visitors are often tempted to speed past the town without stopping. For those who do venture into the town itself, they are greeted with, what has now become, a clean, bright, lively place, with Fore Street, Bampton Street, Market Walk, and Phoenix Lane generally buzzing with shoppers. Pedestrianisation has not brought the end of town centre shops as once some feared. Although, as we have seen, many fine buildings were lost to post-War development, such wanton destruction seems to have ceased. Tiverton still retains some of its most cherished architectural gems; the Castle, Saint Peter's Church, the three almshouses, and Old Blundell's, for example, still testify to the ancient market town.

As the hub of Mid Devon Tiverton has attracted many of the key facilities of the area. Recently we have seen the construction of a Leisure Centre, the combined District Council Headquarters and Library building, as well as a new Hospital, and soon we may even have an Arts Centre. The town has the only cinema in the District, as well as the largest Museum and the largest College. Blundell's School, and its satellite Saint Aubyn's, are flourishing and continue to attract pupils from near and far. Indeed, the recent rapid influx of people has created such a demand for places in the local schools that they have never been so full.

With such growth all around no-one can say Tiverton is stagnating. It is a lively town with, so it seems, a promising future, but its people would do well to cherish its heritage. The challenge, surely, is not to halt development, for that is futile, but rather to welcome newcomers and share with them our knowledge of past Tivertonians and their deeds. They, too, will then be able to take an appropriate pride in the town of Princess Katherine, John Greneway, Peter Blundell, Oliver Peard, Martin Dunsford, John Heathcoat, Thomas Ford, and many, many more who have made it what it is.

Bibliography

Abbreviations

BLib	British Library
CRO	Cornwall Record Office
D&C	Dean and Chapter of Exeter Cathedral
DCNQ	*Devon and Cornwall Notes and Queries.*
DCRS	*Devon and Cornwall Record Society*
DevHist	*Devon Historian*
DRO	Devon Record Office
HMC	*Historic Manuscripts Commission.*
JBritArchAss	*Journal of the British Archaeological Association.*
LRO	Leicestershire Record Office
NDRO	North Devon Record Office
PDAS	*Proceedings of the Devon Archaeological Society.*
PRO	Public Record Office
PSANHS	*Proceedings of the Somerset Archaeological and Natural History Society.*
SRO	Somerset Record Office.
TDA	*Transactions of the Devonshire Association.*
TivLib	Tiverton Library
TivMus	Tiverton Museum

Works cited

ADB	1966	*Australian Dictionary of Biography 1788-1850.* 2 vols.
Andrew, K.	1964	*Elizabethan Privateering: English Privateering During the Spanish War 1585-1603.*
Andriette, A.	1971	*Devon and Exeter in the Civil War.*
Anglo-Saxon Chronicle	1996	translated and edited by M. Swanton.
Annals EIC	1810	J. Bruce (ed.) *The Annals of the Honourable East India Company.*
APC	-	*Acts of the Privy Council.*
Authers, W.	1974	'Notes from the Nineteenth Century Records of the Tiverton Congregational Church', *TDA vol*

		106, pp.34-5.
"	1975	'Plymouth Brethren in Tiverton', *DCNQ vol 33*, pp.130-1.
Banks, M.	1904	*Blundell's Worthies.*
Baring-Gould, S.	1920	*A Book of Devon.*
Barnett, G.	1995	*Richard and Maria Cosway, a Biography.*
Bayly, L.	1619	*The Practice of Pietie.*
Black, J.	1987	'The Discovery of the Cullompton Church Decorations', *Devon and Cornwall Notes and Queries, vol 36*, pp.35-6.
Blaylock, S.	1986	'A Survey of Greenway's Porch at St Peter's Church, Tiverton', *PDAS vol 44*, pp.85-105.
"	1988	*Tiverton Castle: Observations in the Gatehouse Tower.*
Bluecoat School Minute Book	-	kept at the East Devon College.
Blundell, J.	1712	*Memoirs and Antiquities of the Town and Parish of Tiverton.*
Blundell's MSS	-	the archives of Blundell's School
Blundell's Register	1904	A. Fisher (ed.), *Register of Blundell's School pt 1.*
Bourne, J. (ed.)	1986	*Georgian Tiverton: The Political Memoranda of Beavis Wood 1768-98, DCRS new series vol 29.*
Bourne, K.	1982	*Palmerston: The Early Years 1784-1841.*
Bristol	1900	F. Bickley (ed.), *The Little Red Book of Bristol, vol II.*
Brockett, A.	1958	'Nonconformity in Devon in the 18th Century', *TDA vol 90*, pp.31-59.
Brown, A.	1991	'Prehistoric Activity at Bolham', in Maxfield 1991, pp.57-61.
Burkitt, T. & Burkitt, A.	1990	'The Frontier Zone and the Siege of Mount Badon: a Review of the Evidence for Their Location', *PSANHS, vol 134*, pp.81-93.
Burrage, C.	1912	*The Early English Dissenters in the Light of Recent Research (1550-1641).*

CalCommComp	1889-92	*Calendar of the Committee for Compounding 1643-60. 5 vols.*
CalTreasB	1904-57	*Calendar of Treasury Books 1660-1718. 32 vols.*
Cameron, A.	1996	*Thomas Glass MD, Physician of Georgian Exeter.*
Case, H.	1907	*The History of the Baptist Church in Tiverton 1607-1907.*
Chalk, E.	1935	'Notes on the Members for Tiverton (Devon)', *TDA vol 67*, pp.315-47.
"	1936	'Tiverton Letters and Papers 1724-1843', *Notes and Queries vol 170*, p.21 et seq.
Chanter, J. (ed.)	1919	'Tenth Report of the Committee on Church Plate', *TDA vol 51*, pp.80-113.
Chapman, S. (ed.)	1978	*The Devon Cloth Industry in the Eighteenth Century: Sun Fire Office Inventories 1726-1770, DCRS new series vol 23.*
Charities 1826	1826-30	*The Report of the Commissioners Concerning Charities: Devon. 3 vols.*
Cherry, B. & Pevsner, N. (eds.)	1989	*Devon.* (2nd edition).
Churchwardens' Accounts	-	in Saint Peter's Church and Devon Record Office.
Clarendon	1888	*Clarendon's History of the Rebellion.*
Clark, E.	1960	*The Ports of the Exe Estuary.*
Clark, G.	1995	*The Charity Commission as a Source in English Economic History.*
"	2001	*The Secret History of the Industrial Revolution.*
Clarke, P.	1971	'The Neolithic, Bronze and Iron Age, and Romano-British Finds from Mount Batten, Plymouth, 1832-1939', *PDAS, vol 29*, pp.137-61.
Clinker, C.	1978	*Clinker's Register of Closed Passenger Stations and Goods Depots.*
Close Rolls	1902-63	*Calendar of Close Rolls 1227-1509.*

		60 vols.
CommAdvMoney	1888	*Calendar of the Committee for the Advancement of Money 1642-56.* 3 vols.
Compton	1986	A. Whiteman (ed.), *The Compton Census of 1676.*
Cornwall, J.	1977	*Revolt of the Peasantry 1549.*
Craig, F.	1969	*British Parliamentary Election Results 1918-49.*
"	1977	*British Parliamentary Election Results 1832-85.*
Cromwell	1945	W. Abbott (ed.), *Writings and Speeches of Oliver Cromwell.*
Cruwys, M.	1952	'Records at Cruwys Morchard', *TDA vol 84*, pp.1-19.
CSPDom	1856-1924	*Calendar of State Papers Domestic 1547-1704.* 95 vols.
CSPEastIndies etc	1862-92	*Calendar of State Papers, the East Indies etc. 1513-1634.* 5 vols.
CSPFor	1861-1969	*Calendar of State Papers Foreign 1547-94.* 34 vols.
Darvall, F.	1934	*Popular Disturbances and Public Order in Regency England.*
de la Mahotière, Mary	1997	*Hannah Cowley: Tiverton's Playwright and Pioneer Feminist 1743-1809.*
Devon Eyre	1985	H. Summerson (ed.), *Crown Pleas of the Devon Eyre of 1238, DCRS, new series vol 28.*
DNB	1917	*Dictionary of National Biography.* 22 vols.
Dobson, C.	1980	*Masters and Journeymen: A Prehistory of Industrial Relations 1710-1800.*
DSN	1892-	*Devon and Somerset News.*
Dunsford, G.	1904	'The Autobiography of Martin Dunsford, The Historian of Tiverton', *TDA vol 36*, pp.219-225.
Dunsford, M.	1790	*Historical Memoirs of the Town and Parish of Tiverton.*
Dyer, A.	2000	'Appendix: Ranking Lists of English Medieval Towns', in D.M. Palliser

		(ed.), *The Cambridge Urban History of Britain vol I 600-1540*, pp.747-70.
Earle, P.	1977	*Monmouth's Rebels: The Road to Sedgemoor 1685.*
ECA	-	*Exeter Customs Accounts* at the Devon Record Office.
Eden, F.	1797	*The State of the Poor, vol 2.*
EFP	1768-1918	*Trewman's Exeter Flying Post.*
Elton, G.	1977	*Reform and Reformation: England 1509-1558.*
Enrolled Deeds		transcription by J. Tangey, held in the Devon Record Office.
Evans, J.	1881	*The Ancient Bronze Implements, Weapons and Ornaments of Great Britain and Ireland.*
Exeter	*1980*	Exeter Museums Service (ed.), *Folk Festivals and Traditions of Devon*
ExeterAss	1963	A. Brockett (ed.), *The Exeter Assembly: The Minutes of the Assemblies of the United Brethren of Devon and Cornwall 1691-1717, DCRS new series vol 6.*
Exeter Freemen	1973	M. Rowe and A. Jackson (eds.) *Exeter Freemen 1266-1967, DCRS Extra Series vol 1.*
Flanagan, R.	1991	*'Parish-Fed Bastards': A History of the Politics of the Unemployed in Britain 1884-1939.*
Freeman, B.	1927	*The Yeomanry of Devon 1794-1927.*
Garrett, C.	1938	*The Marian Exiles.*
Gentleman's Magazine	1731-1868	*The Gentleman's Magazine.*
Gesta Stephani	1976	edited by K. Potter.
Gibb, M.	1938	*The Lord General.*
Gillett, E. (ed.)	1945	*Elizabeth Ham: By Herself 1783-1820.*
Gilmour, L.	1992	*Riot, Risings and Revolution.*
Glasscoe, M.	1987	'Late Medieval Paintings in Ashton Church, Devon', *JBritArchAss, vol 140*, pp.182-90.
Glassey, L.	1979	*Politics and the Appointment of Justices of the Peace 1675-1720.*
Gore Allen, W.	1958	*John Heathcoat and His Heritage.*

Grant, A.	1983	*North Devon Pottery: The Seventeenth Century.*
Grant, N.	2000	'St Petroc in Devon', *DevHist, vol 61*, pp.10-6.
Gray, H.	1924	'The Production and Exportation of English Woollens in the Fourteenth Century', *English Historical Review, vol 39*, pp.13-35.
Greaves, R.	1986	*Deliver Us From Evil: The Radical Underground in Britain 1660-3.*
Gregory, A.	1932	*Recollections of a Country Editor.*
Grenville 1763-5	1962	J. Tomlinson (ed.) *Additional Grenville Papers 1763-5.*
Griffith, F.	1988	*Devon's Past: An Aerial View.*
Gruenfelder, J.	1981	*Influence in Early Stuart Elections 1604-40.*
Hadfield, A.	1970	*The Chartist Land Company.*
Hadfield, C.	1955	*Canals of Southern England.*
"	1967	*The Canals of Southwest England.*
Halsbury, Earl of	1960	'The Pleasure of Scale', *TDA, vol 92*, pp.19-35.
Harding, Lt.-Col. W.	1845	*The History of Tiverton.*
Harmon, R.	1968	*Susanna, Mother of the Wesleys.*
Harris, R.	1985	'J.N. Singleton: First Headmaster of the First Factory School in the South West', *DevHist vol 30*, pp.13-7.
Harrowby MSS	-	originals at Sandon Hall, photocopies at the Devon Record Office.
Hase, P.	1988	'The Mother Churches of Hampshire', in J. Blair (ed.), *Minsters and Parish Churches*, pp.45-66.
Haslam, J.	1984	'The Towns of Devon', in J. Haslam (ed.), *Anglo Saxon Towns in Southern England*, pp.249-83.
Hateley, R.	1977	*Industrial Locomotives of South West England.*
HC18th	1975-6	*House of Commons Sessional Papers of the 18th Century 1715-1800.* 147 vols..
Henning, B.	1983	*The House of Commons 1660-1690*

vol I.

Henson, G.   1831   *Henson's History of the Framework Knitters.* (reprinted in 1971)

HMC Lords   1887-1977   *House of Lords Manuscripts, HMC, 17ᵗʰ Report.*

HMC Pine Coffin   1876   *Manuscripts of John Richard Pine Coffin at Portledge, North Devon, HMC Vᵗʰ Report, Appendix.*

HMC Portland vol I   1891-3   *Manuscripts of the Duke of Portland, vol 1, HMC XIIIᵗʰ Report, Appendix.*

HMC Portland vol IV   1897   *Manuscripts of the Duke of Portland, vol 1V, HMC XVᵗʰ Report, Appendix.*

HOPG3   1878-89   *Home Office Papers of George III. 3 vols.*

Hoskins, W.   1935   *Industry, Trade and People in Exeter 1688-1800.*

"   1954   *Devon.*

"   1959   *Devon and Its People.*

Hughes, J.   1857   'The Restoration of St Peter's Church, Tiverton', *Transactions of the Exeter Diocesan Architectural Society, vol 6,* pp.37-46.

"   1862   'Proceedings of the Congress', *JBritArchAss,vol 18,* pp.232-52.

Incledon, B.   1790   *Donations of Peter Blundell and other Benefactors to the Free Grammar School at Tiverton.*

IPM MS   transcripts from *Inquisitiones Post Mortem* at the PRO (kept in the Westcountry Studies Library, Exeter).

Jarvis, K. & Maxfield, V.   1975   'The Excavation of a First-Century Roman Farmstead and a Late Neolithic Settlement, Topsham, Devon', *PDAS, vol 33,* pp.209-65.

JCTP   1920-38   *Journal of the Commissioners for Trade and Plantations. 14 vol.*

Jenkins, J.   1982   *The Removal of Blundell's: Town and Gown in Tiverton 1846-82.*

JHC   1776-   *Journals of the House of Commons, 1547-.*

John, E.	1982	'The Age of Edgar', in J. Campbell (ed.), *The Anglo-Saxons,* pp.160-91.
Kanefsky, J.	1977	'Railway Competition and Turnpike Roads in East Devon', *TDA vol 109,* pp.59-72.
KEO	-	collection of deeds etc kept at the Knightshayes Estate Office, abstracts and index held at the Tiverton Museum.
Kerridge, E.	1985	*Textile Manufactures in Early Modern England.*
Kowaleski, M.	1995	*Local Markets and Regional Trade in Medieval Exeter.*
Lang, R.	1971	'London's Aldermen in Business 1600-25', The Guildhall Miscellany *vol 3, number 4,* pp.242-64.
Leach, J.	2000	'Limeburning in Tiverton', *DevHist vol 60,* pp.8-14.
Leicester Journal	1759-	*The Leicester (and Nottingham) Journal.*
Little, B.	1953	*Exeter.*
London	1905	C. Kingsford (ed.), *Chronicles of London.*
Lorne, Marquis of	1892	*Viscount Palmerston.*
LPFD	1864-1910	*Letters and Papers Foreign and Domestic 1509-47.* 21 vols.
Mahood, A.	1952	'Some Notes on Blundell's School', *TDA vol 134,* pp.52-80.
"	1953	'Tiverton Drawing-Master 1796', *DCNQ vol 25,* p.133.
Matthews, A.	1934	*Calamy Revised.*
Mawer, A. & Stenton, F.	1932	*The Place-Names of Devon, Part Two.*
Maxfield, V.	1991	'Tiverton Roman Fort (Bolham): Excavations 1981-1986, *PDAS, vol 49,* pp.25-98.
Memoirs of the Family of Dunsford	-	manuscript held by the family.
Mercurius Politicus	1650-60	*Mercurius Politicus.*
Miller, E. (ed.)	1991	*The Agrarian History of England and Wales vol III, 1348-1500.*
Miller, K.	1995	*The History of Tiverton Town*

		Football Club.
Moger Wills	-	transcripts of wills made by O. Moger, kept in the Westcountry Studies Library.
Monmouth	1985	W. Macdonald Wigfield (ed.), *The Monmouth Rebels 1685, Somerset Record Society, vol 79.*
Mowat, C.	1955	*Britain Between the Wars 1918-40.*
Murray Wills	-	transcripts of wills made by Sir O. Murray, kept in the Westcountry Studies Library.
Nash, A.	1988	'The population of Southern England in 1086: A New Look at the Evidence of Domesday Book', *Southern History, vol 10, pp.1-28.*
Nicholls, L.	1960	*The Trading Communities of Totnes and Dartmouth in the Late 15th and Early 16th Centuries.* Unpublished M.A. thesis, University of Exeter.
Norman, C.	1975	'Four Mesolithic Assemblages from West Somerset', *PSANHS, vol 119,* pp.26-37.
Obituary 1936	1936	'Obituary Notices – The Rev. Edwin Spencer Chalk', *TDA vol 68*, pp.25-7.
Obituary 1942	1942	'Obituary Notices – Alfred Thomas Gregory', *TDA vol 74*, pp.30-1
O'Gorman, F.	1989	*Voters, Patrons and Parties.*
Oliver, Rev. G. & Jones, P.	1853	'The Will of Katherine, Countess of Devon, Daughter of Edward IV: Dated May 2, 1527', *Archaeological Journal vol 10*, pp.53-8.
Orme, N.	1976	*Education in the West of England 1066-1548.*
"	1991	*Unity and Variety.*
Oswald, N.	1977	'Epidemics in Devon 1538-1837', *TDA vol 109*, pp.73-116.
Palmer, S.	1970	'The Stone Age Industries of the Isle of Portland, Dorset, and the Utilisation of Portland Chert as Artefact Material in Southern England', *Proceedings of the*

		Prehistoric Society, vol 36, pp.82-115.
Palmerston	1979	*The Palmerston-Sullivan Letters 1804-63, Camden Society 4ᵗʰ series vol 23.*
Parliamentary Papers	1801-	*House of Commons Sessional Papers 1801-.*
Parry, J.	1871	'A Brief Sketch of the Early History of Bideford', *TDA vol 4,* pp.400-8.
Patent Rolls	1901-86	*Calendar of Patent Rolls 1216-1582.* 71 vols.
PC Unbound pt I	1967	*Privy Council List of Unbound Papers, List and Index Society vol 24.*
Pearce, S.	1972	'Stone and Bronze Implements Found in Devon', *PDAS, vol 30,* pp.236-8.
Pengelly, W.	1876	'Devonshire Gleanings from Notes and Queries', *TDA vol 8,* pp.537-796.
Platt, C.	1996	*King Death: The Black Death and its Aftermath in Late-Medieval England.*
Poor 1822	1822	*Supplemental Appendix to Report from the Select Committee on Poor Rate Returns, House of Commons Papers.*
Porter, J.	1984	'The Incidence of Industrial Conflict in Devon, 1860-1900', *TDA vol 116,* pp.63-75.
"	1989	'The Decline of the Devonshire Wrestling Style', *TDA vol 121,* pp.195-208.
PortsDock	1987	*Portsmouth Dockyard Papers 1774-83, Portsmouth Record Series vol 6.*
Prideaux, E.	1918	'The Medieval Sculptures from the Church of St Peter, Tiverton', *Archaeological Journal vol 75,* pp.209-40.
Protestation 1641	1973	A. Howard (ed.), *Devon Protestation Returns 1641.*
Rackham, O.	1986	*The history of the Countryside.*
Radford, G.	1903	'Nicholas Radford, 1385(?)-1455',

		TDA vol 35, pp.251-78.
Redvers	1994	R. Bearman (ed.), *Charters of the Redvers Family and the Earldom of Devon 1090-1217, DCRS new series, vol 37*.
Reed, A.	1988	'French Prisoners of War on Parole in Tiverton 1797-1812', *DevHist vol 36*, pp.10-4.
Reed, M.	1978	*Pilton – Its Past and People*.
RegLacy III	1968	G. Dunstan (ed.), *The Register of Edmund Lacy, Bishop of Exeter, 1420-1455, vol III. DCRS new series vol 13*.
RegMorton	1991	*Register of Archbishop Morton of Canterbury, part II, Canterbury and York Society vol 78*.
RegStafford	1886	F. Hingeston-Randolph (ed.), *Register of Bishop Stafford of Exeter*.
Richmond, L.	1989	'From the Archive: Blundell's School, Tiverton, Devon', *SPAB News vol 10, no. 4*, pp.17-8.
Ridley, J.	1972	*Lord Palmerston*.
Roberts, S.	1985	*Recovery and Restoration in an English County: Devon Local Administration 1646-70*.
Roe, D.	1981	*The Lower and Middle Palaeolithic Periods in Britain*.
Rowse, A.	1950	*The England of Elizabeth: The Structure of Society*.
Saint Peter's	-	collection of deeds and papers held in St Peter's Church, Tiverton.
Saint Peter's Benefaction Book	-	held in St Peter's Church, Tiverton.
Schoyen, A.	1958	*The Chartist Challenge*.
Shapland Scrapbooks	-	in private hands.
Shorter, A., Ravenhill, W. & Gregory, K.	1969	*Southwest England*.
Shortt, Capt. W.	1846	*JBritArchAss, vol 1*, p.140.
Silvester, R. & Berridge, P.J. & Uglow, J.	1987	'A fieldwalking Exercise on Mesolithic and Neolithic Sites at Nether Exe', *PDAS, vol 48,*

		pp.15-26.
Skinner, E.	1906	'Old Tiverton or Twyford', *TDA, vol 38*, pp.380-90.
"	1906	'French Prisoners in Tiverton from 1797 to 1811', *DCNQ vol 4 pt I*, pp.257-60.
Smiles, S. & Pidgley, M.	1995	*The Perfection of England.*
Smith, G.	1990	'A Neolithic Long Barrow at Uplowman Road, Tiverton', *PDAS, vol 48*, pp.15-26.
Snell, F.	1892	*The Chronicles of Twyford.*
South Molton Gazette	1872-	
SpanishComp	1973	P. Croft (ed.) *The Spanish Company, London Record Society vol 9.*
SPD George I	1977	*State Papers Domestic George I (SP35) part I, List and Index Society vol. 139.*
Stedman	1962	S. Thompson (ed.) *The Journal of John Gabriel Stedman.*
Stephens, W.	1958	*Seventeenth-Century Exeter.*
Stoyel, M.	1994	*Loyalty and Locality: Popular Allegiance in Devon During the English Civil War.*
Subsidy 1332	1969	A. Erskine (ed.), *The Devonshire Lay Subsidy of 1332, DCRS new series, vol. 14.*
Subsidy 1543-5	1986	T. Stoate (ed.) *Devon Lay Subsidy Rolls 1543-5.*
Suetonius	-	*De Vita Caesarum*
TG	1856-	*Tiverton Gazette*
Thomason	1642-6	Thomason Tracts, a collection of news pamphlets, kept at the British Library.
Thorn, C. & Thorn, F. (eds.)	1985	*Domesday Book: Devon, Part Two.*
Todd, M.	1987	*The South-West to AD1000.*
Trelawne	-	collection of Trelawne papers held at the Royal Institution of Cornwall
Ugawa, K.	1962	'The Economic Development of Some Devon Manors in the Thirteenth Century', *TDA, vol 44,* pp.630-83.
unknown	1964	'Congregationalists at Tiverton 1661', *DCNQ vol 29*, p.60.

Varley, D.	1971	'John Heathcoat (1783-1861), Founder of the Machine Made Lace Industry', *Textile History vol 1*, pp.2-45.
VCHSom vol II	1906	*Victoria County History of Somerset, vol 2.*
Walker, J.	1714	*An Attempt Towards Recovering an Account of the Numbers and Sufferings of the Clergy of the Church of England…*
Ward, W.	1953	*The English Land Tax in the 18th Century.*
Warne, A.	1969	*Church and Society in Eighteenth Century Devon.*
Wasley, G.	1994	*Devon At War.*
Webb, S. & Webb, B.	1908	*English Local Government: The Manor and the Borough.*
Welsford, A.	1973	*A Church ands its People Through 900 Years.*
"	1979	*Catalogue of the Books in the Newte Library, St Peter's Church, Tiverton.*
"	1984	*John Greenway 1460-1529.*
Wesley	1829-31	*The Works of the Rev. John Wesley.* 14 vols.
Western Times	1829-	*Western Times*
Whetham, C. & Whetham, W.	1907	*Colonel Nathaniel Whetham.*
White, B. (ed.)	1971	*Association Records of the Particular Baptists of England, Wales and Ireland to 1660. Part 2.*
White's 1850		W. White (ed.), *History, Gazetteer and Directory of Devonshire.*
Whiting, R.	1977	*The Reformation in the South West of England*, unpublished Ph.D. thesis, University of Exeter.
Wickham, P.	1992	'Shrinkhills', *History Today, vol 42*, pp.62-3.
Wilson, C.	1941	*Anglo-Dutch Commerce and Finance in the Eighteenth Century.*
"	1965	*England's Apprenticeship 1603-1763.*
Woodward, E.	1938	*The Age of Reform 1815-70.*

Yonge   1848   *Diary of Walter Yonge Esq., Camden*
                                     Society 1ˢᵗ series, vol 41

Youings, J.   1967   'King James' Charter to Tiverton,
                                     1615', *TDA vol 99*, pp.147-63.

Index of Persons and Places

Persons and places used to provide background information or as examples are not included, unless they relate specifically to Tiverton.

Kenyon, E.H.W. 303
Kiddells Court 242,254
Kidwell, North (Uplpwman) 282
Killerton (Broadclyst) 296
King Edward's View 294
King of Prussia 181
King St 279,286,339
King's College (Cambridge) 45,65,204
King's Head Inn (Lowman Green) 181
King's Head Inn (Westexe) 181
Kirby, Edward 155
Knackershole 307
Knight, Rev. William 265
Knightshayes 16,91,188,191,226,
252,254-6,272-3,276,278,
283,288,292,304,322,344
Knightshayes Estate 252,272-3,352
Knightshayes Estate Office 272
KwikSave 351
Lace Factory 178,207-9,211-2,214-5,
218-9,223,227,231,235,240,
242,248,252,258,269,272,282,
285,289,292,294,296-7,300,
302,309,312-3,321,325,328,
330,333,336,338,344,347,351
Lake, John 343
Lambe, Sir John 98
Lamotte, Alexandre 202
Lampray, Richard 72
Land family 60
Land, Lewis 83
Land, Thomas 70
Landbote 28
Lane, Alderman 267
Langbridge, Thomas 118
Langley Bridge 90
Larches, The 320
Lardner, Richard 197
Laud, William 98
Launceston 92
Lazenby, Emily 295,300
Lazenby, Katherine Maud 318-9
Lazenby, Miss 287
Leat 71,79,201,212,240,297
Leat Street 212,332
Lee, Henry 214
Leeuw, David 137

Legh, Alex 40
Legh, Nicholas de 34
Legh, William 57
LeGrove 354
Leigh Barton (Loxbeare) 239
Leigh family 128
Lello, John 343
Leman, Maj. John 167
Lentel, John 231
Leofhere 12
Leofric, Bishop 22
Leofric Road 350
Lewes, John 75,78
Lewis family 154
Lewis, Elizabeth 198
Lewis, George 163,172-3,176
Lewis, Joanna 169,176
Lewis, John 317,322
Lewis, Samuel 137,143,162-3
Lewis, William 126,137,143,
188,192,198
Ley, Mr 195
Liberal Club 291,313
Lime Kiln Road 228
Little Dart 90
Little Park 74,79
Little Silver 18,31,74,149,
310,329,334
Little Tiverton 17-9,24,31,44
Lloyd, Henry 249
Lloyd Maunder 354
Lloyds Bank 300
Lobb, Stephen 122
Lock, Francis 173
Lock, John 102
Lockett, William 212
Lodge or Zephyr Lodge 202
Lodge Estate 298
Lodge Road 279
London 56,61,74-5,80-1,87,
97,130,137,154,161,175,
178,234,304,315,342,344
London family 53
London Joint City & Midland Bank 300
London Westminster & Parr's Bank 300
London, William 102,108
Londonderry Cottages 260